FOUNDATION OF KARL BARTH'S DOCTRINE OF RECONCILIATION

Jesus Christ Crucified and Risen

David L. Mueller

Toronto Studies in Theology
Volume 54

The Edwin Mellen Press
Lewiston/Queenston/Lampeter

Library of Congress Cataloging in Publication Data

This volume has been registered with The Library of Congress.

This is volume 54 in the continuing series
Toronto Studies in Theology
Volume 54 ISBN 0-88946-583-5
TST Series ISBN 0-88946-975-X

A CIP catalog record for this book
is available from the British Library.

The Edwin Mellen Press   The Edwin Mellen Press
Box 450   Box 67
Lewiston, New York   Queenston, Ontario
USA 14092   CANADA L0S 1L0

The Edwin Mellen Press, Ltd.
Lampeter, Dyfed, Wales
UNITED KINGDOM SA48 7DY

Printed in the United States of America

To Marilyn and our children,
Charles David and Mary Elizabeth,
and to loving and supportive parents,
William Arthur Mueller and Mary Martha Mueller

TABLE OF CONTENTS

FREQUENTLY CITED ABBREVIATIONS
USED IN NOTES

WORKS BY KARL BARTH

AdT	Die Auferstehung der Toten
CD	Church Dogmatics
ET	Evangelical Theology: An Introduction
KD	Kirchliche Dogmatik
KM, II	Rudolf Bultmann--An Attempt To Understand Him
ROD	The Resurrection of the Dead
Romans, I	The Epistle to the Romans, 1st. ed.
Romans, II	The Epistle to the Romans, 2nd. ed.
RTM	Revolutionary Theology in the Making
WGWM	The Word of God and the Word of Man

OTHER WORKS CITED

AdG	Klappert, Die Auferweckung des Gekreu-zigten
Anfänge, I and II	Moltmann, ed., Anfänge der dialek-tischen Theologie, Part I and II
AUO	Geense, Auferstehung und Offenbarung
DMMT	Smart, The Divided Mind of Modern Theology
FAU	Bultmann, Faith and Understanding, vol. I
Harnack--Barth	Robinson, ed., The Beginnings of Dialectical Theology, vol. I
KB	Busch, Karl Barth
KM, I and II	Bartsch, ed., Kerygma and Myth, vols. I and II
RT	Rumscheidt, Revelation and Theology

PREFACE

Assessments of the theology of Karl Barth face formidable obstacles. This attempt is no exception. The scope of the Church Dogmatics--not to mention Barth's additional voluminus writings--confronts every interpreter like a climber about to ascend an Alpine mountain chain whose peaks encompass the total horizon! Nevertheless, attempts must be made.

During the past three decades I have been intensively involved with Barth's theology. I first encountered Barth as a seminarian. Subsequently, I wrote a doctoral dissertation at Duke University assessing Barth's theological method. During post-doctoral studies in Basel with Karl Barth in 1959-1960, I heard what were to be among Barth's final lectures on "Ethics as a Task of the Doctrine of Reconciliation" as well as those on "The Christian Life" with their focus on "Baptism as the Foundation of the Christian Life"[1] Teaching courses and graduate seminars on Barth's theology and deeper involvement in the "later" Barth led to engagement with his massive doctrine of reconciliation. Even prior to this research, it was apparent that much of the recent concentration on the cross and resurrection of Jesus in eschatological theologies was incomprehensible apart from Barth's continuing attention to these central pillars of Christian faith during his long career. Hence my attention turned to Barth's doctrine of reconciliation with special reference to its foundations in Jesus' cross and resurrection.

This study of Barth's doctrine of reconciliation is

divided into three parts. Part I, "The Early Barth: Roots and Controversies," (1919-1934), introduces some of the main lines of Barth's developing theological perspective. The first chapter delineates in broad strokes Barth's attempt to develop a theology of the Word of God with its focus in Jesus Christ. Barth's controversies with theological contemporaries in the twenties and up to the Declaration of Barmen in 1934 are sketched against the backdrop of his maturing perspective. In chapter two, Harnack's controversy with Barth in 1923 provides a case study of the dialectical theology engaging a dominant but no longer unchallenged liberalism. This debate also illumines the developing shape of Barth's theology following the publication of two editions of his commentary on Romans (1919, 1922) and something of his direction shortly after exchanging the pastor's pulpit for the professor's lectern. Chapter three analyzes Barth's publication of 1924, The Resurrection of the Dead, based on his exposition of I Corinthians 15. It was a significant book because it assessed a theological foundation which for Barth was non-negotiable; further, it highlighted his earlier emphasis on Jesus' cross and resurrection while also serving to anticipate their central place in his mature doctrine of reconciliation in the Church Dogmatics. Finally, Barth's focus on the resurrection necessitated his continuing critique of liberalism's theological legacy at this point[2] and anticipated increasing confrontations with Bultmann and his developing interpretation in this regard.

Part II, "Toward a Doctrine of Reconciliation: The Barth-Bultmann Debate" (1941-1952), traces their developing theological differences with particular reference to diverging interpretations of the cross and resurrection of Jesus Christ. The causes precipitating these erstwhile theological allies to part ways leading to the "divided mind of modern theology" (James Smart) at mid century is depicted. Their differing views on the cross and resurrection of Jesus also sheds light on developments in theology in the second half of this century down to the present. It is increasingly clear that not only christology, but also the issue of Jesus' cross and resurrection represent a central focus for a right understanding of Christian faith, praxis and all theological reflection.

In Part III, "The Cross and Resurrection of Jesus Christ: Foundations of Barth's Doctrine of Reconciliation in the Church Dogmatics," (1953-1967), I analyze his mature teaching concerning the doctrine he termed "the heart of the Christian message" and therefore the "heart of the Church's dogmatics."[3] Undoubtedly, the doctrine of reconciliation represents the heart of Barth's Church Dogmatics; it is the cantus firmus which resounds throughout Barth's entire theology. His comprehensive treatment is a magnum opus in itself. It is unparalleled in breadth and depth in the history of Protestant theology and perhaps in the entire history of theology. It represents the fulfillment of Barth's mature theological reflection in the Church Dogmatics and gathers together perspectives and emphases characteristic of his theology from its beginnings.

Barth began writing on the doctrine of reconciliation at age sixty-five! The final volume published during his lifetime appeared some sixteen years later in 1967. He wrote the final Preface during the Easter season of 1967. Barth died a year and a half later on December 10, 1968, at the age of eighty-two. Including the published "Fragment" on "The Christian Life," his doctrine of reconciliation involved three volumes in five books (1953-1967) totalling 3,639 pages of text in the original! Although my analysis deals mainly with its foundations in the cross and resurrection of Jesus in

Church Dogmatics, 4:1, that mountain range is formidable in itself.

In Part III, I have found myself concurring with many of the findings of Bertold Klappert's thorough treatment entitled, Die Auferweckung des Gekreuzigten (1971, 1974). Interested scholars will find in Klappert's citations and bibliographies a wealth of German literature dealing with Jesus' cross and resurrection within the context of the larger European discussion of christology. Those willing to engage his rather formidable German prose will be richly rewarded. Though often quoted in German works as the definitive interpretation of Barth on our theme, his work remains untranslated and largely ignored in English studies of Barth. For this reason, I have felt it judicious to engage Klappert's conclusions and theses and to cite them as fully as I have. It is my hope that an increasing number of English speaking theologians will contribute to the critical engagement with Barth's doctrine of reconciliation which characterizes the contemporary German theological scene. Roman Catholic scholars continue to produce important assessments of various aspects of Barth's theology. If my research contributes to this ecumenical dialogue on Barth's theology, and particularly to discussions of the doctrine of reconciliation, I will be gratified.

On occasion, Barth depicted God's reconciling activity in Jesus Christ as the center of Christian faith and doctrine. Other Christian doctrines concerning creation, anthropology and consummation lie on the circumference of the circle and are illuminated by Jesus Christ and his reconciling work at their common center. Shifting the image, Barth held that reconciliation effected in Jesus Christ is the "only place from which as Christians we can think forwards and backwards, for which a Christian knowledge of both God and man is possible."[4] Barth felt keenly the "very special respon- sibility laid on the theologian" seeking the truth concerning God's reconciling work in behalf of humanity in Jesus Christ. "To fail here is to fail everywhere. To be on the right track here makes it impossible to be completely mistaken in the whole."[5]

My writing of this book began during the celebration of the centennial of Barth's birth in 1986. Let me take this means of thanking the Administration and Trustees of The Southern Baptist Theological Seminary, Louisville, Kentucky, for granting me a sabbatical to pursue this research at the Graduate Theological Union in Berkeley, California, during 1985-1986. Library staffs of the Graduate Theological Union and of The Southern Baptist Theological Seminary were most helpful. The Office Services division provided invaluable assistance in the preparation of this book for publication. Eileen Long deserves special thanks in this regard. Robert Shippey, Jr., a doctoral candidate and Director of Continuing Education for Ministry at Southern Baptist Theological Seminary, was helpful in checking references.

This book is dedicated to Marilyn, my wife, a continuing source of strength and a fellow pilgrim on our common journey, and to our two children, Charles David and Mary Elizabeth. It also honors my parents, William and Mary Mueller, who recently celebrated their sixty-third wedding anniversary. Their life of faith continues to be an example and a source of inspiration.

David L. Mueller
The Southern Baptist Theological Seminary
Louisville, Kentucky

[1]Karl Barth, Church Dogmatics, ed. G. W. Bromiley and T. F. Torrance (Edinburgh: T. & T. Clark, 1936-1969), 4:4, Fragment. Cited hereafter as CD. The original Kirchliche Dogmatik (Zürich: EVZ-Verlag, 1932-1967), cited as KD.

[2]For an analysis of Albrecht Ritschl's influential three volume work, The Christian Doctrine of Justification and Reconciliation, see my An Introduction to the Theology of Albrecht Ritschl (Philadelphia: Westminster, 1969), especially pp. 145-180. For Barth's negative assessment of Ritschl, see his Protestant Theology in the Nineteenth Century (Valley Forge: Judson, 1973), pp. 654-661.

[3]CD 4:1, p. 3.

[4]CD 4:1, p. 81.

[5]CD 4:1, p. ix.

PART I

THE EARLY BARTH:
ROOTS AND CONTROVERSIES (1919-1934)

Chapter I

THE EARLY BARTH AND HIS CRITICS (1919-1934)

INTRODUCTION

One of the decisive signs of the impending breach in the ranks of the dialectical theologians was the developing divergence of the perspectives of Barth and Bultmann, the movement's two luminaries. What began as a skirmish between these contemporaries in the 1920's issued in a pitched theological battle by mid-century following Bultmann's publication in 1941 of his programmatic essay, "New Testament and Mythology." Delivered initially as a lecture to pastors of the Confessing Church on April 21, 1941, it soon made Bultmann's demythologizing of the New Testament a divisive event among Protestant clergy, theologians, churches and laity in Germany and beyond. Indeed the theological landscape in post-war Germany down to the present was markedly influenced by responses for and against Bultmann.

Looking back on the history of modern Protestant theology in Germany, one has to include this essay in the company of such epoch making documents as Schleiermachers' Speeches on Religion of 1799, or Martin Kähler's The So-Called Historical Jesus and the Historic, Biblical Christ of 1892, or the Barmen Declaration of 1934, the theological Confession of the Confessing Church in Germany in its battle with National Socialism. It is not surprising that Bultmann's statement of 1941 was to receive ever sharper criticism from Barth. Barth was expelled from his professorship in Bonn to Switzerland by the Nazi state in 1935. The years of World War II account, in part, for his somewhat delayed response to Bultmann's proposal. Yet it is clear that Barth's temporary silence did not mean that Barth's counter offensive was not being prepared.

I.   BARTH'S COMMENTARY ON ROMANS: DIVERGING
     PERSPECTIVES (1919-1922)

Before assessing Barth's major encounters with Bultmann in mid-century, it must be recalled that its origins can be traced to Barth's initial disenchantment with Protestant liberalism which began about 1914 and intensified in the years of World War I. During this period, both Barth and Bultmann were increasingly critical of cultural Protestantism and also agreed in their stress upon the transcendence of God. In addition, they concurred in opposing the liberal attempt to establish faith on the basis of what could be known of the historical Jesus. Barth's reputation as the leader of the so-called dialectical theology was initially secured through the publication of the first edition of his Romans in 1919. James Smart comments that Bultmann's reputation as a "ruthless pioneering" form critic and leading New Testament scholar was established through his first major work, History of the Synoptic Tradition, published in 1921.

     A.   First Encounter with Bultmann

It seemed incongruous to many that Bultmann, the

radical form critic, could write so appreciative a review of the second edition of Barth's Romans published in 1922. The latter was already acknowledged as the foremost opponent of the reigning liberal theology and its historical critical methodology and mode of exegesis. Barth was forewarned of Bultmann's basically positive response in the very first letter of their extensive correspondence. Bultmann writes: "In my review, of course, I have restrained my own objections and wishes in order to concentrate on reaching an understanding if at all possible."[1] Yet Bultmann openly admits that he concurs with Barth's depiction of the relationship of the interpreter to the text in his preface to the second edition. Furthermore, Bultmann remarks that the latter edition made a much deeper impression on him than did the first, and he commends Barth for numerous insightful exegeses.

What are some of their points of agreement? First, Bultmann notes that both recognize that philological and historical explanation of the text represents a necessary dimension of exegesis. In addition, Bultmann also acknowledges that the interpreter can exegete a text correctly only--as Barth holds--if one "has an inner relation to the subject matter of the text."[2] Second, Bultmann agrees that exegetical comprehension reaches its highest level when the interpreter is so identified with the author that he virtually forgets that he is not himself the author. In short, the interpreter feels he can speak in the name of the author and vice versa. Hence Bultmann concurs that the paraphrase as a commentary on the text is the pinnacle of the exegetical art. Third, true interpretation of a text must be undertaken in the light of the subject matter of the entire text.[3] Fourth, Barth has grasped the depth of the Pauline

conception of faith refusing to allow it to be equated
or confused with any human capacity or potential for, or
expression of, religious experience which could be
construed as a basis for self-justification in the sight
of God.[4]

Despite these agreements, Smart observes that
"Bultmann's distance from Barth was evident on every page
of the review."[5] Bultmann errs in identifying Barth's
commentary with liberal theology and its stress on "the
autonomy and absoluteness of religion."[6] Indeed,
Bultmann traces a lineage from the Apostle Paul to
Schleiermacher, Otto and finally to Barth. Yet by the
year 1921, Barth was clearly opposed to Schleiermacher
and even more to the neo-Protestant or liberal theology
deriving from him. Smart comments that Bultmann

> ...misses the point of Barth's radical nega-
> tion of religion because he fails to see how
> central eschatology is for Barth and that in
> defining faith Barth starts not from what
> faith means for man but from the other end of
> things, from the world of God which is every-
> where pressing in upon us. The reality of
> that world is revealed in Christ in its anti-
> thesis to our entire human world so that faith
> is first of all the apprehension of it as
> God's judgment upon us and only then as God's
> transforming grace.[7]

Smart is surely right that Barth always regards
"religion" as the human attempt at self-justification.
It is therefore diametrically opposed to what Paul
designates as "faith." Yet Bultmann fails to see this
radical distinction and equates religion with what Barth
says about faith. This leads him to interpret the
purpose of Barth's commentary as "the demonstration of
the autonomy and absoluteness of religion".[8] Even prior

to Bultmann's review of Barth's second edition of his Romans appearing shortly after its publication in 1922, Barth learned from a Swiss student of Bultmann's in Marburg that Bultmann was giving considerable attention to it. Barth relayed this word to Thurneysen saying that "Bultmann not only has given his lectures on my Romans but has spent the last six hours of his course working over it alone. He takes 'fearful pains' to understand me."[9] Through this channel Barth also learned that the "discussion [of the Romans] ran aground somehow on the question of Christology."[10] It appears that though both agreed that the liberal quest of the historical Jesus was wanting at the point of failing to deal adequately with the kerygmatic nature of the New Testament witness to Jesus as the Christ, Barth, unlike Bultmann, was moving toward a truly incarnational theology. When Barth spoke of the thirty years of Jesus' earthly life as "years of revelation," Bultmann parts company with him decisively. "I confess that I simply do not understand him; here I can only see contradictions."[11] Upon learning in some detail of Bultmann's reservations from his Marburg source, Barth remarked: "So there is still all manner of old leaven to be swept out even in Marburg. ..."[12]

In the preface to the third edition of Romans, Barth notes that he found it strange that the second edition had received a "friendly reception" from Bultmann. Yet Barth adds: "Bultmann complains that I am too conservative."[13] Bultmann had called for Barth to be more critical in distinguishing between the "Spirit of Christ" and "other spirits" which are also heard in Paul's epistle. Barth interprets Bultmann as saying that Paul's opinions must be criticized since "even he fails at times to retain his grip upon what is, in fact,

6

his subject."[14] Contrary to Bultmann's charge that he is not, therefore, radical enough in his exegesis of Paul, Barth states:

> But I must go farther than he [Bultmann] does and say that there are in the Epistle no words at all which are not words of those "other spirits" which he calls Jewish or Popular Christian or Hellenistic or whatever else they may be. Is it really legitimate to extract a certain number of passages and claim that there the veritable Spirit of Christ has spoken? Or, to put it another way, can the Spirit of Christ be thought of as standing in the Epistle side by side with 'other' spirits and in competition with them? It seems to me impossible to set the Spirit of Christ--the veritable subject-matter of the Epistle--over against other spirits, in such a manner as to deal out praise to some passages, and depreci-ate others where Paul is not controlled by his true subject-matter. Rather, it is for us to perceive and to make clear that the whole is placed under the KRISIS of the Spirit of Christ. The whole is litera, that is, voices of those other spirits. The problem is whether the whole must not be understood in relation to the true subject-matter which is--The Spirit of Christ. This is the problem which provides aim and purpose to our study of the litera.[15]

B.   "The historical critics must be more critical
      to suit me." (Barth)

Barth's critical stance toward Bultmann in the above citation is both prophetic of things to come in his ensuing controversy with him and of a piece with his dissatisfaction with the virtually uncontested dominance of the historical-critical methodology among liberal biblical and dogmatic theologians in the first decades of the twentieth century. Their ire already had been incited by Barth's comment in the Preface to the first edition of his Romans. Commenting on the historical distance separating the Apostle's text from the contemporary interpreter, Barth observed that the "differences between then and now, there and here . . . ." may be uncovered by means of the historical-critical method. Yet he maintained that in the last analysis "the purpose of such investigation can only be to demonstrate that these differences are, in fact, purely trivial."[16] Barth also stated openly that he would choose the "venerable doctrine of Inspiration" rather than the former method were he forced to choose between them. Why so? "The doctrine of Inspiration is concerned with the labour of apprehending, without which no technical equipment, however complete, is of any use whatever."[17]

Reactions from the liberal camp to the first edition of Barth's commentary--insofar as they bothered to take note of it--were largely critical. In the preface to the second edition, Barth chafes from the charge that "I have been accused of being an 'enemy of historical criticism.'"[18] Jülicher, Barth's former professor at Marburg, spoke disdainfully of the first edition and of Barth as "an esoteric personage" whose commentary should come under the heading of "Practical Theology." He depicts Barth as a gnostic and Marcionite so intoxicated by "holy egoism" that he is unable to learn anything from, or even listen to, what the Apostle teaches. In short, Barth falls prey to a radical kind of exegesis which repeats his pet themes ad nauseam. As such, his commentary does not contribute to Pauline scholarship.[19]

Bultmann supported Jülicher's negative reaction to the first edition of Barth's Romans in a note appended to his review of the second edition. He writes: "Barth will partly gather from what is said [in this review] and will partly state himself, that, in relation to both the historical-philological exposition and the material evaluation of Romans and Paul, I agree in large measure with what Jülicher said about the first edition. ..."[20] Others dismissed Barth as a speculative theologian, subjectivist, or a "Biblicist." He is seen to be addicted, like Calvin, with "'The Compulsion of Inspiration.'"[21] In reviewing Barth's first edition of the "Romans," Bultmann welcomed its "religious culture-criticism." But he viewed Barth guilty of a "renewal of enthusiasm"--a kind of pneumatic exegesis--which flies in the face of everything cherished in critical biblical investigation. Even worse, Barth "arbitrarily gave support to the Pauline Christ-myth."[22]

In his second edition of the Romans, Barth responds directly to charges that he rejects historical criticism. "I have been accused of being an 'enemy of historical criticism' . . . I have nothing whatever to say against historical criticism. I recognize it, and once more state quite definitely that it is both necessary and justified."[23] Where then is the point at issue between Barth and the historical critical school? It is not the case that Barth appeals to some kind of private warrant for his interpretation of Paul under the direct inspiration of the Spirit; nor does he appeal to some highly nuanced biblical hermeneutic as the key to unlocking Paul's theology. Two statements provide insights into Barth's general hermeneutic: "Criticism (krinein) applied to historical documents means for me the measuring of words and phrases by the standard of that about which the documents are speaking--unless indeed the whole be nonsense."[24] The failure to deal with the "standard," the subject-matter of the text, "the one cardinal question" of the text, is what Barth

saw lacking in many modern liberal commentaries. Often
their authors seemed to restrict their inquiry to what
finally are matters of prolegomena. This accounts for
Barth's rejoinder to the historical critics: "The
historical critics must be more critical to suit my
taste."[25] Barth's passion was for the Sache, the
subject-matter, to which the text pointed. This means:
"The Word ought to be exposed in the words."[26]

This quest requires the exegete to become contem-
poraneous with the text. Barth began his preface to the
first edition with this programmatic statement: "Paul,
as a child of his age, addressed his contemporaries. It
is, however, far more important that, as Prophet and
Apostle of the Kingdom of God, he veritably speaks to
all men of every age."[27] To become Paul's contemporaries
as his witness confronts the exegete leads Barth to
adopt the exegetical method of the Reformers and more
recent Pauline interpreters like Hofmann, J. T. Beck,
Godet and Schlatter. Above all, Calvin provides Barth's
model for an exegetical commentary:

> ...how energetically Calvin, having first
> established what stands in the text, sets
> himself to re-think the whole material and to
> wrestle with it, till the walls which separate
> the sixteenth century from the first become
> transparent! Paul speaks, and the man of the
> sixteenth century hears. The conversation
> between the original record and the reader
> moves round the subject-matter, until a dis-
> tinction between yesterday and to-day becomes
> impossible.[28]

By contrast, Barth portrayed historical critics as
prone to remain "unmoved spectators" in their treatment
of Paul.[29] Becoming a contemporary with the text's
subject-matter is opposed to such a "cool" mode of

interpretation:

> Intelligent comment means that I am driven on
> till I stand with nothing before me but the
> enigma of the matter; till the document seems
> hardly to exist as a document; till I have
> almost forgotten that I am not its author;
> till I know the author so well that I allow
> him to speak in my name and am even able to
> speak in his name myself.[30]

Such aims and claims led Jülicher to charge both Barth
and Gogarten with a total disregard for the contributions of historical scholarship and to depict them as
foes of historical developments within Christendom.
Their malaise was attributed to succumbing to a
neo-gnosticism. Both Jülicher and Harnack noted Barth's
pietism and even his sectarianism. Harnack dismissed
Barth as a Marcionite addicted to dualistic categories.[31]

C.   The 'Infinite Qualitative Distinction....
      God is in Heaven, and You are on Earth.'
      (Kierkegaard)

In his prefaces to both editions of the Romans,
Barth underlines his intention in interpreting the
Apostle Paul. In the first edition's preface, he
writes: "...my whole energy of interpreting has been
expended in an endeavour to see through and beyond
history into the spirit of the Bible, which is the
Eternal Spirit."[32] To facilitate this goal, Barth
utilized a dialectical method in the first edition of
the Romans. This led some critics to accuse him of
speculation, Hegelianism or Alexandrianism. In Barth's
mind, a dialectical method was appropriate because of
what Kierkegaard called the "'infinite qualitative

distinction' between time and eternity and to my regarding this as possessing negative as well as positive significance: 'God is in heaven, and thou art on earth.'"[33] The use of dialectics in the second edition was intended to acknowledge this radical divide between eternity and time and between God and man. That Barth's intention was not to stress a final separation between God and man in dialectical fashion is evident from the following prefatory statement:

> The relation between such a God and such a man, and the relation between such a man and such a God, is for me the theme of the Bible and the essence of philosophy. Philosophers name this <u>Krisis</u> of human perception--the Prime Cause: the Bible beholds at the same cross-roads--the figure of Jesus Christ.[34]

Put more simply, Barth states that his "fundamental assumption" is that "I assume that in the Epistle to the Romans Paul did speak of Jesus Christ, and not of some one else."[35] This theme of Paul's Epistle calls in question any approach to it "with any other assumption than that God is God."[36] This working presupposition in no way precludes wrestling with the text's meaning, but rather requires it. "Paul knows of God what most of us do not know; and his Epistles enable us to know what he knew."[37]

The concern to listen to what the text says--whether it be a text of Goethe or Lao-Tse--is what characterizes Barth's hermeneutic. Hence his purported "biblicism" means for Barth simply that one should "consider well" the text confronting one as reader.[38] "When I am named 'Biblicist,'" wrote Barth, "all that can rightly be proved against me is that I am prejudiced in supposing the Bible to be a good book, and that I hold it to be profitable for men to takes its conceptions at least as seriously as they take their own."[39]

Looking back in 1926 upon the theological landscape as effected by the two edition of his Romans, Barth expressed the wish that the humorous verse penned by a German pastor about a "Hound of God" might apply to him--and hopefully--to others also.

> God needs MEN, not creatures
> Full of noisy, catchy phrases.
> Dogs he asks for, who their noses
> Deeply thrust into--To-day,
> And there scent Eternity.
>
> Should it lie too deeply buried,
> Then go on, and fiercely burrow,
> Excavate until--To-morrow.[40]

Commenting on Barth's wish, Minear writes:

> Barth viewed himself as such a dog, a dog of the Lord, who deplored the reluctance of his exegetical colleagues to burrow more directly into the Scriptures where he scented Eternity. On their part, his colleagues have found it virtually impossible to accept this burrowing as part of their vocation.[41]

II. SEARCHING FOR THEOLOGICAL ROOTS: FROM PASTOR TO PROFESSOR (1921-1922)

In his thirty-fifth year, after a decade of ministry as a village pastor in his native Switzerland, Barth accepted the invitation to become honorary professor of Reformed Theology at Göttingen, a renowned university in northern Germany. The year was 1921. The transition from the life of a Christian socialist pastor of Safenwil to that of a theological professor with its new demands occasioned a good deal of soul searching and apprehension. These feelings were intensified by the dominant Lutheran caste of Göttingen's theological faculty which looked with suspicion at their new Reformed colleague. The acclaim of Göttingen's theological faculty was due largely to the widespread influence which Albrecht Ritschl had exerted there as a Lutheran systematic theologian. He reached the zenith of his influence during the last quarter of the 19th century prior to his death in 1889. After his death, the liberal theology in its Ritschlian form dominated German theology and to some extent in the Anglo-Saxon world. During Barth's theological student days and until the time of his Copernican revolution, he was a somewhat uneasy devotee of the Ritschlian perspective as mediated to him through Wilhelm Herrmann, a Ritschlian.

A. Acquiring the "Necessary Foundations"

In an autobiographical reflection Barth recalls the new challenges he faced as a fledgling professor. He remarks that essentially he wished to say "the same things as were said in Safenwil." However, the context was different. Barth continues:

> Now it was no longer a question of attacking all kinds of errors and abuses. All at once we were in the front rank. We had to take on responsibilities which we had not known about while we were simply in opposition. ...we had been given an opportunity to say what we really thought in theology, and to show the church our real intention and ability...And yet we were far from being ready. ...We had only just begun on a course which each one had to follow laboriously in his own sphere.[42]

In many ways, Barth felt unprepared for his new

academic tasks. He worked assiduously. Gaps in his own
knowledge had to be filled; deeper foundations had to be
laid. "So before venturing on dogmatics," Barth
recalls, "I announced some purely historical
lectures--essentially for my own instruction."[43] The
demands of his new courses forced him "almost always on
a night shift." It required working faster than his
"natural tempo." He complained often of the "mountains
of material which I haven't mastered." He lamented a
"lack of academic agility, an inadequate knowledge of
Latin and the most appalling memory."[44] One principle he
sought to follow was that "if one moves too quickly--
and this often happens for very good reasons--before
doing what really has to be done first (as though this
could wait), one always has to pay the price."[45]

Barth was surprised and gratified by the "sensa-
tional news" in January, 1922, that "I have been made a
doctor of theology by the (Protestant) faculty at
Münster"--"because of his many and varied contributions
to the revision of religious and theological questioning."[46] Busch remarks that Barth was also quite
pleased with the reaction of his young daughter,
Franzeli. She asked: "Would I now be able to make
children well?"[47]

B. A Committed Reformed Theologian

In his earliest lectures, Barth treated theological
topics and texts related to his own Reformed heritage.
Though assigned by the state to teach in the area of
Reformed theology, Barth confessed later in life: "I
can now admit that at that time I didn't even have a
copy of the Reformed confessions, and I certainly hadn't
read them. ... Fortunately it turned out that my theol-

ogy had become more Reformed, more Calvinistic than I had known, so I could pursue my special confessional task with delight and with a good conscience."[48] His first lecture course dealt with the Heidelberg Catechism. On the basis of other lecture courses and research in Reformed theology Busch observes that "Barth became more and more a committed Reformed theologian, and Barth comments that he 'slowly but surely became intent on pure <u>Reformed</u> doctrine.'"[49]

Barth did not preach often during the early days in Göttingen. Beyond his purely academic concerns and preparation, he tried to be available to students experiencing considerable turmoil in the aftermath of the First World War. He instituted a weekly open discussion hour for students in which any and all questions were permitted. Each Saturday afternoon included a walk with those interested in which Barth either "walked and taught" or "taught and walked."[50] At the end of each semester students gathered with Barth for an "exuberant party" marked by parodies written on everything-- including Herr Professor Barth! One ritual Barth enjoyed on these occasions was "to sit at the piano singing the unforgettable 'Song of the Swiss Exiles' to his own accompaniment."[51] Contacts with students proved an immense stimulus to Barth's teaching and development and gratifying personally. He recalls: "What I had missed in Safenwil I now had an abundance of in Göttingen: talking and arguing not only with books, but with people."[52]

C.   A Trusted Friend and New Encounters

Relationships with colleagues were respectful, but
somewhat distant.   This was due, in part, to Barth's
being an outsider--he was Reformed and Swiss!   Carl
Stange, "an apologist for modernism and positivism" and
a "skilled advocate of Christianity," made it clear to
him on one occasion that in Hanover "the Reformed church
means no more than the milleniarian sects!!"[53]   The fact
that Barth's professorship was an honorary post also led
to some embarrassment from his colleagues.   Barth re-
counts:

> ...the faculty even tormented me a bit: they
> wanted to keep me under ... On the black
> notice board where announcements of lectures
> were pinned they put mine next to the lessons
> of the teacher who showed students how to play
> the harmonium ... that was the place of Re-
> formed theology at the time.   A gymnastics
> teacher was another member of our party. ...
> But I survived.[54]

Barth comments: "In the common room I felt small and
despicable among these giants of scholarship"--or like
a "wandering gipsy ... with only a couple of leaky
kettles to call his own who to compensate occasionally
burns a house down."[55]

Barth found himself most attracted to the church
historians, Erik Peterson, a "sardonic individualist ...
who was convinced of the 'transitoriness of earthly
things,'" and to Emmanuel Hirsch, a learned scholar and
specialist in Luther and Fichte.   Hirsch, who later
became one of the most notable German theologians to
rally to Hitler's Nazi cause, was already a "German
nationalist to his very fragile bones. ..."[56]   Notwithstanding, he and Barth had many personal contacts marked

by respectful but sharp theological exchanges. Busch records the following revealing incident:

> As early as February 1922 there was an ex-change of written memoranda between the two in which they expressed their theological dif-ferences in eleven theses and antitheses. Here Barth contrasted his view of the Bible as evidence of the concrete revelation of God with the view of the Bible [à la Hirsch] as a general religious document.[57]

1. <u>Eduard Thurneysen</u>. Contacts with friends and theologians old and new provided further stimulus for Barth. During his decade as a pastor in Switzerland, his closest friend and theological ally was Eduard Thurneysen, Reformed pastor in a nearby village. Their frequent correspondence and visits while neighboring pastors struggling to hear the Word of God within the words of the Bible led to a deep and lifelong friendship marked by a common theological perspective. Their earliest correspondence (1914-1925) published in English as <u>Revolutionary Theology in the Making</u> is a moving and instructive account of the beginnings of the theology of the Word of God evolving out of the struggles, hopes and fears of two young pastors. Barth's departure to Göttingen neither terminated their friendship nor their correspondence. Thurneysen's visit to Barth in 1922 and their continuing exchanges through letters meant, said Barth, "more than my daily bread." Looking back on those early days together, Barth recalled:

> One can...say that to ground theology in the church and especially in the work of the pastor...is a characteristic of the whole theological renewal movement...It should be known, however, on the one hand that Eduard Thurneysen saw the need for a church theology of this kind before anyone else; at any rate,

he stimulated me to work in this direction. On
the other hand, it should be noted that of all
those who have made a reputation and a name
within this new theology, there is hardly
anyone who embodies it as a movement from the
church for the church as characteristically as
does Eduard Thurneysen.[58]

In another moving reminiscence, Thurneysen's singular significance for Barth's self-understanding and
his own theological direction is apparent.

In Göttingen, too, I needed correspondence and
exchange of ideas with him more than my daily
bread. This was just because I knew how my
stories amused him and because I could confide
to him as to no one else my constant cares and
concerns, which seemed to increase rather than
decrease...but also because it was always my
deepest need to hear his judgment on what I
had done. And though I had my star to follow,
as he had his, I had to keep taking my
bearings from him because I had to understand
him and be understood by him in order to
understand myself properly.[59]

2. <u>Friedrich Gogarten</u>. During this period, exchanges and contacts with Bultmann, Gogarten and
Tillich--all of whom were lumped together by some commentators as representatives of the newer dialectial
theology--shed some light on Barth's direction. Though
Gogarten and Barth were already acquainted, the former's
visit to Göttingen in February, 1922, led to further
dialogue. Barth remarks that on that occasion, "we were
at one in some forthright negative views," but in little
else. Each listened to the other lecture. A parting
exchange indicative of diverging paths, Barth recalls as
follows:

"Do you know, Karl Barth, I don't think that
things will turn out as you expect. Before we

> can talk about the Heidelberg Catechism and
> the Epistle to the Ephesians, we must first
> know what history is." I asked him, "But how
> will you discover what history is?" He re-
> plied, "First I must tackle Troeltsch, Dil-
> they, Yorck von Wartenburg and some other
> great figures from the beginning of the
> 1920s.... Well, first of all we must find a
> concept of history and only on the basis of
> that will we be able to read texts like the
> Heidelberg Catechism and the Epistle to the
> Ephesians"... Even then, that is in the
> winter of 1921-22, I noticed... that we did
> not think in the same way. For me it was
> quite the other way round: first of all I
> wanted to study the Heidelberg Catechism and
> the Epistle to the Ephesians. Only then did
> I want to try to understand what "history" is.
> But these were two very different approaches.[60]

Barth's biographer notes that this fundamental difference "began to hamper the development of their
friendship" though it "did not prevent them from following each other's progress with friendly interest in
subsequent years."[61]

3. <u>Rudolf Bultmann</u>. Barth first became acquainted
with Bultmann while working in Marburg in 1909. From the
time of the first edition of Barth's <u>Romans</u> in 1919,
each was conscious of the other's publications. Some
identified both as representatives of the rising dialectical theology. In reminiscing about their relationship
in the twenties some years later, Barth said: "Of
course Bultmann was also involved in the break with
liberalism... I thought I understood him and perhaps he
thought he understood me. Certainly we sometimes said
the same kind of thing."[62] In February, 1922, Barth paid
his first visit to Bultmann in Marburg. Bultmann had
been appointed as professor of New Testament there in
1921. From that post he became the most influential
<u>Neutestamentler</u> of the first half of the 20th century.

Bultmann had arranged for a group of students to meet
with Barth; he recalled meeting students awaiting him
"in a den with plenty of copies of Romans thoroughly
marked in pencil."[63]

We noted that Barth commented in the Preface to the
third edition of his Romans that the second edition had
received a "friendly reception" from Bultmann, but also
that his review revealed some very sharp differences
between them, prophetic of the widening breach which was
to separate them.

4. Paul Tillich. During this same period, Paul
Tillich visited Göttingen. He and Barth were already
acquainted and knew something of each other's work.
Tillich had served as a chaplain in the German army
during the war. In 1919, he was appointed lecturer at
the University of Berlin. Apart from their common interest in Christian Socialism, they were often linked
theologically. In a letter to Thurneysen, Barth writes
that in the first of two lengthy talks with Tillich, two
students "assailed the stranger with incidental questions ...while I filled my pipe or else had no answer
for the moment." He continues: "The most remarkable
things about him are his 'antipathy to orthodoxy' and
his mythology of history, in which the need for the
supernatural, which he otherwise takes pains to sup-
press, comes pouring out." In their second talk, Barth
relates the following incident: "Hirsch took pleasure
in setting us against each other, denouncing Tillich to
me as un-Christian and me to Tillich as unscholarly. Of
course, we did not agree with this type-casting, although there is something in it. We could only make our
peace on our somewhat narrow common front against
Hirsch, and otherwise on the basis that we should think
and expect the best of each other."[64]

In a subsequent exchange initiated by Tillich in
1923 on the use of paradox in the crisis theology of
Barth and Gogarten, he acknowledged the legitimacy of
speaking about God in terms of the language of paradox.
His main rebuke against both is their surrender of the
eternal tension between the divine and the human,
between the yes and the no, in their non-dialectical and
non-paradoxical identification of the Absolute with
salvation-history, and especially, with Jesus Christ.
In so doing, they were in danger of ushering in a new
orthodoxy and supranaturalism. Barth's reply anticipates what was to remain the main point of contention
between them. He finds Tillich committed to a metaphysic and not finally to the Church within which the
saving activity of God is confessed. The former therefore takes precedence over salvation-history and the
revelation of God which has taken place once and for all
in Jesus Christ. Hence there is no circle of faith in
which revelation, canon and the work of the Holy Spirit
are normative for theological reflection. Apparently
both saw quite clearly their diverging perspectives.[65]

In the summer of 1922, Barth announced he would
offer a course on Calvin in the fall. Perhaps the well-
known German saying of Goethe encouraged him in his
quest to discover and appropriate his own familial and
confessional roots. "Master what you have inherited
from your fathers in order that you may rightfully lay
claim to it" (Faust, Part I). Though he had some prior
knowledge of Calvin from Safenwil days and earlier,
Barth was unprepared for his own experience of discovery. Writing Thurneysen, he said that Calvin was like
"a waterfall, a primitive forest, a demonic power,
something straight down from the Himalayas, absolutely
Chinese, strange, mythological; I just don't have the

organs, the suction cups, even to assimilate this phenomenon, let alone to describe it properly."[66]

D.   "The Need and Promise of Christian Preaching"

During the late summer and fall of 1922, Barth
delivered a series of lectures to pastors and church
audiences throughout Germany indicative of his theological position.   Speaking to pastors on "The Need and
Promise of Christian Preaching," Barth related how his
own confrontation with the task of preaching was the
single, most decisive happening in his Christian pilgrimage. No comprehension of Barth's theology is possible
apart from this beginning and its bearing on his entire
later theological development.   This is quite evident in
the Barth-Thurneysen correspondence.   Barth suggests
that those seeking to understand the genesis of the
theology associated with Thurneysen, himself and others
needed to be aware that it "did not come into being as
a result of any desire of ours to form a school or to
devise a system; it arose simply out of what we felt to
be the "need and promise of Christian preaching"--and
this is the subject upon which I wish to speak to you
today."   He then continued:

> May I make a brief personal explanation?   It
> is relevant to the subject.   For twelve years
> I was a minister, as all of you are.   I had my
> theology.   It was not really mine, to be sure,
> but that of my unforgotten teacher, Wilhelm
> Her[r]mann, grafted upon the principles which
> I had learned, less consciously than unconsci-
> ously, in my native home--the principles of
> those Reformed Churches which today I repre-
> sent in an official capacity.   Once in the
> ministry, I found myself growing away from
> these theological habits of thought and being
> forced back at every point more and more upon
> the specific minister's problem, the sermon.

> I sought to find my way between the problem of
> human life on the one hand and the content of
> the Bible on the other. As a minister I
> wanted to speak to the people in the infinite
> contradiction of their life, but to speak the
> no less infinite message of the Bible, which
> was as much of a riddle as life. Often enough
> these two magnitudes, life and the Bible, have
> risen before me (and still rise!) like Scylla
> and Charybdis: if these are the whence and
> the whither of Christian preaching, who shall,
> who can, be a minister and preach?[67]

Along these lines, Barth saw both minister--and
theologian--suspended between human life in its great
need on the one hand and the Bible and its message on
the other. Hence, the critical and ultimate issue
confronting both minister and theologian is--God. In
this crisis true preaching for Barth reckons with a twin
expectancy: first, the expectancy of the congregation
which longs--whether they acknowledge it fully or not--
for a word from God; second, there is the minister who
has listened expectantly to the Bible's witness to the
Word of God and seeks to proclaim that word. In a
typical statement, Barth states his view of preaching.

> As the minister of the people who come or do
> not come to church on Sunday, he must be the
> first to give them the answer; and as the
> minister of the Bible he must be the first to
> be prepared to submit to God's question by
> asking the question about God, without which
> God's answer cannot be given. If he answers
> the people's question but answers it as a man
> who has himself been questioned by God, then
> he speaks--the word of God; and this is what
> the people seek in him and what God has com-
> missioned him to speak.[68]

This was the context in which Barth's nascent
theology was fashioned. He said "it simply came about

that the familiar situation of the minister on Saturday
at his desk and on Sunday in his pulpit crystallized in
my case into a marginal note to all theology. ..."[69]In
1922 he felt it far too grandiose to speak of his theology as a system. He spoke of it as a "viewpoint," a
kind of marginal note, or "as a corrective, as the
'pinch of spice ... in the food,' as Kierkegaard says."[70]

In concluding his address, Barth spoke of the need
for a new Reformation in the Church. Then he added:

> According to the eighth chapter of Romans,
> there is more hope when one sighs Veni Creator
> Spiritus [Come, Creator Spirit], than when he
> exaults as if the spirit were already his.
> You have been introduced to "my theology" if
> you have heard this sigh.[71]

The audience for Barth's second lecture was made up
of "unsuspecting and self-assured" ministers and laity
gathered in support of Die Christliche Welt, a liberal
Christian journal with a social orientation. Upon
completion of his formal theological studies and ordina-
tion in 1909, Barth's first position was as assistant to
the editor of this influential journal. Writing to
Thurneysen of the setting for his address, Barth spoke
of "parade of liberals" who would only hear what he had
to say if he gave them a "lively introduction to 'the
fear of the Lord.'"[72]

His lecture was on "The Word of God and the Task of
the Ministry." His theme recalls some of the major
notes of the first lecture and thus unfolds something of
the heart of what many were designating as "Dialectical
Theology." At the outset Barth concedes that social,
psychological, ecclesiastical and other factors all
contribute to the perplexity which grips ministers. In
the final analysis, however, Barth states: "Our dif-

ficulty lies in the content of our task." He describes
the problematic situation of ministers in three theses:

> As ministers we ought to speak of God. We are
> human, however, and so cannot speak of God.
> We ought therefore to recognize both our
> obligation and our inability and by that very
> recognition give God the glory. This is our
> perplexity. The rest of our task fades into
> insignificance in comparison.[73]

While ministers are aware that the deepest human
longing finds its resolution in God alone, and while
they also know that they should speak of God, they are
conscious that they cannot. This dilemma and embarrassment exists because ministers are--or should be
aware--that God is not at the disposal of his
creatures--even if they be ministers! "The only answer
that possesses genuine transcendence, and so can solve
the riddle of immanence," declares Barth, "is God's
word--note, God's word."[74] Thus though the minister is
aware that the answer must come from beyond--from God--
there is also the consciousness of the brokenness of all
human language about God. In this dilemma, Barth notes
that pastors and theologians seek the answer to the
question concerning God either by appealing to dogmatic
solutions, or by taking the way of self-criticism or
mysticism, or finally, by engaging in theological dialectics. Though all have their place, none finally can
bridge the gap between the human and God himself. Yet
Barth holds that the embarrassment--occasioned by the
crisis of humanity suspended between finite and infinite, earth and heaven--may be a sign of hope. He
concludes:

> It may be that the Word, the word of God,
> which we ourselves shall never speak, has put

> on our weakness and unprofitableness so that
> <u>our</u> word <u>in</u> its very weakness and unprofita-
> bleness has become capable at least of being
> the mortal frame, the earthen vessel, of the
> word of God. It may be so, I say; and if it
> were, we should have reason not so much to
> speak of our need as to declare and publish
> the hope and hidden glory of our calling.[75]

Although the chairman of the ensuing discussion
sought to soften some of the sharpness of Barth's remarks, many of the liberals heard him as a "young Turk"
opposing the liberal establishment. By the time
Gogarten spoke "with heavy, obscure, but good words,"
even a church historian speaking after him confessed to
being quite "stupefied" by what the "young man,"
Gogarten, had said. On Barth's homeward journey from
the "dreamy autumn Thuringian woods, green, red, yellow
and...far, villages...with white gables and timber
frames...," he visited Luther's room in his birthplace
in Eisenach.[76]

    E.   Theological Ancestry: Toward a Theology
         of the Word of God

In the previous address, Barth traced his theological ancestry to a line running back through Kierkegaard,
Luther and Calvin, and finally to Paul and Jeremiah. He
expressly excluded Erasmus and Schleiermacher. With
reference to Schleiermacher, the acknowledged father of
modern Protestant liberal theology, Barth said:

> With all due respect to the genius shown in
> his work, I can <u>not</u> consider Schleiermacher a
> good teacher in the realm of theology because,
> so far as I can see, he is disastrously dim-
> sighted in regard to the fact that man as man
> is not only in <u>need</u> but beyond all hope of
> saving himself; that the whole of so-called
> religion, and not least the Christian reli-

gion, <u>shares</u> in this need; and that one can <u>not</u> speak of God simply by speaking of man in a loud voice."[77]

In the winter semester of 1922-23, Barth offered courses on the Epistle of James and on Zwingli. Though claiming to be open to what Zwingli's humanism might have to say, Barth confided to Thurneysen that he experienced a "negative conversion" in encountering him. He found in the Züricher, Zwingli, "simply the familiar modern Protestant theology, the very image of it, with a few eggshells from the early church thrown in."[78] Busch adds that Barth was disenchanted with Zwingli and "broke off the lectures with a description of the battle of Kappel in which Zwingli lost his life."[79]

Upon turning his attention once more directly to Luther, and especially Calvin, it became evident to Barth that his continuing study of the Reformed heritage had provided access to the larger heritage of the Reformation. Years later Barth recalled that his study of Luther and Calvin while in Safenwil really did not prove fruitful because "the lenses of spectacles" he wore precluded seeing what was really there. In retrospect, Barth pictured his developing viewpoint in Safenwil as still a kind of pre-Reformation one. It was "somehow in a corner along with nominalism, Augustinianism, mysticism, Wycliffe, etc. It was not itself the Reformation, but nevertheless the Reformation later sprang out of it."[80] Thus the soil was prepared for his deep engagement with the Reformation while at Göttingen. He writes:

Only now were my eyes properly open to the Reformers and their message of the justification and the sanctification of the sinner, of faith, of repentance and works, of the nature and limit of the church... .I had a great many things to learn from them... .[So it was that]

I 'swung into line with the Reformation' as
they used to say. ...[81]

Barth recalls that in the year 1922 someone dubbed
the theology of Barth and his colleagues as "dialectical
theology." From the foregoing analysis, it is clear
that the label, "dialectical theology," was not as apt
a designation of Barth's perspective as a "theology of
the Word of God." Theological excavations had "led us,
as it had to, to the Reformers' understanding of the
Bible and of God."[82] Already during the Safenwil days,
Barth had been strongly influenced by the Kingdom of God
theology of the Blumhardts and the Swiss Christian
socialists, Ragaz and Kutter. Barth remembered his
developing perspective as follows: "In contrast to the
historical and psychological account which the
'religious man' tended to give of himself at the
beginning of the century, the characteristic feature of
this theology [i.e. dialectical] was 'its question about
the superior, new element which limits and determines
any human self- understanding. In the Bible this is
called God, God's word, God's revelation, God's kingdom
and God's act. The adjective 'dialectical' describes a
way of thinking arising from man's conversation with the
sovereign God who encounters him."[83]

Barth also recalls that prior to 1919, the nascent
"theology of the Word" had a certain "affinity to existentialism, which was unknown to me at that time" and
also to "phenomenology." Barth remembers that he bought
and read his first Kierkegaard book, The Moment, in
1909, but the Dane made little impression on him at that
time. Then he adds:

He only entered my thinking seriously, and
more extensively, in 1919, at the critical

> turning- point between the first and second
> editions of my Romans. ...What we found parti-
> cularly attractive...was his inexorable criti-
> cism ... using it to attack all speculation
> which wiped out the infinite qualitative
> difference between God and man. ...[His] voice
> seemed to promise to us from near and far the
> dawn of a really new day.[84]

The fact that the dominant liberal theological establishment felt challenged and opposed the rising influence of this neo-reformation theology did not precipitate the latter's retreat. Instead, Barth, Thurneysen and Gogarten took the offensive by creating a new theological journal in 1922. Barth found Gogarten's suggestion that it be named, The Word, "intolerably presumptuous." He responded: "Better to call it The Ship of Fools than this idolatrous encumbrance."[85] They settled on the title suggested by Gogarten's initial article in the first issue of 1923 and entitled it Zwischen den Zeiten (Between the Times). The title proved prophetic in more ways than one.

III. CHRISTOLOGICAL CONCENTRATION: THE CONFESSION OF JESUS CHRIST AS "THE ONE WORD OF GOD" AS DIVISIVE IN CHURCH AND THEOLOGY (1931-1934)

Although the church struggle in Germany began at the very end of the period under consideration in this chapter, it needs to be treated as an epilogue for two reasons. First, in the estimate of Barth and those who stood with him in the church struggle beginning in 1933, the battle to remain faithful to the basic Christian confession of the lordship of Jesus Christ in the face of the inroads of the Nazi ideology within the Church represented a kairotic event for the neo-reformation theology of the Word of God. It occasioned a final division among the ranks of the dialectical or neo-reformation theologians who once stood quite united. Second, Barth regarded the struggle in opposition to the German Christians to be representative of the necessary rejection of the increasing role of natural theology within the history of neo-Protestant or liberal theology.

The background of the German church struggle may be sketched briefly as follows. Hitler came to power in January, 1933. The overwhelming majority of Protestants both in the established Churches, Evangelical (Lutheran) and Reformed, as in the Free Churches were committed to Hitler as "der Führer" and to the National Socialist ideology. Hitler personally appointed his protégé as the ruling Bishop (Reichsbischof) of the Evangelical Church. Those supportive of Hitler's appointee and the "official" Church recognized by the Third Reich were called "German Christians" (Deutsche Christen). The minority movement protesting this alliance of church and state, of Christian faith and national ideology, were known as the "Confessing Church" (Bekennende Kirche). Barth was the best known of the small group of theologians initiating and identifying with this protest movement.

On reading that Gogarten had accepted the dictum of a German Christian leader to the effect that "the Law of God is identical with the law of the German people," Barth was horrified. He regarded Gogarten's defection to the German Christians as symptomatic of the failure of the Church. Barth relived the disillusionment he experienced in 1914 when virtually all of his theologically liberal teachers rendered immediate and uncritical obeisance to the cause of Caesar in the form of Kaiser Wilhelm II and his war policy. Writing Thurneysen in the fall of 1933, Barth complained: "All along the line Christians and theologians have shown themselves to be a much weaker ... and more ambivalent group than we ever dreamt they might be even in the days of our greatest anger in the Aargau [i.e., in Switzerland in 1914]."[86]

It was no longer possible for Barth to walk with Gogarten. After resigning from the Editorial Board of Zwischen den Zeiten, Barth wrote an angry editorial "Farewell" in October, 1933, marking what proved to be the journal's final issue. Looking back on its founding in 1923, Barth wrote:

> When we founded Zwischen den Zeiten ... we thought we were passionately agreed in what we wanted. We rejected the positive-liberal or liberal-positive theology of neo-Protestantism of the beginning of the [20th] century, and we rejected the man-made God we thought we had recognized in its sanctuary. What we wanted was a theology of the Word of God. The Bible had gradually convinced us young pastors that something of this kind was absolutely necessary and we found a model among the Reformers.[87]

In a more pointed vein, Barth reveals his theological estimate of the German Christians and the defection of the Church.

> When we appeared to be fighting together at the beginning of the 1920s, I for my part, always opposed precisely that which can now be seen in concentrated form in the doctrine, mentality and stance of the German Christians. I cannot see anything in the German Christians but the last, fullest and worst monstrosity of the essence of Neo-Protestantism which, if not overcome, will make and must make the Protestant Church ripe for a move toward Rome. I regard Stapel's maxim about the Law of God to be an utter betrayal of the gospel. I regard this maxim [i.e., the identification of the Law of God with the law of Germany] to be a

much worse--because far more fundamental and
concrete--expression than that of the Harnack-
Troeltsch Era of the idolatrous elevation of
the human as God in the manner of 18th and
19th century theology.[88]

Moreover, Barth reminds his readers that those
abreast of his publications and of Gogarten's cannot
have been unmindful of increasing tensions in their
diverging perspectives. He recalls that in his opposition to all natural theology as the foundation for
Christian theology in CD 1:1, he had singled out both
Gogarten and Bultmann as suspect in this regard. In the
text of CD 1:1 written in the summer of 1931, Barth in
effect asked Gogarten: "To what degree is your attempt
to provide an anthropological foundation for theology
different from the natural theology of Catholicism or
neo-Protestantism? I have never received an answer to
my question."[89] Indeed, the widening division between
Barth and Gogarten, and Bultmann and others desirous of
providing an anthropological foundation for theology led
some wag as early as 1928 to comment: "The leaders of
dialectical theology are as disunited as the generals of
the Chinese revolution." With Gogarten's defection to
the German Christian cause in 1933, the Rubicon had been
crossed. Their disunity was no longer a laughing matter. The only basis on which Barth could have continued
as a co-editor of Zwischen den Zeiten with Gogarten and
Merz is crystal clear in this "farewell" to the journal
he helped establish. "My view is that our periodical
could have been the voice of the true church in our
times only if it stood as a modest but unbreakable dam
against the overwhelming tide of the German-Christian
flood."[90]

A. The Rejection of all Natural Theology

Anyone wishing to understand Barth's sharp polemic against the tradition of natural theology in Catholic and Protestant theology must see it within the context of Barth's theological evolution. His disenchantment with Protestant liberalism was due in large measure to its increasing use of natural theology. He became even more aware of, and opposed to, the prominent role played by natural theology in the history of theology from post-apostolic times to the present. From the time of the Middle Ages, Roman Catholic theology utilized a natural theology which allows for a knowledge of the existence of God, the Creator, on the basis of the humanity's capacity to interpret the revelation of God in nature, history and the human consciousness so as to make this knowledge possible. According to Catholic dogma promulgated at Vatican Council I (1869-70), this preliminary knowledge of God as Creator is supplemented by the truths of God attested in the Bible and inter- preted by the Catholic Church. This remains the norma- tive Catholic teaching to the present.

With respect to Protestantism, Barth admits that the Reformers made an occasional "unguarded" use of natural theology. However, Barth does not regard them as advocates of natural theology. Protestant Orthodoxy in the seventeenth century did make formal use of it preparing the way for its inrush and importance in Protestant theology following the Enlightenment. This leads Barth to interpret the history of Protestant theology from about 1750 to the present as replete with illicit attempts to synthesize nature and grace. Thus in varied ways liberal or neo-Protestant theology sought to effect a liaison between a theology based on the

revelation of God in creation with one issuing from the
revelation of God within his covenant history with
Israel coming to fulfillment in Jesus Christ.[91]

To this point, we have seen that Barth increasingly
distanced himself from the liberal theology stemming
from Schleiermacher in which he was schooled and once
espoused. In order to do so, it was imperative to
attack liberalism's use of the tradition of natural
theology. In his first attempt to write a prolegomena
to his dogmatics in 1927, this becomes very clear.
Barth intends to base his theology upon a position
opposed both to Roman Catholicism and its natural theology as a forecourt for all theological construction and
to liberalism in the tradition of Schleiermacher which
allows for a kind of natural theology by beginning
theological reflection on the basis of a universal
religious consciousness. Barth eschews basing theology
on any metaphysic or philosophy. His concern is to
develop a theology grounded on the Word of God. Hence
the entire prolegomena of 1927 is conceived as an exposition of the doctrine of the Word of God. In contrast to liberalism's concern with both the universal
God consciousness and the specific Christian self-
consciousness, Barth's attention is upon the Word of God
addressed to man. Thus at every point Barth intends to
accentuate the priority of God and his Word above the
response of faith. Nor does he allow any fusion of God
and the human in the moment of faith. Already at this
date Barth interprets God and his revelation in terms of
the doctrine of the Trinity regarding the latter as the
bulwark against every anthropocentric and natural theology. Whoever would affirm a natural theology must show
that it has reference to the triune God who makes himself known in his revelation.[92]

Nevertheless, when Barth spoke in 1929 of the human reception of the Word of God, his use of existential categories made his intended emphasis on the priority of the divine initiative and Word less than clear. Hence he could write:

> The Word of God is not only speech, but address. We can never hurry hither or yon, neither into heaven nor into the abyss, in order to perceive or to read it, but it comes to us. That means: the hearing man is as much included within the concept of the Word of God as the speaking God. He is "co-posited" [mitgesetzt] with the Word in much the same manner as Schleiermacher's God is co-posited in the feeling of absolute dependence.[93]

Upon becoming professor at Bonn in 1930, Barth offered seminars on Anselm's theology and theological method. This intensive study bore fruit in Barth's book on Anselm, Fides quaerens intellectum (Faith in Search of Understanding) published in 1931. In one of his revealing autobiographical statements on "how he changed his mind" during the decade, 1928-1938, Barth said:

> The deepening (of my theological position) consisted in this: in these years I have had to rid myself of the last remnants of a philosophical, i.e. anthropological (in America one says "humanistic" or "naturalistic") foundation and exposition of Christian doctrine. The real document of this farewell is, in truth, not the much-read ... Nein!, directed against Brunner in 1934, but rather the book about the evidence for God of Anselm of Canterbury. ...[94]

The latter statement is of a piece with Barth's earlier correction of the existential methodology utilized in his prolegomena of 1927. In the preface to his

revised prolegomena of the doctrine of the Word of God
published in 1932, Barth remarked that it was necessary
to

> cut out in this second issue of the book
> everything that in the first issue might give
> the slightest appearance of giving to theology
> a basis, support, or even a mere justification
> in the way of existential philosophy. ...in
> the former undertaking I can only see a re-
> adoption of the line Schleiermacher-Ritschl-
> Herrmann, and because in any thinkable con-
> tinuation of this line I can only see the
> plain destruction of Protestant theology and
> the Protestant Church, because I can see no
> third possibility between the play with the
> analogia entis [analogy of being], legitimate
> only on Roman Catholic ground, between the
> greatness and the misery of a so-called nat-
> ural knowledge of God in the sense of the
> Vaticanum, and a Protestant theology self-
> nourished at its own source, standing upon its
> own feet, and finally liberated from such
> secular misery. I can therefore only say No
> here. I regard the analogia entis as the
> invention of Antichrist, and think that be-
> cause of it one can not become Catholic.
> Whereupon I at the same time allow myself to
> regard all other possible reasons for not
> becoming Catholic, as shortsighted and lacking
> in seriousness.[95]

The years of the German Church struggle solidified
Barth's opposition to the tradition of natural theology.
He stood staunchly opposed to the German Christians
advocating a synthesis of German National Socialism as
a second source of revelation with the revelation of God
in Jesus Christ. In his estimate, this pernicious
synthesis was not different in kind from others espoused
earlier in Protestant liberalism. All detracted from
the central revelation in Jesus Christ. This accounts
for the decisive significance of the Barmen Declaration,
the theological Confession of the Confessing Church

opposing the German Christians and adopted by the Synod of Barmen, on May 29-31, 1934. Prior to its approval by the Synod of the Confessing Church meeting at Barmen, Barth as the representative of the Reformed Church and two Lutherans were appointed to provide an initial draft. Recalling that occasion years later, Barth commented that while his Lutheran colleagues took a siesta, the "Reformed Church kept awake." Then Barth comments: "I revised the text of the six statements, fortified by strong coffee and one or two Brazilian cigars. The result was that by evening there was a text. I don't want to boast, but it was really my text."[96]

The first article of the Barmen Declaration bears the unmistakable stamp of Barth's hand. It provides the definitive theological basis for the repudiation of natural theology in the form of the National Socialist ideology as a second source of the knowledge of God alongside of Jesus Christ. The first article states:

> Jesus Christ, as He is attested to us in Holy Scripture, is the one Word of God, whom we have to hear and whom we have to trust and obey in life and in death.

> We condemn the false doctrine that the Church can and must recognise as God's revelation other events and powers, forms and truths, apart from and alongside this one Word of God.[97]

Reflecting on the Barmen Declaration a few years later, Barth interpreted it as the first repudiation of natural theology in the history of Protestantism and therefore as "one of the most notable events in modern Church history."[98] In this same passage written about the time of the outbreak of World War II in 1939, Barth wrote words which may serve as a concluding statement regarding the repudiation of natural theology by the Confessing Church and its significance for all theological reflection.

> What it noticed on this occasion was the fact of the unique validity of Jesus Christ as the Word of God spoken to us for life and death. The repudiation of natural theology was only the self-evident reverse side of this notice. It has no independent significance. It affirms only that there is no other help--that is, in temptation--when it is a question of the being or not being of the Church. What helps, when every other helper fails, is only the miracle, power and comfort of the one Word of God. The Confessional Church began to live at the hand of this notice and at its hand it lives to this day. And it is this notice which it has to exhibit to other Churches, as the testimony which it has received and which is now laid upon it as a commission. It will be lost if it forgets this testimony, or no longer understands it, or no longer takes it seriously; the power against which it stands is too great for it to meet it otherwise than with the weapon of this testimony. But it will also be lost if it does not understand and keep to the fact that this testimony is not entrusted to it simply for its own use, but at the same time as a message of the world-wide Church. And it may well be decisive for other Churches in the world, for their existence as the one, ecumenical Church of Jesus Christ whether they on their side are able to hear and willing to accept the message of the Confessional Church in Germany.[99]

Chapter II

THEOLOGIANS IN CONFLICT: HARNACK AND BARTH

I. THE FIRST ENCOUNTER: HARNACK'S DILIGENT STUDENT
(1906-1907)

In the very month of the publication of the first
issue of the new organ of the "dialectical theology,"
Zwischen den Zeiten, the movement came under attack from
Adolf von Harnack (1851-1930). As Harnack's student in
Berlin in the fall semester of 1906-07, Barth learned
from the leading church historian and historian of dogma
in modern Protestantism. Moreover, Harnack's influence
as a major spokesman for the dominant liberal theology
was secured through the publication of his popular
university lectures of 1899-1900 entitled in English, The
Essence of Christianity.[1] During Barth's semester in
Berlin, he was intensely involved in Harnack's seminar
on Acts and his course on the history of dogma. In the
latter, he heard Harnack develop his famous and influential thesis that the development of dogma in the early
church represented an illicit hellenizing of the simple
gospel of the Galilean Jesus. Barth enjoyed friendly
personal contacts with Harnack and admired him both
personally and as a scholar. On a later occasion, Barth
lamented that he was so caught up in studies with Harnack
that he failed to take advantage of the cultural benefits
of Berlin, the great capital city of Germany. Barth

recalls: "I said to myself, 'This is the great moment: here you are with the theologian of the day, why should you be bothered with museums, theatres and concert halls?'"[2]

It is noteworthy that Barth's adoption of the perspective of liberal theology came to flower during his time in Berlin. This process began in Bern, Switzerland, where he began his theological studies in 1904 under the watchful guidance of his father, professor of Church History and New Testament exegesis. Papa Barth was a staunch traditional theologian of the "positive" or conservative persuasion as opposed to the liberal. His apprehensions about Karl's liberalism increased when his son experienced an intellectual conversion through the careful study of Kant's philosophy and Schleiermacher's theology in his second year of study. In the course of his two years at Bern, Barth also received a thorough introduction to the "historical-critical" school of biblical studies. Looking back to his student days there, Barth wrote: "At that time, as a student of nineteen, I smoked much stronger tobacco [i.e., historical criticism] than anything which could be found years later under the brand of demythologizing."[3]

II. THE SECOND ENCOUNTER: A PARTING OF THE WAYS (1920)

When Harnack fired the first salvo in Barth's direction in 1923 in the form of an open letter, Barth was not caught unawares. In 1920, both were on the program of a Student Conference in Aarau, Switzerland. Barth's address of 1920, "Biblical Questions, Insights, and Vistas," was an elaboration of an Easter sermon. In it he contrasted his own approach to the Bible with that of the historical-critical school, and more particularly, the history of religions school, which interpreted Christianity within the larger context of the history of religions. It regarded Christianity as a species of the larger genus, namely, religion.

In no way did Barth dispute the accepted view that the "Bible is the literary monument of an ancient racial religion and of a Hellenistic cultus religion of the Near East."[4] However, in a way which must have been highly distasteful to Harnack, Barth spoke of the need to give "dispassionate attention to the objective content of the Bible" by means of a method which is not to be regarded as uncritical or unscientific. "...it is...clear that intelligent and fruitful discussion of the Bible begins when the judgment as to its human, its historical and psychological character has been made and put behind us."[5] Barth proceeds to anticipate his later critique of the phenomenon of "religion" understood as a human construct in contrast to revelation which has God for its author. He said:

> Suffice it to say that the history of religion got started somehow, or, rather, the history of the untrue in religion, in contrast to what religion really is. For at the moment when religion becomes conscious of religion, when it becomes a psychologically and historically conceivable magnitude in the world, it falls away from its inner character, from its truth, to idols. Its truth is its other-worldliness, its refusal of the idea of sacredness, its non-historicity. I see the decisive characteristic of the Bible--as opposed to the history of religion, of which obviously the history of the Christian church is a chief part--in that the Bible displays a quite striking continuity of faithfulness, constancy, patient hopefulness, and objective attention toward the incomprehensible, unpsychological, and unhistorical truth of

> God. The human attempt to betray and to
> compromise the secret of which all religion
> dreams, has no standing in the Bible.[6]

Busch summarizes some of the other notes Barth
sounded in his address which to Harnack must have been
discordant.

> Barth declared God to be the "wholly other";
> revelation to be the encounter with a cruci-
> fied man; knowledge of God to be recognition
> at the "boundaries of mortality," "the wisdom
> of death"; the divine Yes to be hidden dialec-
> tically in the form of a No; Christian exis-
> tence to be not "owning, feasting and sharing"
> but "relentless searching, asking and
> knocking."[7]

Barth's closing emphasis on the resurrection of Jesus
from the dead and the Easter message which arises
therefrom was a marked departure from Harnack's concentration on the Jesus of history. Barth could say:
"Resurrection--the Easter message--means the <u>sovereignty
of God</u>. Resurrection, the sovereignty of God, is the
purport of the life of Jesus from the first day of his
coming. "Jesus is the conqueror!" sang Blumhardt, and
it is so."[8]

Earlier Harnack had addressed the same conference
on the theme, "What assured knowledge can historians
provide for the interpretation of world events?"
Barth's own strongly eschatological remarks precipi-
tated, he recalled, "a clash with Adolf von Harnack
which was almost of historic significance."[9] In the
discussion following Barth's address, Harnack informed
Barth--in courteous fashion--that his perspective was
responsible for the worst "state of affairs" in theology
since Kierkegaard! A few days later, Barth spoke for an

hour with Harnack and Eberhard Vischer in Basel. Barth wrote Thurneysen about the way he was dressed down:

> The two gentlemen thought that I would do better to keep my view of God to myself and not make it an "export article"(!). Finally, I was branded a Calvinist and intellectualist. Harnack's parting shot was the prophecy that according to all the experiences of church history I would found a sect and receive inspiration.[10]

III. THE THIRD ENCOUNTER: THE HARNACK-BARTH CORRESPONDENCE (1923)

Harnack initiated the correspondence of 1923 through a published letter entitled: "Fifteen Questions To Those Among The Theologians Who Are Contemptuous Of The Scientific Theology." Rightly assuming that Harnack's questions were directed mainly to him, Barth published his reply: "Fifteen Answers To Professor Von Harnack." Since Harnack began by charging Barth and his cohorts with being unscientific, or as foes of the historical-critical methodology in their understanding of the Bible and the beginnings of the Christian church, Barth responded to this issue head on.

> Concerning the title: One who makes a criticism of the form of Protestant scientific theology which since the days of pietism and the Enlightenment, and in particular in the past fifty years in Germany, has established itself as normative, is not therefore necessarily "contemptuous" of "the scientific theology." The point of the criticism is that this theology may have moved further than is good from its theme (first clearly stated by the Reformation).[11]

A.   On Scientific Interpretation of the Bible

Harnack's first questions concern the issue of what constitutes an adequate method of biblical interpretation.   He observes that Barth appeals uncritically to the "religion of the Bible" or the "revelations" spoken of in the Bible as though they constituted a unity and were validated simply by affirming their presence in the "Bible." If Barth does not admit to such an approach, is he not encouraging the view that the "content of the gospel" is ascertainable solely on the basis of untested subjective religious experience?   Would it not be more advisable to insist that the "content of the gospel" cannot be determined apart from "historical knowledge and critical reflection"?[12]

Barth answers that though one can refer to and speak of the "religion" and "revelations" of the Bible, the real theme of the Bible is "the one revelation of God." "Historical knowledge" could make us aware that the revelation of God or the "content of the gospel" cannot be knowable apart from the divine initiative. That is to say, only God can reveal himself--whether that occurs in the past or present. It follows for Barth that in order for reflection on the "content of the gospel" to be "critical," it must respect the order of the relationship between God and man attested in the Bible.   Theology which investigates the God-man relationship attested there would be "scientific" to the extent that it recognizes its continual dependence upon God's making himself known if he is to be known at all. Only in this way is God the "object" of theological reflection.   He is thus never an object among others subject to human control--and certainly not by means of a scientific methodology.

This approach in no way elevates the subjective experience of God into the norm of the knowledge of God. Barth does not deny that "inner openness" and "experiences" in relationship to the Bible do exist on the one hand, and that there are indeed such things as "historical knowledge" and "critical reflection" of the Bible on the other. But in and of themselves, none of the latter--or any other natural or human mental or spiritual capacity--assure the true understanding of the Bible. The latter comes into being "by the power of the Spirit, who is the same as its content, and that [occurs] in faith."[13]

In his second "Open Letter," Harnack states that Barth's concept of "revelation" is obscured in "oppressive fog" while his theological method is "totally unintelligible to me." Whereas Barth contends that the historical-critical or scientific character of post-Enlightenment modern Protestant theology is not proved correct simply because it is modern and dominant, Harnack argues to the contrary. He writes: "I see in the scientific theology the only possible way of mastering an object [epistemologically]. ..."[14] This approach is ancient to the extent that it originated with "thinking men" and modern by virtue of maturing since the Enlightenment.

In his final rebuttal, Barth expresses dismay at the continuing caricature of him as an opponent of historical-critical biblical studies. The issue is not opposition to the historical-critical approach per se; it is rather that some of its advocates are no longer concerned with what the Reformers called "the Word" attested in the Scriptures and known through the Spirit. Instead, historical critics isolate what is purportedly a so-called "simple gospel." But the latter is neither found in the Scriptures nor through the Spirit--and "can be called 'word of God' only as a figure of speech. ..."[15] Barth asks in effect: "Is this 'simple gospel' the sum of what the Scriptures teach as determined by the scientific method?"

Barth notes that Harnack's praise of modern scientific theology clearly omits inclusion of the Protestant Reformers--not to mention the Apostle Paul. Barth asks in effect: "Is it not arrogant to restrict the designation 'scientific' to modern Protestant theology?" Barth's considered reply is that the "basic approach" of the Protestant Reformers, or even of Protestant Scholasticism and medieval theology, may serve as a model for theology in the attempt to be faithful to the real subject matter of Scripture. This does not entail repristination. Their approach is preferable because they had the "concept of an authoritative object," namely, God: in contrast, the so-called scientific theology of Harnack is one "for whom the concept of an authoritative object has become foreign and monstrous because of the sheer authoritativeness of method."[16] The end result of the latter is a rampant relativism with respect to the "object" of theological discourse.

B.   Experience of God Compared with Faith

Harnack's next series of questions focus on Barth's distinction between so-called "experience of God" and the "awakening of faith." Harnack asks initially: "If ... [the latter] is different from ... [the former], how is it distinguished from uncontrollable fanaticism? If it is identical with it, how can it come about except through the preaching of the gospel, and how can there be such preaching without historical knowledge and critical reflection?"[17] Further, if the experience of God "is contrary to or disparate from all other experience," does this not require "radical flight from the world?" Yet would not the latter decision necessarily be "worldly" and casuistic inasmuch as one still remains in the world?[18]

Barth's rejoinder is that the so-called "experience of God" or "religious experience" (Gotteserlebnis) is "as different from the awakening of faith by God as earth is from heaven" and is practically indistinguishable from "uncontrollable fanaticism."[19] This does not preclude that the "experience of God" might be a "more or less clear symptom and witness of the awakening of faith." Regarding faith, Barth writes:

> Faith, however, comes indeed from preaching, but preaching (whatever may be the state of the preacher's "historical knowledge" and "critical reflection") "by the word of Christ." The task of theology is the same as that of preaching. It consists in taking up and passing on the word of Christ. In this why could not "historical knowledge" and "critical reflection" serve by way of preparation?[20]

After considering the radical distinction Barth made between all human religious and moral experience in relationship to God and true faith, Harnack replied that he remained as puzzled as ever about Barth's intent. In his final attempt at clarification, Barth indicates that he simply holds to the Reformation view that faith in God is enabled through the work of the Holy Spirit. "The acceptance of this unbelievable testimony of the Scriptures I call faith."[21] To understand the genesis of faith in this way is not to succumb to any rampant subjectivism. Since the appropriation of the witness to revelation is effected only through enlightenment by the Holy Spirit, Barth speaks of that happening as "miracle." Wilhelm Herrmann, Barth's influential theological teacher, is cited for his well-known insistence that faith is never to be confused with the belief in, or acceptance of, historical facts, apart from any reference to the activity of the Spirit whose activity vivifies the witness of the written word to Jesus Christ.

Barth sums up the distinction he sees between faith and all other kinds of religious experience:

> Therefore I distinguish faith as God's working on us (for only he can say to us, in such a way that we will hear it, what we cannot hear, I Corinthians 2:9) from all known and unknown human organs and functions, even our so-called "experiences of God."[22]

Relative to the charge that his conception of faith is escapist and involves "flight from the world," Barth answers:

> The faith which is awakened by God will never be able fully to avoid the necessity of a more or less "radical" protest against this world, inasmuch as it is a hope for that which is promised but unseen.[23]

In Barth's view, therefore, a theology which failed to comprehend how faith must maintain a

> basic distance...from this world would of necessity also be equally unmindful of the knowledge of God the Creator. Because [of] the "absolute contrast" of God and the world, the cross is the only means by which we as men can conceive of the original and final unity of Creator and creation [creature]. Sophistry

> is not the insight that not even our protest
> against the world can justify us in the sight
> of God, but rather the usual attempt to bypass
> the cross by the help of a trite concept of
> creation.[24]

In his final reply to Barth on these issues, Harnack makes several points. First, he laments that Barth does not distinguish the tasks of preaching and theology. For Harnack, preaching has to do with depicting the task of the "Christian as a witness to Christ" while "the task of theology is the same as the tasks of science in general."[25] Since Barth confuses these two spheres and writes theology more like a witness and prophet than scientifically, Harnack says: "You transform the theological professor's chair into a pulpit. ... I predict to you on the basis of the course of all of church history that this undertaking will not lead to edification but to dissolution."[26] Surely Professor Barth knows that "there is only one scientific method, so there is only one scientific task—the pure knowledge of its object."[27]

Secondly, Harnack states that Barth's insistence on the sharp differentiation between so-called "experience of God" and related terms and "the awakening of faith" through the Spirit remains obscure. Third, though Barth's view that faith arises from the preaching of the "word of Christ" appears correct at first glance, other statements make it clear that he holds it no longer possible—citing Paul—to "know Christ according to the flesh." Harnack asks: "Thus we no longer know the Jesus Christ of the Gospels, the historical Jesus Christ? How am I to understand that? On the basis of the theory of the exclusive inner word? Or on the basis of one of the many other [subjectivistic] theories?"[28]

C.   The God--World Relationship

Harnack raises a series of questions regarding the
God/world relationship in view of Barth's insistence on
their radical separation.   First, how can one hold to
the absolute separation of God and the world given the
fact that the gospel relates and even equates love of
God and neighbor?   Does this not necessitate a high
valuation of morality? Second: "If God and world (life
in God and worldly life) are absolute contrasts, how can
we lead people to God, that is, to what is good?"
Third, if God is wholly unlike anything said concerning
him in the evolution of culture, as for e.g., by Goethe
or Kant, how are individual and cultural atheism avoid-
able?   Fourth, if contra Barth, it is, in fact, true
that what culture and morality reveal of God are simultaneously "contrasts" and "steps" in the evolution of
culture's knowledge of God--then are not "historical
knowledge and critical reflection" required in order to
"grasp and develop this basic insight?"[29] Fifth, if the
insight that "God is love" is the pinnacle of the knowledge of God, why is it that Barth insists on keeping us
suspended in the anxiety and terror of some "transi-
tional points of Christian experience" removed from the
joy and peace which issue from faith?   Sixth, if according to Phil. 4:8, that which is honorable, gracious
and good is commendable, why does Barth drive a wedge
between the true, the beautiful and the good on the one
hand, and the "experience of God" on the other? Should
he not instead relate them to "the experience of God" by
means   of   "historical   knowledge   and   critical
reflection?"[30]

Barth's first response is that it is "precisely the
bringing together in the gospel of love for God and love

for our neighbor that is the clearest indication that the relationship between our "life in the world" and "our life in God" is that of an "absolute contrast" which can be overcome only by the miracle of the eternal God himself."[31] Is it indeed the case, asks Barth, that love of neighbor is so easily realized? According to Harnack, Barth makes the concepts of "neighbor" and "love of neighbor" problematic whereas the gospel "does not see any problems here at all."[32] Barth asks further: "And if we do not love him what is the state of our love of God? Does anything show more clearly than this "heart" (not of the gospel, but of the Law), that God does not make alive unless he first slays?"[33]

Regarding the question of how people can be led to God and the good if God and world are absolute contrasts, Barth answers citing Jh. 6:44 without comment: "No one can come to me unless the Father who sent me draws him; and I will raise him up at the last day."[34] Harnack rebuts this answer as simplistic. It means that "you condemn all Christian education and, like Marcion, sever every link between faith and what is human... . [and] you have the example of Jesus against you here."[35]

What of Harnack's charge that he so radically distinguishes statements about God expressed in morality and culture from God himself that he encourages atheism? Barth admits that statements about God developed in morality and culture may be significant expressions of "experiences of God" within certain cultures in contrast with what might have developed in more primitive cultures. But does Harnack really have high regard for "the statements of the war theologians of all lands" concerning God and his identity with their cause? Barth most certainly has in mind here the disillusionment he experienced on August 1, 1914, when

> ninety-three German intellectuals issued a
> terrible manifesto, identifying themselves
> before all the world with the war policy of
> Kaiser Wilhelm II. ...It was like the twi-
> light of the gods when I saw the reaction of
> Harnack, Herrmann... and company to the new
> situation," and discovered how religion and
> scholarship could be changed completely, "into
> intellectual 42 cm cannons."[36]

The final sentence of their manifesto reads: "We believe that for European culture on the whole salvation
rests on the victory which German "militarism", namely
manly discipline, the faithfulness, the courage to
sacrifice, of the united and free German nation will
achieve."[37] Against this backdrop, Barth's point follows: "As the 'preaching of the gospel' ... these
statements in any case do not come into consideration,
and whether they "protect" culture and the individual
"from atheism," rather than, derived as they are from
polytheism, plant, atheism, may be in each case an open
question."[38]

Barth continues that true statements about God

> can only be made at all when one knows he is
> placed not on some height of culture or of
> religion, but before revelation and therefore
> under judgment, under which, together with all
> human statements on this subject, those of
> Goethe and Kant also stand. Schleiermacher's
> intimidation by "barbarism" is to be rejected
> as unreal and irrelevant, because the gospel
> has as much and as little to do with "bar-
> barism" as it has to do with culture.[39]

Such a view, replies Harnack, "can be understood only as
a radical denial of every valuable insight concerning
God within the history of human thought and morality."[40]
While Barth concedes that in themselves human statements

about God share characteristics similar to those of "all physical and intellectual development," theology ought to "grasp" and "develop" a more important principle. It is that

> between the truth of God (which can indeed also be expressed in a human statement) and our truth there exists only [contrast], only [an] either-or. [It is more urgent for theology in any case, to 'grasp' and to develop 'this' knowledge!] For humility, longing, and petition will always be for our part the end, as they were the beginning. The road from the old to the new world is not one of stages, not development in any sense, but a being born anew.[41]

Barth does not dispute Harnack's claim that the "insight 'God is love' is the highest and final knowledge of God. ..." He states, however, that this confession is always made in "faith in God's promise"; hence fulfillment of this knowledge awaits the eschatological consummation. "Are we perhaps saved other than in hope?"[42] What of Paul's commendation of that which is true, honorable and just in Phil. 4:8 and Harnack's desire to see such virtues as one with the good, the beautiful and the true and thus correlative with the experience of God? Barth answers with reference to Phil. 4:7, which speaks of "... the peace of God which passes all understanding... ." When the peace of God as a divine gift higher than understanding is granted, it "will keep your hearts and minds in Christ Jesus" (Phil. 4:7). When this occurs, the virtues of Phil. 4:8 become possible. Regarding the correlation between the peace of God and other virtues, Barth writes: "There is a connection between it and that which we call good, true, and beautiful, but the connection is precisely the 'dividing wall,' the divine crisis, which is the only basis on which it is possible to speak seriously of the good, true, and beautiful."[43]

Harnack finds Barth's refusal to allow the transition to Christian faith by way of stages to be in conflict with the emergence of "eternal values" in history within the providence of God. Furthermore, Harnack finds Barth in the greatest tension with Reformation Christianity in his constant emphasis on the eschatological tension characteristic of faith and in his insistence on the dichotomy between all human truth and the truth of God. Harnack regards Barth to be guilty of accentuating "what is incomplete in Christianity"--of which all are aware--"to destroy the possession itself, and to make an illusion of the confidence in which we are privileged to live, and frivolity of the joy which should fill our life." The "frame of mind" Barth regards as characteristically Christian can, at best, "be felt by only a few to be the 'peace of God,' and...can by no means be the necessary presupposition for all Christian humility."[44]

To this point it has already become clear that radically different perspectives regarding the Christian faith characterize Harnack and Barth. Where Harnack finds continuity between Christ and culture, Barth finds discontinuity. Whereas Harnack looks with optimism at advancing Western civilization, Barth speaks despairingly of brokenness and decay. Where Harnack sees a merging of the kingdom of man and the kingdom of God, Barth sees radical difference. While Harnack sees the most sublime products of man's ethical and religious consciousness as akin to the divine, Barth finds a radical divide. Whereas Harnack can relish in the status of liberal Christianity and theology in Germany, Barth

finds little which is commensurate with the apostolic
testimony to Jesus Christ in either church or theology.
Where Harnack highlights the humanity of Jesus and his
similarity to the rest of humanity, Barth stresses his
distinctive difference from all others as the Incarnate
Word. While Harnack advocates the progressive realization of the kingdom of God in human history, Barth is a
radical eschatologist. Where Harnack finds solace in the
"simple gospel" of the Galilean Jesus, Barth stands
awestruck before the crucified and risen Christ. To use
the apt phrase of Martin Rumscheidt, the engagement
between Harnack and Barth is "an encounter of different
worlds."

D.   Barth--A New Marcion?

Rumscheidt's astute analysis of the reasons why
Harnack identified Barth as a new Marcion (ca. 130 A.D.)
are arresting and worthy of careful attention, but would
carry us too far afield. Harnack had published his
influential study of Marcion in 1920. He was preparing
the second edition during the period of his literary
exchange with Barth. Marcion and his 'gospel of the
strange God' (the sub-title of Harnack's book on Marcion) were much on his mind. So much was this the case
that Harnack inserted the following footnote--discovered
by Rumscheidt--in the second edition of his book on
Marcion. While Barth is not mentioned by name, Rumscheidt is certainly correct that Harnack identifies
Barth with "Reformed Orthodoxy" and Overbeck with "critical thought." Harnack observes:

> When contemporary philosophy of religion again
> defines the object of religion--the "holy"--
> fundamentally as the "wholly other", as the

> "alien" and the like, and when this definition
> is made by theologians coming from the camps
> of Pietism, Reformed Orthodoxy, Roman Catholi-
> cism or critical thought (der Kritizismus) and
> when they tell us to avoid all proofs and let
> the phenomenon speak for itself, then they
> have every reason to remember the only prede-
> cessor in the history of the ancient Church
> who knew this strange God, called him by name
> and refuted all proofs and testimonies by
> which one might come to know him and believe
> in him.[45]

Here it must suffice to list some of the major points at which Harnack, the historian of dogma and theologian, opposed Marcion's dualism. Rumscheidt identifies the following objections:

(1) Marcion's views are stated in a conceptually inexact, a philosophically and scientifically improper manner, which Harnack calls 'expressionistic.'

(2) Marcion's interpretation of reality leads into fantasy and mythology because of its dualism. The real becomes confused with what is imaginary.

(3) Is man permitted to condemn the world? Even though there is much evil in the world, to answer in the affirmative, as Marcion answered, is presumptuous.

(4) Marcion regards man's morality and the freedom to which he has already attained while still in the world as opposites and not as steps to the real good.

(5) Marcion's view of providence is restricted to God's love and to those whom it seeks out, namely, the redeemed.

(6) Marcion's renunciation of the world as evil and his restriction of himself to the proclamatory work of the gospel is a sign of an inwardness and lovelessness which denies the reformability of the world and its inherent goodness.

(7) Marcion's asceticism denies all value to life; as such, it is simply negative.

(8) Marcion avoids all use of what makes for a more noble humanity and geniality. Thus he dissolves culture. By calling God the "wholly other," even though it is for him a Christocentric conception, he works with a transcendental sphere of reality rather than with history as the sphere of the real.[46]

1. <u>Barth and Marcion compared</u>. It is clear, as Rumscheidt shows in some detail, that Harnack's objections to Marcion parallel, in the main, those he makes against Barth. Since most are addressed elsewhere in our analysis, they need not be repeated here. Yet, it may prove helpful to note the main points of Barth's careful and extensive answer to being labelled a Marcionite. That Harnack had struck a sensitive nerve is evident from Barth's pained reply. "But now you also, highly honored Doctor, have conjured up against me the shadow of <u>Marcion</u> with the assertion that I 'sever the link between faith and the human.'"[47]

Barth protests that Harnack has not really heard what he had to say in his earlier answer to him concerning the totality of human experience--be it moral or religious, or intellectual and critical--as it relates to God. "Have I really made <u>tabula rasa</u> with those human organs, functions and experiences? It is not my intention to do this."[48] Barth states he in no way denies the reality or range of human possibilities either of the believer or unbeliever; nor does he intend to sever everything human--whether experienced by the believer or unbeliever--from God. Barth writes:

> ...I would rather say that the human is the relative, the testimony, the parable and thus not the absolute <u>itself</u> on some pinnacles or

heights of development as one would certainly
conclude from your statements. The human
rather is the reference [Hinweis, or pointer]
(understood or not understood) to the absolute. In view of this the historically and
psychologically discernible, that which we
know in ourselves and others as 'faith' would
be a witness to and a symptom of that action
and miracle of God on us, of that faith, in
other words, which, created through the 'Word'
and 'steeped in the Word' is, as Luther said,
our righteousness before God himself.[49]

Barth's concern is to maintain against Harnack the
distinction between God, the Creator, and the creature.
For Barth, everything human may become the vehicle of
the presence of God through God's grace. But this is
not attributable to some innate human capacity or religious consciousness, but solely to the divine good
pleasure. Barth highlights his sharp disagreement with
Harnack.

...I am indeed content with the testimonial
character of all that which occurs here and
there in time and as a result of man. I explicitly deny the possibility of positing anything relative as absolute, somehow and somewhere, be it in history or in ourselves, or in
Kierkegaardian terms, of going from testimony
to 'direct statement.' If I do not wholly
misunderstand the Bible and the Reformation,
the latter is and must remain in the most
exclusive sense, God's concern.[50]

For Barth, the fact that Scripture testifies that

God becomes man...is true only as the 'Word
and work of God,' as the act of the Trinity
itself. This act can only be witnessed to and
believed because it is revealed. ...When this
reality becomes cognisable here or there, then
the miracle has occurred which we cannot deny,
with which, however, we cannot reckon as with

any other possibility or even with a general truth. We must worship it when it is <u>present</u> (present as the miracle of God!)[51]

Barth writes comparing the manner in which he conceives the relationship between God and the human in contrast to Harnack:

> My rejoinder to your reproof of 'severing' (which I cannot acknowledge as justified), is that you empty faith by asserting a continuity between the 'human' and faith just as you empty revelation by saying that there is a continuity between history and revelation. I do not sever; I do repudiate every continuity between hither and yonder. I speak of a dialectical <u>relation</u> which points to an <u>iden-tity</u> which cannot be established nor, there-fore, presumed by us.[52]

In a suggestive paragraph, Barth seems desirous of avoiding a wholly negative attitude toward certain evidences of the Christian presence in history. Hence he speaks of the "<u>parabolic</u> value" [<u>Gleichniswert</u>] which may be attributed to "'Christian' <u>biography</u>" or to "'Christian' <u>pedagogy</u>," or finally "to all 'Christian' protest against the world." Then he writes: "Parable, parable only can be all 'becoming' in view of the birth from death to life through which alone (but only on the way which God takes and is), we come from the truth of man to the truth of God."[53]

Barth concludes the substantive part of his second and final letter to Harnack by seeking to rebut and lay to rest the Marcionite label affixed to him by his former professor.

> Still in connection with the charge of Mar-cionism, you demand from me a full answer to the question 'whether God is simply unlike

anything said about him on the basis of the development of culture, on the basis of the knowledge gathered by culture and on the basis of ethics'. Very well, then, but may I ask you really to listen to my whole answer. NO, God is 'absolutely not at all that', as surely as the Creator is not the creature or even the creation of the creature. But precisely in this NO, which can be uttered in its full severity only in the faith in revelation, the creature recognizes itself as the work and the possession of the Creator. Precisely in this NO God is known as God, as the source and the goal of the thoughts of God which man, in the darkness of his culture and his decadence, is in the habit of forming. For this NO, posited with finality by revelation, is not without the 'deep, secret YES under and above the NO' which we should 'grasp and hold to with a firm faith in God's Word' and 'confess that God is right in his judgment against us, for then we have won'. This is how it is with that NO: 'nothing but YES in it, but always deep and secretly and always seeming to be nothing but NO'. What lover of contradictoriness might have said that? Kierkegaard or Dostoyevsky? No, Martin Luther!...Is Luther to be suspected then of Marcionism too?...So, why should you not understand me a little better at the same time? Does the human really become insignificant when, in the faith in revelation, its crisis occurs which makes forever impossible every identification between here and the beyond, excepting always the one which it does not become us to express (about the end of all things foreseen in I Corinthians 15:28)? Does it [the human] really not become full of significance and promise, really serious and possible precisely through being moved out of the twilight of supposed fulfilment into the real light of real hope? Is it really not enough for us to have and to behold in the transitory the parable of the intransitory, to live in it and to work for it, to be glad as men that we have at least the parable and to suffer as men under the fact that it is only the parable, without, however, anticipating the 'swallowing up of death in victory' in a spurious consciousness of eternity exactly because the great temporal significat [it signifies] applies to the greater eternal est

[is] and nothing else?   Have I really made
'tabula rasa'?[54]

E.   Sin and Grace

In putting his final questions, Harnack criticizes
Barth for his excessive emphasis on human sin and fallenness.   He asks: "If all sin is nothing but a lack of
[reverence] and love, how can one put an end to this
lack other than through the preaching of God's holy
majesty and of God's love?   How can one dare to mix in
with it all possible paradoxes and arbitrariness?"[55]
Barth, in turn, finds Harnack the advocate of a shallow
view of sin.   He retorts:

> If sin is perhaps something more than "lack of
> respect and love," that is, a falling away of
> man from God and being lost in a likeness to
> God, the end of which is death, then preaching
> (theology) God's holy majesty and love is a
> task which seems not to be able to spare our
> human thinking and speaking from going on
> unexpected paths."[56]

Barth accuses Harnack of engaging in "spectator theology" which makes simplistic critiques of the language
of paradox in the doctrine of sin.   He concludes:
"Anyone who is in a position where he can show a simpler
solution for the same (the same!) task, should show how
it is done.   Historical knowledge tells us that Paul and
Luther were not in this position."[57]

Harnack's final rejoinder is that Barth's view of
sin indicates his addiction to an "extremely sublime
psychology and metaphysics."   This is evident in his
portrayal of the creature as sinner characterized by a
tormented conscience--a view derived from Paul and

Luther. Indeed, Barth's depiction of sin and salvation
is even more complex and paradoxical than the latter
thereby making his model of sin and grace even more
difficult to emulate. Harnack suggests that if Barth
desires to follow the latter--in itself a questionable
procedure--he should also follow them in stressing
forgiveness of sins. In Harnack's estimate, Barth's
extreme Paulinism causes him to by-pass the "simple
gospel" of Jesus regarding salvation. "The simple
gospel out of which Jesus spoke his easily intelligible
and comforting parables for the salvation of souls does
not suit you. ..."[58]

F.   The Knowledge of Jesus Christ and the Gospel

In the initial exchange, Harnack was conscious of
the tension between his concern to base christology on
the historical-critical reconstruction of the Jesus of
history and Barth's focus on the Christ of the apostolic
kerygma. Therefore, he asks Barth: "If the person of
Jesus Christ stands in the center of the gospel, how can
the basis for a reliable and common knowledge of this
person be gained other than through critical historical
study, lest we exchange the real Christ for one we have
imagined?"[59] This brings Harnack back once again to his
insistence that such knowledge is achievable only
through scientific theology. Barth's approach belittles
reason's role and appears to encourage irrationality.
Does not this encourage the free reign of the Gnostic
and the occult? Does Barth really think that such a
theology has any value in the modern world or any "power
to convince"?

Barth turns the tables with respect to the charge
of being antirational and of directing theology's atten-

tion to the realms of feeling and the subconscious. He
reminds Harnack that it is his own liberal tradition
with its "apotheosis of 'feeling'" which landed in "the
fearsome quagmire of the psychology of the subconscious"
while others ended up as devotees of Anthroposophy. In
addition, Barth seems to have Schleiermacher in mind in
asking Harnack: "Who is it that apart from critical
reason thought he could open a particular "religious"
source of knowledge?"[60] Perhaps it is not too far afield
to suggest that Barth may have been thinking here of his
liberal teachers in the tradition of Schleiermacher and
his theology of feeling who were virtually unanimous in
their open support of the war policy of Kaiser Wilhelm
II in 1914.

Barth interprets Harnack's desire that theology
receive the plaudits of science with respect to the
value of its own activity as indicative not of theology's
health, but of its sickness. He counters:

> If theology regained the courage to be objec-
> tive, the courage to bear witness to the word
> of revelation, of judgment, and of the love of
> God, then it could also be that "science" in
> general would have to look for its "firm
> connection and blood relationship" to theol-
> ogy, rather than the other way around. For it
> would perhaps also be better for jurists,
> physicians, and philosophers if they knew what
> the theologians ought to know.[61]

1.   The 'historical Jesus' or 'the Christ' of the
kerygma? In turning to what Barth's conceives as the
right approach to interpreting the person of Jesus
Christ, we face one of the most important theological
issues dividing the liberal, Harnack, and the neo-
Reformation theologian, Barth.   Harnack had stated
clearly that the correct understanding of the person of

Jesus Christ can be ascertained only by means of historical critical study. In adopting this viewpoint,
Harnack identified with what he regarded as the suc-
cessful outcome of the quest for the "historical Jesus"
which had dominated much New Testament scholarship in
the nineteenth century. This quest sought to recover
the human Jesus and his history eclipsed by the dogmatic
and creedal view of Jesus which stressed his deity in
speaking of him as one person in two natures. We noted
that Harnack set forth his own interpretation of the
historical Jesus in his popular book, What is Christianity? In the main, Harnack distilled what he took to
be the result of the critical research into the life and
history of Jesus and made it constitutive for all
Christian faith.

Though not unprepared for Harnack's concentration
on the historical Jesus uncovered by means of
historical-critical research, it was difficult for Barth
to conceive how Harnack could be so assured of his
position. Apparently Barth was of the opinion that both
Martin Kähler in 1892 and Albert Schweitzer in 1906 had
shown indubitably that the "Quest of the historical
Jesus" was a failure. Kähler anticipated the positions
of the early Barth and the form critics of the 1920's in
contending that only the Christ proclaimed in the apostolic kerygma of the New Testament is of decisive significance for Christian faith. While not denying the
main outline of the life of Jesus, Kähler held that the
gospels were not to be read as neutral biographies of
Jesus, but as kerygmatic testimonies informed by a
common faith in the crucified and risen Lord. In the
present, Christ is known through faith alone. Hence, to
regard the Jesus reconstructed by means of historical
criticism as the object of faith was to misconstrue both

the person of Jesus and the nature of faith. By and
large, Harnack and the liberal theological establishment
ignored both Kähler and Schweitzer.[62]

Barth follows the Reformers and Kähler and opposes
Harnack in holding that the true knowledge of Jesus
Christ as "the center of the gospel" is had through
"God-awakened faith" alone. What role then does Barth
accord historical-critical study? Barth answers Har-
nack:

> Critical-historical study signifies the de-
> served and necessary end of those 'founda-
> tions' of this knowledge which are no founda-
> tions at all since they have not been laid by
> God himself. Whoever does not yet know (and
> this applies to all of us) that we no longer
> know Christ according to the flesh, should let
> the critical study of the Bible tell him so.
> The more radically he is frightened the better
> it is for him and for the matter involved.
> This might turn out to be the service which
> 'historical knowledge' can render to the
> actual task of theology.[63]

Harnack finds it inconceivable that Barth could be
speaking about faith in the person of Jesus Christ
without at the same time holding that this involves
knowledge of him as an historical person. The latter can
be had only through historical-critical study. If Barth
accords no place to historical-critical knowledge of
Jesus and its bearing on the life of faith, he necessarily encourages subjectivism, narrow intolerance and
even fanaticism. Harnack writes Barth concerning his
understanding of Barth's attitude toward critical biblical studies: "What you say here in relation to biblical
science may be formulated like this: the most radical
biblical science is always right and thank heaven for
that, because now we may be rid of it."[64]

G.   Primitive Christianity as Eschatological:
     Dispute on Overbeck

Following this statement, Harnack makes a veiled
reference to Franz Overbeck (1837-1905), church historian and a radical critic of the cultural Christianity
which had come to flower in Protestant liberalism, and
associates Barth with his unpalatable ideas. He writes:

> This point of view, known to the point of
> nausea from recent, second-rate Church-
> history, opens up the gate to every suitable
> fantasy and to every theological dictatorship
> which dissolves the historical ingredient of
> our religion and seeks to torment the con-
> science of others with one's own heuristic
> knowledge.[65]

An historical aside at this point with reference to
Overbeck may prove helpful. He was alluded to above in
connection with decisive figures influencing Barth's
theological about-face.   Both Barth and Thurneysen
discovered Overbeck's writings early in 1920 and wrote
approvingly of him.   In the preface to the second edition of his _Romans_ of 1922, Barth speaks of Overbeck's
influence on his revision and "of the warning addressed
by Overbeck to all theologians. This warning I have
first applied to myself, and then directed upon the
enemy."[66]   The "warning" in question had to do with
Overbeck's trenchant critique of what he regarded as the
cultural Christianity prevailing in Europe at that time
and of its total loss of the eschatological perspective
of primitive Christianity. Overbeck, professor of Critical Theology at Basel (1870-97), was Nietzsche's friend
and colleague, and shared his polemical attitude toward
the current state of the Protestant Church and Chris-

tianity. Overbeck pointed repeatedly--with little effect--to the radically eschatological nature of apostolic faith. Barth heard Overbeck's cry in the wilderness and heeded it: Harnack heard it and ignored it.[67]

In his definitive analysis of the Harnack-Barth Correspondence, Martin Rumscheidt illuminates their differing attitudes toward Overbeck and how this affected their own disagreements.

> Harnack sees the root of this anti-scientific, this speculative or metaphysical theology of Barth's in the historical scepticism Barth had inherited from Overbeck. 'I am in no way inclined to become involved in anything regarding Overbeck', he wrote to Barth on 16 January 1923. What Overbeck denied was what Harnack had spent a lifetime in demonstrating; that historical events as such contain in themselves a reference to a final and all-embracing reality, the divine. He also repudiated the harmony Harnack sought to establish between Christianity and culture. So Overbeck writes that 'Christianity must now make clear how seriously its own affirmation is to be taken, that it is not of this world. ... It is impossible to live the Christian life in this world; whoever tries to give himself equally to the world and to Christianity, and believes that he can live in the former while belonging to the latter, must become lost.' And then there were those attacks on Harnack in Overbeck's Christentum und Kultur which, even though they were made in a diary never meant for publication, were not what one might accept as scholarly criticism.[68]

H.   On the Nature of Revelation and the Gospel

These two different perspectives of Jesus Christ are simultaneously a dispute on the nature of revelation. Harnack wrote Barth that his "concept of revelation" was "totally" incomprehensible to him. In Barth's

view, what Harnack identifies as accessible to historical research with reference to the historical Jesus is
nothing other than the highest expression of the human.
We have seen that for Barth revelation is never accessible directly inasmuch as God is not an object at our
disposal and therewith available to human discovery.
Revelation, Barth never tires of stating, has to do with
God's self-disclosure which he alone determines. The
Scriptures are to be understood as a witness to the
revelation of God. Barth continues:

> One does not have to believe it, nor can one
> do it. But one should not deny that it wit-
> nesses to revelation, genuine revelation that
> is, and not to a more or less concealed reli-
> gious possibility of man but rather to the
> possibility of God, namely that he has acted
> under the form of a human possibility--and
> this as reality. According to this testimony,
> the Word became flesh, God himself became a
> human-historical reality and that this took
> place in the person of Jesus Christ. But from
> this it by no means follows for me that this
> event can also be an object of human-
> historical cognition; this is excluded be-
> cause and insofar as this reality is involved.
> The existence of a Jesus of Nazareth, for
> example, which can of course be discovered
> historically, is not this reality. A histori-
> cally discernible 'simple gospel,' discernible
> because it is humanly plausible, a 'simple
> gospel' which causes no scandal, a 'simple
> gospel,' that is, in your sense, a word or a
> deed of this Jesus which would be nothing
> other really than the realisation of a human
> possibility--would not be this reality.[69]

In Barth's reading of the Gospels as kerygmatic
witness it is not possible to isolate bits and pieces
via historical reconstruction, and therefore separable
from the reality of revelation, and designate them as
'the simple gospel'. "All that is comprehensible is

always that other which makes up the historical context
of the alleged revelation."[70] Barth writes further:

> Beyond this 'other' that barrier goes up and
> the scandal, the fable or the miracle threa-
> tens. The historical reality of Christ (as
> revelation, as 'centre of the gospel') is not
> the 'historical Jesus' whom an all too eager
> historical research had wanted to lay hold of
> in disregard of the very warnings made in the
> sources themselves (coming upon a banality
> which has been and shall be proclaimed in vain
> as a pearl of great price). Nor is it, as you
> said, an imagined Christ but rather the risen
> one, or let us say with more restraint in view
> of our little faith: the Christ who is wit-
> nessed to as the risen one. That is the
> 'evangelical, the historic [geschichtliche]
> Jesus Christ' and otherwise, that is, apart
> from the testimony to him, apart from the
> revelation which must here be believed, 'we
> know him no longer'. In this sense I think I
> can legitimately appeal to 2 Corinthians 5:16.
> At this decisive point, that is, in answering
> the question: what makes Jesus the Christ? in
> terms of the reference to the resurrection,
> one is indeed left from man's point of view
> with what you called 'totally' incomprehen-
> sible. And I gladly confess that I would a
> hundred times rather take the side of the No,
> the refusal to believe which you proclaim on
> the basis of this fact, than the talents of a
> 'positive' theology which ends up making what
> is incomprehensible altogether self-evident
> and transparent once again, for that is an
> emptying and a denying of revelation which
> with its apparent witness to the revelation is
> worse than the angriest refusal to believe
> which at least has the advantage of being
> suited to the subject matter.[71]

I. Conclusion: "The Gap that Divides Us"

Both Harnack and Barth terminated their correspondence to one another on a rather negative note.   A
meeting of minds was not imminent.   At the outset of

Harnack's "Open Letter" following Barth's "Fifteen
Answers," Harnack wrote: "Your answers have made a few
things clearer to me, but for that very reason the
opposition between us has become all the clearer."[72]
Having chastised Barth in the course of his "Open
Letter" for his Marcionitic dualism, abstruse metaphysics and for the encouragement of "every theological
dictatorship which dissolves the historical ingredient
of our religion...," Harnack concluded in a pointed
personal vein. "I do sincerely regret that the answers
to my questions only point out the magnitude of the gap
that divides us. But then neither my nor your theology
matters." Harnack's parting words follow--and these must
have been painful to Barth--who had hopes that his
confessional theology would advance the preaching of the
gospel in the church. Harnack said:

> What does matter is that the gospel is cor-
> rectly taught. Should however your way of
> doing this come to prevail it will not be
> taught any more; it will rather be given over
> into the hands of devotional [pietistic]
> preachers who freely create their own under-
> standing of the Bible and who set up their own
> dominion.
>
> Yours respectfully
>
> von Harnack[73]

Barth's lengthy and final response to Harnack's
"Open Letter" reveals his concurrence on "the gap that
divides us." Regrettably, Harnack's replies have not
narrowed it. Indeed, Barth takes offense at the tone of
admonition marking Harnack's "Open Letter" commenting
that though he cannot question the prerogative "of one
of my revered teachers of former times" to adopt this
somewhat condescending stance toward a former pupil, it

makes the task of responding unpleasant. Barth writes
with some edginess in the initial statement of his last
letter that the revered Harnack is so well established
and renowned that he "has no time and no ear not only
for answers different from those he would himself give
but also for questions other than his own. Is there any
further answer to be given to questions? Is the discussion not over?"[74]

Barth presses this point by saying to Harnack that
neither comprehension nor repudiation of Barth and his
colleagues will be possible "without a serious study of
our point of view."[75] Evidently, Barth felt both at the
time of their exchange in 1923 and upon later reflection
that Harnack had little direct knowledge of his writings
or point of view. After examining the evidence,
Rumscheidt surmises that in addition to having heard
Barth lecture twice, Harnack probably had a passing
acquaintance with the two editions of Barth's Romans,
his Overbeck article, and perhaps a few other articles.
We know from Harnack's post card to Barth written during
the course of their exchange in 1923 that he apparently
wrote the fifteen questions on the spur of the moment.
They arose out of his overall impressions of the
theology of Barth and his friends. In short, what he
knew of them, he did not like. That was sufficient to
initiate the exchange between professor and former
student.[76]

Barth's sharpest rejoinder relates to Harnack's
admonition of Barth--not in his usual "role of the
defender of science"--but now as "the defender of the
so-called Christian 'possession.'" Barth asks: "why
the lament about 'sublimity' of my metaphysic and psychology, as if all of a sudden popular intelligibility
were for you the standard of right theology?"[77] Even

more distasteful is Harnack's penchant for evaluating
his theology in terms of the degree to which it departs
from the "'Christianity of the gospels', as if the topic
of our discussion were all of a sudden the Christian
nature of my theology?"[78] Barth confesses his own "angry
thoughts about the connection between the scientific
character of your theology, which causes you to repu-
diate what I (and not only I) call revelation and faith,
and your own Christian position, which comes out into
the open in the idea that Paul's 'saved in hope' must be
suspected as 'problematical.'"[79] Barth notes that he
could register "very sharp words" about such positions
of Harnack. "Yet what else would I do then but seal
this hopelessness on my part too, something that must
not be done?"[80]

In a somewhat more irenic mood Barth closes by
echoing a note sounded early in his final letter,
namely, his willingness both to discuss his position
further and to change if convinced of a better way.
"...I know how frighteningly relative everything is that
one can say about the great subject that occupies you
and me." With some hope mingled with confidence that he
is, at least, on the right track, Barth concludes:

> I would like to be able to listen attentively
> in the future to whatever you also will have
> to say. But at this time I cannot concede
> that you have driven me off the field with
> your questions and answers, although I will
> gladly endure it when it really happens.
>
> Respectfully Yours
> Karl Barth[81]

In his concluding "Postscript" to the exchange,
Harnack assures Barth "that no other desire moved me in

my letter than to reach clarity <u>vis-a-vis</u> a theologian friend."[82] Having the last word, however, Harnack cannot desist speaking to two issues. First, he remarks that it must be understood that "Paul and Luther are for me not primarily subjects but objects of scientific theology. ..." He adds that he views Barth along with them in the category of preachers who give expression to their Christianity as prophets and witnesses. This distasteful mixture of theological discourse with preaching alluded to earlier remains highly suspect. "Scientific theology and witnessing are often enough mixed together in life, but neither can remain healthy when the demand to keep them separate is invalidated."[83] Second, Harnack expresses his continuing dissatisfaction with Barth's use of the concept of revelation. His final word of caution follows:

> Revelation is not a scientific concept. ...There is no future...in the attempt to grasp a "Word" of this kind as something so purely 'objective' that human speaking, hearing, grasping, and understanding can be eliminated from its operation. I have the impression that Professor Barth tries something like this and calls in a dialectic in this attempt which leads to an invisible ridge between absolute religious scepticism and naive biblicism--the most tormenting interpretation of Christian experience and Christian faith![84]

Harnack concludes that this "invisible ridge" on which Barth walks will not prove spacious enough to provide a foothold for many to follow. "Would it not be better for him to admit that he is playing <u>his</u> instrument only and that God has still other instruments, instead of erecting a rigid either-or?"[85]

Chapter III

THEOLOGICAL FOUNDATION: THE RESURRECTION OF THE DEAD (1924)

> "...if the hope of the resurrection be re-
> moved, the whole edifice of piety would col-
> lapse, just as if the foundation were with-
> drawn from it." (John Calvin)

During the early years of his teaching at Göttingen, Barth taught courses in historical and dogmatic
theology as well as in New Testament exegesis. He gave
lectures on Ephesians and James. In addition, he lectured on First Corinthians in the summer semester of
1923. These lectures were prepared for publication on
the basis of a student transcript while Barth was on his
summer vacation following the semester. Though published in 1924 with the title, Die Auferstehung der
Toten (The Resurrection of the Dead), Barth comments in
the preface to the first edition that a precise title
would be, "Exposition of 1 Cor. 15 in the Context of I
Corinthians."[1] During this same year, a collection of
his essays as well as a book of sermons co-authored with
Thurneysen also appeared.[2]

I. BARTH'S PERSPECTIVE ON FIRST CORINTHIANS

In analyzing 1 Corinthians, Barth takes issue with
the more commonly accepted approach to its interpreta-

tion. According to the latter, the epistle is composed of the Apostle's responses to a series of problems, questions, and controversies in the Corinthian church. The dispute in the church over the resurrection in chapter 15 is regarded as a new theme standing in no special relationship to the issues treated in the preceding fourteen chapters. Barth cites Lietzmann's view as typical: "Without internal or external connexion with what has been said before, the treatment of a new theme [the resurrection] then follows."[3]

While acknowledging that the subjects treated in 1 Corinthians, chapters 1-14, are disparate and seemingly unconnected to the theme of the resurrection in chapter 15, Barth poses two questions. First, is there some thread traceable to the mind of Paul which gives the epistle an internal unity? Second, is the theme of the resurrection developed in chapter 15 simply just another along side of earlier ones? Or it is the theme of the epistle making the previously hidden thread visible?[4]

On the basis of his analysis of I Corinthians, Barth opposes the accepted view and proposes his own alternative thesis in answer to the above questions.

> The chapter devoted to the Resurrection of the Dead does not stand in so isolated a relation to the First Epistle to the Corinthians as at first glance might appear. It forms not only the close and crown of the whole Epistle, but also provides the clue to its meaning, from which place light is shed on the whole, and it becomes intelligible, not outwardly, but inwardly, as a unity. We might even say that this central significance of the ideas expressed in the chapter extends beyond the limits of the First Epistle to the Corinthians. Here Paul discloses generally his focus, his background, and his assumptions with a definiteness he but seldom uses elsewhere, and with a particularity which he has

not done in his other Epistles as known to us.
The Epistles to the Romans, the Philippians,
and the Colossians cannot even be understood,
unless we keep in mind the sharp accentuation
which their contents receive in the light of
1 Cor. xv., where Paul develops what elsewhere
he only indicates and outlines, and which
first imports a specific and unmistakable
colour to his ideas in general.[5]

A.   First Corinthians XV: "The Resurrection
     Chapter"

The preceding citation clarifies why Barth feels
compelled to oppose the view that the rejection of
Paul's teaching concerning the resurrection of the dead
by the Corinthian Christians is simply a matter of a
theological difference with him at one point.   For
Barth, to adopt such a stance with respect to the issue
confronting Paul in Corinth is analogous to the modern
view which finds the Apostle's teaching here either
unintelligible, unacceptable, or a matter of indif-
ference. Barth finds it indisputable that though Paul's
antagonists believed in the resurrection of Christ and
some form of future life which is "immaterial" or
"spiritual," they doubt his teaching on the bodily
resurrection. "This is the 'scandal,' stumbling-block,
in question."[6] For Barth, it follows that it is illegitimate to pick and choose what one desires from Paul's
gospel concerning the resurrection of the dead. "Paul
did not describe all his ideas and declarations as
undiscussible conditiones sine quibus non of Christianity, and, where he did so, it was with a varying
emphasis. That he did this here with the greatest
emphasis can scarcely admit of any doubt."[7] Accordingly,
though attitudes toward the Apostle may vary, Barth

states "...it must at least be obvious from the first glance that, in dealing with the Corinthian doubters, he was not concerned with this thing or that thing, but with the whole."[8]

II. THEOLOGICAL AND METHODOLOGICAL CONSIDERATIONS

   A.   The Limitations of Language of the
        Resurrection of the Dead

The attempt to speak about the resurrection of the dead or the resurrection of Jesus Christ is to attempt the impossible. Insofar as these events confront us with God as wholly other and the reality of his revelation, they are never under human control. To this degree, the apostolic testimony to the resurrection of the dead seeks to give expression to that which is ultimately inexpressible. This accounts for what A. Geense terms the "strongly formal function" of the apostolic witness to the resurrection. He adds that this linguistic limitation which Barth's "Theology of the Word of God" takes with utmost seriousness is not to be construed negatively. That is to say, it makes a considerable difference if language about the resurrection stems from the recognition that the reality toward which it points is finally inexpressible because we are confronted with the revelation of God, or whether the limitation of language about the resurrection is simply an accidental mode of expression referring to some other subject matter such as the significance of the cross or the cause of Jesus which continues. This helps to explain why there is both implicit and explicit speech about the resurrection in the New Testament. To the degree that the entire New Testament witness is predicated upon the reality of the resurrection of Jesus from the dead, Barth adopts J. A. Bengel's hermeneutical rule in reading the New Testament witnesses: "They all breathe the resurrection" (spirant resurrectionem).

That fact that much of the language of the New Testament has this formal function and speaks only implicitly of the resurrection is correlated with the substantive fact that whether the language is implicit or explicit, the content attested is the ultimate mystery.[9] Seen in terms of Barth's thesis in interpreting the entire epistle, Paul's language about the resurrection of the dead is implicit in 1 Corinthians chapters 1-14 and becomes explicit only in chapter 15. But whether his testimony to the resurrection be implicit or explicit, all human language pointing to it is limited and broken. Barth observes:

> ...on the one side, death is the last, the absolute last which we can see and understand; on the other side is life, of which we know nothing at all, which we can only comprehend as the life of God Himself, without having in our hands anything more than an empty conception thereof--apart from the fullness that God alone gives and His revelation in the resurrection.[10]

Finally, all our language is inadequate to bridge the chasm between this life and the life to come. Commenting on 1 Cor. 13, Barth highlights Paul's discussion of the limitation of human prophecy, speaking in tongues, or knowledge--none can bridge the final chasm between the believer and God. "Everything which man, even the man who is inspired and impelled by God, can devise here as means, way and bridge is insufficient. And not, indeed, because the earthly, the human, is in itself so imperfect, but because the perfect comes: Because the sun rises all lights are extinguished."[11] Paul writes: "...when the perfect comes, the imperfect will pass away. ...For now we see in a mirror dimly, but then face to face. Now I know in part; then I shall understand fully, even as I have been fully understood" (1 Cor. 13:10-12). Barth therefore understands the fulfillment of the life of love as eschatological: what Paul points to here is not the prolongation of a human virtue, but rather the anticipation of the resurrection of the dead when "the mortal puts on immortality" (1 Cor. 15:54).[12]

B.   The Comprehensive Significance of Language of the Resurrection

The resurrection of the dead and its corollary, the resurrection of Jesus Christ, provide in Barth's view the comprehensive framework within which everything said in I Corinthians is to be understood. This emphasis on the definitive importance of eschatology for all Christian faith recalls Barth's statement to that effect in his Romans.[13] With respect to 1 Corinthians, he thus maintains:

> The Resurrection of the Dead is the point from which Paul is speaking and to which he points. From this standpoint, not only the death of those now living, but, above all, their life this side of the threshold of death, is in the apostolic sermon, veritably seen, understood, judged, and placed in the light of the last severity, the last hope. ...1 Cor. xv. contains the doctrine of the last things.[14]

1. <u>The Doctrine of "Last Things</u>." It is important to Barth that Paul's eschatology in 1 Cor. 15 and the New Testament generally be distinguished from typical Christian ways of construing the "last things." First, the latter is not to be confused with human projections about the end of history which may be conceived either as imminent or distant in time. Nor will Barth allow that eschatology has to do with the cessation of nature as we know it. In both instances, speculations about the "end" are really extrapolations from known causal sequences. Barth in no way denies that these images of "last things" may be "instructive and stimulating" especially to those apparently indifferent to possibilities which may eventuate in history or in the natural order. Second, not even the conception of "physical-metaphysical, cosmic-metacosmic transformations and revolutions of an unparalleled kind" of which the above may be only a prelude is to be confused with the Christian vision. Third, it is not the case that the "last things" attested in the Bible are equatable with a picture of the end of history constructed with "material taken from the Bible and perhaps even from 1 Cor. xv."[15] Concerning the limitations of biblical imagery, Barth observes: "'Everything transitory' is only a parable; that even the objects of the biblical world belong to the passing; that they are meant to serve and not to rule, to signify and not to be, the Bible, at any rate, leaves us in no doubt."[16] Hence, for example, the various images Paul uses to illustrate astounding transformations occurring in nature are not synonymous with the "incomprehensible" transformation which God will effect through the resurrection, yet reflection upon them can assist thinking upon that greater and unsurpassable transformation.[17]

If the latter false ways of speaking about the "last things" are not compatible with Paul, how does Barth interpret the Apostle's perspective? He says:

> Last _things_, as such, are not _last_ things, however great and significant they may be. He only speaks of _last_ things who would speak of the _end_ of all things, of their end understood plainly and fundamentally, of a reality so radically superior to all things, that the existence of all things would be utterly and entirely _based_ upon it alone, and thus, in speaking of their end, he would in truth be speaking of nothing else than their beginning. And when he speaks of history-end and of time-end, he is only speaking of the _end_ of history and the _end_ of time. But once more of its end, understood thus fundamentally, thus plainly, of a reality so radically superior to all happening and all temporality, that in speaking of the finiteness of history and the finiteness of time, he is also speaking of that upon which all time and all happening is _based_. The end of history must be for him synonymous with the pre-history, the limits of time of which he speaks must be the limits of all and every time and thus necessarily the _origin_ of time.[18]

2. _Biblical Representations of "Last Things."_ Barth finds that biblical representations of "last things"--"however primitive they may be in certain circumstances"--have the advantage over similar conceptions in their use of the concept of eternity. God's eternity sets the definitive limit to all time and history. God's eternity is the "_rule_, the _Kingdom_ of God, His absolute _transcendence_ as Creator, Redeemer, and King of things, of history. ..."[19] To comprehend God's eternity in this way precludes confusing "last things" "with a termination of history, however impressive and wonderful it may be. ...But he will also be

removed from the other temptation, to confuse eternity
with a great annihilation, and to make of the end-of-
history an annihilation of history."[20] For Barth, God,
the Eternal One, stands both before and after all time
and history. Hence in speaking of the eternity of God
who transcends both the end and the origin of all that
is, Barth underlines the truth that it is the eternal
sovereign God alone who initiates and terminates time.
Both the origin and end of time attest his sovereignty.

    3. The End as Origin. This stress on God as both
Creator and Consummator leads Barth to make the correlation between the true end of all things effected by God
and the origin of all things in God. Hence he can say:
"Of the real end-of-history it may be said at any time:
The end is near!"[21] Or again: "...we have to do here
with the doctrine of the "End," which is at the same
time the beginning, of the last things, which are, at
the same time, the first."[22] The image of Christ raised
from the dead as the "first fruits" of the future resurrection of the dead is another correlation of first and
last, of beginning and end. The hopelessness of the
human situation envisaged by the Corinthian doubters is
the denial that "God is God" and that he has raised
Christ from the dead. Barth comments: "That is our
hope; the meaning of the resurrection of Jesus consists
in this, that the resurrection is the divine horizon
also of our existence. Life and the world are finite.
God is the end. Hence He is [therefore and therewith]
also the beginning."[23] Put differently, Barth sees
Paul's intention in 1 Cor. 15 to be the juxtaposition of
the recollection of perishing and death facing the
Corinthians with the resurrection of the dead which lies
beyond all human possibilities. Humanly speaking, the
Corinthians can conceive only of death and the void--of

extinction and non-being.

> With the word "resurrection," however, the
> apostolic preaching puts in this empty place
> against all that exists for us, all that is
> known to us, all that can be possessed by us,
> all things of all time--what? not the non-
> being, the unknown, the not-to-be possessed,
> nor yet a second being, a further thing to
> become known, a higher future possession, but
> the source and truth of all that exists, that
> is known, that can belong to us, the reality
> of all _res_, of all things, the eternity of
> time, the _resurrection_ of the dead.[24]

While it is true that the Apostle knows that the dead
are not yet raised, the hope of the resurrection of the
dead "already _effected_ in God" informs everything said
about death and dying in chapter 15. Once again,
Barth's thesis concerning the central importance of
Paul's teaching concerning the resurrection of the dead
for understanding the entire epistle is evident.

> The recollection of death is so important, so
> urgent, so disturbing, so actual because it is
> in fact really the tidings of the resurrection
> behind it, the recollection of the _life_, of
> our life that we are not living and that yet
> is our life. Hence the end of the Epistle is
> also its beginning, its principle that sup-
> ports and actuates the whole, because it is
> not only a termination, but the end.[25]

When viewed as a whole, Barth concludes with the
following estimate about the doctrine of "last things"
developed by Paul in 1 Corinthians 15:

> The ideas developed in 1 Cor. xv. could be
> better described as the _methodology of the
> apostle's preaching_, rather than eschatology,
> because it is really concerned not with this
> and that special thing, but with the meaning

and nerve of its whole, with the whence? and
the whither? of the human way as such and in
itself.[26]

C. The Existential Meaning of Language of the
Resurrection

It was noted above that despite the limitations of
biblical imagery pointing to the "last things," it does
serve to sensitize and awaken readers to the reality of
God and his ultimate purposes. Barth can say: "Without
any doubt at all the words "resurrection of the dead"
are, for him [Paul], nothing else than a paraphrase of
the word 'God.'"[27] While Barth knows that the paraphrase
is not identical with its referent, he regards it as a
"necessary paraphrase and concretion."[28] Otherwise one
might think of God in terms of some sort of abstract
dominion over the world, or of God who limits all
things, or even of God as Spirit. Though all of these
are possible and even "pious" ideas of God, Barth contends that such conceptions lay no real claim upon the
whole self. The self may remain in the attitude of a
spectator toward God. But the understanding of God as
the One who raises the dead is the attestation that he
is indeed the Lord. Hence for Barth the tie between God
and my existence is highlighted and becomes acute in
speaking of him as the one who raises the dead. He
writes: "God is the Lord of the body! Now the question
of God is posed acutely and inescapably. Body is man,
I am body, and this man, this I, is God's; I can no
longer plead dualism; I cannot retire to a reality
secured against God. ..."[29]

D.   The Critical Function of Language of the
     Resurrection

Geense is quite right to call attention to the way
Barth's language about the resurrection has more than
simply an existential import for him. The paraphrase of
the concept of God by the words, "resurrection of the
dead," exercises a critical function with respect to the
shape of Christian existence in the world. Thus all of
Paul's ethical injunctions in 1 Cor. chapters 5-6 are
directly related to the Lordship of Jesus Christ, crucified and risen (e.g., 1 Cor. 5:7-8; 6:9-11). Sexual
libertinism and illicit concourse with prostitutes is
rebuked with the word: "The body is not meant for
immorality, but for the Lord, and the Lord for the body.
And God raised the Lord and will also raise us up by his
power. Do you not know that your bodies are members of
Christ?" (1 Cor. 6:13-15). Barth comments: "Christianity brings not peace but unrest into natural life; it
transforms it into the body of Christ, into a member of
the body of the risen Lord, who, as such, should be
sanctified."[30] Or even more sharply, Barth comments on
1 Cor. 15:44:

> ...it is raised a (God-) spiritual body, the
> end of the ways of God is corporeality. Only
> with this definition does the idea of God,
> with which, in fact, Paul is alone concerned,
> receive that unambiguous superiority, that
> critical sharpness, that pregnancy with last
> Judgment and supreme hope, the misunder-
> standing of which is implied in the very words
> 'have not the knowledge of God.' (verse 34)[31]

The most intense criticism deriving from the confession of the bodily resurrection is levied against the

religion and morality of the Corinthians.

> That by resurrection, anything else than
> bodily resurrection could be understood by
> Paul or by the doubters is an assumption to be
> found nowhere throughout the chapter. It goes
> without saying that bodily resurrection is
> meant. Hence they stumble against this very
> obstacle. It is just here that Christian
> monism dashes itself in vain against the
> discontinuity, against the dialectic of Paul-
> ine thought. ...Continued existence after
> death, which they also accept, must still be
> only a spiritual, an immaterial existence!
> Why? Well, of course, so that it must find a
> place in a comprehensive philosophy [along
> side of] this present bodily life. A soul
> which lives on after death may, at least, be
> plausibly asserted, if not perhaps demon-
> strated, without disturbing the picture of
> world uniformity. But the resurrection of the
> body, this same body that we plainly see dying
> and perishing, the assertion, therefore, not
> of a duality of life here and life to come,
> but of an identity of the two, not given now,
> not to be directly ascertained, but only to be
> hoped for, only to be believed in, this is
> manifestly nothing but the ruthless destruc-
> tion of that unity, a "scandal," irra-
> tionality, and religious materialism. Whether
> it be felt as harshly as this, it remains the
> same. This is the "scandal," stumbling-block,
> in question.[32]

The decisive divide between Paul proclaiming a
bodily resurrection and the doubters at Corinth, Barth
describes thus: "In the controversy over the resurrection, two worlds clash (the question of corporeality is
only the extreme point at which they touch); the world
of the gospel (let us repeat: as Paul understands it),
and a religious and moral world which looks very much
like Christianity. ..."[33] In Barth's mind, the Apostle
in no way overestimated the significance of the issue.
"The dispute about the corporeality of the resurrection

is also nothing more than an index of the clash of much deeper and more extensive antagonisms."[34] To regard as "something strange" Paul's stress on the bodily resurrection indicates in Barth's view the stance of "spectators who overlook what is involved."[35]

E.   The Praxis of the Truth of the Resurrection

Paul does not seek to prove his message to the doubters by removing all intellectual difficulties. No apologetic tour de force is provided. In Barth's view, he attacked instead the practical laziness characterizing the Corinthians. He calls them to recognize that their transformation and the redemption of creation are not yet present, but await the "coming of Christ."[36] In the meantime, they are called to a life of hope. Yet something further must be said. In order for Paul's message to be understood, the walk of faith is required. Geense puts well what Barth hears in Paul: "The obedience of faith has an eminent importance for the comprehension of the images, the concepts and the theory Paul proclaimed."[37] Barth concludes his exposition of the section, "The Resurrection as Truth" (vv. 35-49), in this way. Paul

> places man forcibly in the light, or, rather, twilight, of the truth that he is created by God in the middle between Adam and Christ, and tells him: Thou art Both, or rather thou belongest to both, and just as both jointly describe God's way, from the old to the new creature, so thy life also is the scene across which this path leads, so must thou, too, make the journey from here to there. In other words, he jerks the questioner and spectator out of his comfortable position and sets him right in the midst of the battle, in which the resurrection is truth. He who recognizes

> himself in Adam and Christ no longer, in fact,
> asks: With what body shall we come again: as
> if it were a marvellous fairy-tale which he
> must "believe." He knows that what is in
> question is this, his body (but the resurrec-
> tion of this body), and gives God the honour
> in fear and trembling, but also in hope. Not
> in the theory, but only in the praxis of this
> battle, is it to be understood: the Resurrec-
> tion as truth, but here it is to be under-
> stood.[38]

III. BARTH'S EXPOSITION OF FIRST CORINTHIANS XV

A. "The Resurrection Gospel as the Foundation of the
   Church" (vv. 1-11)

> Now I would remind you, brethren, in what
> terms I preached to you the gospel, which you
> received, in which you stand, by which you are
> saved, if you hold it fast--unless you be-
> lieved in vain. (vv. 1-2; RSV cited unless
> noted)

Barth underlines the major thrust of the discussion
above in accentuating that the "critical assumption of
the Epistle" expressed in this and in the opening verses
is that the gospel Paul preached "is not a personal
sentiment or opinion or tendency of Paul; ... nothing
new, but the old; nothing accidental and peripheral, but
the foundation and the centre, by virtue of which they
are Christians."[39] The foundation of the church and of
their faith is the gospel which Paul proclaimed. For
the Apostle, this foundation is impregnable and steadfast. The salvation of the Corinthians "is reality in
the message, which they have received and in which they
stand."[40] Central to this message received and believed
is the declaration that Christ has been raised from the
dead. It is not the case, according to Barth, that Paul

regards his hearers as apostates from this truth. Rather, his call to the church is "to keep in memory the message declared unto it, the accepted, the fundamental, the saving message."[41]

> For I delivered to you as of first importance what I also received, that Christ died for our sins in accordance with the scriptures, that he was buried, that he was raised on the third day in accordance with the scriptures, and that he appeared to Cephas, then to the twelve. Then he appeared to more than five hundred brethren at one time, most of whom are still alive, though some have fallen asleep. Then he appeared to James, then to all the apostles. (vv. 3-7)

1. <u>The Historicity of the Resurrection</u>. Barth disagrees with a widespread view which interprets Paul and the tradition as intending to provide a "'resurrection narrative,' a narrative of the historical fact 'the resurrection of Jesus,' or even (Lietzmann) a 'historical proof of the resurrection.'"[42] Barth adds: "How tempting it is to read verses 3-11, for example, with the eyes of historical intelligence, whereby it would make a small difference to the infertility of the yield whether one was resolved to deny or recognize the so-called miracle."[43] Indeed, given the context of this passage, Barth asks "whether all that Paul means here might not have the effect, not of disconnecting the <u>historical position of the question as such</u>, but of <u>relativizing it</u>."[44] Barth paraphrases Paul and adds his own comment as follows:

> 'It was not, and is not, my idea to deliver to you the gospel in this perfectly definite outline which I preached unto you [verse 2], but I have so delivered it as I myself received it'--i.e. the gospel of the primitive

> Church has no other meaning than my gospel.
> It will profit you nothing to try to get
> behind Paul in order to procure a gospel that
> is alleged to be simpler and more acceptable,
> for if you go behind Paul you will stumble at
> the first step upon the same riddle that you
> think only Paul and Paulinism confronts you
> with now.[45]

It may seem that the sequence of verbs in vs. 3ff.,
namely, "died," "was buried," "was raised," "appeared"
are intended to provide a "so-called resurrection report, a narrative of events." Barth questions this
supposition on account of the "unhistorical addition" of
the phrase, "for our sins," following "he died." After
the latter phrase and the "he was raised," there is the
addition of the phrase, "in accordance with the scriptures." Moreover, the phrase, "he was raised," is
followed by a series of "he appeared." But the latter
do not come in the form of an historical proof of the
phrase, "he was raised." For Barth, the decisive reason
against taking vs. 3ff. as a kind of historical proof is
apparent if the phrase, "he was raised," is compared
with v. 13: "But if there is no resurrection of the
dead, then Christ has not been raised. ..." Barth
comments:

> The whole meaning of verses 12-28 is, indeed,
> this--that this historical fact, the resurrec-
> tion of Jesus, stands and falls with the
> resurrection of the dead, generally. What
> kind of historical fact is that reality of
> which, or at any rate the perception of which,
> is bound up in the most express manner with
> the perception of a general truth, which by
> its nature cannot emerge in history, or, to
> speak more exactly, can only emerge on the
> confines of all history, on the confines of
> death?[46]

2. <u>The Resurrection and History: Barth's View</u>.
The point Barth accents here is that neither the general
resurrection nor the resurrection of Jesus Christ from
the dead is comprehensible within the ordinary understanding of history or historical occurrences. That
Jesus dies and was buried signifies the end of his
historical life. History symbolized in the words, "he
was buried," is

> illuminated in the most dazzling manner, from
> the <u>frontier</u> of history, which is described by
> the words "who died" on the one hand, by the
> words "he rose again" on the other hand, while
> the words "he was seen" is the rendering of
> the many-voiced testimony (verse 15) that the
> boundary has been <u>seen</u>. In <u>history</u>, to be
> sure! But <u>in</u> history, the <u>frontier</u> of his-
> tory. ...[47]

Hence that Christ died for human sin would not make the
"<u>frontier</u> of history" visible apart from the testimony
that "God raised up Christ" (v. 15).

As in his subsequent writings, Barth already here
inveighs against all attempts to reconstruct the sequence of Jesus' appearances. All of the incongruities
between Paul and the Synoptics and between the Synoptics
and John are evident. Moreover, while the Gospels do
provide the tradition of the empty tomb, they "do not
make the least secret of the fact that the sight of the
empty tomb and the sight of the risen Lord was something
<u>toto</u> <u>coelo</u> different. ..."[48] Hence the zeal of some who
focus on the empty tomb as though it were the touchstone
of Easter faith is misplaced. Though Barth accepts the
tradition that the "tomb is doubtless empty," he observes that Paul stresses the appearances of the risen
Lord following the early tradition he received. "...He

who died for our sins and rose again on the third day,
He, the crucified and risen Lord, <u>appeared</u>, the boundary
of history and of mankind, the end and the beginning in
one."[49]

In the testimony to the appearances of the risen
Christ in these verses, the accent lies not upon what
was seen by the disciples, but on the One who appeared.
Liberal commentators are misguided in regarding the
appearances either as "objective" or "subjective" vi-
sions experienced by the disciples; positivists or
conservatives also are wide of the mark in the attempt
to establish a chronicle of the "historical facts."[50]
Concerning the latter banal reconstruction, Barth comments:

> As if this "positive" manner of asserting the
> resurrection of Jesus were not in fact the
> secret denial of the very thing which we would
> fain assert, the resurrection as the deed <u>of</u>
> <u>God</u> whom no eye has seen nor ear heard, who
> has entered no human heart, neither outwardly
> nor inwardly, not subjective and not objec-
> tive, not mystical nor spiritistic and not
> flatly objective, but as a historical divine
> fact, which as such is only to be grasped in
> the category of revelation and in none other.[51]

The total thrust of the apostolic witness is upon
the appearances of Jesus Christ. "Only the appearance,
that which He did, is, at any rate, the substance of the
gospel, and, we can now very well say, the central
substance of the gospel which Paul himself received and
delivered, and to which it is his present intention to
recall the Corinthians."[52] Paul removes all possibilities for the Corinthians to ground their faith in some
other gospel. The risen Christ lives: that is the
fundamental article of faith on which the church stands

or falls. In no way is this to be "understood as a continuation of human experiences, and insights of a higher and the highest kind, but only as the witness of God's revelation, as the really genuine Easter gospel, within the very Church of Christ."[53]

It is axiomatic for Barth that God alone can authenticate himself or that "revelation...can...only be proved by revelation." Yet in Barth's view it is significant that "the gospel of the primitive church" regarding the death and resurrection of Christ is attested by Paul to be "in accordance with the scriptures." "Paul knows that he is in harmony with the "scriptures" when, on the grounds of revelation, he testifies that Christ died for our sins and rose again on the third day."[54] Paul envisages the prophets and fathers of the Old Testament as unified in their anticipation of the "turning-point from death to life, from the end to the beginning, from an old to a new world...believing, and promising in many different tongues nothing else than this one."[55] That the Apostle singled out no single passage but spoke directly of "the scriptures" attesting that "Christ died for our sins," Barth interprets as his attempt to claim the entire "Holy Narrative" as corroboration.

Evidently, the Corinthians desired the forgiveness of sins. Barth interprets Paul's declaration to them to be that forgiveness is not secured through the death of Jesus alone. Or again:

> Would it not be a sentimental illusion to glorify the suffering of Christ in itself, and to found one's faith upon the sentiment of Jesus which is therein preserved? Is the Crucifixion, with the bitter inquiry of God with which it ended, adapted for the founda-

tion of a general religious truth that our
sins are to be taken from us?[56]

In order for the power of sin to be overcome, a greater
power must prevail. Here too, and at every point, Barth
interprets Paul to be confronting the Corinthians with
the radical import of the resurrection of Jesus from the
dead. Hence, in order for the forgiveness of sins to be
a reality for the Corinthians and for all, a further
Word of God must be spoken. Barth writes:

> Is not, for our absolution, a "And God spoke"
> necessary, and where is this to be found on
> Golgotha, or how could we hear it there, if we
> had not already heard it beyond all tombs as
> Easter gospel?[57]

3. "He appeared also to me."

> Last of all, as to one untimely born, he
> appeared also to me. For I am the least of
> the apostles, unfit to be called an apostle,
> because I persecuted the church of God. But
> by the grace of God I am what I am, and his
> grace toward me was not in vain. On the
> contrary, I worked harder than any of them,
> though it was not I, but the grace of God
> which is with me. Whether then it was I or
> they, so we preach and so you believed. (vv.
> 8-11)

Barth interprets these verses as the Apostle's
completion of his commendation of the gospel of the
resurrection. He does so by trying to turn the attention of the Corinthians away from his person to the
truth which alone mattered. He had not only "delivered
that which he had received from others" to them as a
faithful transmitter of the tradition of the primitive
church: here he also speaks directly as a witness

attesting the revelation of the risen Lord to him and thus "as an <u>originator</u>" of the resurrection tradition. That Christ appeared to him as to "one untimely born, ...the least of the apostles," in Barth's words--"an abortion beside the healthy children of the house"--is due solely to God's grace. Thus the Apostle can say "By God's <u>grace</u> I am what I am" (v. 10). Barth paraphrases Paul's message in this way:

> 'By His <u>grace</u> I am ...!' The self-evidence of the truth was not in vain, my life was more laborious than that of others, I came in a thicker crowd, but all that is grace. Not I! I deserve and claim and am nothing. I live only by grace. But what I do by grace, that I <u>must</u> do, and I must be taken for what I am. Thus, no value attaches to any distinction between me and others. They, too, can only preach the risen Lord and the resurrection. Hear them or hear me! but hear! There is only one gospel, one faith, one salvation, one ground upon which we stand and ye with us.[58]

B.   "The Resurrection as the Meaning of Faith"
      (vv. 12-34)

> Now if Christ is preached as raised from the dead, how can some of you say that there is no resurrection of the dead? But if there is no resurrection of the dead, then Christ has not been raised; if Christ has not been raised, then our preaching is in vain and your faith is in vain. We are even found to be misrepresenting God, because we testified of God that he raised Christ, whom he did not raise if it is true that the dead are not raised. For if the dead are not raised, then Christ has not been raised. If Christ has not been raised, your faith is futile and you are still in your sins. Then those also who have fallen asleep in Christ have perished. If for this life only we have hoped in Christ, we are of all men most to be pitied. (vv. 12-19)

Barth interprets the Apostle's controversy with the Corinthians set forth in this section to be a "repugnant work of destruction." Such is the case because Paul contends that the ground on which they presume to stand is illusory; therefore his message consists in a radical "Either-Or." This means that "beside the impossible, unbelievable, inaccessible gospel of the Resurrection of the Dead there is left only the abyss of an utterly radical skepticism towards everything divine, even towards everything that is humanly highest, holding the danger that somebody may fall into it and be unable to get out."[59]

1. The Resurrection of Jesus Christ as the Vindication of God. The major point in Paul's argument which Barth singles out has to do with the way in which the Corinthians' belief in the resurrection of Christ seemingly involved treating it "as a remote miracle... [which] had no fundamental and no vital significance for them."[60] Paul argues that since the resurrection of Christ is the foundation of the gospel, how can they deny the resurrection of the dead? Barth understands Paul's aim above all else to be to hold that the resurrection of Christ was the vindication of God as God! That Paul could argue from Christ's resurrection to that of others is predicated on the deeper assumption that in that event God vindicated himself as God. This means that henceforth all reality must be viewed in that light; i.e., the resurrection of Jesus from the dead. Barth writes:

> If that be true, if the end of history set by God is here, if the new eternal beginning placed by God appears here, then that which has appeared from God applies to the whole of history within the scope of this horizon, then the miracle of God to Christ is immediately

and simultaneously the miracle of God to us, and not a miracle about which it may be asked: What has it to do with us? If we see God at work there, then what is true there is also serious for us here and now, then our life, too, it goes without saying, is placed in the light which proceeds from that horizon of all that we call life. Not yet in fulfilment. We are, indeed, still living this life, as yet, we, indeed, only know time; it is the "not yet" which separates us from the resurrection. But we are living the life limited by that horizon, we are living in time for eternity, we are living in hope of the resurrection, it is that which cannot be denied, if Christ's resurrection is to be understood, not as miracle or myth or psychic experience (which all come to the same thing), but as God's revelation. For it just means in fact: "God is God, Either-Or, yes or no, but not: He is God there, but not here in Corinth, but not for us." Christ is risen, but we know and are living only this unending, horizonless life, lacking a last promise.[61]

2.   The Resurrection of the Dead as the Basis of Faith. The denial of the general resurrection by the Corinthians is taken by Paul--in a manner unexpected to his readers--to entail the denial of Christ's resurrection. That is to say, if life is finally simply a "tale told by an idiot, full of sound and fury, signifying nothing," then Christ is not risen! Barth puts it bluntly: "If God is not God in our life, then He is also not that in the life of Christ."[62] If the Corinthians were right that the dead are not raised, then the resurrection of Christ would not be an event sui generis! If it could be "interpreted as a miracle, myth, or inward experience, in this way or that; it then belongs, in any case, to the sea of life, among the many shapes and events, which may be explained in this way or that."[63]

In short, Christian faith has meaning insofar as it is established and grounded in God's saving activity. To deny either the resurrection of the dead or the resurrection of Jesus Christ means for Barth to profess a faith without foundations in revelation. It means that faith would be directed to "the human something in Christ, whose divine resemblance is there asserted."[64] But preaching a human Jesus--no matter how noble--would be "futile" since realistically one could say of Jesus only that he is a dead "Messiah." If Christ be not risen, preaching could no longer be "a kerygma, 'proclamation'; for kerygma is based on revelation, and revelation is in fact denied."[65]

For Paul, the hope of forgiveness now and of a future bodily resurrection stands or falls--as does all else in his proclamation--with the reality of Christ's resurrection. One of Barth's summary statements must suffice: "Either God is known and recognized as the Lord and Creator and Origin, because He has revealed Himself as such, or there is no revelation in history, no miracle, no special category "Christ."[66] The faith of the Corinthians will prove itself illusory. God, the Creator and Consummator, is not the whence and whither of their confidence. Barth sees their faith as without an object; it is faith turned in upon itself. The Corinthians are therefore in danger of exchanging faith for a religion without revelation. "The Christian faith does not live of itself, but by its relation to the faithfulness of God. If this is withdrawn--and the denial of the resurrection, Christian monism, means that it is withdrawn, that the relation to God becomes the relation to the unending--then the faith falls back upon itself."[67]

Following Paul, Barth sees the Corinthian delusion

issuing in a "double self-deception." That is, they are deceived both about this life and the life to come. In both cases, their faith can never issue in confidence. "The gospel of a risen Christ, so far as it is not fundamentally preached and accepted as God's word for all time, is flatly a rebellion against the truth of God."[68]

3. The Resurrection of Jesus Christ as the Basis of Hope.

> But now is Christ risen from the dead, and become the first fruits of them that slept. For since by man came death, by man came also the resurrection of the dead. For as in Adam all die, even so in Christ shall all be made alive. But every man in his own order: Christ the first fruits; afterwards they that are Christ's. [Full stop after autoû]. At His coming, then cometh the end [in this last period] eîta [is not third member to aparché and épeita, verse 23, but closer definition to en tê parousía; tò télos does not mean "the rest," and not even the "end," but adverbially, like 1 Pet. 3:8, "finally"], when He shall have delivered up the Kingdom to God, even the Father; when He shall have put down all [his own] rule and all authority and power [here dash instead of full stop]--for He must reign, till He hath put all His enemies under His feet--[dash instead of full stop] the last enemy that shall be destroyed is death, for [it is written]: He hath put all things under His feet. But when He [Christ] saith: all things are put under Him! [dash instead of comma]--it is manifest that He is excepted, which did put all things under Him--[dash instead of full stop]--and when all things shall be subdued unto Him, then shall the Son also Himself be subject unto Him that put all things under Him, that God may be all in all. (vv. 20-28; Barth's translation using the KJV)

Barth finds the clue to interpreting Christian faith within the kingdom of Christ in terms of our lives

in relationship to the first and second Adam. The
Corinthians did not comprehend the significance of the
Second Adam, the risen Christ, either for their life in
the present in the face of death or in terms of their
ultimate resurrection. They had fallen prey to a kind
of realized eschatology in which what Christ had effected was "something finished and satisfying in itself."[69] Barth reasons that such a stance makes light of
death as the final enemy yet to be overcome. In this
loss of hope in the resurrection of the dead, they have
compromised the power of Christ raised from the dead
whom they profess. Among the Corinthians, "blind
Nature, or fate, stands between God and men as an indissoluble knot, with which one somehow compounds (reli-
giously, if possible), whereas he [Paul] sees the Lord
striding from struggle to struggle and finally approaching the inconceivable supreme victory."[70] Christians
live in the interim between promise and fulfillment,
between the "already" and the "not yet."

Concerning the stance of believers marked by hope,
Barth writes: "To know the revelation of God in Christ
means to place oneself within its promise, not prolep-
tically in a supposed fulfilment."[71] Barth follows the
exegesis of Zündel and Hofmann in vv. 20-28 holding that
Paul does not provide us with an

> eschatological mythology, but in impetuous
> crowding metaphorical language expresses the
> following clear ideas: Christ as the second
> Adam is the beginning of the resurrection of
> the dead. Perfection is the resurrection also
> of His own, and therefore the very fundamental
> thing that was denied in Corinth. This per-
> fection is, as the abolition of death general-
> ly, His highest and at the same time His last
> act of sovereignty. As yet He is not ful-
> filled (vollzogen), His power is still in
> conflict with the other penultimate powers,

and to that extent we are now standing in His
Kingdom, awaiting that last, but only just
awaiting. When He is fulfilled, then His
Kingdom, as a special Kingdom beside the
Kingdom of God...is at an end. To this end
has the Kingdom in fact been given him, that
God should be all in all. Therefore this "God
all in all," and hence the general resurrection of the dead, is the meaning, misconceived
in Corinth, of the resurrection of Christ, the
meaning of the Christian faith.[72]

The Corinthians' adoption of a Christian monism
confuses the interim reign of Christ with the final
reign of God. "That God is all in all, is not true, but
must become true."[73] True believers hold to a "Christian
dualism" which acknowledges the tension between promise
and fulfillment. They look to Christ who will finally
overcome "every rule and every authority and power" (v.
25), opposing the final reign of God. "Faith, i.e., to
be in the Kingdom of Christ, means to await the resurrection."[74]

Otherwise, what do people mean by being baptized on behalf of the dead? If the dead are
not raised at all, why are people baptized on
their behalf? Why am I in peril every hour?
I protest, brethren, by my pride in you which
I have in Christ Jesus our Lord, I die every
day! What do I gain if, humanly speaking, I
fought with beasts at Ephesus? If the dead
are not raised, "Let us eat and drink, for
tomorrow we die." Do not be deceived: "Bad
company ruins good morals." Come to your
right mind, and sin no more. For some have no
knowledge of God. I say this to your shame.
(vv. 29-34)

Presupposing Paul's critique (vv. 12-34) of the
Corinthian version of Christianity as nonsense because
it does not acknowledge "this meaning of the Kingdom of

Christ, i.e. of the Kingdom of <u>God</u>, i.e. the <u>abolition</u>
of <u>death</u>...,"[75] Barth addresses the difficult and critical issue of baptism on behalf of the dead (v. 29). In
opposition to a dominant tradition which refuses to
allow that Paul countenanced vicarious baptism on behalf
of the dead, Barth finds the latter the most tenable
reading. Vicarious baptism was known both to Jews and
Greeks. Paul acknowledges the primitive practice in
Corinth without injecting a value judgment. Yet because
the Apostle is able to criticize the Corinthians and all
modes of faith and praxis from the "supreme height" of
the reality of the resurrection of Jesus Christ from the
dead, he can speak to this "Greek-Christian border-line
possibility in all its ambiguity. ...."[76]

Barth interprets Paul's statement to the Corinthians regarding vicarious baptism for the dead as
saying in effect:

> ...its meaning is the putting not only of
> those now living, but of those already dead in
> connexion, in communion with Jesus Christ. In
> doing so you affirm the resurrection of the
> dead, you pass over fundamentally the boundary
> of human possibilities, which is drawn once
> and for all by death; you acknowledge Jesus
> Christ as the Lord of Life and Death.[77]

Paul's call to the Corinthians to "come to your
right mind" (v.34) and to leave their "intoxicated or
comatose state" is radicalized in his word: "For some
have no knowledge of God" (v. 34). Their sin, according
to Barth, is that they are "captivated by the dream of
an inner-worldly Christianity, without the hope which is
also the <u>goal</u>, without the end which is also the <u>begin-
ning</u>, you are still tarrying in your sins."[78]

C.   "The Resurrection as Truth" (vv. 35-49)

> But some one will ask, "How are the dead
> raised? With what kind of body do they come?"
> You foolish man! What you sow does not come
> to life unless it dies. And what you sow is
> not the body which is to be, but a bare ker-
> nel, perhaps of wheat or of some other grain.
> But God gives it a body as he has chosen, and
> to each kind of seed its own body. For not
> all flesh is alike, but there is one kind for
> men, another for animals, another for birds,
> and another for fish. There are celestial
> bodies and there are terrestrial bodies; but
> the glory of the celestial is one, and the
> glory of the terrestrial is another. There is
> one glory of the sun, and another glory of the
> moon, and another glory of the stars; for star
> differs from star in glory. So it is with the
> resurrection of the dead. What is sown is
> perishable, what is raised is imperishable.
> It is sown in dishonor, it is raised in glory.
> It is sown in weakness, it is raised in power.
> It is sown a physical body, it is raised a
> spiritual body. (vv. 35-44a)

1.   "How are the Dead Raised?" Barth follows an
exegetical tradition which maintains that what is said
in 1 Cor. 15 and similar biblical passages should be
understood "in a 'real' and not in an 'ideal' sense."[79]
That Paul's opponents denied the resurrection of the
dead is the expression of their addiction to an "antago-
nistic Christian-unchristian philosophy."[80] Their query
concerning how the dead are raised (v. 35) purportedly
has to do with "the limitations of human knowledge."
The standpoint from which Paul answers gives rise to
Barth's title for this section, "The Resurrection as
Truth" (vs. 35-49). He notes in passing that an alter-
nate title might have been, "The Conceivability of
Resurrection." But such a title is not really descrip-
tive of Paul's intention and argument. Hence he provides neither philosophical speculation about the idea

of resurrection nor an apologetic defense thereof before the world. It is truly "an attack, not indeed, upon the world, but, for the sake of the world's salvation, upon Christianity, [from the vantage point of revelation]."[81] Thus, Paul shows through preaching "how we ought to think from the standpoint of Christ, of revealed truth."[82] Already presupposed in Paul's argument (vv. 35-49) is the "intimation: The resurrection as reality, the conclusion of the chapter, verses 50-58."[83] In contrast to the exegetical tradition which views the resurrection of the dead in terms of the "internal processes" of nature, Barth sees us introduced rather to "the origin of 'nature,' its creation and redemption, and the reality here becoming, or rather, not becoming, visible is the reality of which Paul, with the whole Bible, also speaks."[84]

The question as to how the dead are raised has to do with the enigma of how there can be life beyond death. How can one speak of an unknown existence beyond death which is somehow identical with human life prior to death? "What kind of life is that of which, by its definition, we can have no conception?"[85] In verses 36-41 the Apostle introduces a "general answer" pointing to analogies to the resurrection in the realm of nature. These images or metaphors of the resurrection speak (1) of something in nature perishing, seemingly dying, and growing once again and (2) of "the variety of appearances of the same thing in the order of time."[86] Following Calvin, Barth speaks of these analogies as a kind of "prelude to the resurrection."[87]

2. Bodily Resurrection. "So also," writes Paul, "is the resurrection of the dead" (v. 42). Several dimensions of Barth's interpretation of Paul deserve notice. First, in turning to the resurrection of the

dead, there is a "transition to something of a totally
different species, the step from the figure to the
reality. No proof is adduced, only room is created in
thought."[88] Second, man is the subject for whom the
change or synthesis from death to life must be effected.
Third, when Paul speaks of human weakness and corrupti-
bility, he sees this focused in human life terminating
in death. Fourth, the resurrection for Paul is bodily
resurrection. Barth writes:

> The corruptibility, dishonour, and weakness of
> man is, in fact, that of his corporeality.
> Death is the death of his body. If death be
> not only the end--but the turning point, then
> the new life must consist in the repredication
> of his corporeality. To be sown and to rise
> again must then apply to the body. The body
> is man, body in relation to a non-bodily,
> determined, indeed, by this non-bodily, but
> body. The change in the relationship of the
> body to this non-bodily is just the resurrec-
> tion.[89]

Paul's words are: "It is sown a physical body, it
is raised a spiritual body" (v. 44a). This transition
cannot be "merely non-bodily existence. Of such Paul
knows nothing whatever. The persisting subject is
rather just the body. It is "natural" body this side,
"spiritual" body beyond the resurrection. ...This
re-predication is the "resurrection of the dead." And
this antithesis brings us to the logical high-water-mark
of the chapter."[90]

> If there is a physical body, there is also a
> spiritual body. Thus it is written, "The
> first man Adam became a living being"; the
> last Adam became a life-giving spirit. But it
> is not the spiritual which is first but the
> physical, and then the spiritual. The first
> man was from the earth, a man of dust; the

> second man is from heaven. As was the man of
> dust, so are those who are of the dust; and as
> is the man of heaven, so are those who are of
> heaven. Just as we have borne the image of
> the man of dust, we shall also bear the image
> of the man of heaven. (vv. 44b-49)

Barth disallows interpreting the transition of
which Paul speaks here to be conceived in terms of the
relationship which God maintains between us as spiritual
beings and himself as Spirit. Nor again, can the hope
of the resurrection have to do with the "pious" recognition that God is indeed the Lord over all. To be sure,
Barth contends that for Paul the words, "resurrection of
the dead" are "nothing else than a paraphrase of the
word 'God.'"[91] But final trust that God is indeed "the
Lord" means that one is bound to God in one's bodily
existence before death and after death.

> The Spirit, not our pinch of spirit and spiri-
> tuality, but God's Spirit triumphs not just in
> a pure spirituality (Geistsein), but: it is
> raised a (God-) spiritual body, the end of
> God's way is corporeality.[92]

In the fifth place, several further dimensions of
Barth's conception of bodily resurrection must be noted.
He will not allow vv. 35-44a to be "interpreted as an
attempted biological demonstration of the reality of the
resurrection." The "God-spiritual body" of v. 44a
"might much rather be called a thanatological magnitude."[93] Unlike the transformations of certain bodies
alluded to earlier by Paul, the spiritual body is not
given and perceptible. To be sure, Paul's argumentation
sees the former as standing in the relationship of the
relative to the Absolute--something which the Corinthian
doubters--apart from being foolish, might have observed

(v. 36). Yet neither empirically nor by way of "theoretical knowledge" does Paul allow access to the truth of the resurrection of the dead. "The words 'it is raised a spiritual body'...constitute the absolute miracle."[94] This "offensive combination" of spiritual and body flies in the face of those who might wish to maintain some view of the immortality of the soul. Paul has no conception of such. It is not the case that the spiritual body can be inferred from the natural body. Barth observes:

> That I am God's, in the concrete sense described, is plainly something New, which is added to this fact. Paul's purpose here is not proof, but description of the truth of resurrection. Exactly as I am, shall I and will I be God's. ... That which persists is not the soul (the latter is the predicate, which must give place to something else), but the body, and even that, not as an immortal body, but in the transition from life in death to life. It is not that, however, which Paul wants to indicate here, but the positive aspect. Exactly in the place of that which makes me a man, the human soul, is set that which makes God, God, the Spirit of God, that is the complete sovereignty of God, that is the Resurrection of the Dead. But exactly in this place! To wish to be God's without the body is rebellion against God's will, is secret denial of God; it is, indeed, the body which suffers, sins, dies. We are waiting for our Body's redemption; if the body is not redeemed to obedience, to health, to life, than there is no God; then what may be called God does not deserve this name. The truth of God requires and establishes the Resurrection of the Dead, the Resurrection of the Body. But the fact that it does so is not to be deduced from something else. Paul knows this already.[95]

Finally, Barth finds it suggestive that Paul regards human nature in terms of the first Adam, the
earthly and earthy man whose image we bear, and the last
Adam, "the man of heaven," whose image "we shall also
bear." (vv. 45ff.) The link providing an "indirect"
identity between the two Adams Barth locates in human
corporeality. The divine intention for humanity has to
do with the transition from our present life in relationship to the first Adam to that in relationship to
the Second Adam still future. But the "change in predi-
cation" which is our resurrection from the dead, the
"reversal from the God-created to the God-created Adam
[is] the change which is to be effected nowhere else
than by and in the palpably visible bodily life of
man."[96] That this continuity ultimately will obtain
between what we now bear in the image of the first Adam
and what we shall bear in the image of the second Adam
is not to be confused with a present possession. That
"we shall also bear the image of the man of heaven" (v.
49) means that the reality of our spiritual body is a
future reality for which we hope. "But between past and
future lies the resurrection."[97] The pneumatics at
Corinth are not already in possession of their spiritual
bodies. They and we await "that which is only given
from God, the absolute miracle."[98]

D.   "The Resurrection as Reality" (vv. 50-58)

I tell you this brethren: flesh and blood
cannot inherit the kingdom of God, nor does
the perishable inherit the imperishable. Lo!
I tell you a mystery. We shall not all sleep,
but we shall all be changed, in a moment, in
the twinkling of an eye, at the last trumpet.
For the trumpet will sound, and the dead will
be raised imperishable, and we shall be
changed. For this perishable nature must put

on the imperishable, and this mortal nature
must put on immortality. When the perishable
puts on the imperishable, and the mortal puts
on immortality, then shall come to pass the
saying that is written: 'Death is swallowed
up in victory.' 'O death, where is thy victory?' 'O death where is thy sting?' The
sting of death is sin, and the power of sin is
the law. But thanks be to God, who gives us
the victory through our Lord Jesus Christ.
Therefore, my beloved brethren, be steadfast,
immovable, always abounding in the work of the
Lord, knowing that in the Lord your labor is
not in vain. (vv. 50-58)

Barth chooses to entitle this final section "The
Resurrection as Reality" inasmuch as Paul "simply proceeds from the resurrection as reality, and testifies to
it for what it is. Why is? Yes, why? Could Paul
himself make any different answer than: because God is
and because He has revealed Himself?"[99] The identity
between the physical or natural body and the spiritual
body only can be from above, from God. It is neither
effected through the power of the natural process, nor
by virtue of an immortal soul or spirit within man, nor
yet again by reason of any human powers. Moreover,
though Paul saw "in death the door to the true life...,"
dying, in itself, is not yet the resurrected life. The
"mystery which Paul here [verse 51] discloses is...the
synchronism of the living and the dead in the resurrection."[100] That is to say, whether dead or living, we
shall be changed. The resurrection, the crisis which
concerns all peoples in all ages, means, as surely as it
is God's decisive word to mankind: "In Him they all
live. ...That He calls is what decides the reality of
the resurrection, not that we live, and not that we
die."[101]

For Barth, the resurrection of the dead is the

eschatological verification that God is <u>God</u>! Otherwise dualism, or the endless cycle between life and death, in which sin and death finally reign supreme would be the last word. What is more, apart from the resurrection of the dead, "...Christianity is not truth, and the word of promise could not be taken seriously."[102] "When the perishable puts on the imperishable, and the mortal puts on immortality, then shall come to pass the saying that is written: 'Death is swallowed up in victory'" (v. 54). However, the "then" of the resurrection of the dead is still future. Prior to the revelation of that "mystery" when "we shall all be changed," we live within the tensions of this life "with the yet greater tension of <u>faith</u>."[103] Therefore, we do not live as those without hope. Barth writes:

> As <u>God's</u> <u>gift</u>, the victory, the "reality of the resurrection," is <u>present</u>; is [a] valid word spoken to us, not to be forgotten, not to be dragged down into the dialectic of <u>our</u> existence, not to be restricted, not to be weakened, not to be doubted. But just for this reason everything depends upon this "victory" being and remaining God's gift "through our Lord Jesus Christ" present in hope.[104]

Barth commends Calvin's assertion that "if the hope of the resurrection be removed, the whole edifice of piety would collapse, just as if the foundation were withdrawn from it. ..."[105] Yet it is precisely the theology of the Apostle Paul "with its word of the resurrection in the centre" that attests it is possible to live in faith and hope--"steadfast, unmovable, always abounding in the work of the Lord" (v. 58).[106]

If we emulate the Apostle, that "centre is not a matter about which we should always be talking--Paul himself did not do so--but we should always be <u>thinking</u> of it."[107]   In that vein, Barth concludes: "...the reality of the <u>resurrection</u>, ...the truth of Christianity is exclusively <u>God's</u> truth, its absoluteness is exclusively <u>God's</u> absoluteness.   What remains to <u>us</u>, what falls to us? (verse 57).   'Thanks be to God.'"[108]

IV.   BULTMANN'S REVIEW OF BARTH'S THE RESURRECTION OF THE DEAD: THE SECOND ENCOUNTER (1926)

Bultmann's review of Barth's The Resurrection of the Dead appeared in 1926.   James Smart is no doubt correct in maintaining that Barth and Bultmann stood closer in their theological perspectives during this period than at any other time.   Indeed, he contends that Bultmann's review discloses "not just an approximation of Bultmann's views to Barth's but an inclination of Barth at least in some measure to follow Bultmann in the reduction of theology to anthropology."[109] Though the latter is overstated, there is certainly considerable agreement in their interpretations of 1 Corinthians.

A.   Some Agreements and Questions on First Corinthians

Let us look at some of these points of agreement. Though not uncritical of the dangers inherent in Barth's theological as opposed to a strictly historical-critical mode of interpretation, Bultmann contends that both have their rightful place and "belong together in a unity." More significant to Bultmann is Barth's identification of the resurrection of the dead as the theme of Paul's letter thereby enabling Barth to use it as a norm for criticizing some of Paul's concepts. Expressed somewhat

differently, by regarding Paul's eschatological proclamation informed by his belief in the resurrection of the
dead as the clue to understanding 1 Corinthians, Barth
derives from Paul himself what appears to be the hermeneutical key to interpreting the totality of human
life in this world and also his hope of the resurrection
of the dead. Thus, Barth can interpret Paul's phrase,
"resurrection of the dead," as another way to speak of
"God." That the resurrection renders everything human
relative is an example of Barth's "material criticism"
which Bultmann applauds. Barth also rightly exercises
"material criticism" of Paul in minimizing the significance of his depiction of the parousia of Christ. Yet
Bultmann finds that Barth did not go far enough in this
direction. Thus he tends to speak only of Paul's figurative mythological language without a thorough going
criticism of Paul and therewith a re-interpretation.[110]

B. Some Disagreements and Questions on First
Corinthians

As we have seen Bultmann supports Barth's view that
the inner unity of 1 Corinthians is to be found in
Paul's teaching on the resurrection of the dead in
chapter 15. However, Bultmann prefers to say that the
Apostle's eschatological proclamation provides the
underlying unity to the epistle even within the consideration of the rather disparate topics of chapters
1-14. A major disagreement relates to Barth's thesis
that the epistle's climax is in chapter 15. Bultmann
counters in arguing: (1) Even Barth's "interpretation
of chs. 12-14 is the climax of his book."[111] (2) This
corresponds, in Bultmann's view, "to the fact that chs.
12-14 constitute the climax of the letter if the unity

of its contents is accepted. If the theme of 1 Corinthians is the 'last things'--not as an object of speculation but as a reality in the life of Christians--then
the climax of the letter is actually ch. 13. ..."[112] The
point of the argument in chs. 12-14--which Barth interprets rightly--is that even the highest human and
spiritual gifts are fragmentary and will "pass away."
(3) Bultmann concurs with Barth that agape-love is
divine both in origin and consummation. Then he adds:
"In that community the indescribable eschatological
event becomes real, so far as love is really present in
it. ...the preaching of 'love' is preaching the resurrection of the dead."[113]

C. Agreements and Disagreements on First
Corinthians XV

What are Bultmann's specific criticisms of Barth's
interpretation of 1 Corinthians 15, the resurrection
chapter? He agrees with Barth's view that the "Last
things" interpreted as the "end of history" are to be
distinguished from the "Last things" which transcend
everything temporal and historical as the final activity
of God. While Barth criticizes "Christian eschatolo-
gists" who take Paul's mythological elements and trans-
pose them into a picture of a this-worldly end of history which is not the eschaton of which Paul speaks, he
does not--according to Bultmann--apply this criticism to
Paul himself. The Apostle must also be criticized for
speaking about the "end of history" with the aid of
"material from Jewish or Jewish-gnostic apocalyptic.
..."[114] Bultmann thus contends that Barth needs to be
more thorough in criticizing Paul's imaging of the "Last
things" on the basis of the Apostle's depiction of the

"Last things," that is, in terms of the Apostle's picture of God as the origin and goal of all that is. Barth
should make a clean break in his re-interpretation of
the mythological imagery in chapter 15 by seeing it, as
he himself said, as the 'attempt to say the impossible.'
Therefore, Bultmann applauds Barth's stress upon the
existential import of the real end of history when he
says: "Of the real end of history it is possible at
every time to say: the end is near!"[115] In short,
Bultmann agrees with Barth that Paul's speech about the
resurrection of the dead has reference to human existence, but access to the resurrection is not had via
speculation, mysticism or anything human.

Bultmann concurs with Barth that for Paul the
resurrection of the dead meant bodily resurrection. Yet
Bultmann emphasizes that the resurrection of Christ
already makes our resurrection in the present a reality
(15:20-22). Clearly, the future resurrection is not
conceived in terms of the immortality of the soul or in
terms of some kind of continuity based on monistic
thinking. Yet Bultmann finds that Barth's failure to
clarify what Paul "understands by 'body' (sōma)" makes
"his exegesis pay the penalty."[116] Bultmann can further
agree that Barth's interpretation of faith (1 Cor.
15:12-19) is correct. "The miracle of Christ's rising
from the dead means for Paul the establishing of the
unique category, Christ."[117] Within this context, Bultmann regards it to be untenable for Barth to maintain
that Paul does not intend vv. 3-11 as an historical
proof of the resurrection of Jesus Christ from the dead.
Bultmann continues: "I can understand the text only as
an attempt to make the resurrection of Christ credible
as an objective historical fact."[118] But Bultmann sees
Paul's apologetic leading him to contradict what he

affirms about death and resurrection in vv. 20-22 which
"cannot be said of an objective historical fact."[119]

Bultmann finds that while Barth rightly sees the
parousia of Christ as essentially one with his resurrection (vv. 20-22), for Paul the parousia is a second
event following after the resurrection and both are
"objective, 'historical' events."[120] A greater difficulty
for Bultmann is Barth's tendency to diminish the significance of death and therewith the miracle of the resurrection of the body by making it appear that Paul
teaches that man really is not transformed in the resurrection: "...he merely acquires a different kind of
material." Or again, Bultmann can say that Barth tends
to substitute the concept of 'body' (sōma) with the
Greek concept of 'form' (eîdos) "gained from the obser-
vation of nature."[121] That is not to say that Barth is
wrong to interpret the resurrection body as a "spiritual
body." But Bultmann contends that this cannot be found
in 1 Cor. 15:44, but is borrowed by Barth "from the
first half of the chapter and partly from statements of
Paul such as Rom. 6."[122]

Both with regard to the concept of "body" (sōma)
and at other points in Barth's exegesis, Bultmann calls
for "much more rigorous exegetical work and of closer
analysis of the text if assured results are to be attained."[123] Hence though Bultmann admires the genius of
many of Barth's paraphrases, he finds that Barth
re-interprets or explains away some of Paul's ideas as
noted above.[124] A final example is found in Barth's
exegesis of vv. 45-58. He is guilty of excluding "the
expectation of 'catastrophic developments' from Paul's
eschatology."[125] Hence Bultmann charges that Barth "has
set the eternal future (futurum aeternum) in place of
the future expected by Paul as in impending cosmic

event. ..."[126] Bultmann contends that had Barth drawn on
other Pauline letters to aid his interpretations, it
would require an equal stress that "to be with Christ"
is to be a "new creation"; and to be the "first fruits"
has to do more with our historical existence as resurrected now in relationship to Christ than with some
relationship to Christ as "the cosmic ground of a future
condition of existence."[127]

Bultmann proposes interpreting the "resurrection
life" and the epistle's leitmotif as follows:

> But this resurrection life is never something
> objective. It is between time and eternity.
> In the judgment of God we are the justified,
> and the 'final possibility' that this may
> become a reality in our temporal life is
> 'love'. Since in the First Letter to the
> Corinthians the dominant theme is not
> justification by faith but the temporal life
> of the believer within time, ch. 13 is the
> true climax of the letter.[128]

PART II

TOWARD A DOCTRINE OF RECONCILIATION:
THE BARTH-BULTMANN DEBATE (1941-1952)

Chapter IV

THE CROSS AND RESURRECTION:
THE BARTH-BULTMANN DEBATE (1941-1948)

INTRODUCTION

An intensification of the Barth-Bultmann debate was occasioned by Bultmann's 1941 lecture and its subsequent publication entitled "New Testament and Mythology." It was only after the end of World War II, however, that the literary debate surrounding Bultmann's proposals grew more intense. In 1948, H. W. Bartsch introduced Bultmann's republished essay and the reply of five critics to German readers with the title, Kerygma Und Mythos, noting that "no single work which has appeared in the field of New Testament scholarship during the war years has evoked such a lively discussion as Bultmann's original manifesto, New Testament and Mythology."[1] In 1953, the German New Testament scholar, Günther Bornkamm, prefaced his essay in another collection dealing with the continuing debate for and against Bultmann as follows:

> It has been a long time since a theological publication has precipitated such a storm in theology and church and far beyond their borders, and along with it such a passionate literary and vocal discussion, as has Bultmann's essay. And it appears that this storm intends to continue to shake us in the forseeable future causing us to grasp for air.[2]

An interpreter and former Bultmann pupil notes that he intended his proposal as a catalyst within the Confessing Church concerning what constituted the proper form of preaching. Schmithals comments that in a sense the increasingly sharp reactions to Bultmann's proposals were unanticipated.

> The surprising thing is that it was only this particular article which involved Bultmann in a crossfire of conflicting views. For the article does not propose any new programme, but merely sums up in a systematic way what Bultmann had been teaching and publishing for twenty years. All his work had been 'demythologizing', even when this term did not occur.[3]

What does Bultmann propose?

I.   BULTMANN'S OFFENSIVE: DEMYTHOLOGIZING THE NEW TESTAMENT (1941)

The problem which Bultmann addresses in his program of demythologizing the New Testament message is as follows. The New Testament presupposes a mythological view of the world and portrays the event of redemption in mythical terms. According to the New Testament's Ptolemaic cosmology, the world was composed of three stories, heaven, earth and hell. The earth was the scene of the conflict between the supernatural power of God and Satan's demonic forces holding humanity captive. The latter's liberation is through the supernatural coming of a new aeon marked by the advent, life, death and resurrection of Jesus Christ which atones for human sin and abolishes death's power. An imminent cosmic catastrophe will soon occur marked by the return of the risen Christ as Judge. At that time, the dead will be raised and the final judgment will take place. Believers will receive their reward and "Sin, suffering and death will then be finally abolished."[4]

Bultmann traces this New Testament mythological world view to Jewish apocalyptic mythology and Gnostic redemption myths. He emphasizes, however, that though the New Testament kerygma is expressed in terms of this mythological world view, it is not to be confused with the latter; it is merely the shell which encloses it. The interpreter's hermeneutical task is to extract the kerygma from its antiquated mythological conceptuality.

According to Bultmann, several reasons warrant the present need for the demythologization of the New Testament's mythical world view. First, it represents a prescientific cosmology and mythology no longer tenable for people today living with a changed world view informed by modern science and cosmology. Second, modern persons do not see the self as subject to interference from, or control by, supernatural powers which suspend the orderly course of nature in bringing about human salvation.[5] To demand acquiescence to such outdated notions as prerequisites to faith or the acceptance of the New Testament message today must be viewed as irrational and meaningless. Furthermore, such a requirement places a false stumbling block which has nothing to do with the essential Christian message in the path of the potential believer.

To engage in demythologizing the New Testament and post biblical ecclesiastical creedal statements based on it does not eliminate its essential message, but enhances it. He says: "If the truth of the New Testament proclamation is to be preserved, the only way is to demythologize it."[6] This approach is justifiable on two grounds. First, the nature of myth itself calls for such an existential interpretation as consonant with its intended meaning. Bultmann states: "The real purpose of myth is not to present an objective picture of the world as it is, but to express man's understanding of himself in the world in which he lives. Myth should be interpreted not cosmologically, but anthropologically, or better still, existentially."[7] If the New Testament's mythological language is left in tact, one overlooks that references to the transcendent world are illegitimately identified with processes in this world. Yet precisely this uncritical indentification of the transcendent world with occurrences within this world demands interpretation. "Hence," Bultmann writes, "the importance of the New Testament mythology lies not in its imagery but in the understanding of existence which it enshrines. The real question is whether this understanding of existence is true."[8] Second, the New Testament mythological language invites a critical interpretation or translation of its meaning because of its inherent inconsistencies and contradictions. For example, persons are seen, on the one hand, as determined by cosmic or transcendent forces, and on the other, as determining their destinies through their own decisions. Furthermore, contradictory mythological images abound such as affirmations of the pre-existence of Christ as the Son of God alongside of depictions of his virgin birth.[9] For these reasons, an existential interpretation of the mythological language of the New Testament is indicated and salutary.

A. Existential Interpretation

Bultmann's aim is to discover the view of human existence contained in New Testament mythological

language, which, when interpreted existentially, confronts modern persons with the possibility for human
fulfillment. He finds that the New Testament speaks of
human existence on two different levels. First, following Paul, Bultmann contends that man is depicted as
unredeemed or in a state of inauthentic existence. This
is the Pauline "sphere of the flesh." In this state,
humans sin by making perverse choices in their attempt
to find security in the world. This results in human
existence being characterized by care and anxiety and
issues in subjection to the powers of sin and death.[10]
Second, opposed to this inauthentic life marked by sin,
Bultmann finds the New Testament's mythological language
pointing to a redeemed existence or authentic life.
This is the life of faith. "Such a life means the
abandonment of all self-contrived security. This is
what the New Testament means by 'life after the Spirit'
or 'life in faith.'"[11] This mode of existence involves
reliance upon God's grace who grants forgiveness of sin
and freedom from all attempts at self- salvation. In
this "eschatological existence" the believer is "no
longer in bondage to anything in the world," but lives
rather through continuing decisions in faith and hope
directed toward God and in love of neighbor.

Bultmann concedes that Martin Heidegger's philosophical existentialism provides a picture both of
authentic and inauthentic existence which formally has
many similarities to his own Christian vision set forth
above. But whereas philosophical existentialism holds
that human beings can realize authentic existence by
means of inherent human capacities, Christian faith
denies this possibility due to humanity's radical fallenness. Bultmann underlines this difference: "Faith in
the sense of obedient self-commitment and inward

detachment from the world is only possible when it is faith in Jesus Christ."[12] The divergence between these two views of authentic existence comes into focus in the following statement: "Here then is the crucial distinction between the New Testament and existentialism, between the Christian faith and the natural understanding of Being. The New Testament speaks and faith knows of an act of God through which man becomes capable of self-commitment, capable of faith and love, of his authentic life."[13]

We ask: what is the aim of Bultmann's existential interpretation of the New Testament witness to Jesus Christ and therewith of his theological method? He answers that his hermeneutic seeks to determine the saving significance of the Christ event attested in the kerygma for human existence. Bultmann believes that the kerygma's testimony to Jesus Christ as the eschatological event provides the possibility of a new self-understanding. Admittedly, the New Testament uses mythological language to express the saving significance of Jesus of Nazareth, a "concrete figure of history." But for Bultmann, such affirmations are different from mythological language concerning Christ's pre-existence, virgin birth, or from reports of Jesus' purported miracles--all of which--as well as the facts which can be established about his life--are not, in and of themselves, crucial for faith. Mythological language has meaning only as testimony to the "historical figure of Jesus and the events of his life" as he is a "figure and event of salvation. If that be so, we can dispense with the objective form in which they are cast."[14] Or put differently: "We can see meaning in them only when we ask what God is trying to say to each one of us through them."[15]

B.   The Saving Event of the Cross

At issue here is the manner in which Jesus' crucifixion may be said to have saving significance. Bultmann finds that the kerygma locates the center of God's
saving activity in the cross and resurrection--not in
the proclamation of the historical Jesus as held by many
19th century liberal theologians. He also contends that
the New Testament interprets Jesus' crucifixion mythologically by means of a "mixture of sacrificial and juridical analogies...which have ceased to be tenable for us
to-day."[16] In addition, the language of atonement is
limited in pointing only to the forgiveness of sin and
the remission of guilt; other more comprehensive images
attest the cosmic significance of the cross as the
"judgement of the world and the defeat of the rulers of
this world (I Cor. 2:6ff.), [and thus] the cross becomes
the judgement of ourselves as fallen creatures enslaved
to the powers of the 'world.'"[17]

Bultmann, however, rejects conceiving of faith in
the cross as the acceptance of some objective happening
long past. Quite the opposite is the case: "To believe
in the cross of Christ does not mean to concern ourselves with a mythical process wrought outside of us and
our world, with an objective event turned by God to our
advantage, but rather to make the cross of Christ our
own, to undergo crucifixion with him."[18] Or again:
"...the cross is not just an event of the past which can
be contemplated, but is the eschatological event in and
beyond time, in so far as it (understood in its significance, that is, for faith) is an ever- present
reality."[19] Hence the existential relevance of the cross
is actualized when it is proclaimed as "the event of
redemption" which "challenges all who hear it to appro-

priate this significance for themselves, to be willing to be crucified with Christ."[20]

   C.   The Resurrection as the Expression of the
        Saving Significance of the Cross

What   importance   can   the   resurrection have--seemingly "a mythical event pure and simple?"[21] According to Bultmann, cross and resurrection constitute a unity. All who are not contemporaries of the cross of Jesus as an historical event are dependent on the New Testament witness to his resurrection which attempts, in mythological symbols, to convey the saving significance of the cross. Given our modern world view, Bultmann finds it impossible to regard the resurrection of Jesus as an "historical fact," or a "miraculous proof," or as the "resuscitation of a dead person."[22] He takes the New Testament statements about the resurrection of Jesus as intending to teach that Jesus' death on the cross is not only a human death, but also the redemptive eschato-logical act of God which conquers the power of death and provides the possibility of each person's new self-understanding. In summation, Bultmann asserts:

> In this way the resurrection is not a mytholo-gical event adduced in order to prove the saving efficacy of the cross, but an article of faith just as much as the meaning of the cross itself. Indeed, faith in the resurrec-tion is really the same thing as faith in the saving efficacy of the cross, faith in the cross as the cross of Christ.[23]

The first Easter event was not, therefore, some objective, historical occurrence which had to do with the raising of the crucified Jesus from the dead.

Rather, "If the event of Easter Day is in any sense an historical event additional to the event of the cross, it is nothing else than the rise of faith in the risen Lord, since it was this faith which led to the apostolic preaching."[24]

How then does one come to have faith or believe in the saving efficacy of the cross? This becomes possible through the continuation of the apostolic preaching originating on the first Easter which proclaims that the "death of Christ...is both the judgement and the salvation of the world... .Through the word of preaching the cross and the resurrection are made present. ..."[25] It always has happened and always will happen in this way. "Christ meets us in the preaching as one crucified and risen. He meets us in the word of preaching and nowhere else. The faith of Easter is just this--faith in the word of preaching."[26]

II. BARTH'S COUNTER OFFENSIVE: ASSESSING BULTMANN (1948)

The first of Barth's concerted responses to Bultmann's demythologizing agenda appeared in his doctrine of Creation (CD 3:2) dealing with anthropology and published in 1948. In a section entitled "Man in His Time," Barth begins with an analysis of "Jesus, Lord of Time." Like all other men, Jesus--though existing in a special unity with God throughout his life--has a limited life span. But unlike all other men, Barth interprets "the history of the forty days between His resurrection and ascension" as his "second history."[27] In light of Jesus' resurrection from the dead, Barth speaks of "Jesus, Lord of Time." Within this context, he sets forth both something of his own position on the resurrection and engages Bultmann.

A.   Defining Bultmann's Dogmatic Presuppositions

At the outset of his critique, Barth commends
Bultmann: "...we must at least give him credit for
emphasising the central and indispensable function of
the event of Easter for all that is thought and said in
the New Testament."[28]   Yet he laments that Bultmann's
entire New Testament exegesis and interpretation is
"always controlled by a set of dogmatic presuppositions
and is thus wholly dependent upon their validity."[29]   He
enumerates them in a series of questions which may be
identified with the following issues.

1.   The Resurrection and Existential Interpretation.   "Is it true that a theological statement is valid
only when it can be proved to be a genuine element in
the Christian understanding of human existence?"[30]

2.   The Resurrection and Historical Research.   "Is
it true that an event alleged to have happened in time
can be accepted as historical only if it can be proved
to be a "'historical' fact" in Bultmann's sense?--i.e.,
when it is open to verification by the methods, and
above all the tacit assumption, of modern historical
scholarship?"[31]

3.   The Resurrection and Faith.   "Is it true that
the assertion of an event which by its very nature is
inaccessible to "historical" verification, of what we
may agree to call the history of saga or legend, is
merely a blind acceptance of a piece of mythology, an
arbitrary act, a descent from faith to works, a dis-
honest sacrificium intellectus [sacrifice of the intel-
lect]?"[32]

4.   The Resurrection and the Modern World View:
"Is it true that modern thought...'shaped for good or
ill by modern science'. ...is so binding as to determine
in advance and unconditionally our acceptance or rejection of the biblical message?"[33]

5.   The Resurrection and the Mythical World View.
"Is it true that we are compelled to reject a statement
simply because this statement, or something like it, was
compatible with the mythical world-view of the past?"[34]

With these questions before us, we turn to Barth's
response to the major issues raised.

B.   Assessing Bultmann's Dogmatic Presuppositions

1.   The Resurrection and Historical Research. The
second of the above hermeneutical presuppositions is
most decisive for Bultmann and likewise for Barth since
it concerns the former's view of reality. For Bultmann
it is axiomatic that one can speak of an event as historical only when its occurrence can be established by
means of the methodology of modern historical scholarship. It follows of necessity that he cannot allow the
resurrection as an historical event since it cannot be
established by such means. One must therefore speak of
it as a mythical event whose significance is appropri-
able only when it is seen as the expression of a
Christian's new self-understanding.

Barth concurs that the occurrence of the resurrection cannot be verified by means of the method of modern
historical science. He disagrees, however, with the
further conclusion that this rules out the possibility
of the resurrection's occurrence or that all events
occurring in space and time must be amenable to ordinary
historical verification.

> It is sheer superstition [Barth writes] to
> suppose that only things which are open to
> "historical" verification can have happened in
> time. There may have been events which hap-
> pened far more really in time than the kind of
> things Bultmann's scientific historian can
> prove. There are good grounds for supposing
> · that the history of the resurrection of Jesus
> is a pre-eminent instance of such an event.[35]

For Barth, therefore, "...in spite of Bultmann, we must
still accept the resurrection of Jesus, and His subsequent appearances to His disciples, as genuine history
[Geschichte] in its own particular time."[36]

In distinction from the cross, the raising of Jesus
from the dead is a new eschatological act of God. Since
it is not open to historical verification, it may be
attested appropriately in the language of saga and
legend. That is not to say that no events within space
and time occurred when the risen Lord encountered certain people: yet this Easter time as the time of revelation is history of a special kind--akin to the history
of creation--but it does have "a tiny 'historical'
margin."[37] The latter margin can be subjected to historical research.

Distinguishing the Ground of Faith and the Object
of Faith. Perhaps Barth's major criticism of Bultmann is
the following:

> R. Bultmann "demythologizes" the event of
> Easter by interpreting it as "the rise of
> faith in the risen Lord, since it was this
> faith which led to the apostolic preaching."
> ...This will not do. Faith in the risen Lord
> springs from His historical manifestation, and
> from this as such, not from the rise of faith
> in Him.[38]

Barth notes that Bultmann "can also speak of 'the self-manifestation of the risen Lord,'" but this statement remains ambiguous since he regards it as equatable with the disciples' acknowledgment of the saving significance of the cross. Barth writes pointedly with respect to Bultmann's subjectivization of the appearances of the risen Lord:

> The "self-declaration" of the "Resurrected" is staged in the minds of the disciples and nowhere else. Nothing happened between Him and them. There was no new, and in its novelty decisive and fundamental, encounter between Him and them to give rise to their faith. They alone were engaged in this history. He was not. They were quite alone.[39]

Here Barth puts his finger on a weak point in Bultmann's interpretation of the resurrection, namely, "the distinction between the Risen One as the ground of faith on the one hand and the origin of Easter faith in the disciples on the other."[40] To be sure, Bultmann speaks of the witness to the risen Jesus as unveiling "the meaning of the cross," and regards the latter as "'the act of God' on which the faith and preaching of the Church are founded."[41] Yet Barth objects to Bultmann's equivocal language: the "act of God" refers solely to the faith and insight granted the disciples into the meaning of the cross. Barth presses his critique of Bultmann's view:

> Their faith had no object distinct from itself, no antecedent basis on which to rest as faith. It stood majestically on its own feet. The "act of God" was identical with their faith. And the fact that it took place, that they believed, is the real content of the Easter history and the Easter time, the real burden of the Christian message. ...Jesus

Himself had not risen. In its simple and
unqualified sense, this statement is quite
untenable.[42]

On the basis of such arguments, Barth accuses
Bultmann of identifying the rise of Easter faith and the
Easter kerygma with the resurrection of Jesus. In this
way, the reality of the resurrection is shifted from its
reference to the crucified Jesus to an event which
happened to, and within, the disciples. Thus the distinction between the risen Lord and the disciple's faith
evaporates. The difference between the risen Lord as
the ground of faith and the faith of the disciples as
its consequence is surrendered as the two merge into one
another. The alternative direction is for Barth, in
fact, the right path to follow: "Jesus Himself did rise
again and appear to His disciples. This is the content
of the Easter history, the Easter time, the Christian
faith and Christian proclamation, both then and at all
times."[43]

We may get the difference between Barth and
Bultmann in focus by recalling the disputed issues
between them outlined above and expanding Barth's
critique.

Barth and Bultmann on the Resurrection and Historical Research. It would seem plausible to expect Barth
and Bultmann to arrive at similar conclusions regarding
the role of historical research as it bears on Christian
origins, and more specifically, on Jesus of Nazareth as
a historical figure. Both cut their theological eye
teeth on the historical-critical method. Through the
influence, in part, of Martin Kähler, one of Bultmann's
most influential teachers, both came to the conclusion
that the "quest of the historical Jesus" was finally a
"blind alley" insofar as it did not deal adequately with

the fact that the total New Testament witness to Jesus Christ, including that of the Gospels, was shaped by the story of his passion and resurrection. Both also agreed with Kähler that faith in Jesus as the Christ was not finally dependent upon the shifting findings of historical research concerning his life. Both are dubious about establishing any exact chronology of the life of Jesus and agree at some points on the rabbinic parallels to certain teachings of Jesus in first-century Judaism. In the tradition of W. Herrmann and Kähler, both oppose Protestant Orthodoxy's tendency to equate faith with assent to doctrinal propositions purporting to have historical support. Though Bultmann is more skeptical than Barth relative to what confidently may be attributed to the historical Jesus, neither has serious doubts about the main outline of his historical life. While Barth is more inclined to take the Gospel periscopes individually, or the reconstructed narrative culled from the Gospels collectively, as essentially reliable, Bultmann's form critical research led him to attribute a greater shaping influence on their final form to the faith of the church. They further concur that both Judaic and other current cultural factors exercised influence upon Jesus. Though Bultmann regards language about the pre-existence and incarnation of the Son of God to be mythological, he concurs with Barth that the Gospels are anti docetic in their stress on Jesus' true humanity. Moreover, Bultmann does not take issue with Barth's refusal to equate the Gospel accounts of the life of Jesus as myth. "The Gospels distinguish the life of Jesus from myths proclaiming timeless truth by underlining, though not overstressing, the temporal limitations to which Jesus was subject."[44] Finally, both theologians follow their teacher, Herrmann, in holding

132

that according to the New Testament faith in Jesus
Christ as the way to the knowledge of God involves the
believer's present response to the proclamation of the
kerygma: faith, therefore, is not to be construed
simply as knowledge about the facts pertaining to the
life of Jesus (fides historica).

These points of agreement lead both to reckon with
the facticity of the history of the man, Jesus. Barth's
high christology, however, leads him to far more traditional conclusions concerning God's presence in the man,
Jesus, than Bultmann allows on the basis of his form
critical reconstruction of Jesus' life.[45] Or put differently, Barth is much more positive than Bultmann in
affirming: "It [the New Testament] proclaims salvation
history, and therefore the time of salvation. The
lifetime of Jesus is this time of salvation."[46]

The point of greatest division between our antagonists relates to their differing interpretations of the
resurrection of Jesus from the dead. Their agreement
appears to terminate with the thesis that the resurrection is "the key to the whole" New Testament.[47] Perhaps
Barth has Bultmann in mind in continuing: "We can agree
about this quite apart from our own personal attitude to
the resurrection."[48] At the outset of his Theology of the
New Testament, Bultmann stated: "The message of Jesus is
a presupposition for the theology of the New Testament
rather than a part of that theology itself. ...Christian
faith did not exist until there was a Christian kerygma;
i.e., a kerygma proclaiming Jesus Christ--specifically
Jesus Christ the Crucified and Risen One--to be God's
eschatological act of salvation."[49] Barth sounds the
same note as does Bultmann and in the same year, 1948:
"The Easter history is the starting-point for the Evangelists' portraits of the man Jesus."[50] What is more,

Barth commends Bultmann "for emphasizing the central and indispensable function of the event of Easter for all that is thought and said in the New Testament."[51] This has to be granted even though Bultmann's understanding of that event is quite different from that of the New Testament.

    2. The Resurrection and Existential Interpretation. Bultmann restricts a valid theological statement to one which "can be proved to be a genuine element in the Christian understanding of human existence."[52] This leads him to reject the claim that "the resurrection of Jesus was an event in time and space on the ground that it does not fulfil this postulate."[53] Though Barth concedes that Bultmann is correct to draw this conclusion from his dogmatic presuppositions regarding the nature of a theological statement, he finds such a view incapable of doing justice to either Christianity's major confessional affirmations or to the primary intention of much of the biblical witness. Whereas Bultmann locates the primary reference of all theological statements in the Christian's self- understanding, Barth regards this as secondary to, and derivative from, their primary function of attesting God's activity. He counters Bultmann's thesis thus: "Primarily, they [theological statements] define the being and action of the God who is different from man and encounters man; the Father, the Son and the Holy Ghost. For this reason alone they cannot be reduced to statements about the inner life of man."[54]

    On Bultmann's reading, Jesus' resurrection involves God acting in what appears to be a "nature- miracle." Acknowledgement of such a happening is in no way requisite to a Christian's self- understanding. Barth identifies this restriction of all theological

assertions to statements about man as an "anthropological strait-jacket" and traces it to the tradition of
"W. Herrmann and even further to Ritschl and
Schleiermacher."[55] Yet somewhat cryptically, Barth adds:
"This tradition can just as easily be exploited in the
opposite direction, so as to leave no genuine case
against the resurrection of Jesus."[56]

    3.   The Resurrection and Faith. According to
Bultmann's third methodological presupposition, no event
may be designated as "historical" which is not subject
to "historical verification." While Barth recognizes
that the resurrection's historicity by its "very nature"
is not accessible to such verification, he questions
whether acceptance of its historicity by virtue of being
attested in the language of saga and legend involves
"merely a blind acceptance of a piece of mythology, an
arbitrary act, a descent from faith to works, a dis-
honest sacrificium intellectus [sacrifice of the intel-
lect]?"[57] On Barth's reading of the New Testament witness
to Jesus' resurrection, no evidence indicates that such
a belief involved an "intellectual contortion. For the
New Testament at any rate the resurrection is good news
in which we may believe."[58] Nor does Barth concede that
the prevailing world view made it easier for the initial
disciples to believe in Jesus' resurrection. He contends, on the contrary, that faith in the Easter message
was just as "incredible" to the "educated Areopagites"
as to the "original disciples" who regarded faith in the
risen Lord "made possible only by the resurrection
itself."[59] To maintain that the acceptance of the
resurrection today is an act of intellectual dishonesty
cannot be countenanced. "Hence," Barth concludes,
"there is no real reason why it should not be accepted
freely and gladly even to-day."[60]

4. <u>The Resurrection and the Modern World View</u>.
Bultmann's thesis is that our contemporary world view
shaped by modern science is not only superior to the
ancient mythical world view, but also necessitates the
critique of biblical statements informed by the latter.
Barth queries: "Is this modern view so binding as to
determine in advance and unconditionally our acceptance
or rejection of the biblical message?"[61] He chides
Bultmann for his addiction to the "well-known Marburg
tradition with its absolute lack of any sense of humour
and its rigorous insistence on the honesty which does
not allow any liberties in this respect."[62] Barth cites
disapprovingly Bultmann's oft-quoted statement ex-
pressing his perspective and determining his interpretation of the New Testament:

> It is impossible to use electric light and the
> wireless and to avail ourselves of modern
> medical and surgical discoveries, and at the
> same time to believe in the New Testament
> world of demons and spirits.[63]

The "shudder" this statement creates in Barth is coupled
with the question whether the "Marburg Kantians" and
Bultmann have not overstated the finality and closedness
of the modern world view. Furthermore, Barth asks: "Is
there any criticism of the New Testament which is inescapably posed by the 'situation of modern man'"?[64] While
not denying that modern Bible readers may presuppose a
modern world view and the promptings of "common sense,"
Barth speaks of those who may feel a "duty of honesty"
which is "more compelling" than the former. He concludes:

> What if they felt themselves in a position to
> give a free and glad and quite factual assent

not to a _fides implicita_ in a world of spirits
and demons but [rather] to faith in the resurrection of Jesus Christ from the dead? What
if they have no alternative but to do this?[65]

5. The Resurrection and the Mythical World View.
The last of the presuppositions Barth attributes to
Bultmann is related to that just treated. It calls for
rejecting statements which originate within, or are
compatible with, the ancient mythical world view. Barth
questions whether a statement's truth is determined by
its compatibility with a world view of the past. "Is
not Bultmann being a bit too heavy- handed in expecting
us [either to accept or] to reject this mythical world
view in its entirety? After all, is it our job as
Christians to accept or reject world views? Have not
Christians always been eclectic in their world
views--and this for very good reasons?"[66] Though Barth
cautions against making the ancient world view sacro-
sanct, he maintains that the biblical witnesses made
cautious and judicious use of "a number of features" of
that world view in attesting Jesus Christ. The fact
that the modern world view makes no allowance for these
features necessitates that Christians "make use of
'mythical' language in certain connections. And there
is no need for us to have a guilty conscience about it,
for if we went to extremes in demythologising, it would
be quite impossible to bear witness to Jesus Christ at
all."[67]

Barth sums up his critique of Bultmann's methodological presuppositions and the way they issue in his
demythologizing program:

When, for instance, Bultmann...dismisses the
connexion between sin and death, or the conception of substitution, or the relation

between death and resurrection, on the ground
that they are particularly offensive and
"obsolete" features in this mythical world-
view, he is perhaps a warning example of what
becomes of a theologian when he all-too-
hastily jettisons the mythical world-view
lock, stock and barrel. To speak of the "rise
of the Easter faith" in the first disciples is
a good thing. But we cannot pretend that this
is an adequate substitute for what is now
rejected as the "mythical" witness to the
resurrection of Jesus Christ from the dead.
As I see it, these are the decisive reasons
why, in spite of Bultmann, we must still
accept the resurrection of Jesus, and His
subsequent appearances to His disciples, as
genuine history [Geschichte] in its own particular time."[68]

C.   Barth's Presuppositions in Interpreting Jesus'
      Easter History

Barth throws down the gauntlet in maintaining that
Jesus has a "further history" after his "first history"
was at an end. "In temporal sequence, it is a second
history--or rather, the fragments of a second history--
of Jesus. It is the Easter history, the history of the
forty days between His resurrection and ascension."[69]
From Barth's perspective, no faithful interpretation of
the Easter events can ignore or deny their objectivity
and actuality. Pointedly Barth states: "Either we
believe with the New Testament in the risen Jesus
Christ, or we do not believe in Him at all. This is the
statement which believers and non-believers alike can
surely accept as a fair assessment of the sources."[70]

1. Problems in Interpreting the Easter History.
Before addressing the meaning of Jesus' being raised
from the dead, it is clear to Barth that even the "fragments of a second history--of Jesus" present the historian with numerous problems. This is due, in the

main, to the fact that those encountered by the risen
Jesus had to do with the "total, final, irrevocable and
eternal mani-festation of God Himself."[71] This accounts
for the difficulty of finding words to attest so singular a happening. Barth notes that the uniqueness of
Jesus' resurrection and appearances strain the limits of
language and makes the "evidence for the resurrection"
necessarily "fragmentary and contradictory, as is actually the case in the New Testament."[72] Whether one
deals with the chronology, duration, or topography
relating to the appearances of the risen Christ, Barth
concludes: "It is clearly impossible to extract from
the various accounts a nucleus of genuine history, quite
apart from the intelligibility or otherwise of the
resurrection itself."[73] Moreover, there are legendary
elements in the witness to the empty tomb and ascension.
Barth concedes that the witness of the Easter narratives
both to the empty tomb and the ascension "are alike in
the fact that both are indicated rather than described;
the one as an introduction, the other as a conclusion;
the one a little more definitely, though still in very
general terms, the other much more vaguely."[74] Nevertheless, these signs--attested at points by a narration
with legendary accretions--are indispensable signs of
the centrality of the event of Easter.[75]

2. The Language of Myth and Saga. Earlier we
noted Bultmann's refusal to accept any event as having
occurred and therewith as historical which cannot be
verified in accordance with the canons of modern historical methodology or which is incompatible with our
modern world view. Judged by these standards, the
traditional interpretation of Jesus' resurrection must
be regarded as myth pure and simple. Thus argues Bultmann; not Barth. He contends that much of the Bible's

witness to God's activity, or the history of salvation, does not lend itself to what modern historians regard as historical narrative. Admittedly, biblical witnesses knew no nuanced distinctions respecting what constituted true "history" as do Bultmann's scientific historians. In disagreement with the latter, Barth holds that biblical testimony often uses the language of saga when "the immediacy of history to God--emerges."[76] For example, such is the case in a paradigmatic way in the case of the Genesis creation accounts. God's initial creative activity eludes all possibilities of historical reportage, but is not, on that account, totally non- historical. "Only occurrences within the existent reality of nature can be historical. But at this point we have to do with occurrences on the frontier of the non-existence and existence of nature. If there can be any accounts of such occurrences at all, they certainly cannot be 'historical.'"[77]

For this reason, Barth interprets the creation accounts in terms of the genre of saga. In fact, the creation accounts are "pure saga"--an exception to the rule among the literary genre found in the Bible--even as those texts in which "we have pure and more or less incontestable 'history'" are also the exception to the rule.[78] For the most part, biblical texts are a mixture of history and saga. "To put it cautiously," Barth writes, "it [the Bible] contains little pure 'history' and little pure saga, and little of both that can be unequivocally recognised as the one or the other. The two elements are usually mixed. In the Bible we usually have to reckon with both history and saga."[79]

Two of Barth's definitions are necessary to understand distinctions he makes between varying literary genre found in the Bible's testimony to God's activity.

Regarding his definition of saga, Barth states: "...I am using saga in the sense of an intuitive and poetic picture of a pre-historical reality of history which is enacted once and for all within the confines of time and space."[80] Thus understood, saga is often characterized by both divination, which intuits those "events" which transcend the ordinary historical continuum, and poetry--

> the articulated form of this divining vision and therefore of the historical emergence seen in this way. In this kind of divination and poetry narrative saga arises distinct from history and in connexion with it--and woe to the history which lacks this connexion. For the most part, it has to do with the constitutive events of history, with its origins and roots. ...Where divinatory and poetical saga is not allowed to speak, no true picture of history, i.e., no picture of true history, can ever emerge. It is just as necessary as pure "historical" perception and expression.[81]

3. Beyond "Historicism" in Interpretation. In this treatment of saga and related literary genre, Barth's subsequent explicit critique of Bultmann's interpretation of the resurrection accounts is anticipated in all essentials. Though Bultmann is not singled out in the following citation on the limitations of a narrowly "historicist" conception of history, he was certainly in Barth's consciousness as he began work on the first volumes of "The Doctrine of Creation" in the war years following the publication of Bultmann's essay of 1941. He writes:

> We must dismiss and resist to the very last any idea of the inferiority or untrustworthiness or even worthlessness of a "non-historical" depiction and narration of history. This is in fact only a ridiculous and middle- class

habit of the modern Western mind which is
supremely phantastic in its chronic lack of
imaginative phantasy, and hopes to rid itself
of its complexes through suppression. This
habit has really no claim to the dignity and
validity which it pretends. It acts as if
only "historical" history were genuine history, and "non-historical" false. The obvious
result is to banish from the portrayal and
understanding of history all immediacy of
history to God on the pretext of its non-
historicity, dissolving it into a bare idea!
When this is done, the horizon of history
necessarily becomes what it is desired to
be--a highly unreal history, a more or less
explicit myth, in the poor light of which the
historical, what is supposed to be the only
genuine history, can only seem to be an ocean
of tedious inconsequence and therefore demoni-
ac chaos. We must not on any account take
this course. In no way is it necessary or
obligatory to maintain this rigid attitude to
the "non-historical" reality, conception and
description of history. On the contrary, it
is necessary and obligatory to realise the
fact and manner that in genuine history the
"historical" and "non-historical" accompany
each other and belong together."[82]

Barth traces the historicist conception of history
to the close of the seventeenth century. "Both Liberalism and orthodoxy are children of the same insipid
spirit, and it is useless to follow them."[83] Their common
presupposition was that "the Bible declares the Word of
God only when it speaks historically"--a view, Barth
charges, "which must be abandoned, especially in the
Christian Church."[84] It led first to an "uncertainty of
faith" inasmuch as it proved difficult to distinguish
between what was "historical" and thus the Word of God
in the Bible and saga. In Protestant Orthodoxy, it was
argued rigidly that since the Bible provided nothing but
"historical" accounts, it was therefore the Word of God
in toto. In opposition to the latter, Protestant

Liberalism attempted to discard sagas and "to penetrate
to a 'historical' kernel which is supposed to give us
the true, i.e., 'historical' Word of God"--a procedure,
Barth contends, in which "we do not lose only a sub-
sidary theme but the main point at issue, i.e., the
biblical witness."[85] He finds all these views operate
with a faulty hermeneutic. The fact that each presupposes the "equation of the Word of God with a 'historical' record is an inadmissable postulate which does not
itself originate in the Bible at all but in the unfor-
tunate habit of Western thought which assumes that the
reality of history stands or falls by whether it is
'history.'"[86] Barth inveighs against this prevailing
characteristic of Protestant theology from Orthodoxy
down to, and including, Bultmann as follows:

> For after all, there seems no good reason why
> the Bible as the true witness of the Word of
> God should always have to speak "historically"
> and not be allowed to speak in the form of
> saga. On the contrary, we have to recognise
> that as holy and inspired Scripture, as the
> true witness of God's true word, the Bible is
> forced to speak also in the form of saga
> precisely because its object and origin are
> what they are, i.e., not just "historical" but
> also frankly "non-historical."[87]

This latter approach to Holy Scripture therefore
precludes prejudgments as to where and how the fallible
witness of prophets, apostles, and others known and
unknown may become a living testimony to God, and thus
the Word of God heard in faith. "We are not less truly
summoned to listen to what the Bible has to say here in
the form of saga than to what it has to say in other
places in the form of history, and elsewhere in the form
of address, doctrine, meditation, law, epigram, epic and

lyric."[88] Any biblical tradition within the history of the covenant inspired by the Spirit of God and attesting his mighty acts may become, through the witness of that same Spirit, the living Word of God to his church. "And this is the case...too where they speak non- historically or pre-historically."[89]

It would take us too far afield to analyze the way Barth's approach to Scripture is developed within his larger and comprehensive doctrine of the Word of God. Yet it is within that context representing the heart of the Prolegomena to his Church Dogmatics (CD I:1 and CD 1:2) that Barth already made all of the decisions which determine his critique of Bultmann's program. In developing his view of "Dogmatics as a Function of the Hearing Church," Barth maintains that the theologian should adopt the stance of the biblical witnesses. Being a witness to God's revelatory activity is integral to every biblical testimony and tradition. Concerning this decisive characteristic of biblical prophets and apostles, Barth writes:

> By the attitude of the biblical witnesses, we mean that orientation of their thinking and speaking which is still that of witnesses to the revelation of God even though they are conditioned by their historical and biographical situation, by their particular speech and outlook, by their concrete situation and intention. They are witnesses. ...They are called by God in the face of all other men to be witnesses of His own action. ...they believe and therefore speak.[90]

D. Barth's Interpretation of Jesus' Easter History: "Jesus, Lord of Time"

Barth introduces his theological and christological

understanding of the human creature with the following
proposition:

> Man lives in the allotted span of his present,
> past and future life. He who was before him
> and will be after him, and who therefore fixes
> the boundaries of his being, is the eternal
> God, His Creator and Covenant-partner. He is
> the hope in which man may live in his time.[91]

    1.   Jesus in His Time: the Contemporary of All
Human Beings. Like all other human beings, Jesus' life
is temporally limited and therewith finite. In opposition to all docetic views of Jesus' humanity, Barth
underlines his historicity. "Like all men, the man
Jesus has His lifetime: the time bounded at one end by
His birth and at the other by His death... ."[92] Yet in
this time of his lifetime, "...He lives as the One He is
in virtue of His unity with God."[93] He lives thus as
God's representative to mankind and as mankind's representative before his Father. That Jesus enjoyed this
special relationship with God, his Father, accounts for
the New Testament witness that his lifetime is the time
of salvation. In this sense, Barth underlines that
already in his lifetime, Jesus is "Lord of Time."
Indeed, he is "the Contemporary of all men." This is
attested in that as the representative of God's grace,
Jesus "gives man what is right, what is his due. And he
represents the gratitude of man, and thus gives God what
is right, what is His due."[94] Thus in the man Jesus in
his time, Barth sees the definitive and unique answer
given once and for all concerning the question of the
right relationship of all human creatures in all time to
God, their Father. It is along these lines that Barth
speaks of "Jesus, Lord of Time." As the one called and
elected of God, the Son actualizes the divine will in

behalf of humanity. Jesus is, therefore, the contemporary of all human beings. "...He is the Contemporary of them all because He lives for God and for them all."[95]

2. "Jesus, Lord of Time:" "Raised from the dead." The thesis that Jesus was the Lord of time even within the limits of his temporal life Barth finds attested in the Johannine teaching "that Jesus Christ 'is come in the flesh' (1 Jn. 4:2), that the Logos became flesh and 'tabernacled' among men (Jn. 1:14). ..."[96] Yet Jesus' lordship over time finds its primary validation in his "second history," the "Easter history, the history of the forty days between His resurrection and ascension."[97] That Jesus was raised from the dead is the key to everything said about him in the New Testament. That occurrence is not to be construed as "a timeless and non-historical truth" or simply as the apostolic memory of his life and death of which the disciples were eyewitnesses. On the contrary, Barth insists that "when the New Testament speaks of the event of Easter it really means the Easter history and Easter time. ...it happened 'once upon a time' that He was among them as the Resurrected."[98]

That Jesus was raised from the dead is the starting point for the entire apostolic witness concerning him--not just that he was confessed as "Lord of Time." On the basis of such passages as 1 Jn. 1:1, Lk. 24:36f., and Jn. 20:24f., Barth rejects any docetic conceptions of the resurrected Jesus. These and other texts underline that it was none other than the man, Jesus, who was raised from the dead. Barth concludes:

> The Resurrected is the man Jesus, who now came and went among them as such, whom they saw and touched and heard, who ate and drank with them, and who, as I believe, was still before them as true man, vere homo.[99]

Apart from this New Testament emphasis upon the bodily
and physical resurrection of Jesus, Barth contends that
"we have no guarantee that it was the decisively acting
Subject Jesus Himself, and thus precisely the man Jesus,
who was active in the Easter history."[100]

3. "Jesus, Lord of Time:" "He Appeared" in the
Mode of God. Not to be overlooked is the complementary
truth "that the man Jesus appeared to them during these
days in the mode of God."[101] This does not mean in an
adoptionist vein that Jesus became divine or the Son of
God by virtue of his resurrection. Rather, the deity of
Jesus which lay veiled within his humanity was unveiled
and disclosed by his resurrection and appearances to his
disciples.

> "God was in Christ" (2 Cor. 5:19)--this was
> the truth which dawned upon the disciples
> during the forty days. He was not both veiled
> and manifest, both manifest and veiled, in
> Christ. He had been veiled, but He was now
> wholly and unequivocally and irrevocably
> manifest. For the disciples this was not a
> self-evident truth, nor a discovery of their
> own, but a conviction that went utterly
> against the grain.[102]

The fear and unbelief of the disciples was not overcome
as Bultmann proposes by means of a

> reassessment and reinterpretation in meliorem
> partem of the picture of the Crucified, but in
> an objective encounter with the Crucified and
> Risen, who Himself not only made Himself
> credible to them, but manifested Himself as
> the "pioneer of their salvation" (Heb. 2:10)
> and therefore the "pioneer and perfecter" of
> their "faith" (Heb. 12:2). This being the
> case, He was among them as God Himself.
> ...God Himself, the object and ground of their
> faith, was present as the man Jesus was pre-
> sent in this way. That this really [once was

and] <u>took</u> <u>place</u> is the specific content of the
apostolic recollection of these days.[103]

4. <u>"Jesus, Lord of Time:"</u>   <u>the Risen Kyrios</u>. The
authority and finality of the risen Jesus' speech and
acts during his appearances attest his divine authority.
The "Great Commission" given to the Eleven to "make
disciples of all nations" (Mt. 28:19) is testimony to
his special divine status and authority. This accounts
for the acknowledgment of Jesus as <u>Kyrios</u> by the apostolic community. Barth traces the origin of this title
"signifying absolute deity" not primarily to an interpretation grounded in the intensity of the experience of
contrition on the part of the disciples, but rather to
the activity of the risen Jesus himself.

> He has appeared and acted as <u>Kyrios</u> among
> them. It is not they who have given Him this
> name, but God. And God has given it by exalt-
> ing Him above all things ... (Phil. 2:9) out
> of and after His death on the cross. Hence
> this name is inseparable from His person, and
> His person inseparable from this name.[104]

It is, therefore, on account of Jesus' resurrection
from the dead that the apostle's affirmation that they
had once known him "after the flesh" (2 Cor. 5:16) is
superseded by the confession of him as <u>Kyrios</u>. This
conclusion calls in question any view of the Gospels
which does not recognize that everything recorded about
the life, ministry and death of Jesus is said in "recollection of the resurrection of Jesus."[105] For Barth this
precludes any reading of the Gospels which concentrates
"attention upon a human Jesus who is not the <u>Kyrios</u>
because He is not risen... ."[106] Such an approach is
faulty because its hermeneutic and methodology do not

reckon with the way the Gospels actually originated. For it was by means of the "post-history" of Jesus, his "Easter history," in which he was revealed to his disciples as "the appearance of God," that the definitive breakthrough to understanding his person took place. Barth underlines this crucial point in the thesis- like statement: "The Easter time is simply the time of the revelation of the mystery of the preceding time of the life and death of the man Jesus."[107]

5. "Jesus, Lord of Time:" His Empty Tomb and Ascension. Since Barth's fuller exposition of the resurrection will be examined more extensively when we treat his doctrine of reconciliation below, it must suffice here to note briefly the lines along which he treats the traditions of the empty tomb and ascension. In our exposition of Barth's view of the resurrection of Jesus to this point, it is clear that he focuses on Jesus' appearances. He notes that these accounts are replete with elements of saga and legend. The attendant obscurity obtains because the stories are "describing an event beyond the reach of historical research or depiction."[108] Unlike the appearance stories, the empty tomb and ascension which delimit the beginning and ending of the Easter time "are both indicated rather than described... ."[109] This fact suggests to Barth that both are signs pointing to the risen Christ who is the true content of Easter faith.

Barth concedes that the New Testament texts make it clear that the "empty tomb was obviously a very ambiguous and contestable fact (Mt. 27:62f.; 28:11f.). And what has happened around this sepulchre is a warning against making it a primary focus of attention. The empty tomb is not the same thing as the resurrection. It is not the appearance of the Living; it is only its presupposition."[110] As an "indispensable sign" of the preceding resurrection, the empty tomb "with its backward, downward, earthward reference, is to show that the Jesus who died and was buried was delivered from death, and therefore from the grave, by the power of God; that He, the Living, is not to be sought among the dead (Lk. 24:5)."[111] Here, too, Barth refuses to dismiss the empty tomb tradition because it is couched in the genre of legend. "It still refers to the phenomenon ensuing the resurrection, to the presupposition of the appearance of Jesus. It is the sign which obviates all possible misunderstanding. It cannot, therefore, but demand our assent, even as a legend."[112] This is all the more the case because historically the rejection of the empty tomb tradition is always coupled with the rejection of the risen Jesus.

Barth interprets the ascension as a sign marking the end of the Easter history as "it points forward and upward." Misconceptions concerning the ascension's significance abound due, in part, to the "worst perpetrations" of Christian art. "There is no sense in trying to visualize the ascension as a literal event, like going up in a balloon."[113] The upward reference has to do with the exaltation of Jesus to "the God-ward side of the universe" where "existing and acting in the mode of God," he is to be "accepted as the One who exists in this form to all eternity."[114] Barth underlines the import of Acts 1:9 which reads: "A cloud received him out of their sight." He regards the biblical imagery of the cloud to refer not only to God's hiddenness, but also to a future revelation and consummation. This gives the ascension story its forward reference. This accounts for what Barth refers to as its "joyous character"--rather than being a farewell marked by sorrow.

Seen in this light, the ascension is a sign testifying Jesus' lordship over time. Barth describes the proleptic nature of the sign of the ascension in these words:

> The ascension is the proleptic sign of the parousia, pointing to the Son of Man who will finally and visibly emerge from the concealment of His heavenly existence and come on the clouds of heaven (Mt. 24:30). ...As this sign, the ascension is indispensable, and it would be injudicious as well as ungrateful on any gounds to ignore or reject this upward and forward-looking sign.[115]

III. BARTH IN BASEL: "CHURCH DOGMATICS...THIS PRIMARY TASK"--AND...

During the late forties, Barth's energies were directed toward the completion of his lectures on the doctrine of Creation. Perhaps in response to detractors' predictions that his theology "from above" could never issue in an adequate doctrine of Creation or the creature, Barth's published a comprehensive treatment appearing in four part volumes, each of great length, beginning in 1945 and concluding in 1951. Following the publication of his anthropology in 1948, the doctrine of providence appeared in 1950. Co-editor, T. F. Torrance, captures Barth's aim in stating that for Barth "providence is...to be understood on the presupposition of the election of grace fulfilled in Jesus Christ and the covenant of grace actualised in salvation history. This means that belief in providence cannot be linked to a world view. It is explicit faith derived from the knowledge of Jesus Christ."[116] In the Preface Barth observed that critics commented pro and con on the "formal systematisation" characteristic of the earlier volumes on creation. He continued:

If I had and have any such concern, it is to hold fast at all costs and at every point to the christological thread, i.e., to what I have recently been accused of under the label and catchword "Christomonism."...And my question to those who are dissatisfied is whether with a good conscience and cheerful heart Christian theology can do anything but seriously and finally remember "Christ alone" at each and every point.[117]

A. Rapprochement with Bultmann?

In May of 1947, Bishop Wurm, President of the Council of the Evangelical Church in Germany, sought Barth's counsel regarding a Marburg pastor's misgivings about Bultmann's reference to "the legend of the empty tomb" and "the marvel of the resurrection." In his letter Bishop Wurm supports Pastor Bruns and raises his own questions with respect to Bultmann's denial that "Christ's physical body was transfigured."[118] He continues:

At this decisive point the church has no authority to teach otherwise than the apostles. I believe that the Bultmannian theory goes far beyond the concern for a sober assessment and solution of the epistemological problem to become a presentation which includes the negation of the fact itself, if not for him, probably for many of his hearers and for the community.[119]

Barth replies promptly to the Bishop's inquiry and sends Bultmann a copy. The latter also had received a copy of Wurm's letter to Barth. Barth begins by recalling that Bultmann was in the "front ranks of those who were then attempting a reorientation of evangelical theology along the lines of a clear confrontation, brought to light in exegesis and systematics, between the human subject and the divine revelation that encounters this subject."[120] Before dealing with Bultmann's questionable christological conclusions, Barth feels it necessary to address his "methodological presuppositions" from which the former derive and which alone are "either theologically or ecclesiastically serious and significant."[121] Barth portrays Bultmann's approach as follows:

> In my view the decisive and distinctive fact about Bultmann's way is that he regarded it as indispensable to base the reorientation on a (then the most recent) philosophical ontology or anthropology. He thought he could take from this ontology a definite "preunderstanding of man" which is normative for theology, too, and in accordance with which the confrontation of man with a distinct Other could be described as a general phenomenon of the uniqueness of human existence. From this standpoint we then have to understand what the Bible calls God's revelation as a specific—the Christian—determination of human existence.[122]

Utilizing this "existential schema" as the norm for interpreting the New Testament, Bultmann was able—in part, due to his outstanding intellect and expertise as the leading German New Testament scholar—to shed light on the meaning of the New Testament witness at many points. Barth also recalls that some of Bultmann's exegetical conclusions led him to identify with the Confessing Church in the German Church struggle in the thirties. Notwithstanding Bultmann's positive contributions, Barth judges the outcome of Bultmann's methodology harshly:

> ...the question remains whether that programmatic basing of theology on some philosophical ontology will not sooner or later, in some way or another, necessarily mean the overthrow of

theology, and whether this has not actually
happened in the case of Bultmann too. In my
view this question has to be answered in the
affirmative. What the Bible calls God's
revelation, according to my understanding of
its witness, is not to be explained as merely
one determination of human existence. And the
explanation of revelation as a determination
of human existence is inevitably truncated and
twisted when it is forced into the framework
of that "preunderstanding," where it can have
the significance only of a Christian instance
of the general human encounter with some
Other.[123]

Barth concludes that Bultmann's methodology represents "a return to the theological method"--later proved
untenable--of "Lessing, Schleiermacher and De Wette"--in
short, to that of theological Liberalism.

With respect to Bultmann's disputed "christological
conclusions," Barth remarks:

I regard these as unavoidable on Bultmann's
presuppositions. Within the "preunderstanding"
which underlies his theological exegesis and
systematics the only possible exposition of NT
statements about the messiahship, the divine
sonship, the vicarious death, the resurrection, and the coming again of Jesus Christ is
one according to which these are to be seen as
conceptual objectifications, influenced by the
imagination of the NT age, of that which the
encounter with God mediated through Jesus
Christ signifies for man. I reject these
conclusions along with Bultmann's presuppositions. ...I...do not hesitate to say that I
have to regard them as "heretical," i.e.,
incompatible with the confession of the
church. ...Those who do not want to finish up
where he does must learn from this brave,
learned, and perspicacious man not be begin
where he does.[124]

Barth addresses next pastor Bruns' complaint that
Bultmann speaks about the "legend of the empty tomb" and

"the marvel of the resurrection." Barth finds it disturbing that Bruns' letter gives no evidence of knowledge of the "decisive presupposition of Bultmann's
theology. ...He does not see that one must attack
Bultmann, if at all, on the basis of his combination
with a specific philosophical ontology."[125] Conceding
that Bultmann's speaking about "the legend of the empty
tomb" and "the marvel of the resurrection. ...could in
themselves be taken in a good sense," Barth remarks that
"the term 'legend' may simply denote the literary genre
of the Easter stories of the Gospels (a necessary one in
virtue of their unique content)."[126] The resurrection of
one who was dead and is alive again "cannot be reported
in the form of a 'historical' narrative but only as
'saga' or 'legend.' This term says nothing about whether
what is reported really happened or not. A legend does
not necessarily lack substance."[127] Likewise, describing
the resurrection as a "marvel" may be appropriate as the
initial response both of believers and unbelievers to
the witness to the resurrection. Barth adds, however,
that Bultmann impermissibly associates the legend of the
empty tomb with "myth" and "has in mind the idea that
what the 'legend' narrates never really took place."[128]
Moreover, Bultmann speaks of the resurrection as a
"marvel" because "he wished to put the fact of the
resurrection truly and definitively in the realm of
credulous fancy."[129]

    In Barth's opinion, it would have been much more
instructive had pastor Bruns seen that what Bultmann
says about the "empty tomb" stands "in the context of a
negative conclusion that embraces the whole of
christology."[130] Barth continues:

        The "empty tomb" is in itself only one repre-
        sentative of that to which the NT writers bear

witness: that the eternal Word of God really
came in the flesh, that in the there and then
to which they refer he came as a Jew to us
Gentiles, that he suffered for us, went down
to death, and was exalted to glory. The
"empty tomb" is not on its own "a fact of
salvation history." What must be confessed as
a fact of salvation history in opposition to
Bultmann and to so many docetic or docetizing
heretics both old and new is the living Lord
Jesus, the Christ of Israel, who is as such
the Savior of the world--in contrast to a
principally timeless Christ-idea which is
embodied in this Jesus but can also be
abstracted from him. That this confession is
not possible with a denial of the "empty tomb"
but only with (incidental!) recognition of
it--this context and this alone can make the
"empty tomb" a worthy theme of theological
discussion. This is what is not expressed in
any way in the accusations and complaint of
Pastor Bruns.[131]

In response to the Bishop's question regarding the
best way to deal with the charges against Bultmann,
Barth suggests the following. First, he asks wryly
whether it may not be the case that Bultmann's detractors "are not much nearer to Bultmann in their presuppositions than they think, whether they have an inner
right, then, to complain about him."[132] Second,
Bultmann's "original purpose and positive qualities"
should not be overlooked when the issue of his "heresy"
is raised. Third, "a contesting of heresy which misses
the essential point, well-meaning though it may be, has
always been more dangerous to the church than the heresy
in question."[133] Reminiscent of his advice in the face of
the threat of the German Christians, Barth counsels once
more that the church confront the issue of its "Confession" on a broad and comprehensive basis. Thus Barth
concludes that "in the matter of Bultmann, I can give no
other advice than either to go into the matter in its

totality or to let it be."[134] Fourth, it may well be the
case that if the church is alert, a "heretic" like
Bultmann "might be indirectly salutary to the church as
a 'pike is in a pond of carp.'"[135] Finally, and more
substantively, Barth suggests that if Bultmann were
surrounded by a church which in its life and witness, in
its relations to state and society, "were to put into
practice even a little its belief in the Risen Lord,
then not only would it be practically immune against the
heresies of the Bultmannian conclusions and theses but
it would also have in reply to Bultmann the one argument
which could perhaps cause him to abandon his basic
position. ..."[136] Hence Barth's considered view is that
if the situation is so perilous in Marburg, it would be
best if "Bultmann and his students are encompassed not
only by a 'believing' but also by a living community.
...Certainly the presence, as I see it, of an intellectual and spiritual error in the theology of Bultmann
cannot be met by the mechanical measures that Pastor
Bruns has in view but only in the freedom of the
Spirit--the Holy Spirit and the human spirit!"[137]

Shortly after this correspondence, Barth travelled
to Germany where he personally discouraged any initiation of ecclesiastical procedures against Bultmann.
Following the publication of his anthropology containing
the critical remarks and queries put to Bultmann later
in the summer of 1948, Barth "vainly attempted a reconciliation with Bultmann in Basle over the critical
passages in the Church Dogmatics, III, 2."[138]

B.   Teaching and Students, Colleagues and Faculty
      Affairs

The post-war influx of theological students to

Basel from all parts of the globe put added pressures on the theological faculty and especially on Karl Barth. Contrary to his own wishes to have his former student, Georg Eichholz, appointed to a vacancy in theology at Basel, the theological faculty voted for a "counter-balance" to Barth, and Hendrik van Oyen, a Dutch ethicist, was appointed.[139] Barth continued with his regimen of lecturing in dogmatics four hours each week in addition to offering weekly seminars both in German and French and English colloquia fortnightly. Barth states that he found increasingly that the seminar format is probably the most fruitful part of academic instruction.

> The student should be learning, by means of important texts, to <u>read</u>: at first to become aware, quietly and completely, of the content of these texts, to understand what he has read in its historical context, and finally to adopt a critical attitude towards it. ...It is a matter of preparing the student for <u>teaching</u> by his active participation in <u>research</u>.[140]

Among the doctoral and post-doctoral students studying with Barth in this period were Felix Fluckiger, Eduard Buess, James Leitch, James M. Robinson, Friedrich Herzog, Max Geiger and Heinrich Ott. While engaged with these advanced students in thesis research and intensive exchanges in seminars, Barth kept in view that both they and the majority of his students were preparing for the pastoral ministry. Hence the practical task of preach-ing and teaching in the church--so long emphasized in his theology--undergirded his own pedagogy. In July of 1950, Barth communicated something of this concern in a letter to his student, Heinrich Ott, who, after Barth's retirement, was to be appointed to one of the posts in theology in the theological faculty at Basel. Busch provides the following excerpts from Barth's letter:

> He [Barth] thought that people would notice "at every turn" if these would-be teachers had never made 'the 'kerygma,' to which there was so much appeal, their own responsibility, if they had never presented it in its canonical Old and New Testament form, with humility and patience, with delight and love, in preaching, instruction and pastoral work, serving a real community, instead of always just thinking about it and talking about it...That produces those academic theologians who are sometimes interesting but in the last resort always sterile because they have dissected the matter for so long and have lost their sense of proportion. All they can do is regard their standpoint as an absolute one and disport themselves arrogantly, proudly and vainly. They keep saying that what is important is unimportant and what is unimportant is important; they keep putting forward their own more or less arbitrary assertions in lectures and sermons--and are really in earnest only when there is yet another dispute in the faculty politics of which they are so fond.[141]

The appointment of Karl Jaspers to the philosophical faculty in Basel in 1948 seems to have been quite agreeable to Barth. In a letter to his son, Christoph, Barth spoke of him as one "who has the gift of directing the attention of his colleagues, with all their disparate concerns, to the ultimate questions of human existence and keeping it there... ."[142] He reports that Jaspers held forth in the largest lecture hall while "mine is the more modest" one. "There are plenty of gifted young men going up and down the steps linking the two rooms, like angels up and down Jacob's ladder. I wonder whether a hundred and thirty or so years ago there was a similar connection between the place where Hegel and Schleiermacher lectured in Berlin, perhaps the other way round." In a light vein Barth comments that the gossip among students concerning whether theology is the "handmaid" of philosophy or visa versa is one which, as "professionals," "we [Jaspers and Barth] may consider ourselves both to be above it." Barth concludes his remarks about Jaspers to his son as follows:

> We are agreed in our concern for knowledge of the mystery which both limits and governs the microcosm and the macrocosm. Each of us sees it from quite a different perspective and so from the first words each of us utters, our teaching cannot be the same. But we are also agreed that this mystery is intrinsically one and the same--and we are also agreed that it is worth devoting ourselves with all seriousness to bearing witness to it.[143]

IV. BARTH "AGAINST THE STREAM"--AGAIN: CONTROVERSIES (1948-49)

The invitation extended Barth to participate in the First Assembly of the World Council of Churches meeting in Amsterdam in 1948 was accepted after initial hesitation. His wider ecumenical involvements had been minimal before 1948. Advancing years and abating energies led him to refuse many requests to lecture and travel requiring him to neglect the Church Dogmatics--which he once referred to as that "great whale!"

A. Ecumenical Confrontation: Barth and the World Council of Churches at Amsterdam (1948)

Barth not only agreed to address the opening assembly on the assigned theme, "The World's Disorder and God's Design," but also participated in preliminary conferences and studied the preparatory materials. His

address both historically and theologically parallels
the theological method of the Church Dogmatics while
also revealing his critique of a more anthropologically
focused theological method and theology characteristic
of much Anglo-Saxon theology at that time--and to a
lesser degree, of Bultmann and his followers.   His
opening remarks at Amsterdam are typical and depict him
once again going "against the stream."

"The world's disorder--and God's design." May
I begin by asking you to consider the question
whether we must not view and handle this
theme, as a whole and in all its aspects, in
reverse order. It is written, we should _first_
seek God's Kingdom and His righteousness, so
that all we need in relation to the world's
disorder may be added unto us.   Do we not
need, do we not want to take this order of
topics seriously?   God's saving design is
above--but the world's disorder, and therefore
also our own conceptions of its causes, and
therefore also our proposals and plans to
combat it, are all _below_. What this whole
lower realm (including our own churchly existence!) means, can only--if at all--become
clear and understandable to us from above,
from the perspective of God's design. Whereas
from the world's disorder, and also from our
Christian analyses and postulates applied to
it, there is no view, no way that leads out
and up to God's design. We should not try to
begin down below; neither with the unity and
disunity of our churches, not with the good
and bad manners of modern man nor with the
terrifying picture of a culture which is only
technically oriented and only concerned with
production, nor with the clash between a
godless West and a godless East, nor with the
threat of the atomic bomb, and certainly not
with the few considerations and measures by
which we think we might cure all this
calamity. In the material that lies before us
here speak too many voices laden with repress-
ed care and anxiety, and on the other hand too
many voices expressive of all too fond
illusions, for us not to need this warning.
They are symptomatic of the fact that the

questions about the right order of procedure,
which is from the top downward, is not a
question that makes no difference.[144]

While acknowledging that the preparatory studies
give evidence of a concern for pointing secular humanity
Godward, Barth finds them characterized by a "positivis-
tic" mode of speaking rather than by the "Christian
realism" called for. He continues:

> But here arises a further question: Should we
> not also come to the clear understanding that
> by "God's Design" is really meant His plan;
> that is, His already come, already victorious,
> already founded Kingdom in all its majes-
> ty--our Lord Jesus Christ, Who has already
> robbed sin and death, the devil and hell of
> their power, and already vindicated divine and
> human justice in His own person? that by
> "God's Design" is therefore not meant the
> existence of the Church in the world, its task
> in relation to the world's disorder, its
> outward and inward activity as an instrument
> for the amelioration of human life, or finally
> the result of this activity in the Christiani-
> zation of all humanity and, connected with
> this, the setting up of an order of justice
> and peace embracing our whole planet? that
> therefore by "God's Design" is not meant
> something like a Christian Marshall Plan?[145]

Barth approves of speaking of the church as the
Body of Christ, but laments a kind of ecclesiocentrism
which makes it appear that Christ is no longer Lord over
his church; indeed, by stressing constantly what the
church must do to correct the world's disorder, it
appears that God has died![146] Again, Barth calls for the
church to be marked by wholehearted allegiance to Jesus
Christ.

> ...the Body of Christ...means, each in his
> place, each in his way, as have put their

whole hope and trust exclusively in Christ
Himself; in His accomplished work of
reconciliation on the Cross, in His
Resurrection as the sign of the new age which
in Him has already broken through, in His Holy
Spirit whereby He comforts His tempted community and rules and overrules the world for
good, quite differently and far better than we
could do--and finally, in His Second Coming in
glory, whereby the redemption He has
accomplished for the whole creation will be
made gloriously manifest.[147]

B. Reinhold Niebuhr vs. Barth: Aftermath of
Amsterdam (1948-49)

Following the Amsterdam meetings, Reinhold Niebuhr
took strong exception to Barth's position. He accused
him of encouraging quietism and an uncritical "Biblical
literalism" with an emphasis on Biblical authority
eschewing any appeal to "norms of truth or right which
may come to us out of the broad sweep of a classical,
European, or modern cultural history."[148] While dis-
avowing Niebuhr's charges, Barth returned to the major
thrust of his opening address cited above. He felt that
it was all too characteristic of much Anglo-Saxon
theology to think in non-biblical categories which were
determinative in theological construction apart from any
serious scriptural warrant. The "two dimensions" present in Anglo-Saxon thinking have to do with "the contrasts of good and evil, freedom and necessity, love and
self-centeredness, spirit and matter, person and
mechanism...and in this sense, God and the world or God
and man."[149] While not denying that these categories have
their place, Barth charges that Anglo-Saxon theologizing
in this framework does not engage the "third dimension"
attested in the Bible having to do with the mystery of
God and his activity. Barth points to this "third

dimension" of concern to "Continental" theology:

> ...the Bible...knows not only these two
> dimensions but also a third that is decisive
> --the word of God, the Holy Spirit, God's free
> choice, God's grace and judgment, the Crea-
> tion, the Reconciliation, the Kingdom, the
> Sanctification, the Congregation; and all
> these not as principles to be interpreted in
> the same sense as the first two dimensions but
> as the indication of <u>events</u>, of concrete,
> once-for-all, unique divine <u>actions</u>, of the
> majestic mysteries of God that cannot be
> resolved into any pragmatism.[150]

1. <u>Continental vs. Anglo-Saxon Theology</u>. The tenor of Barth's remarks reveal deep feelings about the breadth of the chasm separating Continental from Anglo-Saxon theology. That Reinhold Niebuhr--whose name in American theology was often associated with the camp of neo-orthodoxy in its critique of Liberalism--should be the one who fired off this salvo against Barth added to the latter's feeling of betrayal. Niebuhr's initial critique of Barth's Amsterdam address was entitled, "We are Men and Not God." While acknowledging that all Christians would concur with Barth's accent upon the redemptive work of God in Christ as the fountainhead of Christian faith, he interprets Barth's position as a radical form of "realized eschatology" encouraging Christian withdrawal from the complexities of the world's dilemma and the "tortuous and difficult task of achieving a tolerable justice."[151] In short, Niebuhr finds Barth guilty of failing to maintain the prophetic stance he exemplified and encouraged in his own person and theology in the fight against Naziism and the perni-cious nationalism of the German Christians. On account of his emphasis on the victory already achieved prolep-tically in Christ and the revolutionary Christian hope

associated therewith, Barth's theology provides no real help in confronting the social, economic and political issues confronting the church and Christians in times not marked by absolute crisis. Niebuhr ends his critique in approving Barth's initial theological reminder "that we are men and not God, and that God is in the heavens and that we are on earth." But in closing, Niebuhr remarks:

> The wheel is come full circle. It is now in danger of offering a crown without a cross, a triumph without a battle, a scheme of justice without the necessity of discrimination, a faith which has annulled rather than transmuted perplexity--in short, a too simple and premature escape from the trials and perplexities, the duties and tragic choices, which are the condition of our common humanity. The Christian faith knows of a way through these sorrows, but not of a way around them.[152]

That Barth had not anticipated the vigor of Niebuhr's disagreement with him and the "Continental" theology is evident in his pained and pointed reply:.

> In the light of what I have read of his writings, of a good talk which I had with him here in Basle and of his speech at Amsterdam, I had in all good faith looked on him as belonging to the dissenting element among the Anglo-Saxons, and now I find him to my utter surprise--et tu, Brute--entering the lists against me, as spokesman of the "Anglo- Saxon world." This particular mistake troubles me.[153]

As in the case of the earlier identification of Bultmann with Barth in the ranks of the dialectical theologians, here too, the earlier sympathies of Niebuhr with Barth are in dissolution. In his closing reply to

Niebuhr, Barth complains of being caricatured. These theological giants appear like ships passing each other at night. In his final attempt to be understood, Barth maintains that the single point he intended in his address was to call in question the "equivocal way of proceeding from below upwards." This procedure resulted in an "inner uncertainty" and a "striking overburdenedness" in the documents prepared for Amsterdam. Barth rests his case with regard to the chasm between diverging theologies and its two protagonists as follows:

> If I was mistaken in all this, it is a proof of something that I will mention only in passing--namely, the obviously great difficulty for the Anglo-Saxons and "us" to understand one another, let alone to judge one another rightly and even to engage in a fruitful interchange and perhaps to arrive in the end at common insights and decisions.[154]

Chapter V

BARTH AND BULTMANN: THE CONTINUING DEBATE
AND FINAL ENCOUNTERS (1950-1952)

I.   THE WIDENING DEBATE ON DEMYTHOLOGIZATION (1945-1955)

The intensification of the debate between Barth and Bultmann paralleled the broadening controversy surrounding Bultmann's views both within churches and among theologians of all persuasions following the end of World War II in 1945.   Barth published his first systematic response to Bultmann--delineated above--in 1948.   In that same year, the first volume of the German series Kerygma und Mythos appeared introducing Bultmann's essay and the response of his critics to a wider public.

A.   The Growing Ecclesiastical Debate

Reginald Fuller kept English readers abreast of the continuing controversy surrounding Bultmann in the second English volume of Kerygma and Myth remarking: "From about 1950 the debate spread far beyond the confines of Lutheranism and the German-speaking countries, and in 1955 Kerygma und Mythos, IV, appeared with contributions from the Swiss, Scandinavian, and Anglo-Saxon worlds."[1] In his 1954 article, "The Present State of the Debate," Hans-Werner Bartsch located the post-war spark fanning the flames of the controversy.   "Quite likely the trouble began with the ill-advised activities of some of Bultmann's younger pupils, who as pastors or assistant clergy in Wurtemberg parishes were alleged to be teaching in the day schools and from their pulpits that Jesus never did any miracles or rose from the dead."[2] It was reported that some young Bultmannian disciples were using the parody of the Apostles Creed "a la Bultmann" produced by Hermann Sasse:

> . . . not conceived by the Holy Ghost,
> Not born of the Virgin Mary;
> Suffered, indeed, under Pontius Pilate,
> Was crucified, dead, and buried:
> He did not descend into hell;
> The third day he rose not from the dead:
> He ascended not into heaven,
> And therefore sitteth not at the right hand of God
> the Father Almighty:
> From whence therefore he shall not come to judge
> the quick and the dead.[3]

An indication of the depth and extent of the Bultmann debate within German churches of Germany is evident in the pronouncement of the Bishops of the United Evangelical-Lutheran Church of Germany read from the pulpits of member churches in 1953. Though not mentioned by name, Bultmann comes under heavy attack in the following paragraph:

> In recent years a new anxiety has arisen within the Church, and with good reason. Some theologians in our universities, eager to find new ways to commend the gospel message to the modern world, have set about "demythologizing" the New Testament, as they call it. In so doing, they are in danger of reducing parts of the New Testament, and even of abandoning it altogether. They rightly perceive that the New Testament is couched in the language and thought forms of the age in which it was written. But we are bound to ask whether this

> movement is not leading to a denial of the
> facts to which Scripture bears witness. ...We
> appeal to the congregations to hold fast to
> the confession of Jesus Christ, the incarnate,
> crucified and risen Lord, who lives and reigns
> at the right hand of the Father, and who will
> come again in glory.[4]

Such ecclesiastical declarations make it obvious how Barth could be claimed as an ally by the more conservative wing of the German churches in their opposition to Bultmann. Barth certainly provided ammunition for those wishing to pierce Bultmann's theological armor at vulnerable points. Yet Barth seemed more reticent than in former days to debate either his detractors or opponents. In the preface to his anthropology written in 1948 on his sixtieth birthday, Barth chided his uninformed adversaries: "They ought to be glad that they did not come up against me at an earlier period when I had a greater taste for controversy."[5]

B.   Barth Contra Bultmann: Intensified Debate

Nonetheless, Barth's debate with Bultmann did not abate. He recalls that a few years after the war increasing numbers of German theological students crossed the border to study theology in Basel. Concerning the more serious and aggressively theological German students, Barth observed: "These Germans were again a source of amazement to other nationalities and especially us Swiss because of their delight in mulling everything over and discussing it."[6] Among their chief concerns were questions about Bultmann. In the course of Barth's seminar in the summer of 1951 on Schleiermacher's, The Christian Faith, Busch notes that "Bultmann's burning questions were constantly in the background... ."[7]

The widening intensity of the Bultmann controversy in the early fifties led Barth to accede to student pressure in Basel "to tackle the arguments of the Marburg teacher directly."[8] His projected seminar in the winter semester of 1951-52, "Kerygma and Myth," resulted in a "room...crammed full of people--more than ever before."[9] Regarding his approach to the seminar, Barth wrote: "The interest of the students make it inevitable that this time the questions raised by Bultmann and those prompted by him, and the arguments used on both sides, should dominate the discussion in a lively and sometimes heated fashion. It could not be our concern to resolve them in any way."[10]

II. BULTMANN ANSWERS BARTH: "THE PROBLEM OF HERMENEUTICS" (1950)

In the year 1950, Bultmann's first public reply to Barth's extensive attack on his position appeared with the title, "The Problem of Hermeneutics." In this essay, he surveys the history of hermeneutics and applauds the way in which, through the influence of Schleiermacher and later Dilthey, interpretation of texts was seen to require more than simply reconstructing the past as practiced by the earlier "historical school." Heidegger and Fritz Kaufmann built on the approach of Dilthey and give rise to what Bultmann calls an existential mode of interpreting texts. Through its application, the understanding of human existence enshrined in the text and its relevance for interpreting both the historical existence of the original author and the contemporary interpreter may be determined. Appropriate questions put to the text guide the quest for understanding the text: Bultmann designates this as the "prior" or "pre-understanding" with which one comes to the text. Bultmann thus maintains the axiom: "The presupposition of every comprehending interpretation is a previous living relationship to the subject, which directly or indirectly finds expression in the text and which guides the direction of the enquiry."[11] Though the interpreter's interest guiding inquiry of the text may be quite varied, Bultmann contends that the attempt to uncover the understanding of existence enshrined within texts is an especially appropriate line of investigation of poetic, philosophical and religious texts. He describes the function of this hermeneutical principle:

> ...the object of interpretation can be established by interest in history as the sphere of life in which human existence moves, in which it attains its possibilities and develops them, and in reflection upon which it attains understanding of itself and of its own particular possibilities.[12]

Bultmann appears to have Barth and other critics in mind in posing the "dubious" question "whether objectivity in the knowledge of historical phenomena, objectivity in interpretation, is attainable."[13] He answers that it is a misconception to make natural science based upon nature the model for

> the comprehension of historical phenomena; for these are of a different kind from those of nature. They do not exist as historical phenomena at all, without the historical subject which comprises them. For facts of the past only become significant for a subject which itself stands in history and is involved in it; only when they have something to say; and that they only do for the subject which comprehends them."[14]

A.   Divergent Approaches Compared

In conclusion, Bultmann shows how his hermeneutic stands opposed to that of his detractor, Barth.   The first point at issue relates to Barth's rejection of Bultmann's axiom that the interpreter of the New Testament--like the interpreter of any kind of literature--comes to the text with a "prior understanding of the subject."[15]   He appears to have Barth in mind as holding "that the subject about which the Holy Scriptures, and especially the New Testament, speak is the action of God, of which there can be absolutely no prior understanding, as the natural man does not have a previous relationship to God, but can only know of him through the revelation of God, that is, to be precise, by his action."[16]   Bultmann's rejoinder is that "man, of course, can have just as little a prior understanding of God's action becoming a reality in an event, as he can of other events taken as events."[17]   However, to comprehend any historical event requires that one "must certainly have a prior understanding of the historical possibilities within which they gain their significance and so their character as historical events."[18]

In the case of comprehending biblical texts as "records about events as the action of God," there would need to be a "prior understanding of what may in [any] case be termed the action of God--let us say, as distinct from man's action, or from natural events."[19]   To Barth's apparent rebuttal that one cannot know God or what his action might be prior to his revelation of himself, Bultmann states that "we have to reply that man may very well be aware who God is, namely, in the inquiry about him.   If his existence were not motivated (whether consciously or unawares) by the inquiry about

God in the sense of the Augustinian '<u>Tu</u> <u>nos</u> <u>fecisti</u> <u>ad</u>
<u>Te, et cor nostrum inquietum est, donec requiescat in</u>
<u>Te</u>', then neither would he know God as God in any mani-
festation of him."[20]   In Bultmann's view, therefore,
there is an "<u>existentiell</u> [ontic] knowledge about God"
in the quest for salvation or in the quest for an answer
to the meaning of one's personal existence.   But the
interpreter's prior understanding with which he comes to
the New Testament as, for example, with the question
concerning salvation, does not necessarily find corroboration in the New Testament.   "The inquiry directed
at the New Testament must be prepared for a correction
of the notion it brings with it in hearing what the New
Testament has to say."[21]

    It must be noted that Bultmann makes a clear dis-
tinction between the rigorous scientific or phenomenolo-
gical analysis of human existence by means of a "philosophical, or existential analysis of human being" as a
prerequisite for interpreting what the New Testament
says about human existence on the one hand, and on the
other of "paying simple heed to what the New Testament
says--which is directed towards an <u>existentiell</u> understanding of the self, and not towards an existential
knowledge."[22] The former philosophical interpretation of
human existence and knowledge of the appropriate categories arising therefrom do provide the necessary backdrop for making "Scripture itself speak as a power which
has something to say to the present, to present-day
existence."[23] Bultmann concludes with the characteristic
emphasis of his hermeneutic, namely, the identification
of the quest for self-understanding and the inquiry
about God.

> If the object of interpretation is designated
> as the inquiry about God and the manifestation
> of God, this means, in fact, that it is the
> inquiry into the reality of human existence.
> But then interpretation has to concern itself
> with the abstract facets of the existential
> understanding of existence.[24]

A second and related issue Bultmann addresses is Barth's rejection of his existential interpretation of the New Testament. Bultmann finds his own view warranted because a theological statement "can only be valid when it can show itself to be a genuine component part of the Christian understanding of <u>human</u> existence."[25] Barth's rejoinder is that theological propositions which are "interpretations of scriptural pronouncements" have the being and activity of God as their primary referent; secondarily, they refer to an understanding of Christian existence. Bultmann takes sharp exception to Barth's accusation that his method reduces theological statements to "propositions about the inner life of man." He counters in holding that existential interpretation in no way understands the inner self as though it were isolated from that which encounters it. Rather, "the latter existential interpretation seeks to contemplate and to understand the real existence (in history) of man, who exists only in a living connection with what is 'different' from him--only in encounters. And existential analysis is concerned with the relevant abstract sphere in which that might occur."[26]

In the third place, Bultmann questions whether it is legitimate for Barth to agree that the resurrection is not a historical fact which can be established by means of "historical science" on the one hand while still asserting on the other that the resurrection and

other events "have really taken place as history in time
far more certainly than everything which the 'historian'
can establish as such... ."[27] According to Bultmann, this
is double-talk and he demands that Barth "give an
account of his body of abstract categories!"[28] He continues: "It is perfectly clear that Barth is interpreting the pronouncements of Scripture by means of an
imported body of abstract categories."[29]

A fourth criticism of Barth has to do with
Bultmann's charge that he is, indeed, guilty of exempt-
ing the events of salvation-history knowable to faith
from all verification by historical canons otherwise
universally applicable. Such a view makes it difficult
to distinguish faith from blind assent. "In what sense
is Barth appealing to an imperative of truthfulness,
which is of a higher or different kind from that for-
bidding us to consider anything true, which contradicts
the truths actually presupposed in the understanding I
have of the world--the understanding which is the guide
for all my activity."[30] Whereas Bultmann views his own
"existential interpretation of myth" as a methodical
attempt to discover "the possibility of a valid meaning
for the mythical picture of the world," Barth's eclectic
approach to myth fails to clarify "his principle of
selection" and results in "only arbitrary assertions."[31]

III. BARTH'S REPLY: "RUDOLF BULTMANN--AN ATTEMPT TO
     UNDERSTAND HIM" (1952)

Before Barth published his critique of Bultmann
growing out of his seminar and his further "Attempt to
Understand Him" appearing late in 1952, he was paid a
visit by Bultmann in Basel in April, 1952. The two
aging warriors gathered with friends at the Charon, one

of Barth's favorite local haunts. Busch relates that
Barth "put his questions" and "found his Marburg friend
more open than ever before to his objections."[32] Char-
lotte von Kirschbaum was present and reported Bultmann's
response in a letter: "He [Bultmann] thought that he
should think through the matter of the "objective subject" of faith again. That was indeed a gap."[33]

Barth prepared his further questions to Bultmann in
an essay in the summer of 1952 and published it with the
ironic title, "Rudolf Bultmann--An Attempt to Understand
Him." He prefaces his remarks saying: "I must confess
I know of no contemporary theologian who has so much to
say about understanding, or one which has so much cause
to complain of being misunderstood."[34]

A.   The Placement of Bultmann in the History of
      Theology

Before considering the substantive questions Barth
puts to Bultmann in this essay, it may prove helpful to
refer first to his continuing attempt to locate Bultmann
"in the history of theological development."

1. Bultmann: a Modern Rationalist? Bultmann's
name suggests one who above all else champions the
modern world view in contradistinction to the Ptolemaic
and mythological world view dominant in antiquity, the
Bible and much of Christian history. As the children of
modernity stemming from the Enlightenment, much of what
appears in the New Testament is both obsolete and unintelligible to us, according to Bultmann. Barth remarks:
"He looks like a rationalist with the austere Marburg
passion for sincerity! A new David Friedrich Strauss!"[35]
By adopting the "modern world view and modern thought as
his criterion," Bultmann stands squarely in the

tradition of modern thought more exercised about
methodological issues than with substantive results.[36]
Though Barth maintains the truth of his critique of
Bultmann at this point, he reminds too facile critics
that demythologizing represents only the negative side
of the latter's program which is intended "to make room
for his existentialist interpretation. ..."[37] Moreover,
whereas Barth finds Strauss, the nineteenth-century
rationalist, absolutizing the modern world view,
Bultmann "knows it is only relative." The fact remains,
however, that for Barth understanding Bultmann in this
regard would be made simpler had he "said so in so many
words."[38]

　　　2. Bultmann: a Modern Apologist? Or is it preferable, Barth asks, to interpret Bultmann in Schleiermacher's tradition sharing the common concern "to make
Biblical exegesis, theology in general, and preaching in
particular, relevant and interesting for its cultured
despisers?"[39] Much commends this interpretation although
Bultmann finds it annoying. Clearly, his demythologization of the gospel and its translation into existential
categories so as to commend it--properly understood--to
his contemporaries is important. Yet Barth concludes:
"...this is only one side of his work, and hardly the
most important side for him."[40]

　　　3. Bultmann: a Scientific Historian? Another
possibility is to regard Bultmann as a scientific
historian in the "great tradition" of nineteenth-century
scientific historical inquiry. His impressive produc-
tivity as an "academic scholar" lends credence to those
who so interpret him. Yet Barth rejects this understanding of him as, at best, partial. Rather than
viewing him as a scientific historian approaching the
New Testament asking, "what actually happened," Barth

finds his handling of the texts reveal "the skill of a very determined systematic historian."[41] Barth designates the agenda informing Bultmann's method as follows: "There is a good deal of intellectual, if not spiritual pathos in his writings, the onesidedness of which has a rather sectarian attraction, and is certainly strongly religious. And this has nothing to do with pure history."[42]

4. Bultmann: a Proponent of a New Philosophy? Another interpretation sees him as yet another theologian in the history of the church who has adopted some philosophy as the medium through which best to express Christian faith. That Bultmann discovered Heidegger's existentialism to be just such a vehicle is not sufficient reason, according to Barth, to dismiss him. "There is an element of philosophy in all theological language."[43] What Barth finds problematic in Bultmann is that he "attaches such an exclusive importance to his use of existentialism, and indeed it is the very hallmark of his theology which is what makes it such a problem."[44] Hence it is comprehensible why some interpret Bultmann primarily as a philosophical existentialist. On the other hand, Barth notes that Bultmann has warned critics making this charge that he uses existentialism as a tool to facilitate the translation of the gospel. It was Buri—and not Bultmann—"who said that one particular type of existentialism was the only true theology."[45] Notwithstanding Bultmann's protests against being interpreted primarily as a philosopher rather than as a theologian utilizing existentialism—in Barth's words—"merely as a tool"—the latter comments wryly: "A tool which turns out to be the key to open all, or nearly all, the locks is a very remarkable one indeed."[46]

5. <u>Bultmann: a Lutheran</u>? "Yes," answers Barth. "Let me boldly suggest that the nearest solution will be that Bultmann is simply a Lutheran--<u>sui generis</u>, of course!"[47] This hypothesis is tenable since Melanchthon, the first Protestant systematician and "faithful disciple of the young Luther," is "apparently already moving consciously and exclusively within the anthropological triangle of law, sin and grace, law being interpreted as natural law."[48] In short, Barth finds the anthropological and soteriological concentration of the young Luther and Melanchthon to be characteristic of much of the subsequent Lutheran tradition including Kierkegaard, the pietist Tholuck, Albrecht Ritschl, and Wilhelm Herrmann, acknowledged by Bultmann as his influential teacher. Barth surmises that it was probably Herrmann--before Bultmann even knew of Heidegger--who influenced him by "... his constant simplification of the Christian message, his emphasis on its ethical and anthropological aspects."[49] Barth finds this Lutheran concentration on the "application of salvation to man" typical of Bultmann as well. While conceding that Bultmann's Lutheranism is "not the whole story," Barth concludes: "Bultmann's work is inconceivable apart from his Lutheran background."[50]

Earlier in his essay, Barth comments further on Bultmann's theological lineage in connection with the "Tübingen Memorandum" drafted by two Protestant theological faculties and containing comments for and against Bultmann. This Memorandum published in 1952 states that Bultmann's theology combined two theological strands found in twentieth century theology, namely, the "return to the Reformation and its theology, the other the liberalism of the eighteenth and nineteenth centuries."[51]

While agreeing that Bultmann's roots are traceable
first of all to the liberal tradition, Barth suggests he
is better understood as "one of the pioneers of form
criticism." The latter approach displaced the dominant
"history of religions school" in the twenties of this
century. Barth recalls that he and others of like mind,
including Bultmann, were interested in the possibility
that form criticism would provide something better than
the results of liberal exegesis. "It looked like the
beginning of a new appreciation for the objective
character of the New Testament documents."[52]   That
Bultmann, the form critic, could identify himself with
the dialectical theologians surrounding Barth and join
in the publication of its journal, Zwischen den Zeiten,
Barth explains as follows:

> All of us found in the kerygma (which, as
> Bultmann has himself so frequently emphasized
> since, is directed against the history of
> religions school) a common terminology for our
> enterprise. We thought we understood him and
> we believed he understood us. We were all
> trying to hear and reproduce better the real
> message of the New Testament.[53]

To Barth's chagrin, Bultmann carried this better understanding of the New Testament in the direction of translating it from one language into another--a move neither
anticipated by his colleagues nor intrinsic to that
methodology. Barth laments: "I still cannot see how it
was [as] a form critic that Bultmann came to set such
store by translation as his primary concern, as he has
done since."[54]

The designation by the Memorandum of the Reformation heritage as the second strand of Bultmann's theology, Barth accepts only with reservations.   On the

positive side, it may be that Bultmann was influenced by
the aforementioned Lutheran focus on soteriology and
justification. That Barth himself may have directed
Bultmann to the Reformation may be the case even though
Barth notes that his own recovery thereof did not provide the initial impetus to his own reorientation.
Nonetheless, Bultmann, "in all essentials a Lutheran,"
did cast in his lot with the circle of dialectical
theologians in the twenties. Barth views his move thus:

> As a form critic he was able, and as a thinker
> stimulated by the Reformation and particularly
> by Luther (though no doubt indirectly, rather
> than directly) he was bound, to give his
> support to the "theology of the Word" as it
> was called in those days, and to put the
> kerygma at the centre of his theology.[55]

6. Bultmann: a Theologian in the Enlightenment
Tradition. The fact that Bultmann carried out his
program of "understanding" and "expounding" the New
Testament in the direction of "translating" it into a
new conceptuality precludes identifying him with the
Reformation tradition. Barth cites approvingly the
authors of the "Tübingen Memorandum" who locate Bultmann
in the theological tradition responding positively to
the Enlightenment. "For more than two centuries theology has been preoccupied with the Enlightenment, the new
understanding of man and the world based on reason and
revelation which had penetrated the whole of Western
civilization."[56] In contrast to the Reformers, who in no
way found it necessary to establish theological judgments by appeal to norms extraneous to the Bible and its
theme, it appears that Bultmann embraces the Enlightenment tradition in his concentration on what Barth terms
"the problem of translation." He continues: "For that

was the theme of the anti-Reformation, or at least the
un-Reformation, during those two hundred years. I would
like to know where Bultmann stands, but this problem
baffles me, I am afraid."[57]

B.   Bultmann's Theological Agenda

It may prove instructive to follow Barth's analysis
of Bultmann's position and his own further responses and
questions.
      1. Bultmann's Intention. In order to clarify the
discussion for and against Bultmann which appears to be
in a rut, Barth states his view of what he conceives
Bultmann to be about. "First, I hope I am not wrong
when I say that Bultmann's primary aim is to present the
New Testament as the document of a message (kerygma,
proclamation, preaching)."[58] It follows for him that the
New Testament cannot be understood if "our object is to
extract general or theoretical propositions about God,
the world or man, or even neutral historical data about
events which happened long ago, or the record of religious, mystical devotional or even ethical experiences
which happened once and can happen again to-day."[59] The
sole possibility for appropriating its meaning is to
believe the message, the Word of God, it proclaims.
Through faith's response to that word, one is confronted
by God. This "existential" act of appropriation "en-
ables us to understand ourselves by understanding the
message."[60]
      Barth's caveat at this point recalls his objection
to equating response to the gospel with a new self-
understanding. He fears that Bultmann's correlation of
the appropriation of the message with self-
understanding leads to a preoccupation with the believer

rather than with the One who is trusted. Moreover,
Barth finds all self-understanding to be called in
question through God's approach. "How can I understand
and explain my faith, of all things, unless I turn away
from myself and look to where the message I believe in
calls me to look?"[61]

2. Translating the New Testament Message. It is
further clear to Bultmann that the "unique message" of
the New Testament which bears witness to the Word made
flesh is expressed in the language, ideology and thought
forms of its times. Though the interpreter must first
comprehend the New Testament in its original form, it
can only become meaningful to hearers in later ages when
translated into a contemporary idiom. Barth sums up
Bultmann's intention along these lines: "The substance
of the message may be the same, but its form must be
different to-day from that of yesterday. Its form must
be understood and expounded anew to-day."[62]

While acknowledging that the task of translating
the gospel into different thought forms is a perennial
necessity for the preaching and teaching church, Barth
finds this to be a second order rather than a first
order task. Whereas Bultmann appears to focus attention
on the need to reinterpret the ancient medium in which
the New Testament message is expressed, Barth's primary
concern is the Subject of the message. Or to use his
earlier language, it appears that Bultmann is obsessed
with the translation of the message into a new form
rather than with its substance. It seems to Barth that
Bultmann and his modern predecessors are the "blessed
possessors" of the New Testament message who need only
to translate it for their contemporaries. Barth concludes with this question to Bultmann: "Does not what
the New Testament says in its particular historical

form, or rather, does not he who meets me as I read it, stand out in almost every verse, in gigantic proportions? Does not it--or he--continually cry out for a new enquiry about himself?"[63] If this, in fact, is the case, is it not precipitant to concentrate on translating the gospel for modern man apart from a continuing wrestling with the One with whom we have to do?

3. <u>The Content of the Kerygma</u>. Decisive for Barth's analysis is his depiction of Bultmann's understanding of the content of the kerygma. In the latter's view, the kerygma always concerns the "two factors which govern all human existence." First, it reveals the nature of human existence as fallen. Second, it proclaims a new mode of existence calling for acceptance. The response of faith which issues in the transition from the state of inauthentic to authentic existence is brought about in unity with a third factor Barth describes as follows: "This is the saving act of God as experienced and known to faith and completed in the transition just mentioned. This succession, not in time but in fact, is a constant theme of Bultmann's, and is integral to our understanding of him."[64]

C.   Barth's Critique of Bultmann's "Kerygma"

Barth opposes Bultmann's position directly: "I cannot say I recognize in this translation the basic pattern of the New Testament message."[65]   He identifies Bultmann's approach with Melancthon's formula: "This is to know Christ, to know his benefits."

1. <u>Bultmann's Subjectivism</u>. While admitting the rightful place of this stress on the appropriation of the saving grace of Christ in contrast to an "abstract objectivism," Barth accuses Bultmann of adopting an

"abstract subjectivism" as a "kind of systematic principle." That is to say, he gives priority to the
believer's appropriation of the kerygma while Barth
finds that the New Testament accentuates the priority of
the saving act of God in Christ. For Bultmann to affirm
the latter means to speak primarily about human experience. The fact that he adopts this principle precludes
his doing justice to the pattern of the New Testament
even though he may appeal to modern ways of thinking.[66]

2. On Inauthentic Existence. Barth alludes to yet
a further difficulty in Bultmann's depiction of the
nature and knowledge of man's existence as fallen.
First, he finds his equation of the mode of inauthentic
existence as reliance on the sphere of tangible reality
and authentic existence as reliance upon the intangible
reality to be abstract and Platonic rather than biblical
in provenance. Moreover, he fears that even though
Bultmann states that the pre-understanding which fallen
humans have of their condition is corrected and deepened
by hearing the New Testament message, his conceptualiza-
tion of fallenness tends toward abstraction and does not
approximate the radical human fallenness addressed by
the gospel. Barth's contention is that human self-
understanding which views fallenness in terms of human
vacillation between the tangible and intangible spheres
is still abstract and not equatable with the judgment on
human sinfulness declared in the Word of God
encountering man. In adopting a rather Platonic and
abstract way of understanding sin, Bultmann follows the
Protestant orthodox line which conceives of sin in terms
indebted to the natural law tradition. Barth suggests
his own more concrete and christocentric approach in
speaking about the knowledge of sin in concluding his
critique of Bultmann: "For in describing sin

abstractly, apart from what God has done to remove it, he is, by and large, following the line of orthodoxy."[67]

3. On Authentic Existence. Bultmann's interpretation of authentic existence and the life of faith also meets with Barth's disapproval. He questions whether the natural man's pre-understanding already affords the vision of authentic existence requiring only to be filled out by the kergyma. Moreover, Bultmann's typical depiction of the Christian life--as "detachment from the world"--though echoing certain Pauline notes--is too formal and legalistic to encompass the New Testament view of the life of faith as one of gratitude to a gracious God. And once again, Bultmann is able to speak of God's saving act in Jesus Christ only secondarily, "...as a reflection in the mirror of Christian existence... ."[68]

4. On the Transition from the Old Life to the New Life. A still more serious flaw in Bultmann's rendering of the kerygma relates to the way the transition from the old life to the new is related to Jesus Christ. On the one hand, Barth finds him stating that the kerygma grounds the transition from inauthentic to authentic existence in the "Christ event." This stress provides for the linkage of the kerygma with the life, preaching and death of Jesus of Nazareth. On the other hand, Bultmann understands the transition as the "Christ event." Though according to the latter view, the transition had its origin in Jesus Christ, the kerygma is now equated with the transition in itself. Barth asks: "...is the content of the kerygma not the man Jesus, but the transition, and the obedience of faith which that transition demands?"[69]

5. Soteriology Absorbs Christology. In this dispute, Barth observes that Bultmann rightly insists

"on the unity of christology and soteriology, and the kerygma as the proclamation of this unity."[70] It is quite another matter when Christology is merged into soteriology. Barth juxtaposes what he perceives to be the way the New Testament relates Christ and the kerygma and Bultmann's way as follows:

> Kerygma of the Christ event? That I could understand. But it is hardly what Bultmann means. Christ event in and through the kerygma? That is what he seems to mean. And I cannot understand that as a reproduction or translation of the New Testament kerygma. That Christ is the kerygma is what the New Testament appears to say, not that Christ is the kerygma.[71]

Barth finds puzzling the manner in which a robust New Testament christology and its account of the transition—beyond all human possibilities—from the old life to the new through Christ is replaced in Bultmann with a kerygma about the transition itself which is only loosely related to Jesus Christ. "What if the point of [the] kerygma is the summons of faith it addresses to its hearers and the demand that summons imposes upon them? Is the kerygma, thus conceived, a gospel—a kerygma in which nothing is said of that in which or of him in whom its recipients are to believe? What is it but a new law?"[72] It seems to Barth that Bultmann is in danger of transposing the New Testament kerygma which points to an "act of God" into that which speaks rather of a human act of obedience through which the transition from the old to the new life is realized.

D. Cross and Resurrection: Center of the Christ
Event and the Kerygma

In order to comprehend Bultmann's view of the
kerygma, Barth finds it crucial to determine what
meaning he attaches to the assertion that "the Christ
event took place 'for us,' pro nobis?"[73] The issue is
whether Bultmann means to say something more than that
the kerygma is a matter of great concern or significance
for us.

1. The Cross. For Bultmann the first element
constituting the Christ event is the cross. The cross
refers in the first instance to the historical crucifixion of Jesus. A second dimension has to do with
appropriation of its significance by the believer. This
occurs when the word of the cross proclaimed in the
kerygma is heard in faith as the judgment on man's
inauthentic existence. "For the death of Jesus Christ
means that it sets man on the way to a radical, mortal
judgement on his inauthentic being."[74] Barth takes this
to mean that the death of Jesus Christ acquires saving
significance "as the believer appropriates the cross of
Christ and undergoes crucifixion with Jesus Christ."[75]
In this sense, Barth states that Bultmann's point is
that the event of appropriation "is an act of God, the
act of God." Barth continues: "For the origin and
purpose of both--the crucifixion of Jesus Christ as a
historical event and man's faith in its significance--
occur in the sphere of the invisible and intangible and
are, therefore, identical with God."[76]

Barth raises several questions about Bultmann's
interpretation. First, he admits that the cross has
"cosmic" significance, but rejects holding that it "only
acquires this significance by being taken up into the

kerygma and evoking the obedience of faith."[77] Instead
he claims that the New Testament describes the cross in
terms of its "inherent significance" which accounts for
the fact that "it can become significant in the kerygma
and for the faith of its recipients."[78] Second, Barth
admits that the New Testament and Bultmann speak "of the
passion and death of Jesus as being completed in the
life of the believers. ..."[79] However, he disagrees with
Bultmann's contention that faith is incomplete apart
from the believer's personal appropriation of the
significance of the cross. He fears Bultmann's interpretation of faith is too introspective thereby loosing
its grounding in that which took place "without him and
in spite of him, something which took place for him on
God's initiative in the death of Jesus Christ. ...Bult-
mann's doctrine of the cross looks suspiciously like
Catholic passion mysticism."[80] Third, Barth agrees with
Bultmann's point that the New Testament "proclaims the
death of Christ in such a way as to include faith in its
significance as God's incomprehensible--and we might
even say paradoxical--act of salvation."[81] On the other
hand, Barth holds that the New Testament teaches that
the death of Jesus Christ--despite obscurities--is
intelligible and meaningful in itself. Barth depicts
something of the "contours and colours" he finds in the
witness to Jesus Christ in the New Testament. "I think
I can see light falling from both sides here: it was
not just anybody who was crucified, it was God the Lord
who humbled himself and became a servant and man; he was
the servant exalted by God to be the Lord, vindicated as
the witness and prophet of the kingdom of God."[82]

Barth concludes his critique of Bultmann's tendency
to reduce the saving significance of the cross to its
actualization in the present moment of faith. For

Bultmann, Jesus is, as it were, the inaugurator of eschatological salvation. For Barth, as noted in his debate with Reinhold Niebuhr, eschatological salvation has been actualized and effected once in behalf of all through the cross of Jesus Christ. Barth fears that in Bultmann's view the cross tends to be a brute fact, leaving unclear how or why it is God's saving act. Most disturbing is Bultmann's flirtation with the view that Jesus went to the cross "to prove his divine Sonship and demonstrate the supreme paradox of his faith. ..."[83] Bultmann's evident difficulty in finding any inherent significance in the cross is related to the problematic nature of his view of the Christ event as a whole. This comes to expression in a "notorious passage from Bultmann himself" which presents Barth with a real stumbling block in his attempt to understand him. Bultmann wrote: "The saving efficacy of the cross is not derived from the fact that it is the cross of Christ: it is the cross of Christ because it has this saving efficacy."[84] Barth comments: "I should find it difficult to expound it [i.e., the latter statement] in any sense consistent with the New Testament message."[85]

2. The Resurrection. Barth turns to the analysis of Bultmann's view of the resurrection constituting the second element of the kerygma and the Christ event. He reiterates that for Bultmann the resurrection refers to "the revelation of the saving significance of the cross."[86] Thus the resurrection has to do with the emergence of the "Easter faith" in the disciples who therewith acknowledge the significance of Jesus Christ and his cross as saving. In Bultmann's account, this faith gives rise to the kerygma and the church.

Barth interprets Bultmann as teaching that the link between cross and resurrection obtains because the

saving significance of the cross is renewed continually
through the rise of faith. This total happening is what
Bultmann terms the "eschatological event of redemption."
The rise of Easter faith in this view seems to Barth to
refer solely to the subjective and noetic appropriation
of the event of redemption. "Yet apparently even here,
nothing can be said about its being an act of God on its
own right quite apart from its happening in the kerygma
and in faith."[87]

As in the case of the crucifixion, Barth finds
Bultmann guilty of robbing the resurrection of Jesus
Christ of all objectivity. He is not able to speak of
Jesus being raised from the dead or of appearing to his
disciples. All references to his resurrection are
reinterpreted to refer to the rise of faith within the
disciples. Barth asks:

> Does everything indeed depend on the priority
> of the personal resurrection of Jesus Christ
> over every other resurrection there may be in
> the kerygma, in faith, in the Church or in the
> sacraments? Can we give the same priority to
> our own resurrection in him?.. .[Bultmann]
> seems to think that in the kerygma Jesus
> Christ is on his way to rising in us. And
> that is just why I cannot understand him.[88]

Barth completes his assessment of Bultmann's interpretation of the cross and resurrection by contending
that the latter has replaced the objectivity of the
cross and resurrection of Jesus Christ as acts of God
with the transition from inauthentic to authentic existence. He writes:

> Here then it would seem is the act of God
> which is presupposed in the dialectic of human
> existence, or rather in man's transition from
> the old existence to the new. In its ontic

aspect it is crucifixion; noetically it is the Easter event. This is the Christology contained in Bultmann's soteriology and deducible from it.[89]

E.   Bultmann's Demythologizing

It is Barth's opinion that Bultmann's coining of the word, demythologization, represents a "barbarism" and is "unnecessarily provoking." It accounts, in part, for the widespread negative reaction to his position. In point of fact, Barth has addressed some of the positive conclusions of Bultmann's exegesis which he deems more important than the "negative side" of his program evident in "demythologizing proper."

Since the outlines of Bultmann's demythologizing program were treated above,[90] our discussion must be restricted to major questions Barth raises. First, it may be recalled that for Bultmann the contemporary interpreter of the New Testament must reinterpret those elements in the New Testament reflective of "the distinctive world view of late Judaism and Hellenistic gnosticism...[and] everything that corresponds to that world view in the New Testament portrayal of salvation."[91] Bultmann separates himself from liberal exegetes who excised the latter in his aim to reinterpret the New Testament's mythological imagery into language and imagery which is comprehensible today. Barth asks: "Is the essential meaning of these elements and the function they fulfil still recognizable in spite of the different form in which they are expressed?"[92] Put differently, Barth asks whether the intent of New Testament imagery dealing with the transcendent, or the pre-existence and post-existence of Jesus Christ, or the eschatological consummation can be understood only when

it has been translated into a contemporary idiom?
Barth's surmise is that Bultmann and his followers have
lumped these elements "together as a series of curiosities" without due attention to the context in which they
occur in the New Testament and "the value attached to
them in their context."[93]   Moreover, Barth finds it
puzzling that Bultmann locates these "structural
idiosyncrasies" through his historical analysis "treating them separately" as "the problem of all problems for
New Testament exegesis. ..."[94]

Bultmann's reinterpretation involves all of the
essential elements of the kerygma "except those...which
are untranslatable, such as the three-storied universe,
Satan and the demons, the angels, the virgin birth, the
empty tomb and the ascension."[95] The remaining "important elements" calling for re-interpretation Barth
designates as follows:

> There is sin, death; God, his revelation in
> Christ and in Christ alone; the Holy Spirit,
> the divine sonship of the believers, the
> Church and even the sacraments and the escha-
> tological hope, the last being the dominant
> principle.[96]

These elements call for "existential translation"
in Bultmann's view because they "are couched in the
thought and language of the world of those days."[97] On
the basis of this "cardinal principle of criticism,"
Bultmann demythologizes the mythological language in
which "the divine is described in terms of this world,
the other side in terms of this side, the non-objective
as objective."[98] The New Testament writers use the
language of myth to speak of the "power or powers" which
humans experience as the "ground and limit" of their
world and of their "own activity and sufferings.   In

this form myth is an expression of man's self-understanding."[99] Since the mythological view of the world and of human existence portrayed in the New Testament are obsolete and not essential to the message itself, Bultmann finds their reinterpretation justifiable. This is demanded not only because Bultmann finds this process begun in the Gospel of John, but also because the modern understanding of self and world require it if the New Testament is to be intelligible.

1. Barth's Further Questions. Barth raises several issues about demythologizing. First, is it not more appropriate for an interpreter to come to any text in an attitude of openness without prejudging between form and substance? And is it not true that Bultmann comes to the text already knowing that it must be translated in order to be comprehensible? "Is not Bultmann's very concept of myth, the infallible criterion which dominates his hermeneutics, quite alien to the New Testament?"[100]

Second, Barth queries whether Bultmann's call for honesty on the part of the exegete entails being responsible primarily to modern canons of thought "or to the actual text he is trying to understand, and to the criterion to be derived from its spirit, content and aim?"[101] Third, Barth questions whether it is correct to maintain that all mythological language is meaningless today. "Why should not the divine be described in terms of human life, the other-worldly in terms of this world, the non-objective as objective?"[102] Fourth, is it not the case that Bultmann has adopted "too formal a definition of myth" which fails to deal adequately with "the content rather than the form" of the New Testament? Barth concedes that New Testament writers borrowed much of their imagery from their environment, but "it could hardly have occurred to them to produce their message as the proclamation of general cosmic truths disguised as a tale about the gods and their doings."[103]

Given Bultmann's "crude definition of myth," the decisive theological issue is the way the demythologized kerygma speaks of the relationship between God and the world. Barth's critical reservations and questions deserve citation:

> Is the demythologized kerygma allowed to say anything about God's having condescended to become this-worldly, objective and--horror of horrors!--datable? ...Nor can it admit that it originated in the concrete fact that the disciples saw with their own eyes, heard with their ears, touched with their hands, in space and time, not only the dereliction of the Word made flesh hanging on the cross, but also the glory of the same Word made flesh risen from the dead. ...Apparently the demythologized kerygma must remain silent about what causes faith. ...Apparently the kerygma must suppress or even deny the fact that the cross and resurrection of Jesus Christ, the total Christ event, is the event of our redemption, that it possessed an intrinsic significance of its own, and that only because it has that primary significance has it a derived significance here and now. ...Apparently the kerygma must suppress or even deny the fact that the Christ event has founded a community which throughout its history has had a Lord distinct from itself, a Lord whom it follows in discipleship. All this would, it seems, have to go by the board if we demythologized the New Testament à la Bultmann. What is the purpose of the alleged mythological elements if not to demonstrate that we are not left alone in this human, worldly, this-worldly, objective existence of ours, that our faith does not depend on some unknown distant deity, some supracosmic transcendent, non-objective reality? ...How else can all this be expressed except in the way Bultmann calls mythological? ...What service is it to modern man, ourselves included, to suppress the cardinal truth of

the kerygma like this? I am most embarrassed: much as I am loath to charge Bultmann with heresy, I cannot deny that his demythologized New Testament looks suspiciously like docetism. Perhaps this has something to do with his inability to make anything of the Old Testament. It is too historical, too down to earth for him! ...And perhaps it also has something to do with his difficulties over the synoptic Jesus. ...I cannot as yet see how this all fits together, but I must confess that if interpreting the New Testament means demythologizing it, and if demythologizing it means what Bultmann with his definition of myth means by it, it seems to have singularly little to do with the gospel of the New Testament.[104]

F.   Bultmann's Existential Interpretation

Once Bultmann has isolated the "problematic elements" of the New Testament, the issue is how they can be reinterpreted. Barth explains Bultmann's intention as follows:

...the only honest exegesis, dogmatics and preaching is the existentialist interpretation. By this he means one which exposes the specifically Christian self-understanding enshrined in the mythological form. Existentialist interpretation understands and explains the New Testament affirmations as existential statements.[105]

This "anthropological" mode of interpretation is warranted because both the message of the New Testament and the mythological idiom in which it is expressed are expressions of human self-understanding.

In Barth's estimate, this approach has great appeal. First, it claims to capture the "real meaning" of the New Testament. Second, it does so by excising the New Testament's mythological language offensive to modern hearers thereby ridding Christian preaching and teaching of a false stumbling block. This existentialist mode of translating its offensive conceptuality makes it unnecessary for modern hearers of the gospel to sacrifice their honesty by accepting an obsolete mythology; the demythologized gospel confronts them with a real choice between faith or unbelief. Barth concedes that this program was highly attractive to the disillusioned post-war generation of theological students in Germany. It seemed to offer them "something to believe and preach. ..." Barth comments: "Demythologizing makes theology so simple. It allows it to concentrate on essentials. ...to get rid of some of the awkward elements in the New Testament canon. ..."[106]

1. Barth's Questions. Again, Barth questions certain assumptions of Bultmann's hermeneutic. First, he adopted the early Heidegger's existentialism as the philosophy. This meant that Bultmann affirmed Heidegger's concept of the "prior-understanding." The latter has to do both with the conception of human understanding itself and with a particular way of comprehending man's self-understanding informed by Heidegger's analysis of human existence. In adopting Heidegger's notion of the pre-understanding in approaching the New Testament texts, Bultmann is committed to viewing human existence within the polarities of inauthenticity and authenticity, past and future. More pointedly, it means that he approaches the New Testament with the supposition that it is concerned first and foremost with an understanding of human existence. Everything which Bultmann says about human existence and the Christ event is determined by this prior understanding. Indeed, according to Barth, the only dimension of the human transition from inauthentic to

authentic existence which Bultmann does not derive from
Heidegger is his "description of the transition as an
act of God."[107]

While admitting Heidegger's significance and
influence both on modern philosophy and theology, Barth
faults Bultmann for canonizing his philosophy more as
the "queen" than the "handmaid" of his theology. Since
Bultmann himself does not think that there is only one
true philosophy, Barth surmises that the sole reason for
his lionization of it is "because it is the philosophy
par excellence of our day and age."[108] However, since
other philosophies abound, why assume that existentialism alone merits such exclusive attention? Barth
finds it more than questionable that existentialism is
the only philosophy through which the gospel may be
communicated to persons today. Also of note is the fact
that the later Heidegger's philosophy went beyond the
anthropological focus of Sein und Zeit (Being and Time)
of 1927 which influenced Bultmann so greatly. On a more
substantive level, Barth comments: "I do not see why I
have to don this particular strait jacket in order to
understand the New Testament."[109] Or again: "Must we
become existentialists on principle, and existentialists
of this particular brand? Is it the indispensable
prerequisite for the understanding of the New Testament,
of all things?"[110]

In the second place, Barth is unconvinced by Bultmann's insistence that myth requires to be understood
solely as the expression of human self-understanding.
Historically, myth's referents far transcend the human
sphere and therewith an exclusively anthropological
interpretation.

Thirdly, the more serious theological issue Barth
raises has to do with the way Bultmann's hermeneutic

restricts the New Testament witness to what it says
about human self-understanding. "After all," Barth
comments, "it is the message of Jesus Christ; it asserts
an event between God and man, and it is just as certainly couched in the form of a human testimony."[111]
Hence Barth senses an anthropological reductionism
operative in Bultmann which is in danger of losing the
"Christ event which is determinative of all else, controlling and dominating it."[112] This coupled with Bultmann's general failure to deal with the priority of the
divine activity has "made it difficult, if not impossible, for us to recognize the New Testament message in
this new existentialist garb."[113] The fact, as we saw
above, that Bultmann speaks of the transition from
fallen existence to the believer's new existence in
terms of the "Christ event" represents his break with
existentialism. But Barth laments that Bultmann does
not clarify how it is legitimate to speak here of an act
of God. "Yet even Bultmann himself is not sure whether
the retention of an act of God is compatible with demythologizing, and I do not think he has answered his
question satisfactorily."[114] All of this leads to Barth's
personal comment regarding whether Bultmann's mode of
interpreting the New Testament leads, in fact, to an
authentic commendation of the gospel. "Speaking for
myself, I must say I find it hard to imagine how Bultmann could inspire me to study theology, to preach, or
even to believe."[115]

G.   Summation: "Bultmann has forsaken our road..."

Barth's concluding assessment in his attempt to
understand Bultmann deals with two issues. First, what
is involved in "understanding the New Testament?"[116]

Barth takes it to be axiomatic that "to understand the
New Testament kerygma means to understand in faith the
Word of God to which it bears witness."[117] Such a stance
precludes making one's pre-understanding (Vorver-
ständnis) in Bultmann's sense the absolute precondition
for hearing the witness of the text. Clearly, Barth
knows that all come to the New Testament with particular
preconceptions by which we try "to incorporate and
domesticate its strange elements. But have we any right
to elevate all this into a methodological principle? To
defy that strangeness with a 'thus far and no
further'"?[118] It really makes no difference whether this
pre-understanding is shaped by a world view, particular
philosophy or some combination thereof. Whatever the
shape of such a prior understanding, it precludes an
"open-minded approach" to the text. "Let the New Testament serve as the catalyst of our capacity to understand. Do not make our capacity to understand the
catalyst of the New Testament!"[119] Barth cites a statement from Luther's Table Talk as indicative of the
proper approach to the Scriptures:

> Holy Scripture wills to have humble teachers
> who reverence and fear the Word of God,
> teachers who say continually: "Teach me,
> teach me, teach me!" Pride resists the
> Spirit![120]

The second issue concerns "the concept of understanding as such." Barth proposes the axiom: "Biblical
hermeneutics is not so much a specific application of a
general hermeneutics, but the pattern and measure of all
others."[121] Barth alludes often to the utmost open
mindedness possible as a hermeneutical principle
applicable to the reading of any text--including that of

the Bible. This kind of sympathetic listening without prejudgments characterizes all healthy interpersonal relationships as well as much sound therapy and pastoral counselling. Barth speaks of it here in terms of the ideal for interpersonal communication. To realize this ideal in terms of human relationships or in sympathetic comprehension of texts like Goethe's, "the discipline of the Holy Spirit will undoubtedly be necessary."[122] This same illumination of the Holy Spirit is required in order to appreciate "the Old and New Testaments...as a testimony to the Word of God."[123] By making his doctrine of the pre-understanding the normative presupposition informing his approach to, and exegesis of, the text, Bultmann seems to preclude "all right and genuine understanding. For it appears to compete with the Holy Spirit and unduly to restrict his operation."[124]

In a final historical aside, Barth recalls that in the 1920's he and likeminded colleagues were concerned to free theology from an Egyptian bondage where the false gods of philosophy, ideology, world views and the like demanded final allegiance preempting the Word of God. "Although we did not know the Word, we were seeking to demythologize the belief that man was the measure of his own understanding and of all other understanding."[125] Barth speaks of the road chosen as "long and arduous," marked by "many bypaths and false turnings" which repeatedly required "recalling ourselves and our colleagues to the main road." Barth then adds: "Now, as I see it, Bultmann has forsaken our road and gone back to the old one again. He has gone back to the old idea of understanding which we had abandoned. Here is the main reason why I don't want to pursue my attempt to understand him any farther, at any rate for the time being."[126]

Barth surmises that Bultmann's theology may prove dominant in the second half of our century because "younger generations have never known the Egyptian bondage first hand. ..." That is, the bondage of liberalism. Not knowing that captivity, it is not surprising that the "younger" generation "have just found out that there is nothing better than radical criticism, whereas we had found out that there was something even more important."[127]

In conclusion, Barth recalls his final remarks to his "Kerygma and Myth" seminar of 1951-52. He reminded his students how Israel longed for "the flesh pots of Egypt they had left behind, and how soon they got tired of the manna and the quails." Barth writes:

> I ended with a pious hope which I should like to repeat here. If theology in the second half of our century becomes a theology of demythologizing and of existentialist interpretation, with a prior understanding as its sine qua non and its own framework of imagery, let us at least hope that Israel will not be punished with too many quails![128]

H.   Appendix: the End of the Road?

Before publishing his essay, Barth received the second volume of Kerygma und Mythos (1952) dealing with further contributions for and against Bultmann and the latter's response.   Barth expressed regret that Bultmann's reply failed to note significant questions put to him by W. G. Kümmel and Fritz Buri. He chides Bultmann by citing Buri's article calling for a "dekerygmatizing" of theology. Buri wrote: "The kerygma is a last vestige of mythology to which we still illogically cling."[129] Barth views Buri's article as a frontal attack on the "very foundation of his [Bultmann's] theology," which "makes out a good case for itself." With respect to Bultmann's silence regarding Buri, Barth states: "I for one would be most eager to know what the master and his pupils had in mind to counter Buri's arguments."[130] Clearly, Barth never had any sympathy at all for the theology of Buri, his liberal theological colleague at Basel. He wrote his son, Christoph, that "his impression of Buri's theology was that he 'has taken off the bathing trunks which Bultmann is still wearing.'"[131]

Barth's despair over the prospect of any instructive advance in his debate with Bultmann expressed earlier in his own essay is deepened by virtue of this latter publication.[132] He complains of a lack of give and take on both sides as positions harden through repetition. Bultmann's "doggedness" and refusal to budge at all leads to a break down of all real communication. "Can he understand anyone but himself and his own programme? Does it surprise him that there are others who cannot identify themselves with him, cannot understand him, and cannot help misunderstanding him?"[133] It appears that the entire debate "is in danger of getting bogged down in sterility and boredom. ..."[134] This must be the case when the New Testament itself is neglected. "Must demythologizing become a subject of discussion for its own sake? ...Must everyone be concerned with it, and with nothing else? ...No doubt Bultmann will put me in my place. There seems little point in going on with the game any further. Much better to mind our own business."[135]

The sharpness of some of these final comments about Bultmann may have led Barth to dedicate the second edition of his Protestant Theology in the Nineteenth Century to his old friend and nemesis, Bultmann. In a letter to Barth from Marburg dated April 25, 1952, Bultmann wrote: "It was a great and very delightful surprise, when I returned to Marburg, to discover your dedication in the second edition of your Prot. Theol. Receive my sincere thanks and pardon me that for the moment they can only be brief. ...With happy memories of our meeting at the Charon [a Basel hotel] I send sincere greetings, Yours, Rudolf Bultmann."[136]

As soon as his essay on Bultmann was published, Barth sent him a personal copy with his handwritten inscription and the caption: "'O Angel, pardon me!'" (The Marriage of Figaro, 2nd Finale), from the author."[137]

IV. THE FINAL CORRESPONDENCE: THE WHALE AND THE ELEPHANT (1952)

A. Bultmann's Reply: the Issues which Divide Us

Bultmann's letter to Barth is dated November 11-15, 1952. The English translation of sixteen pages makes it by far the lengthiest letter written by either in their correspondence spanning just over forty-four years. In response to Barth's charge that he is difficult to understand, Bultmann appears to echo a statement of the early Barth. He writes: "'Do I understand myself?' For at least when I took the path of demythologizing I did not realize where it would lead, even though I thought I was certain as to its direction."[138]

1. On the View of Reality: Several major differences with Barth surface in his initial comments and later in his letter. First, he insists that a theologian must clarify his epistemological and, more especially, his ontological commitments showing how they are related to philosophy. Concerning these matters,

204

Bultmann writes:

> But I think I always saw one thing clearly,
> namely, that the decisive thing is to make it
> clear with what concept of reality, of being
> and events, we really operate in theology, and
> how this relates to the concepts in which not
> only other people think and speak of reality,
> being, and events, but in which we theologians
> also think and speak in our everyday lives.
> Ontological reflection is thus needed, and I
> think that this may be seen in my essay on the
> christological confession of the World Council
> and the so-called "Abschliessende Stel-
> lungnahme" ["definitive position"] (the title
> is not mine) in Ker. u. Myth., II. If such
> ontological reflection is part of the business
> of theology--and your questions have not made
> me doubtful but simply confirmed me in the
> belief that it is so--it follows that theology
> must concern itself with philosophy, and today
> with the philosophy which has posed the
> ontological question afresh; it must clarify
> its relationship to this.
>
> If you think you do not understand me, is it
> not partly because you do not perceive this
> task, which is in my view posed for theology,
> and consequently have not wrestled seriously
> with existential philosophy? So many of your
> misunderstandings would not, in my view,
> otherwise be possible, e.g., your constant
> discrimination against existential analysis as
> anthropology (in the traditional sense), or
> your trivializing of the distinction between
> "existential" and "existentiell" in the
> amusing note. ...[139]

2. On Existential Interpretation. Second, Bultmann addresses Barth's negative attitude toward the
necessity for translating the New Testament into a
modern idiom to facilitate the preaching of the contemporary church. This requires the excision of the
mythological and cosmological language associated with
the ancient and antiquated world view of the Bible.

I am convinced that this is possible only when
the link between proclamation (in the Bible as

well as the traditional preaching of the
Church) and a dated view of the world is
radically severed. Ultimately we need to be
rid of any link to a world-view of
objectifying thinking...; but first we need
liberation from the mythological world-view of
the Bible, because this has become totally
alien...today, and because the link with it
constitutes an offense--a false one--and
closes the door to understanding. Liberation
from it cannot, in my view, be trivialized as
an incidental or secondary matter; it must
rather be achieved with full and open
criticism.[140]

Bultmann asserts that modern man as technological
man lives his daily life in accordance with "the world
view which is projected by objectifying science, but he
is increasingly aware...that he cannot understand his
own existence in terms of this world view."[141] It is by
virtue of this deepening self-awareness that Bultmann
finds modern man open to the insights of existential
philosophy. However, even though Barth should take more
notice of the prevalent influence of existential
philosophy in terms of its popular influence throughout
Europe, and increasingly in the Anglo-Saxon world, a
heightened self-understanding may arise through
literature and poetry as well as through Heidegger and
existential philosophy. Bultmann remains undaunted in
affirming: "At root nothing matters more than that the
situation of modern man demands an existential interpretation of proclamation. But you do not seem to see
this problem as I do, and therefore you obviously cannot
understand me."[142]

Relative to this issue, Bultmann adds several
comments. He accuses Barth of failing to comprehend
that the new self-understanding which obtains in faith
does not entail an obsessive focus on the new self to

the neglect of the One who encounters him. Nor is it intended to mean that the believer is already a "blessed possessor" of truth. Often Barth and other critics fail to make what Bultmann takes to be a very important distinction. Concerning it, he writes:

> Existential self-understanding (<u>existentielle</u> <u>Selbstverständnis</u>) is being confounded with the existentialist understanding (<u>existentialen</u> <u>Verstehen</u>) of human Being elaborated by philosophical analysis. The affirmations of the latter are certainly meant to be timeless truths...and may pass as such. But existentialist analysis points so to speak beyond itself, by showing (what in itself would be a timeless truth) that existential self- understanding can be appropriated only existentially. In my existential self-understanding (<u>existentielle</u> <u>Selbstverständ-</u> <u>nis</u>) I do not learn what existence means in the abstract [that would be an existentialist understanding], but I understand myself in my concrete here and now, in my concrete encounters.[143]

It follows for Bultmann that even as love for another person which brings a new self-understanding is not a timeless truth effective as a possession, but is vital only with renewed encounters with the one loved, so in like manner, "the self-understanding granted by faith never becomes a possession, but is kept pure only as a response to the repeated encounter of the Word of God, which proclaims the act of God in Christ in such a way as continually to represent it."[144] Barth is wrong to see the translation of the New Testament message as different from understanding it existentially. "I can understand the NT as a word that encounters me only if I take it to be spoken to my existence, and in under-standing it thus I already translate it."[145] Bultmann concurs with Barth that when the understanding of a text issues in faith, this "can be understood only as the gift of the Holy Spirit."[146]

For Bultmann, form criticism makes the issue of translation acute because it points to the difficulty of identifying the original kerygma. "It does not lie plainly before us in certain statements."[147] Accordingly, the Bible's message as the theme of theology calls for continued retranslation. Had not Barth once said that "dogma is an eschatological quantity?" And does not translating the message always involve combating prevailing false self- understandings? Barth fails to see that the Reformation's recovery of the gospel did, in fact, involve a critique of the Roman Catholic view of human existence. Modern theology has to be applauded rather than denigrated for addressing

> that which underlies the modern view of the world and man. The mistake of theology for more than two centuries is really that it did understand the theme correctly, but it did not wrestle with the self-understanding of modern man, but with its scientific objectifications --which is why it also did not question the NT in the matter of self-understanding.[148]

Bultmann agrees that God's action is the starting point for the New Testament witness. But the fact that this is expressed in the "objectifying language of myth" poses the decisive question: "Can the reality of which the NT seeks to speak be grasped by objectifying thought?"[149] Bultmann's aim is to show modern man that the objectifying mythological thought of the Bible is not the real offense. However, although modern man is not committed to the ancient mythology, he is likewise addicted to a false self-understanding based on "objectifying thinking." He, too, tries to find his

security in the objective world he controls.   Bultmann
concludes:

> The thrust of NT thinking, to the degree that
> it is opposed to modern man, lies precisely in
> its shattering of man's certainty and its
> showing him that he can exist authentically
> only in the surrender of certainty and by the
> grace of God. The true offense is at root one
> that is posed for the will. ...Everything
> depends on interpreting the NT "existentially"
> in order that the thrust of its thinking may
> be shown to be in opposition to modern man.[150]

3.   On Sin, Salvation and the Christ Event.
Several of Bultmann's rejoinders deal with disagreements
with Barth about the knowledge of sin, the transition
from the old life to the new and the manner in which
this transition is related to the death and resurrection
of Jesus Christ.   These may be grouped together in order
to see important points of tension between them.   First,
Bultmann rejects Barth's insistence that the knowledge
of sin is "completely new"--that is, knowable only
through Christ.   If that were the case, sin would be
unintelligible. He therefore contends that "existential
analysis" can recognize the phenomenon of sin.   However,
it is only through the confrontation with the Word of
God that the self acknowledges existentially that its
previous quest for security apart from God represents a
false self-understanding and is therefore sin.   Second,
it is not the case that Christian preaching must speak
about the "saving act of God" after one has spoken about
Christian existence; but Bultmann affirms "it is my
conviction that one can do this without harm and that it
must be done today."[151]   Third, regarding the charge that
he subsumes christology beneath soteriology, Bultmann
reiterates that they are a unity.   "Certainly Christ as

God's act precedes my faith. ...But it does not follow
from this that christology must precede soteriology in
theological explication."[152] Fourth, to Barth's charge
that he reduces the "Christ event" solely to the "event
of transition" from the old life to the new, Bultmann
replies that the kerygma "really speaking about God's
act...is itself God's act."[153]

Fifth, though Barth can cite New Testament texts in
which the cross of Jesus Christ has an intrinsic significance apart from faith, this is evidence of a mythological way of speaking which calls for interpretation.
Bultmann states: "I can understand significance only as
a relation."[154] Sixth, Barth held that Bultmann under-
mined the complete efficacy of the suffering and death
of Jesus Christ by accentuating its repetition in the
life of believers. Bultmann asserts that it is a "new
concretization of faith. Faith is in itself already the
(believing) repetition of the suffering and death (and
therewith the resurrection) of Jesus Christ. What else
can it be?"[155] Seventh, Bultmann finds Barth's emphasis
that salvation has been actualized, and not simply
inaugurated, in the death of Jesus Christ to be a somewhat unclear way of saying that it is an "eschatological
happening." Whereas Barth locates the Christ event in
the past, Bultmann states that "my own concern is to
understand the eschatological event as one that cannot
be given a fixed date in this world but is always
present (in proclamation). ... To me the paradox seems
to be that for our vision, for which time is the setting
of the eschatological event, this event seems to be temporal although it puts an end to time."[156] Eighth, there
is what Bultmann cites as his "famous-infamous"
statement which Barth referred to as the "notorious
passage." It reads: "The saving efficacy of the cross

is not derived from the fact that it is the cross of
Christ: it is the cross of Christ because it has this
saving efficacy."[157] Bultmann elaborates his understanding as follows:

> this simply means that it is not possible to
> establish first that Christ's crucifixion is
> the saving event and then to believe (for that
> would mean seeing Jesus as Christ before
> believing him to be so), but that the cruci-
> fixion can be seen as the saving event (and
> Jesus as Christ) only in faith; though
> naturally in such a way that I first believe
> and then confirm that the crucified one is
> Christ. To believe in Christ and understand
> the crucifixion as the same event are one and
> the same thing.[158]

Ninth, with regard to Barth's insistence that one
should speak about the risen Christ "in himself and as
such," Bultmann retorts: "This kind of talk seems to me
to be necessarily mythological. Indeed, it is only in
the kerygma about him and in faith in him, not in historical processes seen in space and time, that the glory
of Christ is beheld or believed."[159] In short, Barth's
attempt to hold to the objectivity and historicity of
the risen Christ is a residue of mythological thinking.
Paraphrasing Barth's emphasis, Bultmann asserts:

> The statement that the first disciples beheld
> the 'glory' of the incarnate Word in a
> resurrection from the dead in time and space,
> that they saw this with their eyes, heard it
> with their ears, and touched it with their
> hands, I regard as sheer mythology; nor does
> it seem to me to catch the real meaning of 1
> John 1:1. And your 'so human, so worldly...,'
> while it may not contradict Luke, certainly
> contradicts John (cf. e.g., 14:18ff.).[160]

Bultmann concedes that the kerygma does not say
that "Jesus Christ moves toward his resurrection in us."

However, the latter phrase could be interpreted as integral to the eschatological event. "Even then, of course," notes Bultmann, "I would say not 'moves toward,' but that the resurrection of Jesus Christ realizes itself 'in us.'"[161]

4. On Hermeneutics and Demythologizing. Another grouping of Bultmann's replies relate to justifying his hermeneutic and demythologizing program. First, regarding Barth's charge that he has lumped all mythological elements together as "curiosities" and made them the "center" of his exegesis, Bultmann answers that they represent "the starting point of my hermeneutical efforts" inasmuch as they represent a "false offense" to modern man. To interpret them in their New Testament context means to extract "the understanding of existence" they contain. "Their 'common denominator' is the objectifying thinking of myth which obtains in them and which contradicts the real understanding of existence in the NT (the understanding of existence as 'historical' and therefore nonobjectifiable)."[162] Second, Bultmann reminds Barth that the main reason for demythologizing is not because the mythological world view is "outdated but the fact that the thinking of myth (contrary to its true intention) is objectifying. I do not replace mythical thinking with the thinking of an objectifying science."[163] In the third place, Bultmann counters Barth's seemingly "enlightening" question whether emphasis on the prior understanding of the expositor coming to the text precludes openness to, or listening to, the text without prejudice. "I ask the counterquestion: How does the NT disclose itself to thinking that is no longer mythological?"[164] It appears that Barth exerts insufficient "hermeneutical effort" in clarifying the presuppositions governing his approach to

the text. "What does 'openly looking for' [the text's intention] mean for you and how do you attain it?"[165] It is not fair to charge that Bultmann's pre-understanding entails a decision on the text's "limits of intelligibility, but I do try to recognize the factual measure and the factual limits. The 'prior decision' is made concerning me, for I am a man, and a man of a particular age. Hence also I have no 'canon.'"[166] Bultmann regards his prior understanding as "a questioning of the text"-- not a "working hypothesis"--concerning what it says about human existence: "so far as I am concerned you might call the concept of existence my canon, but not the concept of myth."[167]

A fourth point has to do with Barth's dissatisfaction with Bultmann's "too formal a definition" of myth by which it could be insinuated that the New Testament authors "produce their message as the proclamation of general cosmic truths disguised as a tale about the gods and their doings."[168] Bultmann retorts: "The NT authors did not, of course, present 'general' cosmic relations and connections in the form of a story of the gods. But sharing the mythical world-view of their age, they tell the story of the Christ event as a story of the gods, as a myth."[169] Once again, Barth's failure to understand is due to "the fact that you leave undiscussed the concept of reality." In contrast, Bultmann's use of the term myth to identify these "problematical elements" is readily justifiable: "for one thing, because these elements are to be called mythological in the language of scholarship; and for another because the concept of myth denotes a mode of objectifying thinking, and this characterizes the NT."[170] Though Bultmann admits that what he terms "mythological" in the New Testament is synonymous with what formerly was called "supernaturalism," he comments: "...I avoid this term because I want to make it clear that the salvation event is 'supernatural' in a radical sense."[171]

In the fifth place, Bultmann feels he had clarified sufficiently how the "demythologized kerygma" actually does speak of "God's action non-mythologically." Barth is correct that its intention is to affirm that "we... are not alone precisely in this human...existence of ours. ..."[172] Yet this need not be expressed mythologically. Earlier Bultmann wrote as follows regarding the action of God:

> ...I am not talking about an idea of God, but am trying to speak of the living God in whose hands our time rests, and who encounters us at specific moments in our time. But since further explanation is required, the answer may be given in a single sentence: God encounters us in His Word--i.e. in a particular word, in the proclamation inaugurated with Jesus Christ. ...The fact that it originates in an historical event provides the credentials for its utterance on each specific occasion. This event is Jesus Christ.[173]

In the light of such statements, Barth's charge of docetism is wide of the mark. Furthermore, to seek to enforce this charge by reference to Bultmann's patent lack of attention to the "earthly" Old Testament elicits his counter-rebuke regarding Barth's own christocentric reading of it. "What I have seen [of your use of the Old Testament] awakens the suspicion that you do not relate to the OT in its earthly and historical form but use a Christianized OT as an instrument."[174] He concedes to Barth "that I have not thus far explicitly elucidated the significance of the historical Jesus for the kerygma."[175] Yet Bultmann adds he cannot comprehend

Jesus' preaching "otherwise than as the preaching of the law, as Luther also did--with the radicalness, of course, that drives the hearer to cry for the grace of God, so that--from the standpoint of faith--it must itself be understood as a summons to grace."[176]

5. On Philosophy, Theology and the Modern World View. Bultmann also addresses a number of Barth's questions relative to his use of philosophy and its role in theology and to the significance of the modern world view. First, it should be clear that his use of existentialism is misconstrued when viewed as a "philosophical key." That would be the case only if it functioned--in advance of one's being confronted by the claim of the New Testament text--to disclose "the meaning of my existence to me as my own."[177] Since it does not do the latter, there is no reason why existential philosophy should not aid theology in the limited task of contributing to the interpretation of human existence. Furthermore, Bultmann reminds Barth that he should know better than to insist that the self-understanding of which existentialism speaks precludes allowance of any relationships of the human subject to God. He writes:

> For the existential interpretation of human existence says precisely that the human subject...is not without his world, nor even without God...so that self-understanding is also understanding of (God and) the world. ... ...Heidegger has said expressly that his analysis of human being is not anthropology.[178]

Secondly, Barth errs in charging that Bultmann absolutizes the modern world view thereby making it impossible to be attentive to the strangeness of the New Testament message. Bultmann refers to his stated position that every world view is relative--including the modern: "For faith needs to be emancipated from its association with every world view expressed in objective terms, whether it be a mythical or a scientific one."[179] Thirdly, Barth is right to admit that "philosophical fragments" float about "in the soup of all theologians." He is wrong to accuse Bultmann of the systematic use of philosophy; only the latter usage is a critical, and therefore, justified usage. "For I regard it as impermissible," Bultmann states, "to be uncritically satisfied with a 'few philosophical fragments.'"[180] Fourth, Bultmann applauds Barth for saying that the "application of salvation" was the real issue for Luther. It follows that the "understanding of existence was the decisive question for him [Luther]."[181] Fifth, Bultmann grants that Wilhelm Herrmann, his teacher, not only exercised a decisive influence on him, but also prepared him to learn from Heidegger. The fact that trust played such an important place in Herrmann's thought makes it unfair to saddle him with a narrowly anthropological interpretation of the Christian faith.[182]

6. On the Pre-understanding and Other Issues. A final series of Bultmann's responses concern further criticisms of his hermeneutic as it relates to the issues of the pre-understanding and of existential interpretation. First, Barth's equation of the New Testament with the "Word of God" is illegitimate in hermeneutical discussions. Bultmann contends that as a "literary record of history" the New Testament is a human document requiring interpretation according to "general hermeneutical rules." Against Barth, he asserts: "That it is God's Word cannot be made a presupposition from which to deduce hermeneutical rules of a different kind. It can show itself to be God's Word, and therefore validate itself, only in the event of

believing understanding."[183]

Second, Bultmann denies having "canonized" a
pre-understanding. Again, the point is that the
pre-understanding has to do solely with the right question which the interpreter as a modern human being puts
to the text. This in no way precludes the truth that
the Word of God confronts the natural human
self-understanding as something "alien." "Existential
analysis can only clarify in what sense God's Word can
be called an alien one that runs counter to my own
ability to understand."[184] Hence, it is not a matter of
imposing our self-understanding as normative upon the
self-understanding which derives from the text--as Barth
charges. Here again, Bultmann insists that this new
self-understanding which results through faith does not
lie in one's own power. Summing up, he affirms:
"Methodologically I can seek, of course, only an
existential [existential] interpretation; what the
Divinus Spiritus effects is an existential
[existentiell] self-understanding."[185]

In the third place, Barth's charge is that Bultmann
deserted the ranks of the early dialectical theologians
and rejoined liberal exegetes in making human knowledge
controlling in all exegesis. In response, Bultmann
recalls that he adopted Barth's own guideline for
biblical interpretation stated in the preface to the
second edition of the Romans, namely, that the Word of
God attested in the text is to be heard as the norm for
all self-knowledge. Bultmann continues:

> Do you not understand that my point is to show
> how the text must achieve validity as a word
> of address? what genuine hearing means? ...I
> have reflected on this, and existential
> philosophy has helped to clarify things for
> me. I do not intend to reverse the revolution

achieved by you some thirty years ago but to solidify the new path methodologically.[186]

7. Signing off: "I have not seen any answer from you. . .." In concluding his letter, Bultmann notes with that the Epilogue to Barth's essay was obviously "written in irritation." The fact that Bultmann's reply to his critics in Kerygma und Mythos II was published with the caption, "Definitive Position," was an editorial decision and not intended either as his conclusive statement or as a response to all contributors.[187] That some critics cited by Barth are not treated in more detail is due to the fact that their contributions were in Bultmann's hands only shortly before publication deadlines. Moreover, Bultmann contends that his response "already contained indirectly my answer to Buri."[188] Barth's final "reproaches" of "doggedness" and intractability are unjustifiable. "I thought I had sought a discussion, especially with you, by putting to you some concrete questions; and I have not seen any answer from you to the questions that were put in, e.g., 'Zum Problem der Hermeneutik,' . . .."[189] Bultmann holds out hope that Barth might yet respond to these unanswered questions and to the critique of Barth's analysis of Bultmann by Hartlich and Sachs.[190]

Bultmann closes his letter as follows: "To the question: "What is finally and ultimately the theme of this debate?" I can only reply: The theme is the question of hermeneutical method in the service of exposition of the NT."[191] In an irenic and reflective mood, Bultmann seeks to defuse the acerbity of some of Barth's remarks:

And now let me close by continuing your quotation from Figaro:
"How can I be angry?

My heart speaks for thee!"--and adding the last
line of Figaro:
"Sorrow be for ever banned!"
With sincere greetings,

Yours,

Rudolf Bultmann[192]

B.   The "Whale" and the "Elephant"--an Aborted
Dialogue

On Christmas Eve of 1952, Barth penned the last of
the substantive letters he was to write Bultmann.   It
seemed to Barth that he did, in fact, always have Bultmann's concerns in mind.   "...I am constantly listening
to you in my ongoing work as you try to stop me doing
the things that I then obstinately do all the same."[193]

    1.   Barth's Final Reflections.   In a playful and
reflective mood, Barth depicts his difference with
Bultmann along these lines:

> Is it clear to you how things are with us--you
> and me?   It seems to me that we are like a
> whale (do you know Melville's remarkable book
> Moby Dick?   You ought to have a high regard
> for it because of its animal mythology!) and
> an elephant meeting with boundless astonish-
> ment on some oceanic shore.   It is all for
> nothing that the one sends his spout of water
> high in the air.   It is all for nothing that
> the other moves its trunk now in friendship
> and now in threat.   They do not have a common
> key to what each would obviously like to say
> to the other in its own speech and in terms of
> its own element.   A riddle of creation whose
> solution in the eschaton I like to depict as
> Bonhoeffer does by pointing toward the "I
> restore all things" of the Christmas hymn.[194]

Barth locates the main divide separating them in
divergent attitudes toward the relationship of existen-

tial philosophy to theology stressing that for him philosophy's relationship to theology must always be ancillary and not normative. "I cannot change in this matter--as you on your side obviously cannot change either--and the most triumphant expansion of that philosophy over the whole earth could not make the slightest impression on me."[195] While acknowledging that his own use of philosophy is eclectic, Barth injects the following aside which sheds light on his own stance:

> Look, after being Kantian up to my ears in my younger days, after having been tempted no less fully by Schleiermacher's romanticism, after being given later (when studying nineteenth-century theology) an unforgettable impression--I got a sharp taste of this in a seminar on Biedermann--of the radiant certainty with which it was once thought that the first and last word about each and all "understanding" had been heard in Hegel--I am not an enemy of philosophy as such, but I have hopeless reservations about the claim to absoluteness of any philosophy, epistemology, or methodology.[196]

Bultmann's repeated rejoinder that he does not apply existentialism as some kind of "alien canon" in his exposition of the New Testament remains unconvincing. Always and everywhere Barth finds a "consistent 'subjectivising'" in Bultmann's interpretation of the New Testament. Barth remains intransigent in arguing that the preeminent task of exegesis is the search for the "objective content" or the reality of God attested in the texts without obsessive fears of "objectifying" thinking. In this regard, Barth comments: "In your exposition I find the textual element concealed which, I believe, should not merely be brought to light, but brought to light first and decisively."[197]

From Barth's perspective, their mutual inability to understand one another is clarified when Bultmann identifies "the really irksome thing about 'mythological thinking'...to be its 'objectifying.'" Yet when Barth searches Bultmann's demythologized kerygma for what might be its "objective content," it seems "your statements...point to a kind of vacuum and claim to have content precisely in saying nothing beyond the existence of the believing 'subject.'"[198] This accounts for what Barth identifies as Bultmann's "consistent 'subjectivizing'" of the New Testament message. Barth's predilection in interpreting the New Testament lies in the opposite direction:

> ...I have learned precisely from the NT, and will not merely continue but will do so by preference, to objectify first and only long after to 'subjectify.' What a dreadful contrast; my interest in NT 'mythology' is precisely that it 'objectifies' the statements of the NT in such unheard of fashion. And at that you see red![199]

Barth finds this penchant for the objective reality of God's revelatory activity so apparent from a contextual reading of his Church Dogmatics--("which you [Bultmann], you naughty man, are known not to read")-- that no excuse exists for misconstruing Barth's "special interest." This leads Barth to comment:

> At the risk of more headshaking and displeasure I will at any rate venture to whisper one thing to you, namely, that I have become increasingly a Zinzendorfian to the extent that in the NT only the one central figure [Jesus Christ] as such has begun to occupy me--or each and everything else only in the light and under the sign of this central figure. As I see it, one can and should read

all theology in some sense backwards from it:
down to anthropology, ethics, and then
methodology. This is what I have attempted
and am still attempting. I have not become
"orthodox" for this reason. ...Nor have I
attained to "certainty" and the like. ...But
in this light theology has become for me a
very positive business. You must understand--
if you can--why for this reason I cannot do
justice to your postulates and on the other
hand take pleasure in the 'objectifying' that
you forbid. I will not expand on this either
polemically or otherwise. One cannot discuss
the fact that "Jesus lives," as we are both
convinced. But one can, as a theologian,
either refrain from thinking to and from this
"objective" reality. I myself cannot refrain
from doing so, but do it. Hence I have a
different concern from yours. The whole
kerygma-myth problem is for me a question of
second rank.[200]

2. "Peaceful thoughts" and "Best wishes." In a
final reflection on Bultmann's intention, Barth finds
that his "best and most peaceful thoughts" about him
surface when he hypothesizes that Bultmann really intends a theology of the Holy Spirit--perhaps as "the
great Schleiermacher" also intended. Yet, as in the
latter case, it seems that Bultmann would have to make
an important move to satisfy Barth:

...then the relation between the third [arti-
cle on the Holy Spirit] and the second article
[on Jesus Christ] must be clarified, i.e., the
latter must not be dissolved in the former but
set forth in its own dignity over against it.
This is where I balk at you as I do at
Schleiermacher (and often also at the younger
Luther). If you could make a move in this
direction, we would be able to talk easily
about many things. I should no longer view
your statements as being in a vacuum, I would
not need to oppose you so defiantly that I
intentionally "objectify," and I might even,
as you desire, "heidegger" a little with you.

> You for your part...but I will not depict this
> millenial possibility further, simply saying
> that the whale and the elephant would then at
> least find their common theme.[201]

This Christmas letter was to be the last in their correspondence until seven years later! Along with wishing the Bultmanns a good Christmas, Barth expresses the hope that on Bultmann's next visit to Basel they will have occasion to enjoy socializing and listening to Mozart's music--together![202]

PART III

THE CROSS AND RESURRECTION
OF JESUS CHRIST:
FOUNDATIONS OF BARTH'S DOCTRINE OF
RECONCILIATION IN THE *CHURCH DOGMATICS* (1953-1967)

Chapter VI

REVELATION AS THE HISTORY OF RECONCILIATION

I. REVELATION AND HISTORY: THE VIEW OF KARL BARTH[1]

A brief survey must suffice both to clarify the consistent way Barth speaks of the relationship of revelation to history in the Church Dogmatics and to provide the framework for interpreting his doctrine of reconciliation. We may anticipate our conclusion to his resume and keep in view that it is presupposed in Barth's discussion of the paradigmatic events of the cross and resurrection of Jesus Christ. Barth puts his thesis forcefully in the form of a theological axiom: "Revelation is not a predicate of history, but history is a predicate of revelation."[2]

To speak of revelation for Barth means to attend to the ways God reveals himself. The center of God's revelatory activity is Jesus Christ, the Word made flesh. He is the concrete unveiling of the triune God who makes himself known as Father, Son and Holy Spirit. It is this trinitarian conception of God which Barth regards as the distinguishing mark of the Christian view of God. Unlike many modern theologians who sought to commend Christian revelation by subsuming it beneath some supposedly more comprehensive concept of revelation or of God, Barth always affirms the uniqueness and unsurpassability of the triune God who reveals himself and whose activity is

attested in the Bible. Barth's concentration is always
fixed on the actual and concrete self-revelation of God.
Therefore, he opposes starting with conceptions of
revelation determined either by philosophy, metaphysics,
philosophy of religion, comparative religion, the
phenomenon of religion, or any humanly devised conceptuality rather than with the revelation of the triune
God.[3]

Barth's astute Catholic critic, Urs Von Balthasar,
refers to Barth's "pathos for reality" when he speaks
about revelation. This is evidenced in a typical
statement by Barth:

> Knowledge of revelation does not mean an
> abstract knowledge of a God confronting an
> abstract man. Rather, it is a concrete know-
> ledge of the God who has sought man and meets
> him in his concrete situation and finds him
> there. Revelation is a concrete knowledge of
> God and man in the event brought about by the
> initiative of a sovereign God.[4]

Barth's oft repeated phrase depicting the nature of
God's revelation is: "Through God alone may God be
known." Only God can reveal himself. He alone determines when, where, and how he will manifest himself;
moreover, he determines the conditions by which human
beings may know him. Hence, when God reveals himself,
he remains the free Lord of his revelation. This means
that "the very definite order of being which Holy Scripture makes manifest, when in its witness to God's revelation it confronts and relates God and man, divine
facts and human attitudes, enforces an order of knowing
corresponding to it."[5] Furthermore, man cannot speak and
think as though he stood at some point enabling him to
determine what revelation should or must be in advance

of attending to how God reveals himself. Any interpretation presuming that man can adopt a point "midway
between God and man" is based upon a "twofold illusion
and assumption, the claim to know what God can and must
do, to know what is necessary and appropriate to us men
so that revelation between Him and us can become an
event. ... and our claim to know our own needs and
possibilities."[6]

A.   Revelation as a Predicate of History:
     the Neo-Protestant Reversal

It was precisely the latter perspective which Barth
found characteristic of the anthropological theology
which took root in Protestant theology beginning about
the year 1700 and flourished in the nineteenth century.
Barth's critique of this neo-protestantism which also
intended to speak of revelation from a purportedly
Christian perspective is sharp: "Where a man becomes so
arbitrary, where he has assumed this role of judge,
whatever his verdict may be, he has nothing to do with
God or with the God-created fact of revelation."[7]   In
opposing this great reversal, Barth proposes the obverse
alternative: "Divine determination and revelation, and
not man's approval, are the criterion of what is appropriate to God and salutary for us."[8]
    The stance commensurate with the priority of God's
time, or the time of his revelation, to human time and
history necessitates avoiding three major errors typical
of modern discussions of the relationship of revelation
and history.   First, the nature of revelation is not
ascertainable by perusing the "manifold" state of the
human phenomenon of time and history in order to see
whether we "ever come directly or indirectly upon the

phenomenon of revelation."[9] Indeed, Barth even says that "it is the historical as such in its universality and relativity which is the necessary 'offence' to revelation."[10] Since revelation is equatable with the reality of God or of Jesus Christ alone, no thing or phenomenon in history, or history itself, is equatable with him.[11] Second, if the reality of Jesus Christ and the new aeon ushered by him is regarded as problematical, it is a sure sign that the clear and repeated testimony of the biblical witness to "this turning-point of the times and so of God's time..." has gone unheeded.[12] Third, the attempt to speak of revelation as though it could in some way be related to, or identified with, "the deeper ground and content of human history" fails to acknowledge that the brokenness and fallenness of human time and history veils God's revelatory activity. The "crucifixion of Christ" makes it possible to see the "frightfulness and inscrutibility" of human history as the old aeon "by virtue of the unveiling in revelation itself, i.e., in Christ's resurrection."[13]

B. Revelation in the School of Salvation-History: Barth's Critique

In his analysis Barth affirms the attempt of certain more "positive" or conservative nineteenth century theologians to accord priority to the biblically attested history of salvation, or the so-called "mighty acts of God." They legitimately opposed the liberal proclivity to "interpret the reality revealed in Jesus Christ simply as the revelation of the deepest and final reality of man."[14] They isolated the history of salvation "to distinguish it from world history, national history, the history of civilisation and even Church

history. ..."[15] Barth expresses his concurrence both
with the term, Heilsgeschichte, as "materially correct
and important" and with the content ordinarily included
within the history of salvation.

> In the sequence of these events--from creation
> to the dawn of the last time (our own) with
> the birth, death and resurrection of Jesus
> Christ--we have to do indeed with the provi-
> sion and revelation of salvation, or, to be
> more precise, of man's indispensable deliver-
> ance by his reconciliation with God as a
> presupposition of his eternal redemption and
> fulfilment.[16]

On the debit side of the ledger relative to this
school, Barth makes the following entries. In the first
place, this movement failed to arrive at an adequate
definition of the preeminent significance of the history
of salvation in contrast to all other history.

> ...this history of salvation is not just one
> history or element among others. It is not
> just a kind of red thread in the texture of
> all other history, of real history. Those who
> use the expression "history of salvation" must
> take good care that it is not transformed in
> their hands into the secular concept of "his-
> tory of religion," i.e., the history of the
> religious spirit, which as such can only be
> one history among many others in the context
> of history generally.[17]

Secondly, while this nineteenth century salvation-
history school spoke of the revelation in Jesus Christ
as the climax of the history of salvation, his constitutive significance for interpreting all history was not
sufficiently grasped. Barth writes: "...within this
Heilsgeschichte they indeed asserted the once-for-
allness of Jesus Christ over against all others without

being able to make the far reaching significance of this fundamental point clear."[18]

Exponents of the salvation-history school in the twentieth century, including some of Barth's own earlier statements, are criticized for tending to subordinate revelation to, or making it a predicate of, the genus, history.[19] The fundamental flaw characterizing both liberals and the more conservative salvation-history school in interpreting revelation was their failure to be radically and consistently christocentric in viewing all of history in the light of Jesus Christ. They also erred in allowing for possibilities of revelation which bypass Jesus Christ and "the cross and resurrection of Jesus Christ. ..."[20] That God's self-revelation in Jesus Christ is the clue to understanding the entire story of God's revelatory activity in history, Barth takes as the normative scriptural testimony to revelation. The way in which Jesus Christ is the center of what Barth' designates "The Time of Revelation," as well as the entire scope of salvation-history, is clear from his summary thesis:

> God's revelation in the event of the presence
> of Jesus Christ is God's time for us. It is
> fulfilled time in this event itself. But as
> the Old Testament time of expectation and as
> the New Testament time of recollection it is
> also the time of witness to this event.[21]

The mystery of the revelation of God in Jesus Christ is that in him we are confronted with the presence of the eternal God in this man in history. To confess that "The Word became flesh" also means "the Word became time."[22] At this point Barth criticizes certain statements in his commentary on Romans

> where play was made and even work occasion-
> ally done with the idea of a revelation per-
> manently transcending time, merely bounding
> time and determining it from without. Then,
> in face of the prevailing historism and psy-
> chologism which had ceased to be aware at all
> of any revelation other than an inner mundane
> one within common time, the book had a
> definite, antiseptic task and significance.
> Readers of it to-day will not fail to appre-
> ciate that in it Jn. 1:14 does not have jus-
> tice done to it.[23]

In conjunction with his explication of God's eternity within the doctrine of God, Barth further concedes
that in his commentary on Romans and his dialectical
period, he and others stressed--in opposition to the
liberal emphasis on eternity in time or on the divine
immanence--the eternity of God in terms of his "post-
temporality." God's eternity was thus depicted in terms
of a "pure and absolute futurity of God and of Jesus
Christ as the limit and fulfilment of all time." Contrary to Barth's intention, the end result was that
God's eternity was not clarified "in such a way as to
make it clear that we actually meant to speak of God and
not of a general idea of limit and crisis."[24]

In assessing Barth's interpretation of salvation-
history in the Church Dogmatics, Kraus contends that
Barth was forced, as we have seen, to distinguish his
developing vision of salvation-history from nineteenth
century antecedents. In addition, we noted Barth's
critique of his own earlier inability to expound a truly
vigorous incarnational view of revelation. However,
neither Cullmann's nor Bultmann's versions of
salvation-history were acceptable to Barth. He parts
company with Cullmann and his nineteenth century predecessors who, "with a certain mythologising clarity,
separated off the special historical context before and

after Christ as the so-called <u>Heilsgeschichte</u>. ..."[25]
The result is that Cullmann depicts salvation-history as
a kind of objective, horizontal time line whose course
is marked by a vertical intrusion in Jesus Christ.
Barth objects that Cullmann uncritically adopts a non-
biblical philosophy of history. Moreover, he dislikes
Cullmann's quasi-objectification of salvation-history.
He apparently has Cullmann in mind in asserting that
salvation-history "is not just a kind of red thread in
the texture of all other history, of real history."[26] In
distancing himself from Cullmann, Barth accentuates the
constitutive significance of Jesus Christ both for the
comprehension of salvation-history and of all history
from creation to the eschaton in a more consistent way
than Cullmann.[27]

Barth agrees with Bultmann's charge that Cullmann's
vision of salvation-history seem heavily dependent upon
a philosophy of history and that he tends so to objectify revelation that its eschatological character is
eclipsed. Yet Bultmann's view of the Christ event as
the eschatological event whose significance may be
appropriated through faith at any moment of history is
also incomplete. Most problematic is Bultmann's existential perspective which tends to docetism in sundering
Christ from the entire Old Testament covenant history.[28]

II. JESUS CHRIST: MIDPOINT OF THE COVENANT HISTORY
OF REVELATION

In light of this dispute, we are prepared for
Barth's own version of salvation-history. We have noted
repeatedly that in contrast to Bultmann, Barth never
speaks of Jesus Christ as the self-revelation of God in
abstraction from God's covenant with Israel which he

fulfills. The Old Testament covenant history is the
"time of expectation"--the "pre-time to revelation"--
which witnesses to the expected and coming revelation in
Jesus Christ. The witness of the New Testament is the
recollection of the fulfilment of time in Jesus Christ.
Barth writes:

> The reality of revelation is not a determina-
> tion of all history or of a part or section of
> the whole of history. It is history, this
> very definite history, which has not happened
> before and will never happen again, which
> happened once for all, not once in every age
> or once in many, but quite literally once for
> all. Before Christ there was an age of proph-
> ecy about Him, and after Christ and age of
> witness about Him, but that before and after
> are governed by relation to the name of Jesus
> as the midpoint of time. Thus the real tem-
> poral pre-existence of Jesus Christ in proph-
> ecy and His real temporal post-existence in
> witness are identical with this once-for-all
> existence of His as the midpoint of time. The
> midpoint of time--which, after all, belongs to
> time--is the fulfilment of time. That is what
> distinguishes it from all other times.[29]

A.   The Old Testament Covenant History: Prophecy
     and Expectation of Christ

Barth regards it to be of fundamental significance
that God's revelation always has to do with God's
activvity which is sui generis; hence not even the
history of Israel or of the Church as the new Israel are
in and of themselves equatable with revelation. With
reference to the Old Testament, Barth can say:

> The Old Testament is the witness to the genu-
> ine expectation of revelation. This raises
> its time (from the standpoint of revelation or
> in view of revelation) high above the other

times in the time area <u>ante</u> <u>Christum</u> <u>natum</u>
[before the birth of Christ]. What is in
question here is not the independent significance belonging to the history as such which
is attested in the Old Testament. The historical uniqueness of Israel, particularly the
originality of its religious history, is
another matter. ... Revelation is not a predicate which may be attributed or not attributed
to this or that historical reality. ...Reve-
lation in the Old Testament is really the
expectation of revelation or expected revelation. Revelation itself takes place from
behind the peculiar context and content of the
Old Testament.... Apart from this revelation
breaking in from without or from above, or
apart from this alignment to revelation, we
cannot speak of revelation in the Old Testament. ...Like revelation itself, genuine
expectation of it is also surrounded by hiddenness. And here also revelation itself
alone can and will break through this hiddenness. As it makes the decision about itself,
so it does also about the witness to itself.
It makes it its witness and it attests it as
such. So in confirmation of the statement
that revelation, i.e., genuine expectation of
revelation, is to be found in the Old Testament, we cannot ultimately and in principle
point to any other authority than to revelation itself, i.e., to Jesus Christ Himself.
His death on the cross proves the truth of the
statement, and it proves it by the power of
His resurrection.[30]

Barth holds that it was axiomatic for the New
Testament apostolic witnesses to regard the Old Testament history of Israel as "the connecting point" of
their "narrative of Christ" while the latter was "the
truth of the history of Israel, the fulfilment of Holy
Scripture read in the Synagogue." This perspective was
affirmed later by the Roman Catholic Church, the Protestant Reformers and by Protestant Orthodoxy. The only
exceptions were "Marcion in the 2nd century and the
Socinians in the 16th"--both of whom were viewed as

heretics.[31]

B.   The New Testament Covenant History: Witness
and Recollection of Christ

The New Testament attests time fulfilled in Jesus
Christ in terms of its recollection of revelation in
him. "That New Testament history, the history of the
proclamation, of the Evangelists and apostles, takes its
rise in revelation, is no less a miracle than that the
Old Testament finds its goal in the same revelation."[32]
Thus revelation in the New Testament is not that of a
"so-called historical peak" but "breaks in from above...
."[33] In order to be able to recollect the revelation
attested as having happened in Jesus Christ, God must
authenticate himself to us by means of the apostles'
witness.

It is not the case that the hiddenness of God in
the old covenant in the face of the suffering of the
righteous and even of the unrighteous is resolved and
unveiled in some visible theophany in the new covenant.
Barth contends that the "New Testament answer to the
problem of suffering--and it alone is the answer to the
sharply put query of the Old Testament--is to the effect
that one has died for all."[34] But precisely the cross
veils the presence of God and therewith his revelation.
Only by virtue of the resurrection of the one crucified
is the mystery and hiddenness of God in the crucified
Jesus, and therewith the mystery of his revelation,
unveiled. Barth speaks of the way in which in the cross
and resurrection of Jesus Christ the veiling and unveiling of God and therewith of his revelation in his
Son take place.

In the New Testament the hiddenness of God is
recognised to be so profound and comprehensive, because here it does not stand alone but
has a perfectly direct, concrete Beyond,
because here it is limited, yet in this very
limitation is also illumined and verified by
God's revelation. As regards the great centre
of New Testament witness we must now emphasise
the moment, without the consideration of which
it cannot be regarded either as the centre or
as anything else. This centre is the passion,
the suffering, the crucifixion and death of
Christ. But the New Testament never speaks
abstractly about the passion of Christ. It
always appears limited, illuminated and verified by the reality of His resurrection--and
that is what makes it central. Obviously in
the New Testament the resurrection of Jesus,
the aspect of Easter, does not play the part
of a second aspect alongside Good Friday, or
a final aspect following the many other aspects of the rest of the preceding life of
Jesus. True, its special place in the history
is at the end, as the limit of the story of
Jesus' life and death. But its function
extends further, namely, to cover all that
precedes it. Our reading of the Gospels from
the beginning is only right if they are read
from the standpoint of this place ultimately
reached in their narrative. And because this
whole story culminates in the passion, the
function of the resurrection is related directly and comprehensively to the fact that
the rejected One of Israel and the crucified
One of Pilate rose again from the dead. But
the function of the resurrection is to make
the passion of Christ, in which the incarnation of the Word of God was consummated,
clearly and unmistakably revelation, the
realisation of the covenant between God and
man, God's act for us, as reconciliation. The
occurrence of the resurrection is not a second
and further stage, but the manifestation of
this second dimension of the Christ event.
The resurrection is meant when it says in Jn.
1:14: "We saw his glory." The resurrection
is the event of revelation of the Incarnate,
the Humiliated, the Crucified. Wherever He
gives Himself to be known as the person He is,
He speaks as the risen Christ. The resurrection can give nothing new to Him who is the

eternal Word of the Father; but it makes
visible what is proper to Him, His glory. It
is in the limitation, illumination and verification of this event, not otherwise, that the
New Testament views the passion of Christ.
That is why in the passion it sees so powerfully the hiddenness of God.   That is why it
speaks so inexorably of the passing of this
aeon.   That is why it is so naturally aware of
the necessity of the sufferings of this time.
That is why above all it binds man so strictly
and universally under the divine accusation
and the divine threat.   The power of revelation is the power of God's hiddenness attested
by Him in this way.   Therefore it is not just
the passion and energy of a protesting, critical, resigned human No to man and his world
that is operative here.   It is really the
passion of Christ.   And it is the passion of
Christ lit up and made articulate, made a real
"word of the cross" (I Cor. 1:18) by the
supremely wonderful story in the background,
which passes all comprehension and imagination, that "Christ is from His agony arisen,
whereof we must all be glad; Christ will be
our comfort." ...This No is a No which cannot
be ignored or contradicted, a divine No which
reposes upon the divine Yes of revelation,
because, in virtue of what happened at Easter,
the passion in which it takes its rise is the
passion of the only-begotten Son of God, full
of grace and truth.   It is because all things
are become new, and for no other reason, that
the old is done away.   It is only because
Jesus lives that His cross is the sign under
which His Church marches. ...As distinct from
the apostles, the prophets were not "witnesses
of the resurrection" (Ac. 1:22).   But the
resurrection was their final meaning.[35]

C.   Jesus Christ: Midpoint and Fulfillment of
Covenant and World History

Barth's thesis that the New Testament regards Jesus
as the midpoint of salvation-history, or that in his
person he is the fulfilled time of revelation, is predi-

cated upon the resurrection of Jesus. "...if we were to press the question, which was fulfilled time between Old Testament expectation and New Testament recollection, we would have to reply, the forty days in which Jesus let Himself be seen in this way (Ac. 1:3)."[36] Hence the New Testament witness to the risen Lord is the stammering "attestation of the pure presence of God...of an eternal presence of God in time."[37] That singular presence of God in human history was anticipated but not yet realized in Jesus' life and ministry. Hence the recollection of eternal time or of Easter time "as such possesses an absolute uniqueness. Both this recollection and its object fall into the same category, the category of the single event of God's revelation. God's revelation is the one thing that makes possible both the Easter story and the Easter message."[38]

While it is true that the recollection of the special time of Easter always refers first of all to "a happening that once became an event in datable time," that does not exhaust its meaning.

> ...because it is the witness to recollection of revelation, the recollection attested by it is thereby extended. Recollection of eternal time, which is what recollection of the risen One is, is necessarily recollection of a time which overarches our time, and which therefore cannot be confined to the datable time with which it is in the first instance related. Recollection of this time must also be expectation of this same time.[39]

In this sense, the New Testament recollection of the risen Lord always looks in expectant hope to his future. In this way, the recollection of the risen Lord which hopes for his coming again "partakes in fulfilled time."[40] The manner in which recollection of the ful-

fillment of time in the risen Christ is correlated with
expectation in the New Testament witness, Barth expresses as follows:

> If in the New Testament the matter ends with
> a mere recollection, if recollection does not
> actually become expectation, if for it the
> First from whom its witness proceeds is not
> also the Last, the Eschatos, if it is not this
> with the same seriousness, the seriousness of
> a knowledge of the First, the New Testament is
> simply a bit of Ebionite tradition. It is
> often enough regarded as such. But the real
> New Testament says clearly that He who came is
> also He that comes. Not a line of the real
> New Testament can be properly understood
> unless it is read as the witness to finally
> achieved divine revelation and grace and
> therefore as the witness to hope. Aligned
> upon the Archimedean point of the story and
> message of Easter, which have no eschatologi-
> cal intention, it is in the rest of its con-
> stitution and content completely eschatologi-
> cal in intention. In this respect it takes
> its place naturally alongside of the Old
> Testament. It is only the sharpened and
> clarified message of the expectation in which
> Israel was already living. ...The adoption of
> the Old Testament into the Canon of the Church
> really meant far more than a welcome confirma-
> tion of Christ as the fulfilment of ancient
> expectation and prophecy. It was because on
> the basis of Christ's manifestation [that]
> expectation and prophecy constituted the very
> element by which His Church lived, that it
> naturally had to claim and to read as its own
> the book of expectation and prophecy. Every-
> thing depends upon understanding the escha-
> tological trend of New Testament faith, if we
> are to understand this faith itself.[41]

1. Fulfilled Time in Jesus Christ and the Dimensions of Time. Within the Scriptures Barth finds the
witness to the manifold ways in which God makes himself
present to his covenant people in time. This special

history in its different dimensions always has Jesus Christ as its center. Hence it takes the form of Old Testament expectation of him, or it is fulfilled time in him, or finally, it is the New Testament recollection of him. Throughout the referent is to God's time as the living God. As such, it is sui generis. Barth finds it important to distinguish this "third time," the time of God's revelation and presence in our time, from two other dimensions of time. The first dimension of time confessed along with the confession of God as creator is of time "created by God." In Barth's view, created time as part of God's good creation is neither knowable apart from faith nor identical to our "lost time." It was in the beginning, but has been eclipsed. "God-created time remains a time hidden and withdrawn from us."[42] Sinful humanity lives in fallen time. "Between our time and God-created time as between our existence and the existence created by God there lies the Fall. 'Our' time, as Augustine and Heidegger in their own ways quite correctly inform us, is the time produced by us, i.e., by fallen man."[43] The "third time" is the time of God's presence with us in his revelation. Barth puts the distinction thus: "If God's revelation has a time also, if God has time for us, if we really (really, in a theologically relevant sense) know and possess time, it must be a different time, a third time, created alongside of our time and the time originally created by God."[44] Whereas our lost time is limited, evanescent and perishable, God's time which he has for us--"as distinguished from our time that comes into being and passes away, is to be regarded as eternal time."[45] This time of God is identifiable with his presence with us and for us "in Jesus Christ, i.e., Deus praesens."[46]

Following Barth, we may characterize what it means

that "God reveals Himself" in the person and "presence of Jesus Christ as the fulfillment of time." He warns repeatedly that there is no possibility of understanding the relationship of God and his revelation to history if it is forgotten that the movement is always from God to man and not vice versa. Hence to hold with Barth that God "reveals Himself" can mean only "that 'revelation becomes history, but not that history becomes revelation.'"[47] This is but another way of underlining what Barth takes to be the fundamental presupposition of the biblical witness to revelation, namely, that God remains the Lord or that "God is and remains the Subject" where and when he reveals himself.

    2. Marks of the Fulfillment of Time in Jesus Christ. Three characteristics of the fulfillment of time in Jesus Christ are noteworthy. First, the fact that God masters time and fulfills it in his self- revelation in Jesus Christ means that whoever acknowledges him becomes "a partner in this time and so a time-partner or contemporary of Jesus Christ, of the prophets and apostles."[48] In the light of Jesus Christ as the fulfillment of time, faith confesses that "our" ordinary clock time is part of the passing aeon, of lost time, which is "real only in its passing."[49] More positively, by virtue of faith's confession that Jesus Christ is indeed the fulfillment of time one "has now no outlook upon an event, upon history, which is not limited and determined by the history of fulfilled time."[50] Years earlier, Barth--life-long avid newspaper reader-- expressed this insight aphoristically: "When one reads the newspaper, one must not forget that one has read the Bible; and when one reads the Bible, one must not forget that one has read the newspaper."

    Second, true acknowledgment of Jesus Christ as the

fulfillment of time always implicates and confronts fallen humanity seeking to preserve itself and its lost time over against God. That "God in time" confronts us in Jesus Christ in the "form of a servant" in "the time of the years 1-30" is always an offence. Barth reasons that neither God in himself nor time in itself is offensive. "'God in time,' 'God in history'--that is the offending thing in revelation."[51] The refusal to accept the fulfilled time in Jesus Christ is the sin both of Jew and Gentile in the rejection and crucifixion of Jesus Christ. It is repeated whenever the "order of rank" between fulfilled time and our time is denied. Ordinarily, this occurs whenever "the offence of revelation" in its "servant-form" is subsumed beneath a purportedly more comprehensive view of world history. Although the latter perspective marks the great divide in world history by the birth of Jesus, it deals with him and his time as though it were "a time like any other." This view of world history tips its hat to Christ, but is, in fact a "picture of a single, almighty world-time and world-reality... without Christ, without revelation, a hard surface of secularity, smooth as a mirror...there is certainly nothing that we can seriously call a history of 'God's mighty acts.'"[52]

The third characteristic of the revelation of God in Jesus Christ attested in Scripture as the fulfillment of time, "the breaking in of new time into the midst of the old," is that it is a "miraculous event."[53] This is so because God himself is present in our history; our human existence, time and history are as such non-miraculous. The event of a miracle, according to Barth, does not refer to an event "hard to conceive, nor yet one that is simpy inconceivable, but one that is highly conceivable, but conceivable only as the exponent of the

special new direct act of God in time and in history."[54]
Thus Barth regards it to be axiomatic that the presence
of God in Jesus Christ himself, the Word which "became
flesh" (Jn. 1:14), and his activity, entail "wonders."
The latter, in terms of biblical usage, "are occurrences
in time and space that have no analogies."[55]

A proper theological approach to signs and wonders
ascribed to Jesus cannot consist in their historical
verification. Rather, the narrative of Jesus' miracles
or signs are

> fundamentally <u>astonishing</u> stories, they func-
> tion first of all in a formal way as a sort of
> <u>alarm signal</u>. ...they alert the hearer and
> reader to a central fact: this history is
> concerned with a fundamentally <u>new</u> event
> which, although undoubtedly occurring within
> time and space, is not to be identified with
> other events occurring within the limits of
> time and space.[56]

Barth can say that "Miracle is thus an attribute of
revelation. As it were, it marks off the limits of
revelation time from all other time."[57] Thus the signs
are always subordinate to Jesus Christ himself. Hence:
"In a real and decisive sense, therefore, <u>he</u> is the
miracle, the miracle of all miracles!"[58]

Barth finds biblical warrant for maintaining the
unique nature of God's time for us as a special history
which takes place within our history while not being
produced by it or evolving from it.[59] The revelation of
the Word of God through preaching takes place "in his
own seasons" according to Tit. 1:3.[60] According to Mark,
Jesus begins his public ministry preaching the "gospel
of God" and saying: "The time is fulfilled..." (1:15).
In Gal. 4:3, Paul depicts sinful humanity prior to

Christ's coming as being enslaved "to the elemental
spirits of the universe." This is what Barth refers to
as our "fallen time." The Apostle continues: "But when
the time had fully come, God sent forth his Son, born of
woman" (Gal. 4:4). The sending of the Son occurs in
"the fulness of time" (tò pléroma toû chrónou). Concerning this fulness or pléroma, Barth states:

> Pleroma is that which fulfils (fills full) a
> vessel, plan, concept or form. It is there-
> fore, the content, the meaning, the reality
> proclaimed as a possibility in this form.
> "Fulness of time" cannot, therefore, be
> regarded otherwise than as "real time." In
> and with the incarnation of the Word, in and
> with the approach of the kingdom of God--we
> should perhaps say as its precursor or its
> concomitant--it also happens that real time
> breaks in as new time, as the now and to-day
> of the Saviour. Thus in Eph. 1:9f. "God made
> known to us the mystery of His will, according
> to His good pleasure to renew (or--and it
> seems to mean the same thing--to sum up) all
> things in heaven and on earth eís oikonomían
> toû plerómatos tôn kairôn, for the orderly
> bringing about of the fulness of the times
> (i.e., in order that by the renewal time also
> might be fulfilled, become real time).[61]

Barth finds God's dominion over time as the "Living
One" confessed by the author of the Apocalypse. He
seems to have in mind the Old Testament name of God of
Ex. 3:14, "I am that I am," and he hears the Lord God
speak: "'I am the Alpha and the Omega,' says the Lord
God, who is and who was and who is to come, the
Almighty" (Rev. 1:8).[62] Or again: "I am the Alpha and
the Omega, the first and the last, the beginning and the
end" (Rev. 22:13). Barth comments:

> From the fact that God is He who exists and
> therefore is the Living One in the supreme

sense and therefore the Almighty, it follows
that He is not only this, but, as this, also
He who was and He who cometh, Alpha and Omega,
the beginning and the end, the first and the
last. And vice versa, by the fact that He is
the first and the last, it is indicated that
He is truly He who is, the Living One, the
Almighty.[63]

God's dominion and lordship over time is further
evident in that the fulfilled time ushered in through
the presence and reconciliation in Christ marks the
onset of the end of the old aeon of fallen time and the
dawning of the new age of God's time. The defeat of the
former is attested in Jesus' death while his resurrection marks the inbreak and dawning of the new aeon, the
new creation and the new world.[64] It is certainly unfair
of Cullmann to charge that Barth here still operates
with a Platonic view of God's eternity which simply
transcends time. Barth states: "The fulfilment of time
that took place in Jesus is not just an alms from the
divine riches; if, according to Gal. 4:4, Jesus Christ
is the 'pleroma [fullness] of the time,' we have to
remember that, according to Col. 2:9, 'in him dwelleth
all the pleroma of the Godhead bodily.'"[65]

Barth construes eternity's relationship to time in
terms of the Word's assumption of flesh in the incarnation. "The Word spoken from eternity raises the time
into which it is uttered (without dissolving it as
time), up into His own eternity as now His own time, and
gives it part in the existence of God which is alone
real, self-moved, self-dependent, self-sufficient."[66]
This emphasis makes Barth's thesis controlling his
entire treatment of the unique time of salvation-history
as fulfilled time in Jesus Christ comprehensible:
"...the special thing about the time of Jesus Christ is

that it is the time of the Lord of time. Compared with our time it is mastered time and for that very reason real, fulfilled time."[67] Or again: "The entire fulness of the benefit of God's revelation and of the reconciliation accomplished in it lies in the fact that God has time for us, a time which is right, genuine and real."[68]

III. COVENANT HISTORY AND WORLD HISTORY

This exposition clarifies why Barth cannot equate human history with the history of salvation or subsume the latter beneath the former. Since salvation-history as the history of revelation is the true history, all other history is to be seen in its light. He highlights this thesis as follows:

> The history of salvation is _the_ history, the true history which encloses all other history and to which in some way all other history belongs to the extent that it reflects and illustrates the history of salvation; to the extent that it accompanies it with signs and intimations and imitations and examples and object-lessons. No other history can have any independent theme in relation to this history, let alone be a general and true history in the context of which the history of salvation can only be one among others. The covenant of grace is _the_ theme of history. The history of salvation is _the_ history.[69]

Kraus comments on Barth's rigorous consistency in developing this perspective: "The precision and clarity with which Barth's thought moves _from_ the revelation fulfilled in Christ _to_ viewing history is without parallel in the history of protestant dogmatics. Only by proceeding along this way can the reality of the special history of God be acknowledged."[70] That this corresponds fully to Barth's intention throughout his discussion of the relationship of salvation-history to universal history is clear from his programmatic affirmation: "...we can and must speak of revelation first of all in the principal statement, in order subsequently to speak of history by way of explanation. But we may not first of all speak of history in order subsequently or by epithet to speak with force and emphasis about revelation."[71]

A.   Covenant History and Creation

There is evidence of a linguistic shift beginning with the doctrine of God (CD 2:1) and becoming prominent in the doctrine of "The Election of God" (CD 2:2) where we find salvation-history language replaced by covenant-history language. This does not entail Barth's rejection of the traditional conception of salvation-history modified, as seen above, in terms of Jesus Christ as its origin, center and goal. Rather, the line of salvation-history always oriented to Jesus Christ is prominent throughout the remaining volumes of the Church Dogmatics. Hence the history of the covenant is the integrative key to all of the ways and works of God from creation to eschaton. While Barth nowhere surrenders the distinctiveness of covenant history with its center in Jesus Christ in the Church Dogmatics, it appears that on the basis of his christological grounding of the divine election (CD 2:2) he is able to deal with universal history within the doctrines of creation and reconciliation in a more positive light than he did in his prolegomena (CD 1:1; 1:2; 2:1).

This comes clearly into view in the suggestive way

Barth relates "Creation and Covenant" (CD 3:1). In his summary thesis he maintains that according to the biblical creation narratives "the purposes and therefore the meaning of creation is to make possible the history of God's covenant with humanity which has its beginning, centre and culmination in Jesus Christ. The history of the covenant is as much the goal of creation as creation itself is the beginning of this history."[72] This reciprocal and positive relationship is amplified in terms of the twin theses: "Creation as the External Basis of the Covenant" and "The Covenant as the Internal Basis of Creation."[73]

This positive relationship of the covenant of grace to world history is explicated further in Barth's doctrine of providence (CD 3:3). In an illuminating paragraph, Barth delineates this perspective.

> We should certainly not forget or erase the fact that the history of the covenant, and therefore the history which is the meaning of all creaturely occurrence, is within the totality of this creaturely occurrence a [special], particular history selected for this purpose and determined and directed accordingly. It is an astonishingly thin line in a confusion of apparently much more powerful and conspicuous lines which seem to be independent and mutually contradictory, and especially to run quite contrary to the one narrow line of the history of the covenant. That world history in its totality is the history in which God executes His will of grace must thus be taken to mean that in its totality it belongs to this special history; that its lines can have no other starting-point or goal than the one divine will of grace; that they must converge on this one thin line and finally run in its direction. This is the theme of the doctrine of providence.[74]

B.   The Providence of God and the Goal of World
     History

World history is thus ordained with a view to God's
covenant history: hence its contours and direction are
ordered by the "King of Israel" who rules over all. In
the light of the divine intention and rule, the cosmos
and world history may be imaged as a river rather than
as a formless sea, or as a living organism constituted
of different parts making up a whole, or as a building,
"a human work of art," in which each part of the structure has its necessary place in the total structure.
Barth concludes: "That is why we cannot possibly compare world-occurrence as it takes place under the divine
rule with an amorphous and self- diffusing mass, but
only with an organism or building."[75]
     It should not be forgotten that what Barth calls
the "formative economy and disposition" of "all world-
occurrence" in its positive relationship to God's intention for all creation manifest in the covenant history
is not knowable apart from the latter. The particular
is the secret telos of the universal. God's special
history with his covenant people unveils his universal
intention for all peoples. More specifically, already
at the outset of the doctrine of election Barth taught
that God's relationship to the world and human history
can be understood only in the light of the "primal
history" involving the Father and the Son in their joint
determination of the divine electing will in the form of
a covenant of grace. This all-embracing divine determination of Father and Son is thus the origin of God's
intention manifest in the history of the covenant and
hidden in universal history. Barth states this perspective in axiomatic fashion:

248

> There is a history between God and the world.
> But this history has no independent significa-
> tion. It takes place in the interest of the
> primal history [Urgeschichte] which is played
> out between God and this one man and His
> people. It is the sphere in which this primal
> history is played out. It attains its goal as
> this primal history attains its goal. And the
> same is true both of man as such and also of
> the human race as a whole. ...The general (the
> world or man) exists for the sake of the
> particular. In the particular the general has
> its meaning and fulfilment. ...We must think
> at once, then, of Jesus of Nazareth and of His
> people. ... All His work takes place according
> to this plan and under this sign. ...Every-
> thing happens according to this basic and
> determinative pattern, model and system.
> ...The primal history which underlies and is
> the goal of the whole history of His relation-
> ship ad extra, with the creation and man in
> general, is the history of this covenant.[76]

Barth sums up the relationships between world history and covenant history and provides an insight into his christocentric vision of the history of the covenant and its universal scope and goal. Special attention should be paid to the dynamic movement in-volved in the history of the acts of God:

> What this context [i.e., of "world-
> occurrence"] is, is revealed to us in the
> history of the covenant and salvation to which
> the Bible bears testimony. It is grounded in
> the free election of grace. It has its begin-
> ning here in the form of the particular and
> sacred work of God in the creation of the
> world. It continues with the reconciliation
> of the world to God as it was foretold in the
> history of Israel and accomplished in Jesus
> Christ. And when the interim period of the
> proclamation of this work is over, it will
> culminate in the perfecting or redemption
> which consists in the general revelation of
> the creative and reconciling act of God. It
> is in this that we find true economy and

disposition. It is here that creaturely occurrence acquires line and direction, and meaningful sequence and context, and therefore form and character, by the rule of God. It is in the name of Jesus Christ that this economy is comprehended. This name, which is present at both the beginning and the end, is the centre which reveals the economy. It is in this name that it really consists. But at every point in this particular and sacred work, at the beginning and middle and end, we find that its concern is with the world. It is the world which God created in His grace. It is the world which He loved and reconciled in His Son. It is the world which He will finally perfect in Christ. And the opening event in this particular sacred history is the calling into being of a special people, a holy community, whose existence is not an end in itself, but something which has to testify and proclaim to the world the Word of the King to it and the work of the King for it. And this means that the context, the economy, the disposition is not only revealed in the history of the covenant and redemption whose centre is Jesus Christ. In a hidden form it is also present and active in world-occurrence generally. The two spheres are distinguished only by the fact that in the one case it is hidden and in the other it is revealed. From this particular, sacred history we see that even world- occurrence generally had its beginning by the grace of God the Creator, that it was decisively altered and conditioned by the love which appeared in Jesus Christ and was authenticated by His death and resurrection, and that it moves towards its own perfection and therefore to the end of the age in the still future revelation of Jesus Christ. The existence of this particular, sacred history means that we can no longer think of world- occurrence generally as a raging sea of events which has neither form nor direction. World-occurrence is something formed, and it is formed indeed according to the sense revealed in this history. Its unity and order are identical with the unity and order which were manifestly achieved in this history. Its Lord is identical with the One who is called the Lord in this history, and therefore with the King of Israel.[77]

Whether Barth's christocentric interpretation of salvation-history and the manner in which it determines world history really allows for the relative independence of creation and, more particularly, human existence and history over against God, is a critical question which must be raised if not pursued at this juncture.[78]

Something of Barth's mindset as he completed the doctrine of creation and approached that of reconciliation is evident in his remark from the preface of the last volume on the doctrine of creation written in 1951: "...although I still enjoy a fight, gradually I have found more and more meaning in life and death affirmations. ...Saying no is hardly a supreme art, nor is the overthrow of all kinds of false idols an ultimate task."[79]

IV. THE DOCTRINE OF RECONCILIATION IN THE CHURCH DOGMATICS

With the understanding of Barth's portrayal of the relationship of the revelation in Jesus Christ to covenant and world history in view, we are prepared for his treatment of the doctrine of reconciliation. Immediately after submitting the proofs of the final volume of the doctrine of creation (KD 3:4, 1951), the eighth of the Church Dogmatics, Barth left for a summer vacation. In view of its increasing size, "Barth occasionally asked himself whether he was building Solomon's temple or the tower of Babel." In a somewhat self-depreciating tone, he wrote his son, Christoph: "I am quite sure that the angels sometimes chuckle at my enterprise; but I would like to think that the chuckle is well-meaning."[80] Nearing normal retirement age, Barth confided his feelings to Christoph as he confronted the challenge of the doctrine of reconciliation looming like a great mountain before him.

> Oh, what a good time I could be having!-- contemporaries are now close to retirement or have already reached it. If only I had not been so arrogant as to dare to embark on this endless ridge walk twenty years ago! "What use is it?" often enough runs through my head; but then I find that each new vista which opens up on this journey proves so attractive and stimulating that I really would not have things otherwise, and I keep on taking one more step forward.[81]

While vacationing in the summer of 1951, Barth struggled to define the divisions and structure of the entire doctrine of reconciliation in preparation for his initial lectures to begin later that summer. In an exuberant mood, he wrote Christoph about the way he came to clarity regarding an outline: "In Locarno I dreamed of a plan. It seemed to go in the right direction. The plan now had to stretch from christology to ecclesiology together with the relevant ethics. I woke at 2 a.m. and then put it down on paper hastily the next morning."[82] In his introductory lectures on the doctrine of reconciliation later that summer, Barth began to sketch a "first section of the plan which he had 'seen.'"[83]

For Karl Barth, the doctrine of reconciliation represents both the heart of Christian faith and theology as well as the center of his Church Dogmatics. Indeed, the challenges confronting Barth in the exposition of what he termed "the heart of the [Christian]

message received by and laid upon the Christian community and therefore with the heart of the Church's
dogmatics"[84] engaged him for sixteen years! The end
result no doubt ranks as a magnum opus in itself and as
the completion of his life's work. Begun when Barth was
sixty-five years of age, this massive work representing
the final part of his incomplete Dogmatics, appeared
during the years 1953-1967, the last part volume being
published just a year and a half before his death on
December 10, 1968, at eighty-two years of age. It was
published in three volumes, but this required four large
books and an unfinished fragment.[85] Without a doubt,
Barth's comprehensive doctrine of reconciliation is
unsurpassed in the history of Protestant theology and
perhaps in the entire history of the Church universal.
In the Foreword to the first volume, Barth spoke of his
feelings as he confronted "the vast territory of the
doctrine of reconciliation." He continued: "I have
been very conscious of the very special responsibility
laid on the theologian at this centre of all Christian
knowledge. To fail here is to fail everywhere. To be
on the right track here makes it impossible to be completely mistaken in the whole."[86] Concluding his prefatory remarks, Barth wrote: "I am still in good heart.
...although the task is a heavy one I do not have to
stagger under its weight, but year in year out it carries me along with it. I now turn to it again. The way
is long. But 'having still time on the earth...'"[87]

A.   The Significance of the Doctrine of
     Reconciliation in the Church Dogmatics

On occasion, Barth depicts Christian knowledge and
theology in the image of a circle. The doctrines of

creation and of consummation or "last things" constitute its circumference. "But the covenant fulfilled in the atonement [Versöhnung] is its centre."[88] In keeping with his christocentrism, Barth notes that the circumference is visible only from the center. "But we can see it only from this point. ...From this point either everything is clear and true and helpful, or it is not so anywhere."[89] Shifting the image a bit, Barth avers that the reconciliation effected in Jesus Christ is "the only place from which as Christians we can think forwards and backwards, from which a Christian knowledge of both God and man is possible."[90] Hence the focus and continual point of reference for all Christian faith and knowledge is Jesus Christ himself. It is axiomatic that "Christ is the mystery of God, that all the treasures of wisdom and knowledge are hidden in Him and not elsewhere and that they are to be acquired in Him and not elsewhere (Col. 2:3)."[91] From this center, and from here alone, all Christian knowledge is saving and true. It is because reconciliation has taken place that theology as the process of "faith seeking understanding" becomes possible. And while Barth fixes his attention on the work of reconciliation achieved by the Son of God whose condescension took him into the "far country" marked by sin and death, the effects of his reconciling work illumine not only the scope of all of God's saving acts in history but also God's eternal purpose preceding creation and eternity which succeeds all time and history. This is the case because this "sovereign act is the act of God's grace."[92]

The far-reaching significance of the doctrine of reconciliation as the fruition of the long course of Barth's entire theological pilgrimage cannot be gainsaid. In light of the above, one can see that many

earlier statements in the doctrine of the Word of God
(CD 1:1 and CD 1:2), the doctrine of God (CD 2:1), the
doctrine of Election (CD 2:2), and the doctrine of
Creation and the Creature (CD 3:1; CD 3:2; CD 3:3; CD
3:4) were ventured in terms of Jesus Christ as the
center of all of God's ways and works. Barth's doctrine
of reconciliation is the explication of the center of
all of God's activity in Jesus Christ.

Barth wrote the first volume of his Doctrine of
Reconciliation in the midst of what he referred to as
the "rampaging Bultmann controversy."[93] We saw above
that Barth's preoccupation with Bultmann's position at
that time led to his offering a seminar on him and to
his famous essay of 1952 attempting "to understand him."
In expounding this doctrine, Bultmann had not been put
behind him, but was very much in his consciousness
throughout. In the preface to the doctrine of reconciliation, Barth makes the following important statement
regarding how his own treatment of it represented an
ongoing debate with his old Marburg colleague:

> The present situation in theology and also the
> peculiar themes of this book mean that
> throughout I have found myself in an inten-
> sive, although for the most part quiet, debate
> with Rudolph Bultmann. His name is not men-
> tioned often. But his subject is always
> present, even in those places where with his
> methods and results before me I have con-
> sciously ignored him. I respect the man, his
> mind and aim and achievements, and the zeal of
> his following. I only wish that I could do
> him greater justice. But if I have to choose
> between, on the one hand, accepting the rule
> which he has proclaimed and thus not being
> able to say certain things which I perceive
> and which I believe ought to be said, or
> having to say them very differently from how
> I perceive them, and on the other hand saying
> them quite freely, but making myself guilty of

using what he regards as an "obscure conceptuality," then I have no option but to choose
the second. His hermeneutical suggestions can
become binding on me only when I am convinced
that by following them I would say the same
things better and more freely. For the time
being, I am not so convinced.[94]

B.   The Place of the Doctrine of Reconciliation in
     the Church Dogmatics

A brief statement of the structure and contours of
the doctrine of reconciliation unfolded in the Church
Dogmatics provides the necessary backdrop for interpreting Barth's intention and the scope of the entire doctrine. Without a doubt, Barth constructed these four
volumes with devoted care. The attendant symmetry
between the parts of the doctrine in their relationships
to one another and in their contribution to the whole
gives the impression of a well-constructed building.
Though Barth anticipated the overall structure of the
Church Dogmatics in the first foreword in 1932, one
could hardly have predicted the massive grandeur of his
subsequent treatment of reconciliation.[95] However, in
keeping with Barth's image of God's work of reconciliation as the middle or center of Christian faith and
theology, its placement as the climax of the Church
Dogmatics is not accidental. Preceding the doctrine of
reconciliation, he developed his prolegomena in terms of
"The Doctrine of the Word of God" (CD 1:1 and 1:2).
This was followed by the doctrine of God (CD 2:1 and
2:2). The third volume dealt with the doctrines of
creation and the creature as well as with providence and
evil (CD 3:1; 3:2; 3:3 and 3:4). Creation as "first in
the series of works of the triune God was depicted as
the "external basis of the covenant" and the covenant as

the "internal basis of creation."[96] In the fourth volume
on reconciliation, Barth unfolds the way in which God
fulfills the broken covenant between sinful humanity and
himself in Jesus Christ (CD 4:1; 4:2; 4:3; 4:4). From
the center or midpoint of God's reconciling activity in
Jesus Christ, Barth projected a fifth volume on the
doctrine of redemption (eschatology). The latter was
never published. Clearly, the doctrine of reconciliation as the center of Barth's dogmatics sums up what has
preceded and provides the basis for Christian hope in
the future eschatological consummation. [97]

C. The Structure of the Doctrine of
Reconciliation in the Church Dogmatics

Barth constructs the doctrine of reconciliation in
four lengthy chapters constituting four volumes! In
chapter XIII, he provides a masterful analysis of "The
Subject-Matter and Problems of the Doctrine of Reconciliation" under the general heading of "The Work of God
the Reconciler" (par. 57). In the following section,
"The Doctrine of Reconciliation," Barth outlines the
entire forthcoming structure of the doctrine in detail
(par. 58). The symmetry which exists between the parts
and the final shape of the whole doctrine is the fruition of the plan Barth projected two years earlier.

THE DOCTRINE OF RECONCILIATION (SURVEY)

The content of the doctrine of reconciliation
is the knowledge of Jesus Christ who is (1)
very God, that is, the God who humbles Himself, and therefore the reconciling God, (2)
very man, that is, man exalted and therefore
reconciled by God, and (3) in the unity of the
two, the guarantor and witness of our atonement.

This threefold knowledge of Jesus Christ includes the knowledge of the sin of man: (1) his pride, (2) his sloth and (3) his falsehood --the knowledge of the event in which reconciliation is made: (1) his justification, (2) his sanctification and (3) his calling--and the knowledge of the work of the Holy Spirit in (1) the gathering, (2) the upbuilding and (3) the sending of the community, and of the being of Christians in Jesus Christ (1) in faith, (2) in love and (3) in hope.[98]

The doctrine of reconciliation proper is developed in the three following chapters which all deal with different dimensions of Jesus Christ as reconciler. Chapter XIV entitled, "Jesus Christ, the Lord as Servant," unfolds the way in which the eternal Son of God is very God "with us" in Jesus Christ thereby effecting reconciliaton (CD 4:1, par. 59). Here Barth treats what orthodox dogmatics refer to as the priestly office of Christ. Chapter XV, "Jesus Christ, the Servant as Lord," treats him as the true Son of Man who is exalted by God as the Lord in behalf of humanity (CD 4:2, par. 64). This is Christ's kingly office. Chapter XVI, "Jesus Christ, The True Witness," portrays him as the Mediator, in whom God and man form a unity, who fulfills the prophetic office as guarantor and witness of the atonement effected between God and man through him (CD 4:3, par. 69). Within each of the major chapters indicated above, Barth deals with dimensions of human sin which find their definitive illumination in contrast to Jesus Christ, the reconciler (par. 60, 65, 70). There follows in each chapter a development of what the objective reconciliation effected by Jesus Christ means for man's justification, sanctification and calling (par. 61, 66, 71). Final sections in each chapter deal with the subjective appropriation of reconciliation through the work of the Holy Spirit in the gathering, upbuilding and sending of the Christian community (par. 62, 67, 72). The work of the Spirit in each Christian giving rise to a life of faith, love and hope concludes Barth's treatment (par. 63, 68, 73). The special ethics which was to have completed the doctrine of reconciliation appeared only in a Fragment. In it the Christian life was seen as a calling on God viewed in terms of Baptism (foundation), the Lord's Prayer (completion), and the Lord's Supper (renewal), (CD 4:4).

The following chart depicts the structure of the doctrine of reconciliation in Barth's Church Dogmatics.

CHURCH DOGMATICS IV

Church Dogmatics	**CD IV/1**
CHRISTOLOGY	<u>Jesus Christ, the Lord as Servant: True God</u> 59: True <u>God</u>--humbling Himself and therefore reconciling
Person	59:1 The Way of the Son of God into the Far Country=the state of humiliation
Work	59:2 The Judge judged in our Place: the Obedience of the Son of God=the priestly office
Transition	59:3 The Verdict of the Father: the Resurrection
<u>HARMARTIOLOGY</u>:	
Sin as:	60: Pride and Fall
<u>SOTERIOLOGY</u>	61: God's Judgment as the Justification of Humanity
<u>PNEUMATOLOGY</u>	
The Work of the Holy Spirit: a. in the Church	62: Gathering of the Christian Community
b. in each Christian	63: Faith
<u>ETHICS</u> CD IV/4 The Christian Life as calling on God	Baptism--with Water as the <u>Foundation</u> of the Christian life in prayer for the Holy Spirit

260

THE DOCTRINE OF RECONCILIATION

CD IV/2

Jesus Christ, the Servant as Lord: True Man

64: True Man, exalted by God thus reconciled

64:2 The Homecoming of the Son of Man=the state of exaltation

64:3 The Royal Man: the exaltation of the Son of Man=the kingly office

64:4 The Direction of the Son

THE CREATURE

65: Sloth and Misery

66: God's Sending as the Sanctification of Humanity

THE HOLY SPIRIT

67: Upbuilding of the Christian Community

68: Love

The Lord's Prayer--"Our Father"--as (instruction for) the Completion of the Christian life

CD IV/3

Jesus Christ, the True Witness

69: In Unity God and Man and thus the guarantor and witness of reconciliation

69:2 The Mediator, the Light of Life=the unity of both states

69:3 Jesus is Victor: the Glory of the Mediator= the prophetic office

69:4 The Promise of the Spirit

70: Falsehood and Condemnation

71: God's Promise as the Vocation of Humanity

72: Sending of the Christian Community

73: Hope

The Lord's Supper--Eucharist--as the Renewal of the Christian life in the prayer of thanksgiving

It is not our concern in this study to examine the entire scope of Barth's doctrine of reconciliation. We have outlined its three major divisions above, but our analysis will be restricted primarily to the main lines of the doctrine of reconciliation developed in the first major chapter, "Jesus Christ, the Lord as Servant" (CD 4:1, Ch. XIV), with special attention accorded the crucifixion and resurrection of Jesus and their centrality in Barth's doctrine of reconciliation. It could be argued that because Barth lays such stress upon the objective reconciliation effected in behalf of the world in Jesus Christ (par. 59), everything said later in the unfolding of the doctrine of reconcilation is, in some sense, already anticipated in this section entitled "The Obedience of the Son of God." Or put somewhat more guardedly, in Barth's perspective the linchpin of the entire doctrine of reconciliation lies in the truth of the condescension of the Son of God, of the Lord who became a servant, in his identification with, and suffering in the place of, sinful humanity. This condescension of God in behalf of humanity in his Son is authenticated, validated and revealed when the crucified is raised from the dead through the power of God. All of this is the subject matter of paragraph 59. Whatever meaning reconciliation has for the world, the Church, and individual believers must be intrinsic to this event.

It follows, therefore, that although for Barth the work of God through his Spirit is not identical with the reconciliation effected through Jesus Christ once and for all, it must, of necessity, be congruent with it. That is to say, the sphere of subjective Christian existence comes into being and persists solely by virtue of the objective reconciliation effected by God in

Christ. This is what the Reformers meant in teaching that faith lives from its object. Barth agrees. The dimensions of subjective Christian existence evident in faith, love and hope are real and possible only on account of what God did in Christ reconciling the world to himself (2 Cor. 5:19). With this in mind, we turn to the analysis of the first major chapter given to the exposition of the doctrine of reconciliation following Barth's survey of the whole.

Chapter VII

JESUS CHRIST, THE LORD AS SERVANT:
THE OBEDIENCE OF THE SON OF GOD[1]

I.   THE CONDESCENSION OF THE SON OF GOD

Throughout this section, Barth's major concern is to show the manner in which the condescension of the Son of God in Jesus Christ and his obedience in behalf of wayward humanity was for the purpose of restoring it to God through his identification with us, taking our lost cause to himself, and suffering the judgment which otherwise would have fallen to us.

The movement from God to man in the Son's condescension Barth develops in terms of the caption, "The Way of the Son of God into the Far Country." The allusion to the parable of the prodigal son (Lk. 15:11-32) is evident, but Barth does not justify his use of it until he treats "Jesus Christ, the Servant as Lord." Whereas the earlier chapter had to do with the condescension of the Son, the latter has to do with his exaltation as Son of Man which is depicted as "The Homecoming of the Son of Man." Acknowledging that to attempt a "direct christological" interpretation of the parable would be strained, Barth nevertheless adds: "But again we do not do justice to the story if we do not see and say that in the going out and coming in of the lost son in his relationship with the father we have a most illuminating

parallel to the way trodden by Jesus Christ in the work
of atonement, to His humiliation and exaltation."[2] Thus
Barth contends for the legitimacy of a kind of "indirect...typological, or _in_ _concreto_ christological
exposition" which he has attempted.[3]

A.   The Atonement as History

In Barth's view, every sound exposition of what
constitutes reconciliation between God and man must
stress that the movement is from God to man, from above
to below. Reconciliation always has to do with the true
God who wills to be with and for man in Jesus Christ.
Barth distinguishes this event and history from the
universal rule and providence of God. "God became man.
That is what is, i.e., what has taken place in Jesus
Christ."[4]   Barth never tires of insisting that the
"reconciliation of man with God takes place as God
Himself actively intervenes. ..."[5]   He regards the
fundamental apostolic witness to be to the reality of
the presence of God in the condescension of his Son,
Jesus Christ. It is in this way that we are to understand "the way of the Son of God into the Far Country."
All subordinationist interpretations of Jesus Christ
which deny his true deity Barth rules out as incompatible
with the New Testament witness. "When we have to do with
Jesus Christ we have to do with God. What He does is a
work which can only be God's own work, and not the work
of another."[6]

Crucial to interpreting Barth's view of reconciliation correctly is the avoidance of regarding it as in
some way unhistorical or trans-historical. In part, this
represents Barth's own correction of some of his earlier
usage of the concept of primal history (Urgeschichte)

which transcends the plain of ordinary history. More
importantly, the insistence that reconciliation must be
conceived as historical is opposed to Bultmann who views
the cross primarily as "the eschatological event in and
beyond time, in so far as it (understood in its
significance, that is, for faith) is an ever-present
reality."[7] Though Barth also speaks of reconciliation
through the cross as eschatological, he criticizes
Bultmann for the way the concrete reality of reconciliation in Christ looses its historical moorings in his
stress on its ever present existential significance.
This accounts, in part, for the way Barth introduces the
section dealing with the condescension of the Son:

> The atonement is history. To know it, we must
> know it as such. To think of it, we must think
> of it as such. To speak of it, we must tell
> it as history. To try to grasp it as supra-
> historical or non-historical truth is not to
> grasp it at all. It is indeed truth, but
> truth actualised in a history and revealed in
> this history as such--revealed, therefore, as
> history.[8]

Yet it is apparent that the reconciliation enacted
in history lies in the sphere of what Barth elsewhere
designates as Heilsgeschichte or salvation-history. For
"the atonement is the very special history of God with
man, the very special history of man with God."[9] Although
this history is a story which can be told, it simultaneously "underlies and includes, not only in principle
and virtually but also actually, the most basic history
of every man. It is the first and most inward presupposition of his existence. ..."[10] It is always axiomatic
for Barth that all human history is determined by, and
to be understood in the light of, this "special history

of God with man." The latter is never to be subsumed beneath some general concept of history. "The atonement takes precedence of all other history."[11] The history of God's reconciling activity is not reducible to, or identifiable with, the existential experience of the Christian believer. When "it is revealed and grasped and known, it is so in its priority, its precedence, its superiority to all other histories, to the existence of all the men who take part in it."[12]

The preeminent ontological significance of the temporal history of Jesus Christ as the fulfillment of the history of reconciliation determinative for interpreting all human history derives from the fact that it is the actualization of the eternal and gracious will of the triune God. It is because Barth sees a perfect congruity between what is actualized in Jesus Christ in history with the pre-temporal decision of the triune God that one can see the main lines of the reconciling work of Jesus Christ anticipated in his comprehensive doctrine of election published in 1942. In his opening thesis concerning the electing God, he wrote: "The doctrine of election is the sum of the Gospel because of all words that can be said or heard it is the best: that God elects man; that God is for man too the One who loves in freedom."[13] The manner in which this decision preceding all history determines all of God's activity is evident from the following thesis: "The election of grace is the eternal beginning of all the ways and works of God in Jesus Christ. In Jesus Christ God in His free grace determines Himself for sinful man and sinful man for Himself."[14]

B.   Jesus Christ: the Actualization of Atonement

From the foregoing it is already clear that the history of God's reconciling activity has its foundation in the divine decision in eternity; it therefore determines his universal covenant with humanity; it finds decisive expression in his covenant with Israel and reaches its fulfillment in the history of Jesus Christ himself.   In short, Jesus Christ is the climax of the history of the divine condescension. He is the central actor in the drama of reconciliation which relates God to humanity.   Pointedly Barth says: "The atonement is noetically, the history about Jesus Christ; and ontically, Jesus Christ's own history.   To say atonement is to say Jesus Christ."[15]   Bultmann tends to reverse this emphasis by saying, in effect, since it is reconciling, it is the history of Jesus Christ.   Barth, on the contrary, holds that because we are confronted with the subject, Jesus Christ, reconciliation is real.   "For He [Jesus Christ] is the history of God with man and the history of man with God."[16]

It is important to be clear from the outset that Jesus Christ in his person and work is not only indespensable to the initiation of reconciliation, but also in terms of all of its consequences effected through him.   "In all its different aspects the doctrine of reconciliation must always begin by looking at Him, not in order to leave Him behind in its later developments, but to fix the point from which there can and must be these later developments."[17]

This christological perspective determines the total structure of Barth's treatment of the history of reconciliation in the chapter, "Jesus Christ, the Lord as Servant."   The first section (59:1) is entitled "The

Way of the Son of God into the Far Country." Here Barth shows that the deity of Jesus Christ is attested precisely in his condescension. "That Jesus Christ is very God is shown in His way into the far country in which He the Lord became a servant."[18] Thus the deity of Jesus Christ, the subject who effects reconciliation, is manifest in his condescension and saving work. The following section, "The Judge Judged in our Place" (59:2), seeks to answer the question as to why the Lord became a servant. Barth answers: "For in the majesty of the true God it happened that the eternal Son of the eternal Father became obedient by offering and humbling Himself to be the brother of man, to take His place with the transgressor, to judge him by judging Himself and dying in his place."[19] The third section is entitled, "The Verdict of the Father" (59:3). Here the emphasis lies on the way in which God validates the judgment suffered by Jesus Christ on the cross by raising his Son from the dead. "But God the Father raised Him from the dead, and in so doing recognised and gave effect to His death and passion as a satisfaction made for us, as our conversion to God, and therefore as our redemption from death to life."[20]

We may highlight Barth's understanding of the meaning of the Son's condescension to his estranged and alienated creatures by seeing him as the expression of God's interest in, grace toward and unmerited good will in behalf of wayward humanity. Barth writes:

> In the fact that God is gracious to man, all the limitations of man are God's limitations, all his weaknesses, and more, all his perversities are His. In being gracious to man in Jesus Christ, God acknowledges man; He accepts responsibility for his being and nature. He remains Himself. He [cannot] cease [being]

> God. But He does not hold aloof. In being
> gracious to man in Jesus Christ, He also goes
> into the far country, into the evil society of
> this being which is not God and against God.
> He does not shrink from him. ,He does not pass
> by [the man who had fallen among thieves] as
> did the priest and the Levite. ...He makes his
> situation His own.[21]

Fundamental here and throughout is Barth's insistence that God did not surrender his deity in his gracious condescension to his creatures.

> He does not forfeit anything by doing this.
> In being neighbour to man, in order to deal
> with man and act towards him as such, He does
> not need to fear for His Godhead. On the
> contrary. We will mention at once the thought
> which will be decisive and basic in this
> section, that God shows Himself to be the
> great and true God in the fact that He can and
> will let His grace bear this cost, that He is
> capable and willing and ready for this conde-
> scension, this act of extravagance, this far
> journey. What marks our God above all false
> gods is that they are not capable and ready
> for this. ...God is not proud. In His high
> majesty He is humble. It is in this high
> humility that He speaks and acts as the God
> who reconciles the world to Himself.[22]

C. The Apostolic Witness to the Deity of Jesus
   Christ

We have seen that for Barth there can be no adequate understanding of the New Testament witness to the reconciliation effected in Jesus Christ apart from the recognition of his deity. Thus "the way of His incarnation is as such the activiation, the demonstration, the revelation of His deity, His divine Sonship."[23] What evidence leads Barth to this decisive conclusion?

1. Jesus--Qualitatively Other. The reality of reconciliation between God and humanity is grounded in the fact that God himself confronts his needy human family in Jesus Christ, his Son. In Barth's reading of the New Testament--particularly the Synoptics--he finds a "united testimony" to the complete, authentic and individual humanity of Jesus of Nazareth. At the same time it maintains that "in that man there has entered in and there must be recognised and respected One who is qualitatively different from all other men."[24] In no way is it permissible to equate Jesus' deity with humanity's highest evolution. "He is not simply a better man, a more gifted, or more wise or noble or pious, in short a greater man."[25] Rather, "as against all these men and their differences we have in the person of this man One who is their Lord and Lawgiver and Judge."[26] The man, Jesus, exercises a sovereign authority in relationship to all others and is further distinguished from all others as the Saviour. Summing up the New Testament witness to the uniqueness of Jesus, Barth writes:

> In attestation of this understanding of the man Jesus the New Testament tradition calls Him the Messiah of Israel, [the Son of David, the Son of Man,] the Kyrios, the second Adam come down from heaven, and, in a final approximation to what is meant by all this, the Son or the Word of God.[27]

The special dignity ascribed to Jesus in these titles is accentuated in Barth's summary statement: "It [the New Testament] lifts Him--[think of it: always this fellow-man]--right out of the list of other men, and as against this list (including Moses and the prophets, not to mention all the rest) it places Him at the side of God."[28] Barth is aware that his conclusion concerning Jesus as "qualitatively other" does not accord with the findings of many New Testament form critics. Eichholz is undoubtedly correct that Barth's treatment of this issue indicates that he has considered their positions and drawn his own conclusions.[29]

2. <u>The Witness of the New Testament Traditions to the Deity of Jesus Christ</u>. The designation of the deity of Jesus Christ as fundamental in the primitive New Testament witness is maintained, according to Barth, in the post-apostolic period. Here and elsewhere in his Dogmatics, Barth argues for an essential continuity between the witness to the Godhead of Jesus in the New Testament and the christological developments in the early church which issued finally in the dogma of the person of Christ in 451 A.D. at Chalcedon. On this basis, it is impermissible to assume that the patristic church was really involved in the divinizing of the man, Jesus. The use of christological titles in interpreting Jesus does not represent the "free apotheosis of a man."[30] Moreover, the Ritschlian-Harnackian thesis that the development of the logos christology in the early church represented an illicit metaphysical hellenizing of the original witness to the Galilean Jesus and his simple gospel does not accord with the facts.[31] It is rather the case that the knowledge of the deity of Jesus "presupposed and confirmed in the dogma--not the dogma itself--was the decisive point at which the different spirits in the Church...always divided."[32] Put even more sharply, Barth adds: "And to this day there is hardly a point of Christian knowledge and confession which is not positively or negatively, directly or indirectly, related to this one point, to this primitive Christian insight."[33]

The view of F. Loofs and others is that the

christological titles ascribing deity to Jesus Christ
represent a "religious valuation" of him by the disciples or by palestinian or hellenistic communities in
terms of their own ideologies and concepts. Barth
concedes that the apostolic and post-apostolic communities were called to make responsible interpretations of
Jesus in terms of prevailing thought patterns. He cautions, however, that evaluating this process requires
certain considerations to be kept in mind.

First, there "is no discernible stratum of the New
Testament in which--always presupposing His genuine
humanity--Jesus is... seen...or...judged in any other
way than as the One who is qualitatively different. ..."
Second, "there is no discernible stratum which does not
in some way witness that it was felt that there should
be given to this man, not merely a human confidence, but
that trust, that respect, that obedience, that faith
which can properly be offered only to God." Third,
"Allowing for every difference in viewpoint and concept,
the heavenly Father, His kingdom which has come on
earth, and the person of Jesus of Nazareth are not
quantities which can be placed side by side, or which
cut across each other, or which can be opposed to each
other, but they are practically and in effect identical." Fourth, titles purportedly "conferred" on Jesus
may not be viewed as arbitrary ascriptions "which we
might omit or handle otherwise." The titles' witness to
Jesus' deity would still be appropriate "even if it
could be proved and not merely suspected that Jesus
Himself did not expressly speak of His majesty, His
Messiahship, His divine Sonship." Moreover, the titles
finally are subordinate to Jesus himself. Thus the
disciples "do not try to crown Him in this way, but they
recognise Him as the One who is already crowned, to whom

these titles already belong." Fifth, against the backdrop of the "Old Testament concept of God" presupposed
in early Christian communities, the "apotheosis of a
man" or the "exaltation of a man as a cult-god" is
highly unlikely. Sixth, Barth insists that Jesus was, in
fact, what the disciples attested him to be even prior
to their witness. Thus: "He is to them the Christ, the
Kyrios, the Son of Man and the Son of God, the One who
is absolutely different and exalted even before they
describe Him in this way."[34]

These considerations make it untenable to regard
the church's ascriptions of deity to Jesus as arbitrary
valuations. Barth finds the New Testament witness
pointing clearly in the opposite direction. He concludes: Jesus "actually was and is and will be what He
is presented [to be] in the reflection of this witness,
the Son of the Heavenly Father, the King of His kingdom,
and therefore 'by nature God.'"[35] Finally, it is crucial
that Barth finds the confession of Jesus' deity not only
in the primitive apostolic witness, but also--as inti-
mated above--integral to Jesus' own self- witness.
Hence the primitive witness appeals "in some sense to
Himself--that He Himself continually attests Himself as
such. And in relation to others they count on it happening that they too may accept--not their own representation and appraisal of a man honoured by them --but the
Word of Jesus, His self-attestation of His majesty, of
His unity with God."[36]

Klappert underlines the thesis developed above,
namely, that for Barth the confession of the deity of
Jesus Christ is (1) based upon the oldest New Testament
traditions; (2) and derives both from Jesus' confrontation of the disciples as the one who is qualitatively
other and from his own self-testimony. In so doing,

Barth rejects accounting for the christological titles
on religious (Loofs), psychological (Weiss), cultic
(Bousset) or soteriological-kerygmatic (Bultmann)
grounds.[37] In light of the above, Hans Grass identifies
Barth's position correctly:

> The affirmation of the deity of Jesus Christ
> must not be understood as a derivative, but
> rather as a fundamental thesis. It is not a
> question of a statement which believers make
> on account of the impression made by the
> person of Jesus, or one which they have made
> or make in order to express his significance;
> we are dealing rather with a statement of fact
> in terms of which one is to think.[38]

3. The Definition of the Deity of Jesus Christ:
His Suffering and Cross. Having stated what he takes to
be the New Testament witness to Jesus' deity, Barth concedes he "must be more precise" in defining how this
confession was made both in the Gospels and Epistles.
Our question is: what gave rise to the confession of
Christ's deity?

The crucial methodological move which Barth commends is that the deity of Jesus Christ must be read off
from the concrete existence of the man, Jesus. "...the
mirror in which it can be known (and is known) that He
is God, and of the divine nature, is His becoming flesh
and His existence in the flesh."[39] Barth intends this
approach in opposition to arbitrary interpretations of
Jesus' deity which bypass, or abstract from his human
existence.

Confrontation with the human existence of the man,
Jesus, means to be met with "the mystery of His
existence."[40] Contrary to all expectations of what
constitutes deity, the New Testament speaks of the "man

Jesus as the Son of God... [in terms of] that which apparently stands in the greatest possible contradiction to the being of God; the fact that in relation to God-- and therefore to the world as well--this man wills only to be obedient--obedient to the will of the Father... ."[41] Barth finds this amply testified in Jesus' submission to baptism at the hands of John, his resistance to temptation in the wilderness, his entire ministry of servitude, his submission in Gethsemane--in short, in his doing the will of God.[42] That the mystery of the presence of God in Jesus is revealed only indirectly-- contrary to ordinary expectations--Barth underlines in stating: "The true God--if the man Jesus is the true God--is obedient."[43]

Jesus' way of obedience is one of suffering. "...the New Testament describes the Son of God as the servant, indeed as the suffering servant of God."[44] Barth does not regard the suffering of Jesus as acciden- tal or incidental. Rather, he suffers "necessarily and, as it were, essentially, and so far as can be seen without meaning or purpose."[45] While not citing Martin Kähler here, Barth adopts his thesis that the Gospels are passion stories with lengthy introductions. Barth writes:

> The prophecy which occurs three times in all the Synoptics, that the Son of Man must and will be delivered up to men, to the high- priests and the scribes, and finally to Gen- tiles, explicitly reveals the character of the whole story of the man Jesus as a story of suffering--whatever we may think of the place of these passages in the history of the tradi- tion.[46]

Jesus' way of obedience and suffering as the indirect unveiling of his deity involves not only his
condescension in sharing our humanity, but also his
bearing the judgment which otherwise would have been our
lot. Thus the way of Jesus is the way to the cross.
"He is the suffering servant who wills this profoundly
unsatisfactory being, who cannot will anything other in
the obedience in which He shows Himself the Son of
God."[47] In an extensive excursus, Barth cites materials
from the Gospels and Epistles which underline the way in
which the obedience, passion, crucifixion and death of
Jesus are ultimately revelatory of his deity.[48] He
concludes:

> Exegetes old and new have been right in their
> references and comments when they have seen
> all this [that is, the New Testament witness
> to Jesus' obedience, suffering and death] and
> tried to consider the deity of Jesus Christ in
> the light of it. On the other hand, it has
> always led and always does lead to confusion
> where this more precise understanding of the
> human being of God [or the humanity of God]
> and [thus also of] the divine being of the man
> Jesus is disregarded or weakened or not taken
> as the starting-point for all further discus-
> sion.[49]

Later Barth underlines the manner in which the
suffering and death of Jesus reveal his deity. He
interprets the New Testament witness to Jesus' passion
and death to mean that "this human action and suffering
has to be represented and understood as the action and,
therefore, the passion of God. ..."[50] Indeed, this note
is sounded even more starkly in a subsequent, fuller
explication of the way of the life of Jesus under the
sign of the cross. He anticipates again the note dominant in Moltmann's, The Crucified God, in speaking of

Jesus as a criminal dying between two criminals "with
that last despairing question on His lips, as One who
was condemned and maltreated and scorned by men and
abandoned by God. ...In the deepest darkness of Golgotha
He enters supremely into the glory of the unity of the
Son with the Father. In that abandonment by God He is
the One who is directly loved by God."[51] To be sure,
this "secret of the whole" was not disclosed to the
disciples until the resurrection of the one crucified.

In light of Barth's way of tracing the development
of the New Testament witness to the deity of Jesus,
Klappert asserts:

> Barth thus arrives at his fundamental thesis:
> the character of the entire history of Jesus
> as a history of humiliation issuing in the
> cross is the interpretive center of the primi-
> tive Christian confession of the deity of
> Jesus. In fact, in that his entire life, of
> necessity, was in the characteristic form of
> the one who suffers, the Son of God reveals
> his deity. For this reason, Barth regards the
> suffering and cross of Jesus as constitutive
> of the interpretive center which establishes
> the deity of Jesus.[52]

In adopting this thesis, Klappert takes sharp issue with
Pannenberg and others who contend that Barth's procedure
is to establish the deity of Jesus on the basis of the
traditional interpretation of the incarnation.[53]

4. Beyond the God of Theism. By virtue of the
congruity between Jesus and God, his Father, it follows
that the suffering and death of Jesus reveal not only
his own deity, but also the character of the divine
nature. If, as we have seen, Jesus' deity is attested
precisely in his servitude and lowliness fulfilled in
his death on the cross, it is impossible to view God as

some kind of impassive Absolute. Barth's theological
axiom with respect to the determination of the divine
nature is enunciated thus: "Who God is and what it is
to be divine is something we have to learn where God has
revealed Himself and His nature, the essence of the
divine."[54] An abstract and speculative theism might
project the following image of God: "We may believe
that God can and must only be absolute in contrast to
all that is relative, exalted in contrast to all that is
lowly, active in contrast to all suffering, inviolable
in contrast to all temptation, transcendent in contrast
to all immanence, and therefore divine in contrast to
everything human, in short that He can and must be only
the 'Wholly Other.'"[55] In recalling his own image of God
as "Wholly Other," Barth chides himself for some of the
excesses of his language about God in his dialectical
period; more significantly, it refers here to a concept
of God constructed without regard to God's self- revelation. "But such beliefs are shown to be quite untenable, and corrupt and pagan, by the fact that God [,in
fact, is and acts like this in] Jesus Christ."[56] That is
to say, in the light of deity revealed in Jesus Christ,
it is necessary to say that in the freedom of his grace
God reveals himself as relative, lowly, finite, passive,
suffering, immanent, worldly--and human.[57]

Barth gives powerful expression to the origin of
such statements about God as he speaks dialectically
concerning Jesus Christ:

> The Almighty exists and acts and speaks here
> in the form of One who is weak and impotent,
> the eternal as One who is temporal and perish-
> ing, the Most High in the deepest humility.
> The Holy One stands in the place and under the
> accusation of a sinner with other sinners.
> The glorious One is covered with shame. The

One who lives for ever has fallen a prey to
death. The Creator is subjected to and overcome by the onslought of that which is not. In
short, the Lord is a servant, a slave.[58]

This suffices to make Barth's point and to correct what
may be false and abstract images of God--including some
of his own earlier statements. We conclude with Barth's
typical programmatic statement: "It is in the light of
the fact of His humiliation that...all the predicates of
His Godhead, which is the true Godhead, must be filled
out and interpreted."[59]

    5. The Old Testament: the Prefigurement of
Christ's Condescension. Characteristic of Barth's view
of reconciliation effected through the condescension and
death of Jesus Christ is his insistence that it becomes
comprehensible only in the light of its continuity with
God's covenant activity with Israel.[60] New Testament
christological statements relate to one who became
"Jewish flesh," not to "a man in general, a neutral
man," but to "the One who fulfills the covenant made by
God with this people."[61] Docetic christology always
results from severing Jesus from Israel. Jesus is the
Messiah of Israel who, as such, is ordained as the
world's saviour. "The particularity of the man Jesus in
proceeding from the one elect people of Israel, as the
confirmation of its election, means decisively that the
reconciliation of sinful and lost man has, above all,
the character of a divine condescension, that it takes
place as God goes into the far country."[62] This does not
mean that the suffering and death of Jesus is provable
a priori on the basis of God's condescension in the old
covenant. It is more a matter of seeing both continuity
and difference between Jahweh's condescension in behalf
of Israel and its fulfillment in Jesus Christ. The

gracious love of God "who is one with the man Jesus His Son (Jn. 10:30) is the God who years before was not too good, and did not count it too small a thing, to bind and engage Himself to Abraham and his seed, and to the God in this particularity and limitation--'I will be your God.'"[63]

This makes apparent that what happens in the suffering and humiliation of the Son is not without precedent or accidental. There were "provisional representatives" of the "incomparable Son" in the old covenant. Barth depicts the dialectical relationship between the testaments thus:

> The Old Testament, and also the New Testament in its constant implicit and explicit connexion with the Old, makes it quite clear that for all its originality and uniqueness what took place in Christ is not an accident, not a historical novum, not the arbitrary action of a Deus ex machina, but that it was and is the fulfillment--the superabundant fulfillment--of the will revealed in the Old Testament of the God who even there was the One who manifested Himself in this one man Jesus of Nazareth--the gracious God who as such is able and willing and ready to condescend to the lowly and to undertake their case at His own cost.[64]

The way God's condescension in behalf of Israel prefigures its fulfillment in Jesus Christ is highlighted by Barth at three points. (1) Jahweh's election of Israel is an act of his condescension. That the Son of God stands in the place of Israel as God's Son in the Old Testament means "He is the same high God who in supreme humility elected Himself the God of this one small people."[65] The fulfillment lies in the fact that the elect people is represented in the "one Israelite

Jesus." The difference is that "now He [God] Himself
becomes lowly."[66]   (2) God's electing love in the Old
Testament entails his condescension in behalf of a
wayward and rebellious people.   That Jesus becomes
"Jewish flesh," that he is the "Messiah of Israel,"
means that Jesus takes his place in behalf of, and along
side of, this sinful people.   "The Son of God in His
unity with the Israelite Jesus exists in direct and
unlimited solidarity with the representatively and
manifestly sinful humanity of Israel."[67]   (3) Israel,
God's elect people, stands under God's judgment and
accusation on account of their sin and rebellion.   "To
be flesh is to be in a state of perishing before God."[68]
The decisive difference in the New Testament is that God
is identified unsurpassably with the man Jesus.   "He,
the electing eternal God, willed Himself to be rejected
and therefore perishing man.   That is something which
never happened in all the dreadful things attested in
the Old Testament concerning the wrath of God and the
plight of man."[69]

Klappert summarizes the way in which for Barth
God's condescension in behalf of Israel prefigures his
electing love and faithfulness fully expressed in the
suffering of his elect Son:

> God is essentially and necessarily one who
> exists in solidarity with the godless, who
> submits himself to judgment in the cross and,
> as such--in death, in being judged, in soli-
> darity with the godless--neither withholds his
> deity, nor acts precipitantly or peripher-
> ally, or in contradiction to himself as one
> suffering; rather, he is the one who precisely
> here is essentially, actually and necessarily
> the revealing God.   The concentration on the
> condescension of the Son of God himself on the
> cross in its underivable contingent character
> on the one hand and in its necessity on the

other provides the dynamic of Barth's exposition.[70]

II. THE SON'S SELF-ABASEMENT AS GOD'S HUMILIATION

Our analysis of God's condescension in the Son in Barth's theology to this point has dealt with its reality and facticity. This is in keeping with his methodological axiom which dictates dealing with the reality of God's self-revelation prior to asking about its possibility. This axiom is warranted on theological grounds since God is knowable only in terms of his active revelation. Though the being of God transcends his acts outside of himself (ad extra) and has priority in this sense, the being of God is revealed to us and therefore knowable by us only in his acts. Yet God truly reveals himself in his acts. The congruity which obtains between God in himself (in se) and God for us (pro nobis and ad extra) makes it legitimate to ask how God's revelation reflects something essential about his inner being. Barth therefore continues to probe the "outer moment" of the incarnation, namely, its actualization.

A. Incarnation and Humiliation

The first issue here is how God can become incarnate without ceasing to be God. Hence Barth poses the question of the incarnation's "possibility from the standpoint of God. ..."[71] In agreement with the "Christian theological tradition" Barth holds that the incarnation (Jn. 1:14) is correctly interpreted as an act of God's sovereign, free and gracious will. That God was in Christ means further that the possibility of

God's condescension in his Son is intrinsic to God's nature. He has therefore done and revealed that which corresponds to his divine nature. "God can do this."[72] Thus the possibility of the incarnation for God is the necessary corollary of its actualization. God's self-revelation in history corresponds precisely to the eternal and inner nature of God.[73]

That God becomes lowly in the "form of a servant" (Phil. 2:5ff.) is the expression of his "freedom which is that of his love."[74] God does not thereby contradict his nature. Rather, he confirms himself. "The humility in which He dwells and acts in Jesus Christ is not alien to Him, but proper to Him."[75] The incarnation and humiliation of God in the Son is thus never to be interpreted to mean that God has thereby ceased to be God. Barth's programmatic statement on this point is never negotiable in the Church Dogmatics:

> God is always God even in His humiliation. The divine being does not suffer any change, any diminution, any transformation into something else, any admixture with something else, let alone any cessation. The deity of Christ is the one unaltered because unalterable deity of God. Any subtraction or weakening of it would at once throw doubt upon the atonement made in Him. He humbled Himself, but He did not do it by ceasing to be who He is. He went into a strange land, but even there, and especially there, He never became a stranger to Himself.[76]

1. Kenotic Theories. The above discussion already presupposes Barth's conclusion regarding the correct interpretation of the so-called self-emptying (ékénosen) of God in his Son in his incarnation, condescension, obedience and finally death on the cross (Phil. 2:5-11). Barth interprets the Son's self- emptying (Phil. 2:7) in

terms of his "taking the form of a servant." This in no
way means that the Son thereby surrendered his deity.
It is rather that God had the potentiality to "humble
Himself in this form. ...He could be obedient even to
death, even to the death of the cross. He had this
other possibility: the possibility of the divine self-
giving to the being and fate of man."[77] Thus while the
Son of God has his being in the form of God (forma Dei),
he exercised his freedom to be present in the alien form
of a servant (forma servi). This involves the concealment and hiddenness of his Godhead and majesty, but not
its surrender. "He had it and He made use of it in the
power and not with any loss, not with any diminution or
alteration of His Godhead. That is His self-
emptying."[78] Common to the main line of Christian
tradition prior to the kenotic theories of 19th century
theology was the view "that the Godhead of the man Jesus
remains intact and unaltered."[79]

Where does Barth locate the errors in the kenotic
theories? Historically, it began as a debate among 17th
century German Lutheran theologians. The Giessen party
did not deny Jesus' possession of the divine majesty or
Godhead. But they interpreted the kenosis or self-
emptying involved in the incarnation to mean the
"partial abstention of the man Jesus, in the exinanitio
[humiliation], from the use of the majesty imparted to
Him."[80] This view purportedly sought to preserve Jesus'
humanity against docetic views. It became the orthodox
Lutheran view. The 19th century German kenoticists tied
on to this earlier Lutheran tradition and were particularly concerned "to find a place for the historical form
of Jesus in its human limitation."[81] Their error, in
Barth's eyes, was that they moved beyond the earlier
view that Jesus abstained from exercising his majesty or

Godhead while incarnate to assert a "partial or complete
abstention...on the part of the Son of God, the Logos
Himself, from the possession and therefore the power to
dispose of His divine glory and majesty. ..."[82] Barth
interprets the view of Thomasius to the effect that the
"kenosis [self-emptying] consisted in the fact that in
the incarnation the divine logos renounced the attributes of majesty in relation to the world (omnipotence,
omnipresence, etc.), in order that in the man Jesus,
until His exaltation, He might be God only in His immanent qualities, His holiness and love and truth."[83]

In the light of this historical excursus, Barth's
caveats—no, outright repudiation of—this 19th century
kenoticism becomes comprehensible. It is crucial that
Barth reject every kind of kenoticism surrendering the
deity of Jesus Christ. He faults all such christologies
because they surrender the "God...in Christ reconciling
the world to himself" (2 Cor. 5:19). While applauding
the kenoticist's intention to clear away the difficulties of orthodox christology and to make possible a
"historical" consideration of the life of Jesus," Barth
concludes on a sharply negative note:

> But they succeeded only in calling in question
> the "God was in Christ" and in that way damag-
> ing the nerve of a Christology orientated by
> the Old and New Testaments. There are many
> things we can try to say in understanding the
> christological mystery. But we cannot possibly
> understand or estimate it if we try to explain
> it by a self-limitation or de-divinisation of
> God in the uniting of the Son of God with the
> man Jesus. If in Christ—even in the humilia-
> ted Christ born in a manger at Bethlehem and
> crucified on the cross of Golgotha—God is not
> unchanged and wholly God, then everything that
> we may say about the reconciliation of the
> world made by God in this humiliated One is
> left hanging in the air.[84]

On the basis of the reconciliation actualized by
God in Jesus Christ, Barth affirms "that God for His
part is God in His unity with this creature, this man,
in His human and creaturely nature--and this without
ceasing to be God, without any alteration or diminution
of His divine nature."[85] This rules out certain interpretations of the incarnation and humiliation of the Son
in modern kenotic christologies. First, it is not
allowable to interpret the divine condescension and
incarnation as "an absolute paradox." According to this
view, the incarnation is understood as a novum mysterium
[new mystery]; in God's condescension in his Son, we are
confronted "with what is noetically and logically an
absolute paradox, with what is ontically the fact of a
cleft or rift in God Himself, between His being and
essence in Himself, and His activity and work as the
Reconciler of the world created by Him."[86] This ontic
cleavage within the Godhead may be designated as "the
inner-divine Paradox of Being (Seinsparadox)."[87] Such a
view contradicts Barth's basic supposition that God in
his revelation for us (pro nobis) is congruent with God
as he is in himself (in se or a se). It would still be
maintained that in himself God remains immutable and
thus omnipresent, eternal and perfect in all respects.
But in his incarnation and condescension in our behalf,
he became limited and lowly. Yet such a view posits God
in antithesis to himself: we are dealing with God's
determination to be "'God against God.'"[88] Barth admits
that this view is seldom stated so boldly. Such a
view--while not logically or theologically untenable--
Barth rejects because it posits disunity or conflict
within the Godhead. In addition, it must be opposed
because it calls the reality of God's true presence in
the person and work of his Son in question. "On this

view God in His incarnation would not merely give Himself, but give Himself away, give up being God."[89]

A second view of the nature of the paradox involved in the incarnation may be termed the "Existential Paradox" (Existentialparadox). This view is identified by H. Vogel as follows:

> Does the self-revelation of God stand under the sign of a contradiction or is it only the existence of the sinner in relation to this truth [that is, of the divine condescension] that does so? Are we not confronted at the decisive point with an existential paradox [Existentialparadox], i.e., of the contradiction characteristic of man's existence as one who stands in the presence of God?[90]

Vogel's response to his own question is that the self-revelation of God "has to do with God giving himself up to the contradiction of man against God. It is not a matter of a contradiction grounded within or dividing the being of God in himself.... It is rather the contradiction which runs through our existence."[91] Barth's view appears very similar. He insists that the condescension of God in his Son "means His giving Himself up to the contradiction of man against Him. ..."[92] That this does not entail God's ceasing to be God or entering into contradiction with himself is apparent from this statement: "God gives Himself, but He does not give Himself away. He does not give up being God in becoming a creature, in becoming man. He does not cease to be God. He does not come into conflict with Himself."[93]

Third, there is what Vogel terms "the Paradox of Judgment" (Gerichtsparadox). This has to do not only with the judgment of God on the contradiction in which man exists, but also with the fact that God takes this judgment upon himself in Jesus Christ. Barth speaks in similar fashion of the divine humiliation involving "His placing Himself under the judgment under which man has fallen in this contradiction, under the curse of death which rests upon him. The meaning of the incarnation is plainly revealed in the question of Jesus on the cross: 'My God, my God, why hast thou forsaken me?'"[94]

Klappert appropriately stresses that Barth will not allow that God ceases to be God in entering into these contradictions by which he effects our reconciliation. Barth writes: "He also makes His own the being of man under the curse of this contradiction, but in order to do away with it as He suffers it. He acts as _Lord_ over this contradiction even as He subjects Himself to it."[95] This means that God "reconciles the world with Himself as He is in Christ. He is not untrue to Himself but true to Himself in this condescension, in this way into the far country. If it were otherwise, if in it He set Himself against Himself in contradiction with Himself, how could He reconcile the world with Himself?"[96]

Although Barth's major point against allowing some kind of disunity or contradiction within God himself derives from his insistence that this calls God's entire work of reconciliation into question (as is evident from the foregoing quotation), he argues his view further by alluding to Paul's insight that God is "'not a God of confusion, but of peace.'"(1 Cor. 14:33). Barth takes this to mean that whatever God does in reconciliation accords with his inner nature. "In Him," he writes, "there is no paradox, no antinomy, no division, no inconsistency, not even the possibility of it."[97] Hence everything which God does in Christ in entering into the contradiction and curse and judgment which characterize our fallen human existence is harmonious with who he is.

As we saw above ("Beyond the God of Theism"), we must read off who God is from what he does. These are always commensurate. Hence our views of what is possible for God and what stands in contradiction to his nature are determined by what he does--not in terms of our preconceptions concerning what is appropriate or inappropriate to God. Barth concludes: "It is not for us to speak of a contradiction and rift in the being of God, but to learn to correct our notions of the being of God, to reconstitute them in the light of the fact that He does this."[98] The correlative principle which represents the answer to the questions about contradictions and paradoxes within God's nature is then enunciated as follows: "He has therefore done and revealed that which corresponds to His divine nature."[99]

It should be clear that Barth is unwilling to move even a hairsbreadth from his methodological axiom that the God who is "for us" (pro nobis) corresponds directly to God "in himself" (in se). That God's glory is concealed in taking the form of a servant is certainly true. Yet this "concealment, and therefore His condescension as such, is the image and reflection in which we see Him as He is."[100] It is therefore warranted for Klappert to accentuate Barth's thesis that precisely the divine condescension of the Son on the cross as the self-revelation of God determines what may, or may not, be regarded as possible or potential for God. By so reasoning, Barth avoids speaking of the incarnation either in terms of the "a priori methodology of Anselm on the one hand or on the basis of a christology of paradox on the other."[101] Instead, he has moved in a posteriori fashion from the reality of the cross of Jesus Christ as the fulfillment of his humiliation, making the latter constitutive for the Christian understanding of God.[102]

B. The Obedience of the Son of God: the Son's
Humiliation on the Cross

To this point Barth's concentration has been on the
"outer moment" of God's condescension in his Son. In
the form of a servant, Jesus rendered obedience to God,
his Father. It is critical that his outer obedience
reflect his inner obedience. This is, in fact, Barth's
thesis: "The way of the Son of God into the far country
is the way of [His] obedience. This is (in re) the
first and inner moment of the mystery of the deity of
Christ."[103] However, in arriving at this conclusion Barth
pro-ceeds by means of a kind of indirect approach by
attending to what can be read off from the humanity of
Jesus Christ and the reconciliation effected through
him.

Thus he argues that (1) if the "humility of Christ"
is "an attitude of the man Jesus of Nazareth;" and (2)
if the "humility of this man" entails a "free choice
made in recognition of an appointed order, in execution
of a will which imposed itself authoritatively upon
Him,"--in short, in "an act of obedience," and if (3)
"what the man Jesus does is God's own work"; then, it
follows for Barth that by beginning with the humanity of
the Son of God and with what God has effected in him it
can be said (4) that "this aspect of the self-emptying
and self-humbling of Jesus Christ as an act of obedience
cannot be alien to God."[104] Hence to speak of the obedience of Christ is a statement both about the man Jesus
and about God. This assumes that "what the New Testament says about the obedience of Christ, on His way of
suffering, has its basis, even as a statement about the

man Jesus, in His divine nature and therefore in God Himself.[105] Along this line of inquiry, Barth contends that we are confronted with the knowledge of "the other and inner side of the mystery of the divine nature of Christ and therefore of the nature of the one true God--that He himself is also able and free to render obedience."[106]

By identifying the mystery of the deity of Jesus Christ in terms of the special obedience he renders as the Son of God to his Father and therefore in his special relationship as Son to his Father, we may be confronted with the "real key" to interpreting the deity of Jesus Christ. Were this the case, we would be confronted with the "revealed mystery" of the deity of Jesus Christ.[107] In fact, this is the position Barth adopts. He holds that the primitive Christian witness to the deity of Jesus Christ was grounded finally in the belief that God himself was united with the Son in his obedience even to the cross. Barth makes this point forcefully:

> Therefore we must determine to seek and find the key to the whole difficult and heavily freighted concept of the "divine nature" at the point where it appears to be quite impos-sible--except for those whose thinking is orientated on Him [Jesus Christ] in this matter--the fact that Jesus Christ was obedi-ent unto death, even the death of the cross. It is from this point, and this point alone, that the concept is legitimately possible.[108]

Correlatively, what is revealed in the suffering and death of Jesus Christ is constitutive for the New Testament understanding of the true nature of God. Barth contends that we must see and understand "what the New Testament witnesses obviously saw and understood, the proper being of the one true God in Jesus Christ[,] the <u>Crucified</u>."[109]

From this vantage point, Barth enumerates several characteristics "of the self-humiliation of God in Jesus Christ as the presupposition of our reconciliation."[110] First, the humiliation, suffering and death through which Jesus Christ effects reconciliation is an "act of obedience" grounded in the Father's being and will. Second, the obedience of the Son to the Father reveals that what the Son and Father do in unity is neither capricious nor arbitrary. That is to say, the freedom which God exercises to condescend to us in his Son is "not one of the throws in a game of chance" taking place in the divine being. Rather, "It takes place in the freedom of God, but in the inner necessity of the freedom of God and not in the play of a sovereign <u>liberum arbitrium</u> [free will]."[111] Third, the necessity of God's free and gracious activity in his condescension to us in his Son has its correspondence in the necessary obedience of the Son. "Jesus cannot go any other way than this way into the far country."[112] In the case of the obedience of the Father and of the Son, therefore, there is no question of speaking of fate, chance or of something occurring without purpose or meaning. Rather, in the twin obedience of the Father and the Son which effects the world's reconciliation "we have to do with a divine commission and its divine execution, with a divine order and divine obedience."[113] Fourth, by virtue of the congruity between God's gracious humility in which he condescends to us and the obedience rendered by the Son in humbling himself to his Father's will, Barth speaks of God's saving event in the cross of Jesus Christ, his Son, "as worthy of unlimited confidence."[114] This line of reflection indicates the relevance of the knowledge of the necessity of the condescension of the Son of God fulfilled in the cross.

1. Beyond Subordinationism and Modalism. It appears that to reckon with obedience within God himself destroys God's unity and requires thinking in terms of "two divine beings," the one greater and the other lesser. Subordinationism has taken this view and regarded the Son as "a second divine being of lesser divinity. ..."[115] While admitting that subordinationists took Jesus' obedience seriously, Barth faults them for failing to correlate his obedience with his deity or with the presence of God in him. Hence they concluded by accentuating the obedience which Jesus as a lesser being rendered to God. In so doing, they dissolved not only the deity of Jesus Christ, but also the reconciling work of God effected by him. The end result is a christology of a "heavenly or earthly creature standing in supreme fellowship with God and to that extent supremely qualified."[116] Barth's point is unequivocal: "Anyone other or less than the true God is not a legitimate subject competent to act in this matter. ...When we have to do with Jesus Christ we have to do with God."[117]

The Modalists also intended to enforce the divine obedience of the Son and therewith his deity. But the Son's obedience represents only a temporary manifestation or mode of God; in his transcendent nature, he is distinguished from the Son and not identified with the latter's humiliation and suffering. Once again, this calls God's reconciliation through Christ in question. Barth poses the issue thus:

> For if in His proper being as God[,] God can only be unworldly, if He can be the humiliated and lowly and obedient One only in a mode of appearance and not in His proper being, what

294

> is the value of the deity of Christ, what is
> its value for us? It is as the humiliated and
> lowly and obedient One that He is the Recon-
> ciler.[118]

Barth rejects both of these positions as nominalis-
tic and incompatible with the realism characteristic of
the New Testament. The latter presupposes that "God was
in Christ" and therefore that God as "the Reconciler of
the world" is "identical with the existence of the
humiliated and lowly and obedient man Jesus of
Nazareth."[119] Accordingly, Barth insists that only the
latter emphasis accords with an adequate view of Jesus
Christ and his reconciling work. Neither position
harmonizes with the New Testament witness to God or
Jesus Christ. In contrast to his own position which
seeks to make "Jesus Christ, the Crucified," determinative for the understanding of God, the latter do not.
"Both suffer from the fact that they try to evade the
cross of Jesus Christ, i.e., the truth of the humiliation, the lowliness and the obedience of the one true
God Himself as it became an event amongst us in Jesus
Christ as the subject of the reconciliation of the world
with God."[120]

C.   Condescension and Cross in Correspondence to
       God's Triunity

We have seen that Barth has argued that we can
speak of obedience in God on the basis of what has been
revealed to us in the obedience and humiliation of Jesus
Christ. He grants it seems offensive to posit obedience
in God: that is, "that there is a below, a _posterius_,
a subordination, that it belongs to the inner life of
God that there should take place within it _obedience_."[121]

Yet Barth regards it to be illegitimate to presume a priori that the unity of God precludes the possibility of God being "both One who is obeyed and Another who obeys."[122] Nor can this subordination in God himself be rejected from the outset as being unworthy of God on the grounds that it entails some kind of gradation within the Godhead. To this Barth replies: "Does subordination in God necessarily involve an inferiority, and therefore as deprivation, a lack?"[123] Barth answers his own question in asserting that on the basis of the divine obedience visible in Jesus Christ one can draw the "astounding deduction that in equal Godhead the one God is, in fact,...the One who rules and commands in majesty and One who obeys in humility. The one God is both the one and the other."[124] This living God who exists within himself as Father, Son and Holy Spirit and is knowable in his self-revelation is to be distinguished from all abstract and neutral conceptions of God.

It cannot be our purpose to introduce the consistent and dominant Trinitarianism of Barth's Church Dogmatics here. He alludes to his exposition of the triune God even within his Prolegomena where he asserted that Trinitarianism was the distinguishing mark of the Christian doctrine of God.[125] Noteworthy here is the manner in which the obedience of the Son provides the warrant for speaking of the eternal obedience of the Son to the Father within the Godhead. This is in keeping with Barth's adoption of the classical trinitarian axiom that the operations of the Trinity in creation and history (economic Trinity) correspond to the triune life of God himself as Father, Son and Holy Spirit (ontological or immanent Trinity).

Hans Iwand has described the doctrine of the

Trinity as the expression of the christological mystery within the concept of God.[126] Klappert adapts this thesis to what he finds Barth doing: "Barth's Trinitarianism represents the inscription of the reconciliation-event, the inscription of the differentiated unity of cross and resurrection on the doctrine of God."[127] Though Barth speaks of the reflection of the triune God in the world created by him, of the clearer representation of his triune being in the life- in-relationship or co-humanity of woman and man (analogia relationis) as imago dei, these are only prelude to the full correspondence to his nature in his work of reconciliation.

> In the work of reconciliation of the world with God the inward divine relationship be-tween the One who rules and commands in majesty and the One who obeys in humility is identical with the very different relationship between God and one of His creatures, a man. God goes into the far country for this to happen. He becomes what He had not previously been. He takes into unity with His divine being a quite different, a creaturely and indeed a sinful being. To do this He empties Himself, He humbles Himself. But, as in His action as Creator, He does not do it apart from its basis in His own being, in His own inner life. He does not do it without any correspondence to, but as the strangely [con-sequent] final continuation of, the history in which He is God. He does not need to deny, let alone abandon and leave behind or even diminish His Godhead to do this. ...He does not need to be radically and totally above, the first, in order to become radically and totally below, the second. Even below, as this second, He is one with Himself. He simply activates and reveals Himself ad extra in the world. He is in and for the world what He is and for Himself. ...He is as man, as the man who is obedient in humility, Jesus of Nazareth, what He is as God (and what He can be also as man because He is it as God in this mode of divine being).[128]

Some critics like Otto Weber have accused Barth of regarding the history of reconciliation simply as the illustration of what is already predetermined and pre-figured within the transcendent and immanent Trinity. While it is true that the incarnation, humiliation and cross of Jesus Christ correspond to the eternal obedi-ence which the Son renders to his Father, Barth always insists--perhaps in fear of Hegel--that his condescen-sion is always an act of free grace. He insists that God's condescension in the form of a servant means "He becomes what He had not previously been."[129]   It is therefore Barth's intention that the "newness and strangeness," contingency and freedom of the divine condescension "not be put in the shade or weakened by this reference to its [inner]-trinitarian background."[130] That the Son became a servant may be seen in terms of the trinitarian background: "But not even in the being of the triune God is there any analogy for the fact that He does actually do it."[131]

Barth's summary statement provides the conclusion to this entire section (59:1): "The way of the Son of God into the far country, i.e., into the _lowliness_ of creaturely being, of being as man, into unity and soli-darity with the sinful and therefore perishing humanity, the way of His [becoming _flesh_] is as such the activa-tion, the demonstration, the revelation of His _deity_, His _divine Sonship_."[132]

Chapter VIII

THE JUDGE JUDGED IN OUR PLACE:
THE SUFFERING AND DEATH OF THE SON OF GOD

I. THE CROSS OF JESUS CHRIST: THE BASIS OF
   RECONCILIATION

In the first major section of the doctrine of
reconciliation, "The Way of the Son of God into the Far
Country" (59:1), we saw that Barth focused on the Lord
who became a servant in Jesus Christ. "We had to know
who the servant is who is here actively at work as
subject."[1] Accordingly, the Person of Christ and his
deity as the Son of God received the emphasis as the
subject effecting reconciliation. This is the foundation
of everything that follows and the nail on which all else
hangs. In the major section before us, "The Judge Judged
in Our Place" (59:2), attention is fixed on the goal of
the journey of the Son of God. "_Cur_ _Deus_ _homo_? [Why did
God become man?] With what purpose and to what end does
God will this and do this?"[2] In traditional terms, the
emphasis now is on the doctrine of the Work of Christ.
Yet it must be recalled that Barth opposes an artificial
distinction between the person and work of Christ.
Klappert rightly suggests that section 59:1 highlights
the christological aspect of the "working Person" while
59:2 focuses on the christological aspect of the "personal work." Put somewhat differently, we can say that

in 59:1 the person of Christ as reconciler was in the forefront as Barth underlined that "God was in Christ" (2 Cor. 5:19), in 59:2, the stress is on "reconciling the world" (2 Cor. 5:19) through the saving work of Jesus Christ on the cross.[3]

A. Introduction

At the outset of his exposition of the atoning work of Christ, Barth cautions against restricting its significance by concentrating on its existential appropriation as the first order of business. First and foremost--and always--Barth contends that the Scriptures view the reconciliation in Christ as the vindication of God himself and therewith of his gracious will and purpose. Cur Deus homo? Barth answers:

> ... He wills this and does this in an outward
> activation and revelation of the whole inward
> riches of His deity in all its height and
> depth, that He wills and does it especially
> that the world created by Him might have and
> see within it, in the Son as the image of the
> Father, its own original, that He wills it and
> does it for the sake of His own glory in the
> world, to confirm and proclaim His will not to
> be without the world, not to be God in isola-
> tion.[4]

Sola deo gloria! Solely to the glory of God! Here and elsewhere it is apparent that Barth is the true heir of Calvin. Clearly, this does not mean that God's reconciliation of the world to himself serves the gratification of a selfish ego. Rather: "In doing what He does for His own sake, He does it, in fact, propter nos homines et propter nostram salutem [for us men and our salvation]."[5]

Before assessing the manner in which the reconciling work of God comes to its fulfillment in the death
of Jesus Christ on the cross, it needs to be kept in
mind that the event of reconciliation encompasses the
totality of the Christ event. The way of the Son of God
into the foreign country of man's alienated existence,
and therewith the event of reconciliation, encompasses
the incarnation, life and ministry, death and resurrection, and finally the present reign of Jesus Christ as
the exalted Lord in his Spirit. In this section, "The
Judge Judged in Our Place," the focus falls on the way
in which Jesus Christ, the active subject who effects
the reconciliation of the world, becomes himself the
object who is judged on the cross in our place. In his
summary paragraph introducing the entire action, Barth
speaks of the "eternal Son of the eternal Father [who]
became obedient by offering and humbling Himself to be
the brother of man, to take His place with the transgressor, to judge him by judging Himself and dying in
his place."[6] Barth contends that the forensic language
of the New Testament provides him the most comprehensive
conceptuality for interpreting what is common to the
varied New Testament imagery which attempts to depict
and interpret how the Lord of the covenant, the one who
was "qualitatively Other," the Saviour, is the Judge who
was judged on the cross.

B.   Jesus' History as a Passion Narrative

In Barth's interpretation of the New Testament
witness that Jesus Christ died "for us," he emphasizes
that no adequate understanding of the suffering and
death of Jesus Christ is possible if divorced from his
history. During his lifetime, Jesus traveled the way

into the far country whose end was death. For this reason, to speak about reconciliation through Christ means telling a story about what happened "once upon a time." It has to do with what happened to Jesus Christ in his history once and once and for all. What does Barth find when he looks particularly at the "evangelical history" of Jesus recorded in the Synoptics? "What do we find in this history [Historie]?"[7]

The first (1) of the three parts of Jesus' history involves his Galilean ministry. Barth recalls his earlier emphasis in viewing Jesus as one standing "over against" both his disciples and "in marked contrast" to the "whole world of men."[8] John the Baptist preaches of the greater one who is to come after him, saying: "He will baptize you with the Holy Spirit and with fire. His winnowing fork is in his hand, and he will clear his threshing floor, and gather his wheat into the granary, but the chaff he will burn with unquenchable fire." (Mt. 3:11-12). Thus the "baptism of John is...the sign of penitent expectation of the Judge and His dies irae [day of wrath]. And it is to this baptism that Jesus of Nazareth submits. ...He does so as the Judge who has been proclaimed."[9] And even though Jesus then becomes "the evangel" and proclaims the good news of the coming kingdom to his disciples and the multitudes, he is increasingly misunderstood, forsaken, and deserted--even by his disciples. In the course of his ministry, Jesus was truly among the people as the "Lord [who] has shown Himself their Judge...in face of whom they all showed themselves...to be sinful and lost Israel, sinful and lost humanity...and also a sinful and lost band of disciples."[10]

In the second (2) part of Jesus' history, beginning with Gethsemane, Barth notes a remarkable

transition--though it is not unanticipated in the first
part. This is the story of Jesus' passion and death.
"Jesus no longer seems to be the subject but the object
of what happens. His speech is almost exclusively that
of silence and His work that of suffering."[11] This is
the story of Jesus' arrest, trials and persecution,
torture, execution and burial. What takes place is, in
effect, contrary to all expectations. Instead of the
judgment falling upon Israel, "the One whose passion is
enacted in all its stages is the only innocent One, the
One who has indeed divine authority to accuse in the
midst of sinful Israel, the "King of the Jews." In
fact, there is "a complete reversal, an exchange of
roles. Those who are to be judged are given space and
freedom and power to judge. The Judge allows Himself to
be judged. ...He is, in fact, judged."[12] Jesus dies the
death of a criminal--crucified on a cross--"hanging in
shame and agony and helplessness on a Roman gallows.
That is what we are told in the second part of the
Gospel story."[13]

Part three (3) of Jesus' history is the Easter
story which "gathers together the sum" of everything
told before. "The Easter story is the Gospel story in
its unity and completeness as the revealed story of
redemption."[14] It is the account of God's acknowledgment
of Jesus of Nazareth by raising him from the dead. This
"new Gospel history" originating with Jesus' resurrection to life out of death is what gives shape to the
Gospel story as a whole. Barth writes: "The Easter
story is the record of how it [the Gospel story] became
what it was (in all its curious structure a history of
redemption) for the disciples--not by their own discovery but by the act of God in the word and work of
Jesus Himself. It tells us, therefore, that this his-

tory, Jesus Christ Himself as He exists in this history, is significant in and by [Himself]."[15]

1. **The Objective Reconciliation in Jesus Christ** (extra nos). In the preceding quotation, Barth accentuates that reconciliation must be understood first and foremost as an objective event which occurred apart from us (extra nos) in Jesus Christ even though it happened for the world (pro mundo), and for us (pro nobis), and therewith also for me (pro me) and for each person. In emphasizing the objective facticity of God's saving event in our behalf in Jesus Christ, Barth opposes modern Protestantism's concentration on the believer's subjective appropriation of reconciliation through faith to the neglect of its objective ground.[16] Barth insists on the objective nature of the atonement which God effects in Jesus Christ at many points: the following typical depiction underlines how he views what happened in the history of Jesus Christ. It

> took place...that the Son of God fulfilled the righteous judgment on us men by Himself taking our place as man and in our place undergoing the judgment under which we had passed. ...That is what happened when the divine accusation was, as it were, embodied in His presence in the flesh. This is what happened when the divine condemnation had, as it were, visibly to fall on this our fellow-man. And that is what happened when by reason of our accusation and condemnation it had to come to the point of our perishing, our destruction, our fall into nothingness, our death. Everything happened to us exactly as it had to happen, but because God willed to execute His judgment on us in His Son it all happened in His person, as His accusation and condemnation and destruction. He judged, and it was the Judge who was judged, who let Himself be judged. ...In His doing this for us, in His taking to Himself--to fulfill all righteousness--our accusation and condemnation and

> punishment, in His suffering in our place and
> for us, there came to pass our reconciliation
> with God. Cur Deus homo? In order that God
> as man might do and accomplish and achieve and
> complete all this for us wrong-doers, in order
> that in this way there might be brought about
> by Him our reconciliation with Him and conver-
> sion to Him.[17]

While Barth finds Bultmann's preoccupation with the appropriation of the saving significance of the cross important, it is derivative from the import of the cross of Jesus Christ in itself. Speaking of the reconcilia-tion which took place in Jesus Christ, Barth says: "It took place in Him, in the one man, and therefore there and then, illic et tunc, and [also] in [its] signifi-cance hic et nunc, for us in our modern here and now."[18] On the negative side, this means that the subjective significance of reconciliation in the present cannot take precedence over its past objective significance in itself effected through Jesus Christ. The ontological and theological and therewith the methodological prior-ity of the history of Jesus to that of all subsequent believers never must be surrendered. Barth puts this axiomatically: "The relationship between the signifi-cant thing which He is in Himself and the significance which He may acquire for us is an irreversible relation-ship."[19] Barth holds that Jesus' own history is signi-ficant in and of itself and that he attests himself in the witness of the Gospel story to himself. "What is significant in itself has the power to become signifi-cant and will in fact become significant."[20] Faith--whether past, present or future--always lives in ab-solute dependence upon Jesus Christ and his history.

This emphasis on the objectivity of reconciliation marks a fundamental divide between Barth and Bultmann.

"Jesus Christ as He exists in this history [i.e., his own history and the Gospel story he continually empowers] cannot, therefore, be merged into all the significances which do, in fact, come to Him or disappear in them."[21] Thus contra Bultmann and all who subjectivize the reconciliation effected through Jesus by saying it becomes significant only by virtue of the present faith of the believer, Barth replies: "Jesus Christ for us, as a supremely objective happening, is the word of reconciliation on the basis of which there is a ministry of reconciliation."[22]

Although Barth speaks of the universal significance integral to the objective reconciliation brought about through the passion of Jesus Christ in terms of its "historical singularity," he does not assert that its meaning is ascertainable simply in terms of possible historical knowledge of it as such. Only "in the decision of faith" on the part of the individual is the "passion of Jesus Christ" known as "the act of God" which "happened for him, and therefore in very truth for the world."[23] Yet Barth rejects the widely held view that the saving work of Christ only provides the possibility for reconciliation which first becomes actual in faith. Bultmann is wrong to emphasize the latter. As we shall see, Barth finds such a view guilty of failing to acknowledge that the reconciliation of the world to God has already taken place in Christ. Barth cites Bultmann: "By Christ there has been created nothing more than the possibility of zoé [life], which does, of course, become an assured actuality in those that believe." Barth comments: "This is the very thing which will not do."[24] Our existence is already encompassed in that of Jesus Christ. "In our christological basis, in Jesus Christ Himself, everything that can be said of the relevance of His being and activity in our sphere is already included and anticipated."[25]

II.   JESUS CHRIST: THE RECONCILER ON THE CROSS "FOR US"

We are now ready to ask more systematically about Barth's portrayal of what "Jesus Christ was and did pro nobis, for us and for the world." Barth proposes "four related answers" to this question: "A.   He took our place as Judge.   B.   He took our place as the judged. C.   He was judged in our place.   D.   And He acted justly in our place."[26] This fourfold way in which Jesus Christ "was the Judge judged in our place" Barth regards as a definitive and comprehensive statement of his theology of the cross (theologia crucis) based upon the New Testament.   Boldly, Barth comments:

> All theology, both that which follows and indeed that which precedes the doctrine of reconciliation, depends upon this theologia crucis [theology of the cross].   And [all theology] depends upon [the theology of the cross] under the particular aspect under which we have had to develop it in this first part of the doctrine of reconciliation [59:1] as the doctrine of substitution (Stellvertretung).[27]

For Barth, "if the nail of this fourfold 'for us' does not hold," it follows that the entire fabric of Christian faith with its purportedly true doctrine of sin and salvation will prove to be nothing but human mythology destined for decay.[28]

A. Jesus Christ, the Judge who took our Place as Judge

Barth introduces the first dimension of the reconciliation effected by Christ "for us" as follows: "Jesus Christ was and is 'for us' in that He took our place as our Judge."[29]

1. The Judge. We noted above that in his exposition of the history of Jesus Christ recorded in the Synoptics, Barth finds it characteristic that during his Galilean ministry Jesus appears as the one who exercises judgment with sovereign authority. His preaching concerning the coming kingdom and the mighty acts and wonders he does as signs of its coming attest his sovereignty. Judgments he makes relative to his disciples or the larger crowds reveal him to be their superior, Lord and Judge. To be confronted by him and his words and deeds meant to undergo the divine judgment he himself exercised. Barth summarizes the Gospels which attest that "there has passed through the midst of all these men One who is absolutely superior to them, exalted above them, and fearfully alone. ...The Lord has been among them. And in the course, and as the result of His being among them, in fulfilment of His proclamation and work, and as its consequence, the Lord has shown Himself their Judge. ..."[30] As the Judge of the coming kingdom of God, Jesus exposes the sin and unrighteousness of both foes and friends--of all.[31]

2. The Judge who takes our Place as Judge. In a marked departure from the main line of Christian tradition, Barth contends that the true nature of human sin is uncovered only in the light of the revelation in Jesus Christ. He proposes, therefore, to "maintain the simple thesis that only when we know Jesus Christ do we

really know that man is the man of sin, and what sin is, and what it means for man."[32] In sharp contrast to the obedience of the Son of God, human sin has "its root and origin [in] the arrogance in which man wants to be his own and his neighbour's judge."[33] Human sin is unveiled as the flawed attempt to transcend creaturely limits by "trying to be as God: himself a judge."[34] For the human person as a limited creature to act as a "pseudo-sovereign creature" involves, in effect, assuming the prerogative belonging to God alone.

Human sin and fallenness are confronted when "God Himself encounters man in the flesh and therefore face to face in the person of His Son, in order that He may pass on the one who feels and accepts himself as his own judge the real judgment which he has merited."[35] God's saving action in Jesus Christ entails not only a "moral accusation" of man's pride and an "intellectual exposure" of the error of his way. It also means, more importantly, that Jesus Christ as "very man and very God has taken the place of every man."[36] This involves the displacement of man--the usurper--who destroys himself in playing God and seeking to be the final arbiter of his own destiny. In confronting humanity in Jesus Christ, "it is this function of God as Judge which has been re-established once and for all. ..."[37] To be displaced as our own judges by Jesus Christ entails a change in man's being. Barth writes: "He [man] is no longer judge. Jesus Christ is Judge. He is not only over us--a final court which we must finally remember and respect. He is radically and totally for us, in our place."[38]

For Barth, Jesus' ministry makes it clear that man's selfappointed role of being a judge and judging self and others has been terminated. The evangelical prohibition is: "Judge not, that you be not judged" (Mt. 7:1). Barth comments: "The One who forbids men to judge, who restrains and dispenses them from it, is the One who has come as the real Judge."[39] The judgment which Jesus Christ as the true Judge exercises is thus an abasement of man as a bad and false judge. "If this man is my divine Judge, I myself cannot be judge any longer."[40] Klappert's summary puts it well: "Jesus Christ is the true Judge who has come on the scene, who judges in our place, displaces us as judges, removes us from the judgment seat, acts in our place and is in this way for us."[41]

3. Judgment as Liberation and Hope. In addition to the abasement, displacement and jeopardizing of human existence which occurs by virtue of being replaced by Jesus Christ as Judge, something more is involved. Opposing both a venerable theological tradition of late medieval theology and the history of its art--which portrays Christ as the just Judge who metes out punishment or reward--Barth reclaims the biblical tradition which associates God's righteous judgments with his salvific activity. Barth recalls that the Old Testament "Judges" are appointed "to be helpers and saviours in the recurrent sufferings of the people at the hand of neighbouring tribes."[42] Moreover, the function of God or of the Son of God as Judge is not primarily to condemn and reject sinners. Rather, God's righteous judgments are in the service of his mercy: his righteousness is a merciful righteousness.

In expounding the perfections of the "divine loving" within the doctrine of God, Barth had already insisted on the interrelatedness of God's righteousness and judgment with his mercy. He states that in the light of Jesus Christ it can be seen that "the condemning and punishing righteousness of God is in itself and as such the depth and power and might of His mercy."[43] The function of the divine Judge, Barth describes as follows: "...He is the One whose concern is for order and peace, who must uphold the right and prevent the wrong, so that His existence and coming and work is not in itself and as such a matter for fear, but something which indicates a favour, the existence of One who brings salvation."[44]

Jesus Christ is one with humanity as the Judge who is the saviour. "He comes, therefore, as a helper, as a redeemer, as the one who brings another and proper order. ...He comes as the kingdom of God in person. ...to reconcile the world with God, i.e., to convert it to God."[45] This is why Barth can hold "that the fact that Jesus Christ judges in our place means an immeasurable liberation and hope."[46] It is a liberation freeing man from the burden and anxiety of judging others and himself. "Jesus Christ is Judge. The matter is taken out of my hands."[47] This replacement of man as judge gives rise to hope both for humanity and for every person because the one who is our Judge is none other than the saviour who has reconciled us to God.

B.   Jesus Christ, the Judge Judged in our Place

Barth introduces the second saving aspect of Christ's being "for us" in his passion and death thus: "Jesus Christ was and is for us in that He took the place of us sinners."[48] Christ is therefore not only the Judge who takes our place, but also the one who "lets Himself be judged for us... ."[49] This involves his "deepest humiliation" in that he has "to suffer the consequences of our sins, to be the just One for us sinners, to forgive us our sins."[50]

1. <u>The Passion of Jesus in the Gospels</u>. In recounting the Gospel story of Jesus' history, we observed
that the passion narrative marks a radical transition in
Jesus' life. Whereas Jesus is the divine subject exercising judgment in the first part of his ministry, he
"becomes the object of this judgment from ...Gethsemane
onwards."[51] This is contrary to all expectations.
Instead of acting his role as Judge, Jesus is delivered
into the hands of his accusers and judged. Barth depicts
this great reversal of roles characterizing Jesus'
passion:

> Jesus represents men at the place which is
> theirs according to the divine judgment, by
> putting Himself in the place which is theirs
> on the basis of and in accordance with their
> human unrighteousness. Jesus maintains the
> right by electing to let Himself be put in the
> <u>wrong</u>. He speaks for Himself by being <u>silent</u>.
> He conquers by <u>suffering</u>. Without ceasing to
> be action, as action in the strongest sense of
> the word, as the work of God on earth attain-
> ing its goal, His action becomes a <u>passion</u>.[52]

Barth admits that the Gospel story gives little
explanation either of the transition to his passion or
of its meaning. It simply relates that the one who as
Judge exercised judgment in the first part of his ministry was at its end the one who himself was judged.
Despite the reversal of roles, Barth will not allow
Jesus' passion and death to be interpreted as some fate
or accident which contravened his deepest intentions.
Nor does he countenance regarding only the story of the
active ministry of Jesus in the Gospels as significant
thereby minimizing the import of his passion and death.
"Rightly to understand the passion and cross of Christ,

we must not abstract it from the sequence in which this
is clear. We must understand the first part of [his]
story as a commentary on the second, and vice versa.
His passion and the cross are therefore to be understood
as His action. It is as the One who carries His cross
to Golgotha that He comes to judge the quick and the
dead."[53]

The Gospels recount straightforwardly that Jesus
suffers the charge of malefactor, blasphemer, and political agitator in silence: he suffers being accused,
prosecuted and pronounced guilty. He does not try to
save himself. He seeks no self-justification. He makes
no attempt to reject the pronounced verdict. Barth asks
in effect: "Why does Jesus not defend himself and 'his
honour as the One sent by God?'" He replies:

> We can explain this only if He saw the triumph
> of His honour as the One sent by God in what
> happened to Him, in what He had to suffer when
> He was set in antithesis to all other men as
> the one great sinner, because He fulfilled the
> will of God in so doing, because He did what
> had to be done for them and the world taking
> upon Him their sin and in that way taking it
> away from them. If this action is the meaning
> of His passion, then it is meaningful as such.
> The Gospel story says this factually [actual-
> ly]. It does not offer any theological ex-
> planation. It says hardly anything about the
> significance of the event. But in telling us
> what it has to tell, and in the way it does,
> it testifies that we are dealing with the
> event which at bottom cannot bear any other
> theological explanation than that which we
> have here tried to give in actual agreement
> with every Church which is worthy of the name
> of Christian.[54]

2. The Actions of Jesus as the One Judged. In the
most basic sense, when Jesus takes our place as Judge,

he does that for which he was ordained. It is his prerogative to judge. The "inconceivable thing is that He acts as Judge in our place by taking upon Himself, by accepting responsibility for that which we do in this place. "He 'who knew no sin' (2 Cor. 5:21) ...gives Himself...to the fellowship of those who are guilty... and not only that...He makes their evil case His own."[55] Echoing Anselm, Barth views Jesus as "very man," the representative of humanity which bears the accusation and judgment which is its lot; but since he is also "very God," he "can conduct the case of God against us in such a way that He takes from us our own evil case, taking our place and compromising and burdening Himself with it."[56]

That Jesus Christ, the righteous Judge, takes the consequences of our sin and lost cause to himself means that "He is the man who entered that evil way" so that "it can be ours no longer."[57] Christ literally takes our sin to himself. As the one judged in our behalf, he bears the accusation, judgment and curse which otherwise would be ours. In this sense, the Judge has ordained that he himself should bear man's judgment as the one judged. Christ himself is "the Lamb which bears the sin of the world that the world should no longer have to bear it or be able to bear it, that it should be radically and totally taken away from it."[58]

That God's righteous judgment in behalf of the salvation of the world entails such an undeserved benefit for us does not mean that it is not "costly grace" (Bonhoeffer). Nor should it be assumed that the "happy exchange"(Luther)--in which Jesus Christ is judged in the place of sinners and sinners are set free--is only a mock or unreal exchange because Jesus was sinless.

> If anything is in bitter earnest it is the
> fact that God Himself in His eternal purity
> and holiness has in the sinless man Jesus
> Christ taken up our evil case in such a way
> that He willed to make it, and has in fact
> made it, His own. He did not, in fact, spare
> His only Son but delivered Him up for us all
> (Rom. 8:32). And the sinlessness, the obedi-
> ence of this one man ...is that He did not
> refuse to be delivered up and therefore to
> take the place of us sinners.[59]

3. <u>The Consequences of Jesus' being Judged "for</u>
<u>us"</u>. Though the consequences of Jesus' being judged for
us are both implicit and explicit in the above discussion, several features of its significance need to be
underlined. The methodological axiom here and throughout Barth's theology is that true self-knowledge is the
corollary of the knowledge of God in Jesus Christ.
Though Barth seldom mentions Calvin's clear enunciation
of this principle in the opening statement of the <u>Insti-</u>
<u>tutes</u>, his christological modification and use of it is
patent. Accordingly, our knowledge of ourselves as
sinners obtains only through faith in, and knowledge of,
Jesus Christ. Barth puts his thesis thus: "If it is
the case that Jesus Christ made His own our evil case,
our <u>sin</u>, then in Him we obviously have to do with the
reflection, the supremely objective <u>source of knowledge</u>
of that case."[60]

It follows for Barth that inasmuch as the reconciliation Christ effected was total, man's corruption
was likewise total. "The fact that Jesus Christ died
totally for the reconciliation of every man as such...
means decisively that this corruption is both radical
and total."[61] The cure for man's corruption is therefore
either total or it is not truly salvation. This is,
indeed, what occurred through Christ. "...the atonement

made in Jesus Christ, does not consist in a partial
alteration and amelioration of his knowledge and conduct
[as sinner], but in an absolutely comprehensive transforming of his situation, in his total conversion to...
God... ."[62] Barth puts this in the form of an axiom:
"If reconciliation, and therefore the justification of
sinful man, consists in the fact that man himself in his
totality is unreservedly converted to God, then there
can be no reservations with regard to his corruption."[63]
Failure to acknowledge humanity's real and total corruption as unveiled in Christ as reconciler marks a radical
division in Christianity. "We are not one with the
Catholics and humanists--even those in our own ranks--in
the knowledge of Christ, and therefore we cannot be at
one with them in this as in so many other matters."[64]

The judgment which fell on Jesus Christ himself
standing in the place of sinful humanity is therefore
the definitive disclosure of who we are as sinners. As
a consequence, it is not possible "to separate between
us and our sins, between what we are and what we do.
..."[65] Barth puts it well: "Man is what he does. And
he does what he is."[66] Salvation--if it be true salva-
tion--must be total salvation for the sinner as a total
self, a whole self. Thus "there is no place for any
distinction between [man] as the neutral doer of sin,
and sin as his evil deed."[67]

Following Barth, we can summarize what it means
that Christ has taken our place as sinners and suffered
the judgment which otherwise would have fallen on us.
First, by taking our place as sinners, we see who we are
as sinners. Second, by bearing our sin as his own in
our place, our sin is forgiven. Third, by bearing our
sin away by taking our place as the "one great sinner,"
Jesus Christ calls us to turn from our judgment which

has been negated in him and to him in faith as the
source of our righteousness and justification.[68]

C.   The Judge _Put_ _to_ _Death_ in Our Place

Barth delineates the third dimension of God's being
"for us" in Jesus Christ, as follows: "Jesus Christ was
and is for us in that [in our place] He _suffered_ and was
crucified and _died_."[69]   Jesus' passion and death is the
subject of this section. The judgment falling upon him
presupposes the way of his obedience and is its fulfillment at a specific point in history. "The Judge who
judges Israel and the world by letting Himself be judged
fulfills this strange judgment as the man who suffered
under Pontius Pilate, was crucified, dead and buried."[70]
There are three dimensions of this "strange judgment" to
which Barth attends.

1.   The Passion and Death of Jesus as a Divine
Action. It was noted that Barth stressed that whereas
the first part of the Synoptic history portrays Jesus in
terms of his "sovereign action" as Judge, the second
part beginning with his passion depicts him as one who
suffers, is judged and dies on a cross. Barth sees a
reciprocal relationship between these two parts of
Jesus' life. In the passion of Jesus, it cannot be a
matter of Jesus' bowing to fate or chance. Quite contrary: the passion of Jesus was "action in the strong-
est sense of the word. ..."[71] The fact that in the
passion of Jesus "the subject of the Gospel story became
an object does not alter this fact. For this took place
in the freedom of this subject."[72]

Barth takes this view in contrast to a dominant
trend in contemporary scholarship which attributes
Jesus' passion predictions to the Church which puts them

in the mouth of Jesus ex post facto. In speaking of
Jesus' free resolve and acceptance of his passion and
death, Barth further disagrees with all who assess as an
unanticipated fate or calamity. Barth affirms:
"According to the common consent of the Gospels Jesus
Christ not only knew but willed that this should happen."[73] For Barth, the passion and death of Jesus are
comprehensible only in terms of God's intention and
action. Klappert puts this point clearly:

> Inasmuch as Jesus Christ is this subject, this
> sovereign Judge, this qualitatively Other, who
> belongs on the side of God, therefore his
> passion is decisively action. The decision
> with regard to the question of the subject
> active here is at the same time the prelimi-
> nary decision with respect to the question of
> the nature of the passion.[74]

2. The Passion of Jesus Christ as an Action in
Space and Time. The passion of Jesus was not only an
action, but also eventuated in the death sentence being
levied at a particular time and place on him who was the
Judge. Both secular and biblical records record that
the man, Jesus, "suffered under Pontius Pilate, was
crucified, dead and buried."[75] Hence "we are dealing
with an act which took place on earth, in time and
space, and which is indissolubly linked with the name of
a certain man."[76] Marking the passion as a "unique
[einmaliges] occurrence" serves negatively to distinguish it from "a myth which is cyclic and timeless and
therefore of all times."[77] Positively, it means that
Christ "stood overagainst man, the sinner, not only as
God, but rather as man in his place. ..."[78] According
to the Gospels, therefore, the reconciliation of the
world with God happened once for all at a "very definite

318

point in world history which cannot be exchanged for any other."[79]

3. The Passion of Jesus Christ as the Suffering of God. Prior to setting forth Barth's thesis at this critical point, we need to begin by asking him what constitutes the singularity of Jesus' passion as the foundation of our reconciliation with God? First, it is true that "many men have suffered grievously... . perhaps more grievously and longer and more bitterly"[80] than did Jesus. Secondly, it is not the case that the New Testament depicts Jesus' human suffering as different in kind from other human suffering. It was therefore "not the intention of the New Testament, nor...the intention of the Church as it understood itself in the light of the New Testament, that the fundamentally unique occurrence should be found in the human passion as such."[81] Following what he takes to be the clear New Testament perspective regarding the uniqueness of Jesus' passion, Barth states:

> The mystery of this passion, of the torture, crucifixion and death of this one Jew which took place at that place and time at the hands of the Romans, is to be found in the person and mission of the One who suffered there and was crucified and died. His person: it is the eternal God Himself who has given Himself in His Son to be man, and as man to take upon Himself this human passion. His mission: it is the Judge who in this passion takes the place of those who ought to be judged, who in this passion allows Himself to be judged in their place. ...He gives Himself to be the humanly acting and suffering person in this occurrence. He Himself is the subject who in His own freedom becomes in this event the object [who acts in it by allowing himself to be mistreated].[82]

Here a far more radical question than that of theodicy is posed: "It is a matter of the humiliation and dishonouring of God Himself...the question whether in willing to let this happen to Him He has not renounced and not lost Himself as God, whether in capitulating to the folly and wickedness of His creature He has not abdicated from His deity?...Or whether indeed he has died and might be dead?"[83] No! This is not the answer. "That God has intervened in person [for us] is the good news of Good Friday."[84] The answer to the question, therefore, contravenes all human possibilities and expectations. It derives solely from the divine good-pleasure. Has God abdicated his deity? Has he died? "...it is a matter of the answer to this question: that in this humiliation God is supremely God, that in this death He is supremely alive, that He has maintained and revealed His deity in the passion of this man as His eternal Son."[85] Hence, in the passion of the Son of God we are confronted not with a tragic finale to an otherwise significant and heroic life. Instead, Barth speaks of the fulfillment of

> the mission, the task, and the work of the Son
> of God: the reconciliation of the world with
> God. There takes place here the redemptive
> judgment of God on all men. ...In this passion
> there is legally re-established the covenant
> between God and man, broken by man but kept by
> God. On that day of suffering of that One
> there took place the comprehensive turning in
> the history of all creation--with all that
> this involves.[86]

That the passion of Jesus Christ is indeed the turning point in world history according to the New Testament, Barth states thus: "The New Testament has this in mind when in the Gospels it looks forward to the passion

story of Jesus Christ and in the Epistles it looks
forward from it to the future of the community and therefore to the future of the world and of every man."[87]

It should be clear that we have reached what Barth
takes to be the very heart of the reconciling work of
Jesus Christ. Once again, as throughout Barth's exposition of the doctrine of reconciliation to this point,
everything is contingent upon God being decisively and
unsurpassably present in, and identified with, the person
of Jesus Christ. The uniqueness of Jesus' passion and
death is an implicate of, and therefore derivative from,
the person who suffers and dies. Barth puts this
emphatically. "Because it has been a matter of this
person and His mission, therefore, the suffering,
crucifixion and death of this one man was a unique
occurrence."[88]

4. The Suffering of God in Barth's Theology. Our
analysis contends that one of Barth's major contributions
to the reinterpretation of the classical Christian
doctrine of God lies in his stress on the divine suffering. This comes to clearest expression in the doctrine
of reconciliation where God's nature as love is supremely
manifest in the Son's obedience in the far country
fulfilled in his passion and death on the cross. But the
foundation for this emphasis in Barth's theology was
already laid at the very outset of the Church Dogmatics
in his insistence that all Christian speech about God is
trinitarian and christological in focus. He published
the first volume of the doctrine of God in 1940--thirteen
years before the first volume of the doctrine of reconciliation. The entire doctrine of God is developed in
terms of "The Being of God as the One who Loves in
Freedom."[89] In his programmatic thesis summarizing this
section, Barth writes: "God is who He is in the act of

His revelation.   God seeks and creates fellowship
between Himself and us, and therefore He loves us.   But
He is this loving God without us as Father, Son and Holy
Spirit, in the freedom of the Lord, who has His life
from Himself."[90]   Thus God's love is not something
fortuitous or occasional, but constitutive of God as
God.   In a following section, Barth develops "The Perfections of the Divine Loving" in terms of the following thesis: "The divinity of the love of God consists and confirms itself in the fact that in Himself
and in all His works God is gracious, merciful and
patient, and at the same time holy, righteous and
wise."[91]

In harmony with the principle that God's revelation corresponds to God's nature in himself, Barth
completes his doctrine of God with a creative treatment
of the divine election.   As noted earlier, Barth found
it necessary to depart from much of the Catholic and
Protestant tradition on predestination, including that
of Calvin, on account of their common failure to ground
election in Jesus Christ, and therewith in the divine
love rather than simply in the divine sovereignty.[92] That
God's omnipotence is that of his love receives powerful
expression in Barth's fundamental thesis on God's eternal election: "The election of grace is the eternal
beginning of all the ways and works of God in Jesus
Christ.   In Jesus Christ God in His free grace determines Himself for sinful man and sinful man for Himself.
He therefore takes upon Himself the rejection of man
with all its consequences, and elects man to participation in His own glory."[93] Against this larger backdrop,
Barth expands the view of the suffering of God in the
condescension and death of his Son within the doctrine
of reconciliation.

Barth's consistent emphasis on the suffering divine love represents an implicit criticism of the tendency of much Catholic and Protestant orthodoxy to highlight God's absoluteness in stressing the divine impassibility and impassivity. This Greek metaphysical heritage bequeathed to Christian theology by Plato and Aristotle exalted the divine apathy (ápátheia) as the definitive indicator of the self-sufficiency of deity. Moltmann writes: "As actus purus (pure act) and pure causality, nothing can happen to God for him to suffer. As the perfect being, he is without emotions. Anger, hate and envy are alien to him. Equally alien to him are love, compassion and mercy."[94] Our analysis of Barth's doctrine of reconciliation makes it indubitable that any conception of an apathetic God unable to suffer is the polar antithesis of his view of God who freely loves and suffers.

It represents no exaggeration to say that for Barth the suffering of Jesus Christ is essential both to the definition of the deity of the Son and the deity of God. Within his doctrine of God, Barth speaks of God's self-determination in his electing love as his resolve to take the consequences of man's sin and therewith human suffering to himself. He wills this in determining his Son as "the Lamb slain from the foundation of the world. For this reason, the crucified Jesus is the 'image of the invisible God.'"[95] The suffering of God in, with, and under the suffering of Jesus is a dominant theme of Barth's doctrine of reconciliation. He therefore writes that it is "the eternal God Himself who has given Himself in His Son to be man, and as man to take upon Himself this human passion. ...He gives Himself to be the humanly acting and suffering person in this occurrence."[96] The fact that God is the co-sufferer in the suffering of the Son is what makes that suffering unique. "We are not dealing merely with any suffering, but with the _suffering_ _of_ _God_ and this man in face of the destruction which threatens all creation and every individual. ..."[97] This accounts for Jüngel's apt comment that "Barth concludes that lowliness and inner-worldliness cannot be excluded from the concept of the essence of God. God, rather, is really thought of and understood in his divinity only when he can be believed to have suffered even death, without ceasing to be God."[98]

Barth speaks approvingly of the theological tradition of Patripassianism.

> It is not at all the case that God has no part in the suffering of Jesus Christ even in His mode of being as the Father. No, there is a _particula_ _veri_ [particular truth] in the teaching of the early Patripassians. This is that primarily it is God the Father who suffers in the offering and sending of His Son, in His abasement. The suffering is not His own, but the alien suffering of the creature, of man, which He takes to Himself in Him. ...This fatherly fellow- suffering of God is the mystery, the basis, of the humiliation of His Son: the truth [and reality] of that which takes place historically in His crucifixion.[99]

Moltmann applauds Barth's deepening of Luther's "theology of the cross" noting that

> Barth has consistently drawn the harshness of the cross into his concept of God. ...Because Barth thought consistently of 'God in Christ,' he could think historically of God's being, speak almost in theopaschite terms of God's suffering and being involved in the cross of the Son, and finally talk of the 'death of God,' _de_ _facto_, if not in those very words.[100]

Barth's continuing insistence on the identity of God the Father with his Son who is judged does not mean that Jesus Christ is not also fully one with humanity. Were this the case, no atonement between God and us could take place. We would, in effect, be without an advocate or representative. In order, therefore, for a substitutionary view of the atonement to be convincing, it is necessary that Jesus Christ be both the true representative of God and of man. This, in fact, is Barth's position. If either the deity or humanity of Jesus Christ is problematic, a substitutionary theory of the way in which atonement is actual in Jesus Christ becomes unconvincing. Yet it is precisely the complete identification of God with his Son on the one hand and God's complete identification with us in our humanity through the humanity of Jesus on the other which Barth finds in the New Testament's witness to Jesus Christ. The rigorous way Barth presupposed and develops this motif in interpreting what occurs in the reconciliation achieved through Jesus Christ is typified as follows:

> God was true to Himself when He gave His Son to die for us. He did not in this way con- ceal the conflict between man and Himself, let alone ignore or overlook it. He bore it, as it had to be borne, to the bitter end, as it effected Himself as the injured party and man as the violator of His glory. His mercy consists in the fact that He took this con- flict to heart, indeed, that He bore it in His heart. ...For in Him who took our place God's own heart beat on our side in our flesh and blood, in complete solidarity with our nature and constitution, at the very point where we ourselves confront Him, guilty before God. Because it was the eternal God who entered in Jesus Christ, He could be more than the Repre- sentative and Guarantor of God to us. He could also be our Representative and Guarantor towards God. He could be the fully accredited

Representative not only of the divine Judge,
but also of the judged: of fallen Adam in his
sin; of the whole of sinful humanity; of each
individual sinner in all his being and sin-
ning. Because He was God's Son, He could take
humanity to Himself in such a way that in it
He was the Advocate for God to us and to God
for us all--this one man for every man. In
this fully accredited representation of God to
us all and of us all to God, Jesus Christ came
into the midst to bear that conflict to the
bitter end in righteousness, but in the merciful righteousness of God. In this fully
accredited representation He really suffered
our distress as the distress in the heart of
God Himself. He therefore became the object
of divine wrath and judgment and the bearer of
our guilt and punishment. Thus we do not have
here...a raging indignation of God...against
an innocent man whose patient suffering
changes the temper of God, inducing in Him an
indulgent sparing of all other men. ...We do
not have here an abstract justice of God which
is later changed into an equally abstract compassion and indulgence. On the contrary, it
is the actual and terrible wrath of God which
rules according to God's free good-pleasure in
the fulfillment of what is from the first His
merciful righteousness, and it does not need
any change of mood or weakening, but in its
strictest fulfillment it is the self-
expression of the eternal unchangingly good
will of God. And it is not the fact that a
man suffers in patience and innocence which is
the motive force of this happening. There is
no moving of God by the creature on the basis
of which God can then decide on a universal
amnesty. But it is God's own heart which
moves in creation on the basis of His own
good-pleasure. It suffers what the creature
ought to suffer and could not suffer without
being destroyed. It suffers it with omni-
potent vicariousness in virtue of the fact
that it is the heart of the almighty Lord and
Creator, who, since it is His good-pleasure,
cannot be prevented from Himself sustaining
His creature (even in the face of His own
divine wrath), as He has Himself created it.
And if the creature accepts this vicarious
suffering, accepts its own life on the ground
of this divine substitution as a gift of the

> love and grace and mercy of its Lord and
> Creator, this cannot mean that before God it
> hides behind another. ...On the contrary, the
> meaning is that it is dragged out of its
> hiding place and put fair and square before
> the face of God as the face of Him before whom
> it is utterly lost and who alone can now be
> its Saviour from death and its life. It
> means, then, that the creature is cast wholly
> and utterly upon God and bound to God as to
> Him who alone has conducted its cause and will
> conduct its cause in eternity.[101]

Among the strong emphases in this rich passage is
that of the suffering or passion of God himself in the
person of his Son. Far too often the impression given
by casual commentators on Barth's theology is that it
represents a restatement of Protestant orthodoxy with
its purported static and abstract view of God. Nothing
is further from the truth as careful readers of Barth's
Dogmatics are aware. If one mistakenly associates
Trinitarianism with an abstract and abstruse view of
God, one would be guilty of misconstruing both classical Trinitarianism and Barth's more dynamic version
thereof. Eberhard Jüngel's assessment of Barth's Trinitarianism makes unmistakably clear that to speak of God
as triune in Barth's sense necessitates tracing the
dynamic history of God's rich life in his relationships
to creation, to his covenant people, and, most especially, to Jesus Christ. Hence it is appropriate that
Jüngel entitles his paraphrase of Barth's doctrine of
the Trinity, "God's Being is in Becoming."[102]

    5. <u>The passion of Jesus Christ: the Defeat of the
Powers of Sin and Death</u>. It was noted that for Barth
the gravity of human sin is not disclosed fully apart
from the fact that it is borne by the Judge who was
judged in our place on Golgotha.[103] "Sin, therefore, is
the obstacle which has to be removed and overcome in the

reconciliation of the world with God. ..."[104] But sin is also the source of "the destruction which threatens man, which already engulfs him and drags him down" and it must be blocked at its source in the atonement.[105] "Its wages is death (Rom. 6:23). It is the sting of death (I Cor. 15:56). By it death came into the world (Rom. 5:12). And the concept of death in the New Testament means not only the dying of man but the destruction which qualifies or rather disqualifies it, eternal death, death as the invincibly threatening force of dissolution. It is to this place that man moves as a sinner."[106]

In contrast to Bultmann and others who regard the cross of Christ as significant only as it is proclaimed and accepted in faith, Barth insists that as the act of God for us it is first of all, and therefore primarily, significant in and of itself. For the former to be true "presupposes a definite message concerning the passion itself and as such."[107] Bultmann does not go far enough in stressing the facticity or "thatness" of the cross without asking about the "how" and the "what" of the cross, that is, about its content. For Barth, if the cross of Jesus Christ is not significant and saving truth in itself and as such, it can in no way become true by being proclaimed or believed. With the New Testament and the Reformers, Barth insists that faith always looks to Jesus Christ. "New Testament faith does not curve in upon itself or centre on itself as fides qua creditur" [i.e., 'faith which believes' or subjective faith].[108] Hence to ask why the passion of Jesus Christ is significant in itself is neither due to speculative interests nor to an attempt to prove its significance historically.

[On the contrary, it is much more simply a
matter of the question of truth; or more
precisely, a matter of the recognition of the
answer to the question of truth which is given
and included in the act of God for us.] Truth
is the disclosure and recognition of that
which is as it appears to man. ...Christian
experience, as the manifestation of that which
is, i.e., of Him who is, can be true and of
the truth. But it is not so in abstracto, in
itself and as such. It is true to the extent
that it proceeds from the truth, and therefore
from that disclosure and recognition. ...It is
true in and by its source, in and by Jesus
Christ as its basis, upon which it is dependent but which is not dependent upon it.
...For that reason we cannot be content to
define the passion of Jesus Christ as "the act
of God for us," however that may be, but we
must go on to define the act of God for us as
the passion of Jesus Christ. [In it, and in
it alone, is it the "act of God for us." With
it (i.e., the passion of Jesus), the truth of
our Christian-human experience of existence
stands or falls].[109]

In order for the sinner to be reconciled to God,
only God can help. "Where the intervention of God in
person is needed, everything is obviously lost without
that intervention, and man can do nothing to help
himself. That God has intervened [for us] in person is
the good news of Good Friday."[110] For reconciliation to
occur, there must be a correspondence between the power
of sin and eternal death and the impending perdition and
judgment confronting the sinner on the one side and the
judgment which Jesus Christ, the Judge, bears in our
stead on the other. "Our position is such that we can
be rescued from eternal death and translated into life
only by total and unceasing substitution, the substitution which God Himself undertakes on our behalf."[111] That
the Judge is judged for us entailed "treading the way of
sinners to its bitter end in death, in destruction, in

the limitless anguish of separation from God, by deli-
vering up sinful man and sin in His own person to the
non-being which is properly theirs, the non-being, the
nothingness to which man has fallen victim as a sinner
and towards which he relentlessly hastens."[112]

While conceding that one can say that the Judge
suffered the punishment which is the consequence of
human sin, Barth rejects certain Anselmic notions
associated with this doctrine. The concept of punishment is not central to New Testament views of atonement. Its rightful usage necessitates rejecting both
the idea that the suffering of Jesus "'satisfied' or
offered satisfaction to the wrath of God" or that Jesus'
"suffering our punishment" means that "we are spared
from suffering it ourselves. ..."[113]

The decisive issue in the suffering of the Judge is
that in him the actual destruction of the first Adam,
the sinner, and therewith of us, and of sin has taken
place once and for all.

> ...in the suffering and death of Jesus Christ
> it has come to pass that in His own person He
> has made an end of us as sinners and there-
> fore of sin itself by going to death as the
> One who took our place as sinners. In His
> person He has delivered up us sinners and sin
> itself to destruction. He has removed us
> sinners and sin, negated us, cancelled us out:
> ourselves, our sin, and [therewith] the
> accusation, condemnation and perdition which
> had overtaken us. ...The man of sin, the first
> Adam, the cosmos alienated from God, the
> "present evil world" (Gal. 1:4), was
> [defeated] and killed and buried in and with
> Him on the cross. On the one side, there-
> fore, He has turned over a new leaf in the
> history of the covenant of God with man,
> making atonement, giving man a new peace with
> God, reopening the blocked road of man to God.
> [That access had been bolted from within, from
> man's side, and had to be opened once more

from within, from man's side.] That is what
happened when Jesus Christ, who willed to make
Himself the bearer and Representative of sin,
[allowed] sin to be taken and killed on the
cross in His own person (as that of the one
great sinner). And in that way, not by
suffering our punishment as such, but in the
deliverance of sinful man and sin itself to
destruction, which He accomplished when He
suffered our punishment, He has on the other
side blocked the source of our destruction; He
has seen to it that we do not have to suffer
what we ought to suffer; He has removed the
accusation and condemnation and perdition
which had passed upon us [in that he has
cancelled their objectivity to us]; He has
saved us from destruction and rescued us from
eternal death.[114]

It is crucial to highlight the dominant chord
sounded here and everywhere Barth assesses what occurred
in the "passion of Jesus Christ" as "the judgment of God
in which the Judge Himself was judged."[115] By virtue
of the absolute and complete identity between Jesus
Christ and sinners in the judgment which he bore in our
place, Barth speaks of the destruction and negation of
the sinner and of sin which thereby took place. This
quid pro quo is not understood in some symbolic or
figurative sense. Barth understands the atonement as
actualized ontologically and therewith literally. The
radical unity between Jesus Christ and humanity and the
radical judgment he suffered for us in our place makes
it necessary to regard him as our substitute or representative in whom, therefore, the judgment upon the
sinner has been carried out definitively.

Barth suggests that it is appropriate to speak here
of "satisfaction," but not in the sense that Christ's
death pacified the divine wrath. Satisfaction is rather
to be understood to mean "that God has done that which
is 'satisfactory' or sufficient in the victorious

fighting of sin to make this victory radical and total."[116] It is thus that the "No" which is involved in the judgment of the sinner is in the service of the "Yes" of God which underlies it. Barth describes the radical exchange brought about by God's doing what is "satisfactory" thus:

> For the sake of this best, the worst had to happen to sinful man: not out of any desire for vengeance and retribution on the part of God, but because of the radical nature of the divine love, which could "satisfy itself only in the outworking of its wrath against the man of sin, only by killing him, extinguishing him, removing him. ...He has done that which is sufficient to take away sin. ..."[117]

Barth's prediliction for military imagery to describe Christ's reconciling work often is evident in the doctrine of reconciliation. Its usage is traceable to the Romans commentary written against the backdrop of World War I. Typically, Barth pictures God in his reconciling work in Christ doing battle with "the principalities and powers" (Col. 2:15), the powers of sin, death and destruction which hold sinful humanity captive. Paradoxically, the passion and death of Jesus Christ represent a divine action--indeed, it is the victorious climax of the pitched battle between God in Christ and all hostile forces opposing him and enslaving humanity. In his death on the cross, the victim is paradoxically the victor. "He disarmed the principalities and powers and made a public example of them, triumphing over them in him" (Col. 2:15). Clearly, the imagery of the classic "Christus victor" (Christ, the Victor) atonement theory resounds with great force in Barth's depiction of the drama of reconciliation.[118]

D.   The Judge who does <u>Right</u> in our Place

"Jesus Christ was and is for us in that in our place He <u>has</u> <u>done</u> that which was <u>right</u> in the eyes of God and thus in truth."[119] This is Barth's thesis regarding the fourth dimension of the manner in which God is "for us" in the passion and death of Jesus Christ effecting reconciliation.

1.   <u>The Righteousness of God</u>. In speaking to the point of how God is for us in Jesus Christ as "the Judge, the judged and the judgment," Barth acknowledges that these aspects make it appear that reconciliation "<u>seems</u> to be purely negative."[120] This is the case because humanity's enmity against God and usurpation of the divine right of judgment requires that God's reconciling action against man take this "negative form" entailing the suffering and death of his Son. This means that "Jesus Christ has to be the Judge, the judged and in His own person the fulfilment of the judgment. ..."[121] However, the "No" which is carried out in the judgment which falls on Jesus Christ and appears wholly negative is, in fact, in the service of God's grace and thus ultimately positive. Barth defines this action as the righteousness of God. Its source lies neither in the world nor humanity: they contribute nothing to it. In it we are met with God's action alone.

> The Judge, the judged, the judgment--the one Jesus Christ who is all these things and in and by Himself does all these things--is the <u>justice</u> or <u>righteousness</u> [<u>Gerechtigkeit</u>] <u>of</u> <u>God</u> in the biblical sense of the term: the omnipotence of God creating order, which is "now" (<u>nuni</u> <u>dé</u> Rom. 3:21) <u>revealed</u> and <u>effective</u> as a turning point for this present evil aeon (Gal. 1:4) to the new one of a world reconciled with God in Him, this One.[122]

It is apparent here that Barth seeks to correct a
more traditional view of the divine justice which requires satisfaction. He does so by regarding the righteousness of God in Jesus Christ as "identical with the
free _love_ of God effectively interposing between our
enmity and Himself, the work and word of His _grace_."[123]
In addition, Barth recalls his modification of the
traditional dogmatic concept of "judge" alluded to
earlier in defining the divine righteousness as "the
omnipotence of God creating order."[124] Hence God's
righteousness does not refer to something apart from
Jesus Christ on the basis of which salvation occurs.
This means "comprehensively that in this action Jesus
Christ was amongst us and lived and acted for us as _the
just_ or _righteous_ man: 'the just for the unjust.'"[125]

    2. _Jesus Christ, the Righteous Man_. What are the
characteristics of the righteous action of Jesus Christ,
the righteous man, through which he brings about reconciliation between man and God by once again restoring
the order which ought to obtain between them? Barth is
thus asking how Jesus Christ, the righteous man, reveals
the righteous God.

    First, Barth recalls the title of this entire
chapter, "The Obedience of the Son of God" (par. 59), in
stressing that Jesus Christ "lived and acted as the one
man _obedient_ to God."[126] Sin involves man's disobedience,
forfeiture of freedom and unrighteousness: this is the
history of the first Adam who exists "in the wrong
before God." Jesus Christ, the second Adam, is obedient,
free and righteous: he exists in the right before God
and therewith is able to restore the rightful order
intended between man and God. Barth summarizes this
first point: "The atonement is therefore _positively_ the
removal of this unrighteousness by the existence of the

one _obedient_ and therefore free man."[127] Jesus Christ as
the second Adam marks the beginning of a new aeon and a
new humanity in that in his person "this new and obedient and free man" lived and died for all.

Second, Jesus did the right, or acted righteously,
for us "simply in His complete _affirmation_ of this
reversal, this execution of _judgment_ in the _judging_ of
the _Judge_."[128] The obedience of Jesus is synonymous with
his sinlessness. The latter is not to be interpreted as
"abstract and absolute purity," but rather as Jesus'
refusal to maintain his own right against God in his
life and death for us. That is, whereas Barth sees that
humanity sins--every person--sins by usurping God's
prerogative by acting as his own judge--Jesus "takes our
place as sinners" in that he takes "upon Himself this
guilt of all human beings in order in the name of all to
put God in the right against Him. In so doing He acted
justly in the place of all and for the sake of all."[129]
Barth pictures Jesus' way into the far country, therefore, as his way of obedience and penitence on behalf of
the many. In this sense, Jesus was "the one great
sinner. ...the one lost sheep, the one lost coin, the
lost son (Lk. 15:3f.), and therefore ...as the Judge He
is the One who is judged."[130]

E.   Summary

Following Barth we may summarize his entire analysis of the larger question as to why God became man (_Cur
Deus homo_?) and the question of this section, namely,
"what Jesus Christ was and did _pro nobis_, for us and for
the world." Barth's four interrelated answers are: "He
took our place as _Judge_. He took our place as the
judged. He was _judged_ in our place. He did that which

was just in our place."[131]

Barth concludes that the development of his doctrine of reconciliation and, indeed, the whole of his theology, is dependent on this theologia crucis (theology of the cross) and its particular view of representation and substitution. He reiterates his major thesis that the reconciliation Jesus Christ effected "for us" is valid only as the true God (vere deus) is active in the Son.

> Everything depends upon the fact that the Lord who became a servant, the Son of God who went into the far country, and came to us, was and did all this for us; that He fulfilled, and fulfilled in this way, the divine judgment laid upon Him. There is no avoiding this strait gate. There is no other way but this narrow way. If the nail of this fourfold "for us" does not hold, everything else will be left hanging in the [air] as an anthropological or psychological or sociological myth, and sooner or later it will break and fall to the ground.[132]

Chapter IX

THE RESURRECTION OF THE CRUCIFIED: THE AWAKENING, APPEARANCES AND ASCENSION OF THE SON OF GOD

I.   THE AWAKENING OF JESUS: THE REVELATION OF THE
     RECONCILER[1]

Barth's initial exposition of the awakening of Jesus
concentrates on the identity of the person involved. His
basic thesis is that "the raising of Jesus Christ (with
all that it implies for us and for all men) is in the New
Testament comprehended and understood as an act of God
with the same seriousness as the preceding event of the
cross with its implication for us and for all men."[2]
This unique occurrence of the awakening of the one
crucified and buried is developed along three lines.
First, the raising of Jesus is an act of God; second, it
is the exemplary form of God's revelation; and third, it
is a free act of God's grace. We need to examine each
of these emphases.

A.   The Raising of Jesus: the Exclusive Act of God

Jesus' suffering and death on the cross which Barth
interprets as a divine judgment making God's gracious
intention to effect our salvation through his Son
efficacious may also be viewed in terms of Jesus'
obedience or simply as a human act. However, to inter-

pret the cross solely in terms of its "historical" character or "pragmatic context" fails to comprehend its "real meaning" as "the work of God." Thus Barth affirms: "As the judgment of God, the event of Golgotha is exclusively the work of God."[3] Though not stated here, for Barth it is axiomatic that neither one nor the totality of God's saving acts is comprehensible simply in terms of their "historical" setting. Attention also must be given both to God's involvement and to its perception through faith.

That Jesus was raised from the dead on the third day is "unequivocally marked off from the first happening [i.e., the cross] by the fact that it does not have in the very least this component of human willing and activity."[4] Hence the awakening of Jesus "takes place quite outside the pragmatic context of human decisions and actions."[5] Barth therefore holds that the raising of Jesus from death cannot be viewed as "historical" in the same sense as the cross. "Like creation, it takes place as a sovereign act of God, and only in this way."[6] Where the dead are raised, "God and God alone is at work." "To raise (égeírein) the dead, to give life (zoopoieîn) to the dead, is, like the creative summoning into being of non-being, a matter wholly and exclusively for God alone, quite outside the sphere of any possible co-operating factors (Heb. 11:19; 2 Cor. 1:9; Rom. 4:17)."[7]

B. The Raising of Jesus: the Exemplary Form of Revelation

While Barth acknowledges that the New Testament records events such as Jesus' baptism, signs and transfiguration accentuating the unique presence of God in him, the full revelatory significance of these pre-Easter happenings was understood only retrospectively in the light of the event of Easter and the forty days. Moreover, though the disciples were eyewitnesses of Jesus' ministry and some had witnessed his death, "they were, like the rest of Israel, 'fools, and slow of heart to believe' with regard to God's presence in Him."[8] The mystery of "the way of the man Jesus, and of the end of that way on the cross of Golgotha, was first revealed to them and perceived by them when the event was already past, when the man Jesus was dead and buried and had been taken from them...when all bridges between Himself and them...previously...available...had been broken."[9] That the crucified had been raised could not be postulated or surmised; it could be affirmed only "from the divine revelation which had taken place in this event."[10]

Barth rejects Bultmann's contention that the New Testament witness to the raising of Jesus focuses on "a [nature] miracle accrediting Jesus Christ... ." For the disciples, God's raising of Jesus meant the acknowledgment of the "true, original, typical form of the revelation of God in Him and therefore of revelation generally, the revelation which [illumines] for the first time all God's revealing and being revealed (in Him and generally)."[11] Prior to that disclosure, the presence of God in Jesus' ministry and especially in his ignominious death remained partially hidden and paradoxical to his followers. Only on the basis of the revelatory character of the event of Jesus' appearances to the disciples as the one raised from the dead was his identity known and confessed. Barth underlines this point:

> For the first community founded by this event,
> the event of Easter Day and the resurrection
> appearances during the forty days were the
> mediation, the infallible mediation as

unequivocally disclosed in a new act of God,
of the perception that God was in Christ (2
Cor. 5:19), that is, that in the man Jesus,
God Himself was at work, speaking and acting
and suffering and going to His death, and that
He acted as, and proved Himself, the one high
and true God, not in spite of this end, but on
this very way into the far country which He
went to the bitter end, in this His most
profound humiliation, at the place where an
utter end was made of this man.[12]

In sum, that God raised Jesus out of death is the
definitive disclosure of the identity of the Son of God
who became a servant and who suffered and died on the
cross thereby effecting humanity's reconciliation with
God. For this reason Klappert insightfully concludes
that in Barth's view the identity of Jesus Christ as the
subject who reconciles us to God is not established by
means of the correlation between the incarnation and the
raising of Jesus but rather in terms of the correlation
between Jesus Christ crucified and resurrected.[13]

      C.   The Raising of Jesus: the Act of God's Free
            Grace

     - That God was in Christ in the Son's way into the
far country leading to his cross precludes holding that
"Jesus Christ as the Son of God was associated with the
Father as the Subject of His own resurrection."[14]
Pointedly Barth states: "The New Testament does not put
it this way."[15] The awakening of Jesus from the dead is
consistently attributed to the work of God, the Father
(Gal. 1:1, Rom. 6:4). The Son is totally dependent upon
the Father in his dying and death. Crucial to Barth's
argument is the New Testament distinction between the
awakening of Jesus (Auferweckung) "which happened to

Jesus Christ" and his subsequent resurrection appearances. "It is one thing that He 'rises again' and shows
Himself (éphanróthe) to His disciples as the One raised
from the dead (Jn. 21:14). Quite another thing is the
act of this [awakening] (Auferweckung)."[16] In Jesus
being raised through the power of God, we have to do
wholly with an action of God. In being raised by his
Father, Jesus is "a pure object and recipient of the
grace of God."[17] The Son's utter dependence on the
Father is radicalized in his suffering and death. That
He was raised from the dead was God's new and sovereign
act following his death. "It was not the result of His
death. Its only logical connection with it was that of
the sovereign and unmerited faithfulness, the sovereign
and free and constantly renewed mercy of God."[18] He was
raised sola gratia! Through "God's free act of grace"
alone, Jesus was raised from the dead.

Summing up, we ask: to what extent does the raising of Jesus as the exclusive act of God on behalf of
the Son reveal the hidden identity of the Son veiled in
his humiliation on the cross? Barth gives several
answers: First, the raising of Jesus is revelation in
its exemplary form as a singular act of God disclosing
the self-offering of the Son on the cross. Second, the
raising of Jesus is the revelation of the one humiliated
as the Son of the Father: the raising of Jesus as the
act of God in behalf of the Son is the Father's confirmation and revelation of the humiliated one as the Son
of the Father. It is to the one crucified that the
Father grants the name of kurios (Phil. 2:9). Third,
the raising of Jesus is the revelation of the obedience
of the Son in relationship to the Father: that Jesus
was raised is an act of God's pure grace in the Son's
behalf testifying to the faithfulness of the Father

toward his obedient Son.[19] Thus the raising of Jesus as an exclusive act of God is the clear revelation of the subject of reconciliation on the cross! It is the exemplary form of the revelation of God.[20]

II. THE RAISING OF JESUS: THE VALIDATION OF THE ACT OF RECONCILIATION EFFECTED THROUGH THE CROSS

A. The Raising of Jesus as a New Act of God

Barth treats the awakening of Jesus as a divine act entailing a divine judgment. The raising of Jesus from the dead--according to Barth's second major thesis--is "that in relation to the happening of the cross it is an autonomous, new act of God. It is not, therefore, [merely] the noetic converse of it."[21] Though standing in an "indissoluble connection with the event of the cross," the event of Easter has a "particular character" as a "different happening."[22]

Barth speculates that the powers of chaos, sin and death could have effected a final separation between man and God. But according to the "inconceivable love" essential to God's original decision to affirm humanity within his good creation, he chose "in grace not to surrender His own right, and His creature; and therefore to be in the right without giving chaos the last word and supreme power over the creature...to act and demonstrate and reveal Himself as God and Lord of the world after the fulfilment of His judgment on the world... . He did not have to do it, but He was also free to do it."[23] That God's "No" is encompassed in His "Yes" is the miracle of Easter.

B.   The Raising of Jesus as the Verdict of God

The raising of Jesus "is the great <u>verdict</u> <u>of</u> <u>God</u>, the fulfilment and proclamation of God's decision concerning the <u>event</u> <u>of</u> <u>the</u> <u>cross</u>."[24]   Barth accentuates this new act as God's validation, acceptance, acknowledgment, answer, and confirmation "of Jesus Christ, of His life and death."[25]   In raising Jesus, God justified his Son. Paul teaches us that the Son was "vindicated in the Spirit" (1 Tim. 3:16) and "raised for our justification" (Rom. 4:25).[26]

We need to ask: what are the implications of God's new act in raising Jesus after his death on the cross on the one hand and of his verdict pronounced in raising the one crucified on the other? With respect to the raising of the Son from the dead, we have seen that it has noetic significance since it illumines and reveals the person of the subject, the Son, who in his suffering and death actualized humanity's reconciliation to God. In addition, God's new act in raising Jesus "confronted His being in death, that is, His non-being, as the One who was crucified, dead, buried and destroyed, as the One who had been and had ceased to be."[27]   Thus Jesus' awakening was of the "Judge...judged...and...the Priest...sacrificed. He was 'delivered up for our trespasses' (Rom. 4:25). He had delivered Himself up (Gal. 2:20)."[28]

The Father's deliverance of Jesus from death was his "judicial sentence that the action and passion of Jesus Christ were not apart from or against Him [God], but according to His good and holy will, and especially that His dying in our place was not futile but effective, that it was not to our destruction but to our salvation."[29]   Thus   the   divine   approval   and acknowledgment of the Son in raising him from the dead validates the personal work of reconciliation effected on the cross through the Son. It does not mean, however, that the work of reconciliation effected by God through the Son on Golgotha was in need of some kind of completion or supplementation by raising him from the dead.[30]

C.   Summary

First, the awakening of the crucified Jesus from the dead is related to the cross while being a new act of God with its own content. It is neither to be identified with the disciples' believing recognition of the significance of the cross (Bultmann) nor as the completion of the reconciliation effected through the cross. Second, the Father's awakening of Jesus is his acknowledgment of Jesus Christ, the crucified one; it is the Father's judicial validation of the death and reconciling work of the Son effected on the cross. Third, the raising of Jesus from the dead is the efficacious proclamation of the teleological subordination of the "No" of God to his "Yes" concealed under its opposite in the cross. That God raised Jesus from the dead is the justification of God and his electing will; it is the justification of Jesus Christ; and it is the justification of sinful humanity in him. That God's saving work in and through his Son was not finally negated in the cross by the powers of chaos, sin and death is declared in the divine verdict pronounced by God in raising his Son.[31]

III. THE RESURRECTION: THE REVELATION OF THE ROYAL MAN
     EXALTED ON THE   CROSS

Whereas the statements concerning the awakening of
Jesus from the dead in the first two theses had as their
theme the humiliation of the Son and the judgment of the
Judge judged on the cross, the third thesis has to do
with the resurrection as the revelation of the "royal
man" exalted on the cross.   In designating Jesus of
Nazareth as the "royal man," Barth recalls that he is
viewing Jesus Christ in terms of his "kingly office"
(munus regium) in which as the Son of Man or servant, he
is the Lord.   Here the accent falls upon "Jesus Christ
as the true and new man in virtue of his exaltation, the
second Adam" with whom God united himself in the incarnation.[32] Corresponding to the condescension of the Lord
who became a servant (CD 4:1), there is the exaltation
of this servant/Son of Man as the Lord (CD 4:2, par.
64). Barth views the import of "The Exaltation of the
Son of Man" as the "royal man" for completing humanity's
reconciliation to God through him in the following
comprehensive thesis:

> Jesus Christ, the Son of God and Lord who
> humbled Himself to be a servant, is also the
> Son of Man exalted as this servant to be the
> Lord, the new and true and royal man who
> participates in the being and life and lord-
> ship and act of God and honours and attests
> Him, and as such the Head and Representative
> and Saviour of all other men, the origin and
> content and norm of the divine direction given
> us in the work of the Holy Spirit.[33]

Now the focus is on the revelation of the lordship of
the one crucified.

A.   The Resurrection as the Revelation of the
      Royal Man Exalted on the Cross

To what extent, Barth asks, is it precisely the
resurrection which reveals the royal man exalted on the
cross?   This involves the rejection of three false
positions.

First, the resurrection's significance is not
construable as "a continuation of His being in a changed
form which is its fulfilment."[34]   God's saving work in
Christ's passion was complete and perfect in itself.
"The humiliation of God and the exaltation of man as
they took place in Him are the completed fulfilment of
the covenant, the completed reconciliation of the world
with God."[35]

Second and conversely, Barth opposes Bultmann's
view that the resurrection is to be identified with the
rise of faith in the hearts of the disciples and thus as
the expression of their recognition of the significance
of the cross.[36] The resurrection and ascension of Jesus
Christ are acts of God which "take their place alongside" and over against the existence and history of
Jesus Christ which ends with his death.[37] Proclamation
of the resurrection can be construed as the explication
of human faith and thus of a new self-understanding only
secondarily and as a result of this event. The resurrection is not in the first instance the actualization
within the hearts of the disciples of the knowledge of
the royal man exalted on the cross. Rather, the resurrection is to be distinguished from the cross as an
event with its own content and significance.

Third, and finally, the resurrection (Auferstehung)
is not identical with the awakening (Auferweckung) of
Jesus from the dead through the power of God. Jesus was

awakened from the dead: that is God's act. Then he appeared to his disciples: this follows after his being awakened which remains undescribed and unattested in the New Testament. "God awakened Him and thus He is raised."[38] Barth laments: "If only Christian art had refrained from the attempt to depict it [i.e., this miracle]. He comes from this event which cannot be described or represented--that God awakened Him. It is in consequence of this that He appears to His disciples."[39] Jesus thus was raised from the dead exclusively through God's activity; however, the appearances have to do with Jesus' active self-revelation. "The resurrection and ascension of Jesus Christ are the event of His self-declaration."[40]

In this way Barth interprets the resurrection appearances as self-manifestations of the crucified Christ raised from the dead through an act of God, and thus of the one who is identical with the royal man exalted on the cross. Whereas the exaltation of the royal man is grounded in the humiliation of the Son of God on the cross (CD 4:1), the resurrection, as the appearance to his disciples of the one who was raised, is grounded in the awakening of the one crucified. Summing up: the resurrection is not to be identified as a) the completion of the being and activity of the royal man exalted on the cross; or b) as the actualization of the Easter faith of the disciples; or, finally, c) with the awakening of Jesus from the dead (Auferweckung) which event is its foundational presupposition. With these delimitations, we understand the resurrection as the self-testimony and revelation of the royal man exalted on the cross.[41]

B.   The Resurrection as the Revelation of the
     Royal Man Exalted on the Cross

The issue confronting Barth here is why precisely
the resurrection is the revelation of the royal man who
dies upon the cross.   Why does the New Testament not
relate the resurrection primarily to Jesus' proclamation
and ministry as the self-revelation of the new reality
of the kingdom of God?   Or does the resurrection have as
its primary corollary the anticipations of his resurrection in such events as his signs, transfiguration, and
the Great Confession which make clear that "the light of
the event of Easter and the ascension...is not entirely
absent even in the pre-Easter sequence[?]"[42]   Expressed
differently in the vein of Pannenberg, ought not the
resurrection be seen as the confirmation of Jesus'
absolute claim to authority which had been announced in
a preliminary way through his words and deeds?   Or is
Marxsen correct that the resurrection is to be related
to, and interpreted primarily in terms of, the further
actualization of the "Sache Jesu" (Jesus' cause) and
only secondarily related to his death on the cross?
Barth's thesis that the resurrection is the revelation
of the royal man exalted precisely on the cross is
established on several grounds.

First, the resurrection is the revelation of the
reconciling work of Jesus Christ which only comes to its
final completion on the cross--and not before.[43]   Easily
overlooked is an obvious fact: "What was to be re-
vealed--the being of Jesus Christ as very God and very
man, and therefore the humiliation of the Son of God and
the involved exaltation of the Son of Man--was indeed
virtual and potential from the very beginning of His
history and existence, but it was only in His death on

the cross that it was <u>actually</u> and <u>effectively</u> accomplished and completed."[44]   In his pre-Easter ministry,
Jesus was moving toward the completion of his messianic
work. "How could that which had not yet been completed
be revealed as completed?"[45]   Barth interprets the
witness of the Gospels to be that it "is only at the end
and goal of the passion...that there did and does take
place the realisation of the final depth of humiliation,
the descent into hell of Jesus Christ the Son of God,
but also His supreme exaltation, the triumphant corona-
tion of Jesus Christ the Son of Man."[46]   If the "Messianic <u>secret</u> is no more and no less than the secret of
the Messianic <u>work</u>," then the "resurrection and ascension of Jesus Christ are the <u>completed</u> revelation of
Jesus Christ which corresponds to his <u>completed</u> work."[47]
This is Barth's first clarification of why the resurrection is the revelation of the saving work of the Son of
God and Son of Man which came to its completion on the
cross.

Secondly, "the resurrection and ascension of Jesus
Christ are the revelation... .of the divine No and Yes
[<u>finally</u> <u>accomplished</u> <u>on</u> <u>the</u> <u>cross</u>]".[48]   Following
Kähler, Barth understands the Gospels essentially as
passion narratives with brief introductions. They
recount the history of the Servant on the way from Bethlehem to Golgotha; it is the way of the Son's condescension.

> What was revealed in His resurrection and
> ascension was the secret of His way--the way
> which was not just any way, but led from
> Bethlehem to Golgotha, the place where He was
> condemned for us but also acquitted, where in
> and with His life the life of all humanity
> represented in Him was judged, and justly
> rejected and condemned and destroyed, but also
> (because this took place in the loss of His

life) justified and sanctified and saved in
His life by the grace of God. It is in this
way, in the divine No and Yes finally spoken
on Golgotha, that His being was fulfilled as
the humiliated Son of God and exalted Son of
Man. It was in this way that the reconciliation of the world with God was accomplished in
this unity of His being.[49]

Barth's concluding thesis is therefore follows:
"The resurrection and ascension of Jesus Christ are the
revelation which corresponds to this completion of His
work, manifesting it as such, declaring its meaning and
basis."[50] Thus the resurrection is the revelation of the
royal man already anticipated in his words and deeds:
he is the one in whom the divine No and Yes are definitively and completely accomplished in the cross; therefore the resurrection is related primarily to the
exalted man who reigns and rules on the cross.

Thirdly, the resurrection is the revelation of the
man who on the cross was fully conformed to God.[51] In
what way is the resurrection the revelation of the royal
man exalted on the cross? Or put differently: What
does it mean that "His death is the act of the Son of
Man, His cross the dominating characteristic of His
royal office?"[52] Barth responds to this question along
the following lines: it was in his passion and death on
the cross that Jesus is supremely and definitively the
royal man because his solidarity with sinful humanity is
realized there in its greatest depth. There "He was and
is our Brother, and fulfilled His brotherhood with us
... ."[53] There, on the cross, he suffered as the
"Neighbor" for us as his neighbors.[54] Typical of Barth's
many statements is the following:

The definitive form of the elevation and
exaltation of this man, of His identity with

God's eternal Son, was that in which He gave
human proof of His humanity and obedience to
the Father, of His humiliation, of His human
suffering and dying as a rejected and outcast
criminal on the wood of curse and shame. It
was for this that He was sent as the Son of
God. And He was true to His mission as the Son
of Man. In this He Himself recognised and
accepted His determination. This was the
divine decree fulfilled in His life. This had
to be, therefore, the final action in the
story of the elect covenant-partner, the
people Israel, and the beginning of the story
of the new covenant with the whole world, at
which the former had aimed from the very
first, which had always been its meaning and
promise.[55]

Seen in this way, the cross is the definitive sign
of Jesus Christ as the royal man: on the basis of this
event, Jesus Christ is the man who is wholly conformable
to God and his will. In summation, Barth writes:
"...His death...is the clear and complete and consistent
fulfilment of His human abasement, and therefore the
human complement and repetition of the self-humiliation,
the condescension, in which God Himself became one with
us in His Son."[56] Hence "...His cross [is] the dominating characteristic of His royal" office.[57] For this
reason, for Barth the resurrection has the cross as its
primary corollary; it is the royal man exalted and
ruling on the cross who is revealed in his resurrection
from the dead.

C. The Resurrection as the Revelation of the
Royal Man Exalted on the Cross

The resurrection is the revelation of the royal man
elevated on the cross in that it unveils that which was
hidden in the cross. "For the being of Jesus Christ as

Lord, as King, as Son of Man, as true man, is a hidden being."[58] That the servant who suffers is indeed the Lord is hidden from us in the cross; the "Yes" is concealed beneath the "No."[59] In order for us to be able to perceive that the crucified one is God's Son, it had to be revealed to us in Jesus' resurrection. The mystery of the cross, the paradox that the servant is the Lord, is not a problem humanly soluble. The crucified one must come to us: we cannot go to him. Through God alone may God be known! Acknowledgment of this fundamental mystery is possible only because the crucified appeared to his disciples as the risen Lord. We are not left alone and to our own resources in relationship to him. The New Testament witness to the sequence of the events of cross and resurrection both have to be heard. "We have to hear the two sides of the message in their irreversible sequence, the first as the first (which always has to be heard too), and the second as the second. He is the Crucified who as such closes Himself off from us, and He is the Resurrected who as such discloses Himself to us."[60]

D.   The Resurrection as the Efficacious Lordship
      of the Crucified

The resurrection as the revelation of the lordship of the crucified is the disclosure of reconciliation completed through him. As the manifestation of the royal man exalted on the cross, the "event of Easter...is the initiation of His lordship as the Lord of all time."[61] Barth commends Luther for teaching that God's act in the resurrection attests that the crucified "'lives and reigns to all eternity.'"[62] To acknowledge that the crucified one has been given the name which is above every name is to confess that "'Kyrios is Jesus Christ, to the glory of God the Father'" (Phil. 2:10).[63] The Son's elevation attested in his resurrection appearances has cosmic implications: the one crucified and resurrected is the "Lord of Time."[64] Concerning the risen Lord, Barth writes: "Jesus Christ is in fact our Lord, and power flows from Him. The way from the one to the other, from Him to us, is wide open, and He Himself already treads it."[65] By virtue of Christ's resurrection as the royal man, the representative man, we are incorporated into his lordship. Our inclusion in his lordship is not hypothetical: it is not added to by our decision.

"The ascension of Jesus Christ is the termination point of this history of revelation."[66] To confess with the Apostles Creed and the New Testament that Jesus Christ "ascended into heaven" is to speak of a "hidden" dimension. "When He went into this hidden sphere He went to God."[67] Barth stresses the eternal God-manhood of the Mediator, Jesus Christ, who, "by virtue of His ascension, goes to the place of [the] origin of all the dominion of divine power and grace and love. It is not only God who is now there, but as God is there He, this man, is also there. That this is the case is the hidden thing which is revealed in the ascension of Jesus Christ."[68]

From the foregoing it is apparent that the crucified Jesus is the primary referent of the resurrection appearances. His lordship was present--though hidden--in his reconciling work on the cross. Inasmuch as the one crucified was raised and appeared to his disciples, they confessed him as Lord in their present history. In addition, Barth speaks of the final and definitive future fulfillment of Christ's lordship. Klappert

rightly criticizes Moltmann's charge that Barth operates
with a static eschatology which allows for no open
future. As early as his discussion of "Jesus, Lord of
Time,"[69] Barth writes: "He who comes is the same as He
who was and who is."[70] Barth specifically cautions
against some kind of "diffused hope" for the future
"apart from and alongside Him, the last One."[71] This was
a decade before Moltmann's Theology of Hope which, at
times, seems to equate a general "hope for the future"
with Christian hope. Barth affirms: "The hope of the
apostles and the community could only be hope in Jesus.
It could only be a looking to His being in this third
dimension."[72] In that future fulfillment in his parousia, his "glory" will no longer be revealed in a "particular and transitory" form but as "universal and per-
manent, embracing the whole of creation both in heaven
and earth."[73] Barth concludes: "The first community
hoped because it owed its existence to the promise
vouchsafed in the resurrection of Jesus: 'begotten
again unto a lively hope by the resurrection of Jesus
Christ from the dead' (1 Pet. 1:3). Hence it could only
hope in Him, in His coming glory commenced in the resurrection and to be completed in the parousia."[74]

E. Summary[75]

Barth's major affirmations concerning the lordship
of the royal man exalted on the cross and revealed
through his resurrection from the dead may be summarized
as follows.

1. Having been raised from the dead, the resurrection refers to the appearance of Jesus Christ to his
disciples from his first appearance until his ascension.
Thus the resurrection is the revelation of the royal man

exalted on the cross. As such, the resurrection of Jesus Christ (phaneroûn) is neither to be interpreted as the completion of the being and work of the royal man exalted on the cross nor as its actualization in the Easter faith of the disciples: nor is the resurrection to be identified with the awakening of Jesus from the dead which is its presupposition. Inasmuch as the manifestation of the royal man exalted on the cross derives from the self-manifestation of Jesus Christ, it is the resurrection itself which is the revelation of the royal man exalted on the cross, that is, of the man exalted and ruling on the cross.

2. The resurrection is the completed revelation of the royal man who is exalted on the cross. Therefore, the resurrection's primary point of reference is the cross inasmuch as there Jesus Christ first completed the work of the royal man. It was initially on the cross that the divine "No" and "Yes" was fulfilled in Jesus Christ. It was on the cross that Jesus was for the first time the man completely conformed to God. Finally, this is the case because Jesus' earthly activity already was enacted under the shadow of his death; he was already being qualified as man in view of his cross. Inasmuch as the resurrection is the revelation of the royal man whose work is first fulfilled on the cross, its primary point of reference is the cross. Thus whereas in CD 4:1 the cross and the awakening of Jesus from the dead constitute the interpretive center from which the vere deus (truly God) is comprehended, in CD 4:2, cross and resurrection are the interpretive center for comprehending the vere homo (truly man). As the man exalted and reigning on the cross, Jesus of Nazareth is the true man.

3. The resurrection is the revelation of the royal

man who remained hidden beneath the contradiction of the cross. Inasmuch as Jesus Christ is the exalted man initially and definitively on the cross while being simultaneously its opposite in the form of the man who is most abased and hidden on the cross, the resurrection is the revelation of the royal man whose identity basically is veiled on the cross. Therefore, the resurrection has as its primary point of reference the cross as the actual place where the man is exalted and ruling.

4. The revelation of the lordship of the reconciler established on the cross is itself a new act of lordship: the revealed lordship of the crucified is the efficacious realization and preservation of the lordship of the reconciler established on the cross. As the revelation of the lordship of the crucified, the resurrection is the beginning of the preservation of his efficacious lordship. The revelation in the resurrection of the one exalted and ruling on the cross is simultaneously the initiation of the lordship of Christ, the Victor, who manifests the actualized reconciliation.

IV. THE RESURRECTION OF THE CRUCIFIED: AN ACTUAL EVENT IN HISTORY

In this final section, Barth examines the awakening of Jesus and his appearances as occurrences in our space-time continuum--and in this sense--"the historical character of the content of the Easter stories."[76] He treats this as a formal, though important, amplification of his earlier exposition.[77] We noted that Barth views the resurrection as a real happening in history in that it is an implicate of Jesus' being raised from the dead, and therewith as the validation of the reconciliation effected on the cross (CD 4:1); as such, the resurrection is the revelation of the royal man exalted on the cross (CD 4:2).

A. Jesus' Awakening from the Dead as Event--an Implicate of its being a Divine Verdict

That Jesus was raised from the dead "has happened in the same sense as His crucifixion and His death, in the human sphere and human time, as an actual event within the world with an objective content."[78] Critical here is Barth's insistence that Jesus' resurrection cannot be understood apart from his own past lifetime. "...Jesus Christ appears to His disciples, revealing Himself to them as the One who has risen again from the dead... ."[79] Thus the "kerygma tells us, and faith lives by the fact, that God has ratified and proclaimed that which took place for us, for redemption, for our salvation, for the alteration of the whole human situation, as it will finally be directly and everywhere revealed."[80] Along this line, Barth interprets the resurrection accounts essentially as reconciliation stories.

Why does Barth emphasize that Jesus' awakening had the character of an event in relationship to the divine judgment effected on the cross? Why should the judgment pronounced in the raising of Jesus be seen as an objective happening in relationship to the teleology of the cross? Barth answers:

> If Jesus Christ is not risen--bodily, visibly, audibly, perceptibly, in the same concrete sense in which He died, as the texts themselves have it--if He is not also risen, then our preaching and our faith are vain and futile; we are still in our sins. And the apostles are found 'false witnesses,' because

they have 'testified of God that he raised up Christ, whom he raised not up' (I Cor. 15:14f.).[81]

The fact that it is the crucified who addresses his disciples and us in his "concrete otherness" means

> to hear in Him the Yes which has been spoken in and with and under the No of His death and ours, to find ourselves addressed in Him as those who are liberated from judgment and death, as those who are set in fellowship and peace with God... . This address, He Himself as the One who addresses us in this way, is the basis of our faith.[82]

For Barth, faith is not self generated.

> We do not, therefore, only believe that we are called and are the children [of God]--on the basis of a parthenogenesis or creatio ex nihilo of our faith regarded as an act of God. We are the children of God because we who could not say this of ourselves, however strong our faith, are addressed as such by the Son of God who was made flesh and raised again in the flesh... .[83]

Klappert summarizes:

> The character of the awakening of Jesus as an event in space and time is thus an implicate of the divine verdict pronounced in it in relationship to the cross. It is not because the awakening of Jesus is an event in space and time that it is the judgment of the Father; rather, because the awakening of Jesus as a judgment of the Father is related to the cross as an event in space and time, it is an event with an inner worldly objectivity and, to that degree, is the external ground of faith.[84]

B.   Jesus' Resurrection as Event--an Implicate of
     its Revelatory Character

Barth holds that "in the resurrection and ascension
of Jesus Christ we have to do with an inwardly coherent
event."[85] Like his death which preceded, it is distinct
as "an event within the world, in time and space. It,
too, takes place in the body, although not only in the
body."[86] As stated earlier, the occurrence of the
resurrection in space and time is always interpreted as
the revelation of the one exalted on the cross. The event
of the resurrection

> consisted in a series of concrete encounters
> and short conversations between the risen
> Jesus and His disciples... . these encounters
> are always described as self-manifestations of
> Jesus in the strictest sense of the term... .
> self-manifestation means (1) that the execu-
> tion and termination as well as the initiative
> lie entirely in His own hands and not in
> theirs... . Self-manifestation means (2) that
> the meaning and purpose of these encounters
> consists simply and exhaustively in the fact
> that the risen Christ declares Himself to them
> in His identity with the One whom they had
> previously followed and who had died on the
> cross and been buried.[87]

Or as Barth puts it in an earlier excursus on the resurrection: "He had been veiled, but He was now wholly and
unequivocally and irrevocably manifest."[88]
     At this point Barth warns against the quick sur-
render of the corporeality of the risen Jesus.

> It is impossible to erase the bodily character
> of the resurrection of Jesus and His existence
> as the Resurrected. Nor may we gloss over
> this element in the New Testament record...as
> a false dualism between spirit and body as

[some have] repeatedly tried to do. For unless Christ's resurrection was a resurrection of the body, we have no guarantee that it was the decisively acting Subject Jesus Himself, the man Jesus, who rose from the dead.[89]

Jesus' "glorified corporeality," however, is subordinate to the New Testament emphasis "that the relevance of the self-manifestation of the risen Christ is to be found always in the demonstration of His identity with the One who had lived and taught and acted and gone to His death."[90]

It should be clear why Barth accentuates the resurrection as an event in space and time as a corollary of the self-testimony and manifestations of the resurrected one in his identity with the one crucified. He states:

...if it were [only] a supernatural or even [only a] supersensual event which as such would not be experienced or attested by men, it might be all kinds of things, but it would not be an event of revelation. The fact that it was an event of this kind, and had a decisive significance as such, emerges afterwards in the changed attitude of the disciples to their Lord, especially after Pentecost, but even in expectation of Pentecost. But if it was an event of this kind, it was a concrete element in their own history, and therefore a concrete element in human history at large.[91]

Thus Barth argues for the character of the resurrection as an event occurring in space and time and experienced by the disciples on the basis of the continuity between the crucified Jesus and the risen one attested in his revelatory self-manifestations and self-testimony as the risen one.[92] The reality of Jesus' self-attestation to his disciples as risen Lord gives rise to "the knowledge of our love for the One who has first loved us in Jesus Christ."[93]

    C.   The Resurrection Event as a Pre-historical Occurrence with an Historical Implicate

Barth maintains consistently that the Gospels recognize that in the witness to the Easter event and the appearance stories "we are led into a historical sphere of a different [singular] kind."[94] There is first of all no "real account" of Jesus' being raised. "It is simply indicated by a reference to the sign of the empty tomb. Then it is quietly presupposed in the form of attestations of appearances of the Resurrected."[95] Barth further admits that the "account of the resurrection appearances" whether analyzed singly or collectively do not give "us a concrete and coherent picture, a history of the forty days."[96] The Apostle Paul further complicated the picture in providing "another account" of what happened (1 Cor. 15:4-7) and by including "the appearance to himself" on the Damascus road long after the forty days within his list of appearances. Finally, there is the added fact that "reported appearances... came only to those who by them were quickened to faith in the crucified Jesus Christ."[97] Klappert notes, however, that these factors neither lead Barth to force the interpretation of these New Testament accounts of the awakening and appearances of Jesus into such alternatives as "historical-non-historical," "history-kerygma," "History-_Übergeschichte_" (supra-history), nor to develop an ontology of history which would make room for the dimension of historical contingency in general and therewith the contingency of the resurrection event in particular.[98]

Taking what appears to be Troeltsch's definition of what constitutes an historical event as a starting point for discussing the resurrection, Barth counters:

> If in modern scholarship "historical ground" means the outline of an event as it can be seen in its "How" independently of the standpoint of the onlooker, as it can be presented in this way, as it can be proved in itself and in its general and more specific context and in relation to the analogies of other events, as it can be established as having certainly taken place, then the New Testament itself does not enable us to state that we are on "historical ground" in relation to the event here recorded. There is no reason to deplore this. After all that we have seen of the nature and character and function of the resurrection of Jesus Christ as the basis, and in the context, of the New Testament message, it is inevitable that this should not be the place for the "historicist" concept of history.[99]

According to historical canons, death is final and the dead are not raised. "The death of Jesus Christ can certainly be thought of as history [Historie] in the modern sense, but not the resurrection."[100] The awakening of Jesus from the dead and the appearances as events in space-time transcend the realm of what ordinarily counts as "historical." Barth continues:

> It is beyond question that the New Testament itself did not know how to conceal, and obviously did not wish to conceal, the peculiar character of this history, which bursts through all general ideas of history as it takes place and as it may be said to take place in space and time. There is no proof, and there obviously cannot and ought not to be any proof, for the fact that this history did take place (proof, that is, according to the terminology of modern historical scholarship).[101]

Does Barth therefore posit a realm transcending history in the sense of the alternative between "historical" and the trans-historical (übergeschichtlich); or does he reduce the historicity of the resurrection to the genesis of the disciples' faith by which they came to acknowledge the saving significance of the cross as does Bultmann? Barth's position moves in another direction. He states:

> ...we should be guilty of a fundamental misunderstanding of the whole New Testament message if, because the history of the resurrection is not history in this sense, [i.e., as ordinarily conceived,] we tried to interpret it as though it had never happened at all, or not happened in time and space in the same way as the death of Jesus Christ, or finally had happened only in faith or in the form of the formation and development of faith.[102]

Such a statement raises the question as to how accounts "which by the standards of modern scholarship have to be accounted as saga or legend and not history...may still speak of a happening which, though it cannot be grasped historically--is still _actual_ and _objective_ in time and space."[103]

It is essential to note Barth's distinction between the non-historicity of the resurrection as an event transcending human possibilities and causalities on the one hand and the historicity of the resurrection in the sense that as datable and locatable it occurs in space and time on the other. The fact that Jesus was raised from the dead wholly apart from any human cooperation or action through an exclusively divine act does not mean it was not an occurrence in space and time. "It [i.e., the resurrection] begins outside the gates of Jerusalem on the third day after that of Golgotha... ."[104] Thus as an event it "stands in a sequence of time and space" rather than being some nebulous horizon which can be everywhere or nowhere.[105] It is along these lines that Barth speaks of the resurrection as an historical occurrence. "...sound exegesis cannot idealise, symbolise or allegorise, but has to reckon with the fact that the New Testament was here speaking of an event which really happened, as it did when it spoke earlier of the life and death of Jesus Christ which preceded it and later of the formation of the community which followed it."[106]

Thus Barth affirms both the resurrection's historicity insofar as it is related to a particular place and time and its non-historicity insofar as it is exclusively an act of God. The Easter history and Easter time are datable and locatable and, in this sense, have "a tiny 'historical' margin."[107] On the other hand, the resurrection "by virtue of its very nature is inaccessible to 'historical' verification... ."[108] The non-historicity of the resurrection has to do with the fact that as an exclusive act of God it occurs outside of, or without respect to, human activity or natural causality; hence its "content" is not ascertainable by means of the historical-critical method.[109] For these reasons Barth concludes that the resurrection implies the historical plane while at the same time being an event which "cannot be grasped historically" and, to this degree, may be spoken of as a "'pre-historical' happening."[110] As an exclusive divine act, the resurrection transcends the plane of ordinary history; on the other hand, by virtue of its impingement on our space- time continuum in terms of its locatability etc., it implies the historical plane.

In Barth's view, therefore, the resurrection as event can neither simply be identified with its historical facticity on the one hand nor treated abstracted from it on the other. For Barth there is an irreversible correlation between the resurrection as an act of God and its historical facticity. The affirmation that the crucified Jesus was raised from the dead never can be made solely on the basis of historical investigation; as an act of God sui generis, it transcends ordinary historical possibilities and categories. In this sense Barth always has held that revelation is not a predicate of history. Revelation always has to do with God's activity which engages us in our history, but it is not subsumable as a category within it. The fact that the New Testament witness to the resurrection points to a unique miracle effected exclusively through God implies the "historical" dimension within which the risen Lord makes himself known.[111]

Barth's insistence on accentuating the priority of the resurrection as an act of God through which Jesus was awakened from the dead necessitates dealing with it in the context of its New Testament attestation. This precludes (1) a purportedly neutral and objective approach to the resurrection's historical facticity which knows in advance of the investigation of the texts what may be affirmed as "historical." He encourages the continuing need for an historical investigation characterized by the "most impartial and painstaking investigation of the texts which speak of" the event of the resurrection. If such historical investigation "is to be meaningful as an introduction, the 'historical' element to which it addresses itself will have to be the attestation of this event as we have it in the New Testament texts in their character as historical documents. It will not be 'the historical facts' which we have to find (or think we have already found) somewhere behind the texts, and which we then claim as objective reality."[112]   (2) A proper understanding of the New Testament witness to the risen Jesus should not focus more than is the case in the New Testament on the "miraculous character" of his appearances. The focus of the New Testament is on "the Lord Himself who is in the centre of the picture, and not the miracle of His appearing (although this is emphasised too)."[113]   (3) As indicated above, Barth holds that there can be no real comprehension of the facticity of the resurrection if the issue of its historicity is abstracted from the resurrection of Jesus as an eschatological act of God. Barth makes his point as follows:

> The statement, "Christ is risen," clearly implies the statement: "A dead man is alive again" and that his grave is empty. But it only *implies* it. If we *abstract* the latter assertions from the former, they become (whether accepted or denied or "demythologized") *uninteresting* for the understanding of the texts and their witness. They *cannot* be considered as a basis for the knowledge of Jesus Christ--not even if we affirm them "historically" in the sense of the remarkable investigation of H. F. von Campenhausen. ...The Easter-stories and the whole Easter message of the New Testament do not give us any reason to make this kind of abstraction. And, if not all, at least many of the questions that we have to put to them will lose their point if they are considered from this angle.[114]

With respect to the intention of the New Testament witness to the resurrection, Barth contends that the apostolic community "was not interested in any resurrection or actuality of resurrection in general, but in the resurrection of this man, and the resurrection of all

men inaugurated by it. In other words, it was interested in something which is beyond the reach of general
polemics against the concept of a miracle which embraces
nature, and indeed of a general apologetics in favour of
this concept."[115]

D.   Summary

Barth's major theses regarding the resurrection of
Jesus and of the relationship of the cross and resurrection may be summarized as follows:

1.   The raising of Jesus from the dead is exclusively a divine act. As such, it is the paridigmatic
form of God's revelation. It is an act of God's free
grace in behalf of the crucified Son serving to reveal
the Son through whom reconciliation has been actualized
on the cross. Inasmuch as the identity of Jesus as the
reconciler is veiled in the cross, the Father's raising
of him reveals the one crucified as the one through whom
reconciliation takes place (par. 59:1). Along these
lines Barth interprets the crucifixion and resurrection
of Jesus as the paradigmatic events determinative for
affirming the true deity of Jesus Christ.

2.   In his second major thesis, Barth views Jesus
being raised from the dead as God's positive judicial
verdict attesting that the one crucified for us and
thereby enduring the divine negation is vindicated.
Along these lines Barth interprets the unity of the
cross and resurrection of Jesus Christ as the interpretative center for comprehending how the reconciliation of the world with God takes place through Jesus
Christ (par. 59:2).

3. Barth's third thesis is that the resurrection of Jesus reveals him to have been the royal man precisely in his suffering and death on the cross. The obedience of the man, Jesus, to God his Father comes to its fulfillment in the cross. In this sense, Barth views Jesus as the one who was in fact already the exalted royal man on the cross. In that the resurrection reveals the one crucified as the royal man exalted on the cross, it is in light of the cross and resurrection of Jesus that his true humanity is to be interpreted.

4. Inasmuch as God's raising of Jesus from the dead is an exclusive divine act transcending all human and historical possibilities, its content is not historically ascertainable. Since there is no human witness of its occurrence, it is also not historically verifiable. Nonetheless Barth holds that the appearances of crucified Jesus to certain disciples and the empty tomb point to the historical dimension recoverable through historical means and reconstruction. The fact that Jesus' awakening from the dead transcends the ordinary course of historical causality necessitates holding that its "event-character" is an implicate of the confession of the identity of the risen one with the one crucified. Along these lines Barth maintains that the interconnectedness of the cross and the awakening/resurrection of Jesus provides the interpretive center for regarding these occurrences as events happening in space and time.[116]

Chapter X

JESUS CHRIST, CRUCIFIED AND RISEN:
THE UNITY OF HIS CROSS AND RESURRECTION

The preceding analysis of Barth's major theses regarding the interpretation of the death and resurrection of Jesus Christ presupposes the positive relationship and connection he construes between them. We noted that Barth's first thesis was that the raising of Jesus from the dead served to reveal the hidden identity and deity of the Son crucified on the cross. According to Barth's major thesis, the raising of Jesus by God, the Father, was the divine validation of the act of reconciliation effected by the Son on the cross for us. The third thesis depicted Jesus' resurrection as the revelation of him as truly man, the royal man, exalted to lordship on the cross and therewith his true humanity. Along these lines the positive connection and correlation between the death and resurrection of the person, Jesus Christ, has been both implicit and explicit. Barth now turns to an elaboration of this connection.

I.   THE POSITIVE CONNECTION BETWEEN THE CROSS AND
     RESURRECTION

The import of this fourth and final thesis is evident when Barth says: "We come to the point which is decisive for our investigation when we ask...what is the positive connexion between the death of Jesus Christ and His resurrection."[1] To this point we have looked primarily at the connection between cross and resurrection in terms of a "backward reference" from the resurrection to the cross. In this section, Barth accentuates the "forward reference" of the cross to the resurrection. In neither instance, however, can either event be isolated or abstracted from the other or subsumed beneath the other. Barth prefers to speak of the death and resurrection of Jesus Christ as two events in a connected teleological sequence which requires speaking of their reciprocal relationships. Thus "...it is a genuine sequence and correspondence in a differentiated relationship in which both factors have their proper form and function."[2] Insight into Barth's position is afforded by assessing various dimensions of this differentiated relationship.

A. The Differentiated Connection of Cross and Resurrection

Within Barth's treatment of the differentiated connection between cross and resurrection, it is possible to identify several aspects. These are: (1) the aspect of the identity of the subject involved; (2) the material aspect or the content involved; (3) the temporal aspect; and (4) the temporal sequence.

1. The Differentiated Connection of Cross and Resurrection: the Aspect of Identity. It is Barth's view that the raising of Jesus as an exclusive act of God must stand in a relationship to the cross "which is meaningful in substance."[3] He adds that in "the sequence of these two acts of God...there must actually be, and be revealed, the identity of the acting divine

Subject... ."[4] This is the case since the raising of Jesus following the event of the cross constitutes "a unity with the event which precedes...it by being together with the first an event in the existence of the same historical subject... ."[5] The raising of Jesus does not cancel his death; rather, it "had its unaltered terminus a quo in His death in our place. The One who was raised was [none other than] the One who was crucified, dead and, to prove it, buried. The One who was exalted was [none other than] the One who was abased."[6] The awakening of Jesus from the dead was God's creative act establishing the identity between the one crucified and resurrected. Thus the "togetherness of the Jesus Christ of Good Friday and the Jesus Christ of Easter Day" is possible only "as created by the divine verdict... ."[7]

In that the unity between Jesus Christ crucified and risen is established solely on the basis of a sovereign divine action means that it is not deducible from some more comprehensive ontology, view of reality or frame of reference. The Church is "the company of those" who believe that "the crucified Jesus Christ is alive" and who therefore regard this affirmation "as the axiom of all axioms... ."[8] Recalling the Declaration of Barmen of 1934, Barth accentuates that Jesus Christ crucified and risen is "'the one Word of God that we must hear, that we must trust and obey, both in life and in death.'"[9] That Barth intends the Church and his readers not to shy from the far-reaching import of this binding yet liberating axiom for all faith and theological construction is evident in the following statement: The Church "interprets creation and the course of the world and the nature of man, his greatness and his plight, wholly in the light of this Word and not vice versa."[10]

This established identity between Jesus Christ

crucified and risen as the "axiom of all axioms" for-
tifies Klappert's contention that the connection of cross
and resurrection cannot be derived from the incarnation,
the preaching of Jesus or from some prior and higher
principle. Nor is it legitimate for Bultmann to interpret the tie between cross and resurrection as the symbol
of the transition from inauthentic to authentic existence. Nor will Klappert allow the identity of Jesus
and the unity of his cross and resurrection to be
rendered credible in terms of the backdrop of the universal historical horizon of Jewish apocalyptic as Pannenberg proposes.[11]

To proceed from the reality of the identity of the
risen Christ with the one crucified requires the self-
revelation of the risen Christ. His positive self-
attestation "necessarily acquires and has the stamp of
the axiomatic, the first and the last, and therefore the
self-evident."[12] Barth puts this unambiguously: "If
there is any Christian and theological axiom, it is that
Jesus Christ is risen, that He is truly risen[!] But
this is an axiom which no one can invent. It can only
be repeated on the basis of the fact that in the enlightening power of the Holy Spirit it has been previously
declared to us as the central statement of the biblical
witness."[13]

In sum, God's creative act in raising Jesus Christ
from the dead, and therewith the revelation of the
identity of the subject, Jesus Christ, crucified and
resurrected, is further attested in the unveiling of the
identity of the risen Jesus with the crucified in his
resurrection appearances. Thus the identity of Jesus
Christ as crucified and risen is attested in the connection which exists between the cross and resurrection as
acts of God.

2. The Differentiated Connection of Cross and Resurrection: the Material Aspect. Regarding the material unity of the cross and raising of Jesus in this sequence, Barth states:

> They belong together in that in these two events of God with and after one another there is effective and expressed the [one] Yes of the reconciling will of God... .It is our case which is undertaken, our conversion to God which is brought about, both in the one and in the other... .To the making of this alteration and therefore to the reconciliation of the world with God there belong both the free obedience of the Son in His death and also the grace of God the Father in His [awakening]: the event of Golgotha and the event in the garden of Joseph of Arimathea.[14]

It is thus on the basis of the unity which obtains between resurrection and cross that the ontic foundation of reconciliation is secured.

Yet the unity of these two events through which we are reconciled to God entails a definite sequence. However, that does not mean "that their sequence and correspondence is that of a repetition, or that their relationship is that of the unity of two equal factors. ...On the contrary, it is a genuine sequence and correspondence in a differentiated relationship in which both factors have their proper form and function."[15] The unity of the cross and resurrection of Jesus Christ through which the reconciliation of the world obtains requires distinguishing "a terminus a quo and a terminus ad quem: first, a negative event (with a positive intention), ...then a positive event (with a negative presupposition)... ."[16] Thus the unity of cross and resurrection is a differentiated one in which the cross has a forward reference in the resurrection and a positive intention in humanity's justification, while the resurrection has a backward reference and a negative presupposition in the death of Jesus on the cross "for our trespasses" (Rom. 4:25).

Barth finds his exegetical guideline for understanding the positive connection between cross and resurrection in the Apostle Paul as is apparent from his succinct summation:

> ...the positive connexion between the death and resurrection of Jesus Christ consists in the fact that these two acts of God with and after one another are the two basic events of the one history of God with a sinful and corrupt world, His history with us as perverted and lost creatures. The one concerns our trespasses, the other our justification (Rom. 4:25). In a comprehensive sense Jesus Christ "died and rose again for us" (2 Cor. 5:15).[17]

The reciprocal connections between cross and resurrection also enable Barth to speak of their connection in the reverse sequence.

> The justification which took place in the resurrection of Jesus Christ confirmed and revealed in what sense God was in the right in His death...asserting His right against sinful men who, as such, were judged in the death of their Representative, being destroyed and necessarily crucified and dying with Him; but also not surrendering His right over these men as His creatures, and therefore not surrendering the right of these creatures of His, but with a view to re-establishing and maintaining it. The death of Jesus Christ preceded His resurrection. God established and maintained His own right against man and over man, and the right of man [h]imself. This makes it clear in what sense in the resurrection of Jesus Christ He willed to justify both Jesus and Himself, and has in fact done so,

> proclaiming His own twofold right and the
> right of man as His creature as they were
> there established and maintained to be the
> basis and the beginning of a new world, put-
> ting them into force and effect, making it
> plain that the history of the humiliation of
> His Son, the history of His way into the far
> country, is <u>redemption</u> history within <u>univer-
> sal</u> history; against man, and therefore for
> him.[18]

Barth finds the New Testament witness--in spite of
its varied imagery--to be harmonious in sounding the
single refrain that in the crucified Christ the old and
"former things" have been done away while in the risen
Christ the new has come. A "remarkably central verse"
for Barth in this regard is 2 Cor. 5:17: "If any man be
in Christ, he is a new creation; old things are passed
away, behold, all things are become new."[19] In Barth's
estimate, the New Testament communities are unanimous
that the prophetic hopes for the fulfillment of the
promises of God had come to pass in the death and resurrection of Jesus Christ. Barth expresses this powerfully:

> The old, the former thing, has passed away:
> the new has come, has grown, has been created.
> It is "in Christ"--the Crucified and Risen--
> and Christ is in it. In His death its own
> death and that of the world is, in fact,
> already past, and in His life its own life and
> that of the future world is before it. It has
> turned away from the one, it has turned to the
> other. It has <u>put off</u> the one, it has <u>put on</u>
> the other. Its existence looks back to the
> Crucified and forward to the Risen. It is an
> existence in the presence of the One who was
> and will be. He is its <u>terminus a quo</u> and its
> <u>terminus ad quem</u>. It is an existence in that
> alteration, that is, in that differentiated
> relationship between the death and the resur-
> rection of Christ. When a man is in Christ,
> there is a new creation. The old has passed,

everything has become new. This means that the event of the end of the world which took place once and for all in Jesus Christ is the presupposition of an old man, and the event of the beginning of the new world which took place once and for all in Jesus Christ is the goal of a new man, and because the goal, therefore the truth and power of the sequence of human existence as it moves towards this goal. The world and every man exist in this alteration.[20]

The connection Barth affirms between what Otto Weber designates as the "negative-positive event of the cross and the positive-negative event of the resurrection" refers to a unity of two conceptually independent factors which constitute the differentiated relationship of the cross and resurrection in their substantive continuity and sequence. To be sure, Bultmann also can say: "The cross and the resurrection form an inseparable unity."[21] But whereas Bultmann speaks of the paradoxical unity between the cross as historical and the resurrection as eschatological, Barth affirms "the sequence and correspondence of the death of Jesus Christ and His resurrection ...with and after one another [as] the basic events of the alteration of the human situation in which [the reconciliation of the world with God came to completion]. This, then, is the differentiated relationship between the two events."[22]

In light of the differentiated connection between the cross and resurrection of Jesus Christ in its teleological sequence, it is clear that neither event can be equated with, nor subsumed beneath, the other. "The theologia resurrectionis does not absorb the theologia crucis, nor vice versa."[23] Barth summarizes what he takes to be the proper way of speaking of their differentiated connection:

> We do not speak rightly of the death of Jesus
> Christ unless we have clearly and plainly
> before us His [awakening], His being as the
> Resurrected. We also do not speak rightly of
> His [awakening] and His being as the Resur-
> rected if we conceal and efface the fact that
> this living One was [precisely the One cruci-
> fied and the One dead for us].[24]

3. The Differentiated Connection of Cross and
Resurrection: the Temporal Aspect. The radical transition of humanity's relationship to God brought about by
the death and resurrection of Jesus Christ requires
Barth to make a "further distinction in our understanding of this relationship. It is a matter of the
character of the two events which underlie this alteration as temporal events, their relation as they are with
and after one another in time."[25]

The major issue confronting Barth here is the right
conception of the way in which the atonement effected by
Jesus Christ is efficacious and relevant to us in the
present. On the basis of the preceding argument, he
maintains that cross and resurrection constitute a
"togetherness in content" which also involves a "togetherness in time."[26] God's second act in raising Jesus
from the dead means, in Luther's words, that the crucified "lives and reigns to all eternity."[27] That the
crucified is risen means that he is "the Lord of all
time." Barth puts it well:

> That which took place on the third day after
> His death lifted up the whole of what took
> place before in all its particularity [once-
> for-all-ness] (not in spite of but because of
> its particularity) into something that took
> place once and for all. It is in the power of
> the event of the third day that the event of
> the first day...is not something which belongs
> to the past, which can be present only by

recollection, tradition and proclamation, but is as such a present event, the event which fills and determines the whole present.[28]

Barth is well aware that this discussion plunges him willy-nilly into the modern theological controversy on the relationship of faith and history. Barth's conclusion should be evident from our discussion to this point. If the Church truly reckons with the "living Saviour" risen from the dead, then "the Mediator" between God and us "is the same here and now as He was there and then... ."[29] For Barth, the New Testament witness presupposes "the eternal unity, or the temporal togetherness, of the humiliated and the exalted, the crucified and the risen Jesus Christ... ."[30] Earlier Barth maintained that the fundamental issue with regard to Christ's atoning work was not the technical issue regarding the historical distance separating us from him, but rather the theological issue, namely, that in Jesus Christ the holy God confronts sinful humanity. Relative thereto, Barth states: "In and with the overcoming of the real and spiritual problem of the relationship between Jesus Christ and us, the technical problem of the relationship between the then and there and the now and here is also soluble and has in fact been solved."[31] Speaking directly concerning how the crucified Saviour is present as the eternal High Priest and risen Lord, Barth writes:

> The eternal action of Jesus Christ grounded in His resurrection is itself the true and direct bridge from once to always, from Himself in His time to us in our time. Because as crucified and dead He is risen and lives, the fact of His death on the cross can never be past, it can never cease to be His action, the decision which God makes hic et nunc [here and

now] to His own glory and in our favour,
summoning us on our part to responsibility... .[32]

In this proposal, Barth contradicts Lessing who
questions whether a "contingent fact of history" could
be equated with a "necessary truth of reason." Barth
opposes this false alternative in saying:

> The moment of this particular "contingent fact
> of history" was the moment of all moments.
> There is no moment in which Jesus Christ is
> not Judge and High Priest and accomplishes all
> these things. There is no moment in which
> this perfect tense is not a present. There is
> no moment in which He does not stand before
> God as our Representative who there suffered
> and died for us and therefore speaks for us.[33]

Seen in this light, the problem of the historical
distance between then and now and there and here Barth
terms as an "epiphenomenon" of secondary importance.
That the living God himself bridges the gap between what
he effected once in behalf of the world through his Son
by being present as the same One here and now through
his Spirit means more than treating the resurrection in
some vague sense as eschatological. Rather, it means to
confess:

> He who was crucified is risen, and as such, He
> lives unto God (Rom. 6:10). He is the same
> yesterday, to-day and forever. This temporal
> togetherness of the Jesus Christ of Good
> Friday and the Jesus Christ of Easter Day as
> created by the divine verdict is the [funda-
> mental] basis [Realgrund] of life for men of
> all ages. And as such it is the [fundamental]
> basis of the alteration of their situation.[34]

Even though Barth does not name other opponents or treat their respective views on how the reconciliation in Christ becomes effective in the present, he certainly has them in mind. His basic contention is that God alone is able to bridge the gap between who he was in the particularity of Jesus Christ in his history then and our own present today. He understands this in terms of the continuing work of the risen Christ in the Spirit. This precludes accepting any and all attempts to secure continuity with past historical events by means of some kind of continuity based upon ontological, existential or on some kind of hermeneutical grounds. Klappert defines the issue as follows:

> The question of continuity, that is, how is it possible for there to be communication between the judging God and judged man, cannot--in view of the cross--be answered either in existential-anthropological terms [Heidegger, Bultmann], or in terms of the movement of history [Gadamer], or in terms of universal history [Pannenberg]. No act from man's side can bridge this qualitative distance: no anthropological continuum can provide media-tion here... for the cross marks the final and definitive judgment which has taken the right of existence from man. And what kind of mediation still could remain between man who has squandered his right to exist when con-fronted with the crucified? The "continuum," or that which provides mediation in view of this situation, cannot be something general locatable in historical consciousness, or in human nature, or in certain principles of reason, or in existential structures... .[35]

Some of Barth's critics argue that his customary appeal to the contemporaneity of the risen Christ as the solution to the problem of the relationship of faith to the past history of Jesus Christ really represents bypassing the problem. To be sure, we have seen that Barth regards the problem of our historical distance from the Christ event to be a methodological and technical issue subordinate to the deeper theological issue relating to the transition from God to man or from christology to anthropology. The "real scandal" is that Christ's reconciling work then and there has transformed our existence here and now. Barth stresses the same divine initiative in speaking of the transition from God to us in that the crucified attests himself to us as risen, and therewith as contemporary, through his Spirit. This theological reality and truth is of primary significance, but "does not prevent us from taking the problem of distance with the seriousness proper to it."[36] Hence all of the questions relating to the relationship of tradition, recollection, and preaching to the history of Jesus Christ have their rightful place within this larger theological question. If the solution to the theological issue is ignored, the hermeneutical question relating to what Kierkegaard designated as the eighteen hundred years between Christ and us will prove insoluble. I take it that this is what Barth intended in his repeated emphasis that Christ's reconciling work involved his incorporation of our humanity. This was and remains true. Hence Barth writes:

> Our christological basis includes within itself the fact (and with it quite simply ourselves, our participation in that event), that the turn from Jesus Christ to us has already been executed and is a fact in Him, that in and with Him we, too, are there as those for whom He is and has acted. This fact is the subject of a specific second step as we try to follow out the truth of it. Naturally, the first step must precede. Jesus Christ must have come to us in that existence of His

which embraces ours, but is also proper to
Himself and superior to ours.[37]

Looking back on the transition from God to us by
means of his saving acts in the cross and resurrection
in their interrelated connection and unity, Barth
summarizes his position thus:

> The event of Easter Day is the removing of the
> barrier between His life in His time and their
> life in their times, the initiation of His
> lordship as the Lord of all time. ...Thus the
> death and resurrection of Jesus Christ are
> together--His death in the power and effec-
> tiveness and truth and lasting newness given
> to it by His resurrection--the basis of the
> alteration of the situation of the men of all
> times.[38]

4. The Differentiated Connection of Cross and
Resurrection: the Temporal Sequence. Having looked at
the unity of cross and resurrection in time, Barth turns
to yet another aspect of their relationship. "According
to the report and message of the New Testament they are
separated by the gulf between the first and the third
days. They stand to one another, therefore, in a relationship of temporal sequence."[39] The cross stands as
the great divide: on the one side, there is (1) the way
and time of Jesus Christ hastening toward its fulfillment in his death. On the other side of the cross (2) is
the new life and time of the risen Christ manifested
initially during his appearances during the forty days.
Jesus Christ thus confronted his disciples in a sequence
of times whose end was marked in the one instance by his
death and whose new beginning in the other by his being
raised from the dead. "He is the living Saviour in both
of these times, the one after the other, on this side

and the other side of His death; there humiliated, here exalted, the One who lives and rules eternally, in all times, as the Lord of time."[40]

God's verdict attesting and validating the crucified and the reconciliation accomplished by him in raising him from the dead also marks the beginning of the parousia of Jesus Christ. In the first instance, the parousia of Jesus Christ has to do (1) with a "direct form" of his "living presence" in a transformed mode of existence during the forty days marked by the sign of the empty tomb at its beginning and the ascension to the "right hand of God" at its end. Looking at the sequence of times marked by the cross, resurrection, and ascension of Jesus Christ, Barth regards the latter as the beginning (2) of "the time of another form of His parousia, His living [presence]--no less complete and sufficient in itself, but quite different."[41] During this time, Christ is "no longer, or not yet again, directly revealed and visible and audible and perceptible (as He had been) either to the disciples, the community, or the world... ."[42] For the believing community, Christ will be "directly present and revealed and active...by His Spirit... .but not without the mediation of recollection, tradition and proclamation; the living Word of God, but not without... .that mediating ministry... ."[43] This "time of the community in the world" is illumined by, and attests in its faith, life and witness the crucified and risen Christ and the light which shone forth in him for the reconciliation of the whole world. But the fulfillment is still expected in (3) the final form and time of the parousia of Christ. The Church looks to that fulfillment as it lives "between the times." Thus Barth can say:

It is **not yet** the <u>revelation</u> of the altered
creation, of the children of God as they are
transformed by what has taken place for them
and to them in Jesus Christ. It is **not yet**
the time of the resurrection of <u>all</u> the dead.
Obviously, therefore, it is **not yet** the time
of the fulfilment of the [awakening] which has
come to them in Jesus Christ. To that extent
it is **not yet** the fulfilment of His <u>parousia</u>
and presence and salvation in the world reconciled by Him.[44]

Later Barth finds these three forms of the <u>parousia</u> of
Jesus Christ analogous to God's triune being. Hence it
is necessary to emphasize both the unity and distinction
of the times and forms of the <u>parousia</u>--or "effective
presence"--of Jesus Christ. Yet in "all these forms it
is one event... .Always and in all three forms it is a
matter of the fresh coming of the One who came before.
Always and in different ways it is a matter of the
coming again of Jesus Christ."[45]

B.   The Differentiated Connection of Cross and
     Resurrection: its Teleology

We have tried to show that Barth understands the
differentiated relationship of cross and resurrection as
a unity constituted of a "genuine sequence and correspondence...in which both factors have their proper form
and function."[46] On the basis of their reciprocity,
Barth is able to view the cross as a negative event with
a forward referent and positive goal in the resurrection, while the resurrection is a positive event with a
backward referent in the cross as its negative presupposition. In tracing the contours of the differentiated
relationship of cross and resurrection, we do justice to
Barth's analysis.

1. The Reciprocal Connection of Cross and Resurrection: a Summary. Barth delineates the backward and forward references between the death and resurrection of Jesus Christ in terms of the major theses he developed regarding their meaning. Barth summarizes the first thesis in saying that "we have thought of the [awakening] of Jesus Christ as the work of grace of God the Father. But [precisely] this work of grace is wholly and utterly the answer to the work of obedience of the Son fulfilled in His self-offering to death."[47] Thus the awakening of Jesus reveals him as "the one beloved and obedient Son of God."[48] Barth sums up the second thesis as follows: "We have thought of the [raising] of Jesus Christ as God's proclamation and revelation. But what can it proclaim and reveal, what can it disclose, but [precisely] the act of reconciliation and redemption once and for all accomplished in His death, in the judgment fulfilled in Him and suffered by Him, the divine Yes already concealed under the No?"[49] Barth's third thesis may be summarized by stating that the resurrection of Jesus Christ marks the beginning of the revelation of the royal man crucified and exalted on the cross. Thus the resurrection reveals none other than the royal man exalted precisely in his death on the cross. This is the content of the third thesis which illuminates the reciprocity of resurrection and cross. In summarizing the fourth thesis, Barth recalls: "We have thought of the [raising of Jesus Christ] as the other side of his death, [the other side] of the judgment which fell upon Him as our Representative [and substitute], which therefore passed conclusively and irrevocably upon all men and every individual man in Him. But it is wholly and utterly the other side of 'this side.'"[50]

In light of these reciprocal relationships obtaining between the cross and the raising of Jesus from the dead, Barth interprets the cross as a negative event with a positive intent. Yet regarding the reciprocity between cross and resurrection, Barth says: "We have so far spoken of two different acts of God and therefore only of the 'relationship' between them."[51]

2. The Inseparable Unity of Cross and Resurrection. Barth continues immediately to add: "But the time has now come to use a stronger term. For here there are not only two acts of God, but here there is also a single act of God: thus, here those two are to be seen not only in their relationship, but also in their unity."[52] In the unity of these two events "the one Yes of the reconciling will of God was powerfully expressed... ."[53] The unity of cross and resurrection exists by virtue of the common subject active here. "It is the one God who is at work on the basis of His one election and decision by and to the one Jesus Christ with the one goal of the reconciliation of the world with Himself, the conversion of men to Him."[54]

Barth is able to highlight the unity of the cross and resurrection as the center of salvation-history thus:

> In this unity the death and resurrection of Jesus Christ are together the history of Jesus Christ, and as such the redemptive history to which everything earlier that we might call redemptive history in the wider sense moved and pointed, and from which everything later that we might call redemptive history in the wider sense derives and witnesses. Here in the unity of this death and this [awakening] from death that history takes place in nuce. It is an inseparable unity.[55]

The fact of this unity in reciprocity means that neither of these events can be understood aright apart from its reference to the other. Hence to speak of the death of Jesus Christ, one must have his resurrection in view; to speak of him as risen means to remember that "this living One is the Crucified and the One who died for us."[56]

3. The Cross and Resurrection as a Unity with an Irreversible Sequence. Another characteristic of the unity of cross and resurrection is that their reciprocal relationships stand in an irreversible teleological sequence. "It is the unity of a sequence. It is rather like a one-way street. It cannot be reversed."[57] Inasmuch as the death and resurrection of Jesus Christ effecting the reconciliation of the world to God took place one after the other and once for all in an irreversible sequence, it is illegitimate after Easter to preach of faith in the crucified or in the cross abstracted from his resurrection. "...that means that God, and we too, have to do with the Crucified only as the Resurrected, with the [once-for-all] event of His death only as it has the continuing form of His life."[58]

For Barth, the New Testament witness that the crucified is risen precludes any piety, theology, cultic or ascetical exercises focused on the cross as well as all visual representations of "the crucified Christ as such."[59] Every approach which isolates and abstracts the crucified from his resurrection fails since it seeks Jesus Christ apart from "the wholeness of His history as it took place according to the witness of the New Testament!"[60] All such attempts undermine the truth that "there is no going back behind Easter morning."[61] The theological and hermeneutical error involved in isolating the cross from the resurrection is akin to that of isolating his life from his death and resurrection. Regarding the consequences of the former, Barth writes:

> It involves going back to the night of Golgotha as not yet lit up by the light of Easter Day. It involves going back and into the event of judgment not yet proclaimed and revealed as that of salvation. It involves going back into the sphere where the divine Yes to man which He Himself alone can reveal is still inacessibly concealed under His No. It involves going back into the death in which all flesh is hopelessly put to death in and with the Son of God.[62]

Such a theology of the "bare cross" leads in Barth's view to a false view of God's wrath, judgment and law abstracted from his grace. Such theological reflection is a sign of "unbelief, ingratitude, disobedience" and issues in uncertainty. In contrast, Barth calls for theological reflection determined by a right perception of the teleological sequence and relationship between Jesus' cross and resurrection.

> In every age [and for all peoples], post Christum means post Christum crucifixum et resuscitatum. [That is a unity.] The first is included in the second, the death of Jesus Christ in His life, the judgment of God in the grace of God. "Death is swallowed up in victory" (I Cor. 15:54). The relationship can never be reversed. The second is no longer closed up and concealed and kept from us in the first, the life of Jesus Christ in His death, the grace of God in His judgment, His Yes in His No.[63]

This correct perspective on the relationship of cross and resurrection precludes conceiving them in cyclical terms, or in terms of some kind of "eternal recurrence," or in terms of some kind of equilibrium

388

effected there between grace and judgment, between Yes and No. Barth rejects such views as mythological thinking injurious to all Christian life and preaching, teaching, pastoral care and theology. Faithful theology respects God's decision and the way which he has taken in the death and resurrection of Jesus Christ. Obedient reflection acknowledges that

> It was for the sake of His electing that from all eternity He rejected... .It was to make alive that He put to death. And now He has indeed elected and loved and saved and made alive. And the telos of the way which He has gone in the person and work, in the history of Jesus Christ, is our beginning--His electing, therefore, His love, His saving, His making alive.[64]

That Jesus Christ is crucified and risen precludes, however, that his cross and resurrection be taken as the goal rather than as the "starting-point" of theological reflection. The fact that "Jesus lives" means that his followers are those "who hear the message of Easter Day and are obedient to the verdict of the Holy Spirit pronounced there, praying that it may daily be disclosed afresh to us, looking forward in hope to the consummation of His parousia and therefore to our redemption, which is grounded in our reconciliation with God as it has already taken place on His cross, which has already begun in His resurrection, in which the disciples beheld His glory."[65]

Barth sums up how he conceives the unity of the cross and resurrection under examination in this section:

> This is the unity of the act of God in the death and resurrection of Jesus Christ, or,

rather, the unity of the act of God in the person and work of His Son, who was put to death for our transgressions, but who now lives for our justification as the guarantor and giver of our life, having been raised from the dead in our mortal flesh. It is a unity which is securely grounded. It is the unity of an irreversible sequence. It is a unity which is established teleologically. Jesus Christ as attested in Holy Scripture is the One who exists in this unity.[66]

C. The Connection of Cross and Resurrection: Summary Theses[67]

1. The differentiated connection of the cross and raising of Jesus is to be understood with reference to the divine subject known in the sequence of these two acts of God. As such, it represents God's creative establishment of identity between the one crucified and the one raised from the dead. As such, this identification is not to be subsumed beneath any other event such as the incarnation or proclamation of Jesus. Nor is it to be deduced from something higher such as a concept of reality or a concept of history. Nor can it be proved necessary on the basis of some external norm whether existential or ontological. Nor is it to be derived from some other condition such as the claim and corresponding vindication of Jesus. The differentiated connection of the cross and the raising of Jesus as God's creative act of identifying the one resurrected with the one crucified is, by virtue of the one active in it (the Father) and the subject known in it (the Son), the center and axiom of all theology.

2. The cross and the raising of Jesus stand in a reciprocal and particular differentiated connection because the raising of Jesus has a backward reference to

the cross and the cross has a forward reference to the raising of Jesus. Insofar as the raising of Jesus reveals the Son who was obedient on the cross, the subject involved there is disclosed. Insofar as the raising of Jesus proclaims the "Yes" hidden beneath the "No" of the cross, the nature of the judgment carried out there is disclosed. Thus the resurrection is seen as a positive event with a negative presupposition while the cross is seen as a negative event in correlation with the positive event of the resurrection. The differentiated connection of the cross and the raising of Jesus represents a unity involving a genuine sequence of two different factors with different contents and functions.

3. This differentiated connection of cross and awakening is simultaneously the unbreakable unity of an irreversible teleological sequence insofar as the "No" is in the service of the "Yes," the judgment of grace is in the service of the grace of judgment, and insofar as the negative event of the cross has a positive intention. The differentiated connection between these two events when viewed as an unbreakable unity precludes maintaining a balance, equipoise or static equilibrium between them: rather, we are confronted with an irreversible teleology. These events cannot be construed in terms of a yes and a no. Rather, they constitute a teleologically ordered unity to the extent that in both foundational events the one "Yes" of God for the reconciliation of the world is sounded. Thus the connection of cross and resurrection--on account of their sequence as two foundational events and their backward and forward reciprocal relationships--is a differentiated connection with an irreversible teleology.

Chapter XI

CONCLUSION: CROSS AND RESURRECTION
IN THE THEOLOGY OF KARL BARTH

I. THE UNITY OF THE PERSON AND THE WORK OF JESUS CHRIST
    IN THE RECONCILIATION EFFECTED ON THE CROSS[1]

A prevalent criticism of Barth's doctrine of reconciliation is that it represents a reaffirmation of
classical christology constructed upon the dogma of the
incarnation as its foundation. In his adoption of this
christology which moves "from above to below," it is
argued that Jesus' resurrection plays no constitutive
role. Pannenberg and others criticize Barth along these
lines. Others also fault Barth for depreciating the
significance of the passion and cross of Jesus. In
short, Barth is accused of accentuating the person of
Jesus Christ (christology) on the basis of the incarnation at the expense of his saving work.[2]

In agreement with Klappert's extensive elaboration
of this issue, it can be maintained that while not
surrendering the intention of classical christology,
Barth does more than render it more dynamic by synthe-
sizing the doctrine of the two natures of Jesus Christ
with the orthodox Protestant doctrine of the two states
of Christ as Pannenberg contends. It may seem clear that
the flow of the first major section of Barth's doctrine

of reconciliation (CD 4:1, ch. XIV) in its tripartite division makes Pannenberg's thesis tenable. Read from this perspective, the three divisions of Paragraph 59 are interpreted as follows: 1. the incarnation (The Way of the Son of God into the Far Country); 2. the cross (The Judge Judged in Our Place); and 3. the resurrection (The Verdict of the Father). It appears that the history of reconciliation is, in fact, the history of the incarnation completed in the cross and revealed in the resurrection.

In concurrence with Klappert, it should be noted that it is not enough to affirm with Pannenberg that Barth has modified classical christology without asking where he has carried out this modification. Klappert is certainly correct that Barth has carried out this modification explicitly and intentionally within the doctrine of reconciliation.

> W. Pannenberg's interpretation of Barth along these lines is to be credited for recognizing how Barth has rendered traditional christology more dynamic. As evidence Pannenberg points to: the coincidence of humiliation and exaltation; the interpretation of the two natures in the light of the two states and vice versa; the interpretation of the deity in light of the humiliation and of Christ's humanity in light of his exaltation...; developing his christology in terms of the history of Jesus rather than in terms of static categories; the interpretation of "Being as act," and of "act as being ...; and the interpretation of the singular history [of Jesus Christ] as a history with universal significance--all of this can and must--apart from any precise location of it within the horizon of classical incarnational christology, a christology "from above to below"--be understood as its radicalization.[3]

It is noteworthy that Barth gives a clear indication of the manner in which traditional christology is modified in his survey of the doctrine of reconciliation and the problems attending its explication (CD 4:1, par. 58). In paragraph 58:1, Barth provides an initial survey of the "reconciling God" and in paragraph 58:2, he follows with a preliminary description of the reconciled man (CD 4:1, pp. 79ff.). This double movement from above to below and from below to above necessitates that all speech about "God with us" as the "centre of the Christian message" is always "primarily a statement about God and only then and for that reason a statement about us men."[4] The center in whom this movement from God to humanity and from humanity to God is actualized is the one Mediator, Jesus Christ. Thus in paragraph 58:3, "Jesus Christ the Mediator," Barth maintains that it is only in him that there is the confluence of the above and below, of God and humanity. "...that one thing in the middle is one person, Jesus Christ. He is the atonement as the fulfilment of the covenant. In Him that turning of God to man and conversion of man to God is actuality in the appointed order of [their] mutual interrelationship... ."[5] This precludes locating atonement apart from Jesus Christ and his history. "For that reason He who bears this name, and His existence, must really be regarded as the middle point which embraces the whole and includes it within itself, the middle point in which the sovereign act of the reconciling God and the being of reconciled man are one."[6]

In short, Klappert is correct to underline that Barth accentuates the unity of the person and work of Jesus Christ and thus of christology and the doctrine of reconciliation. This is why Barth insists that Jesus Christ "exists in the totality of [H]is being and work

as the Mediator--He alone as the Mediator, but living
and active in His mediatorial office."[7]

Pannenberg errs in accusing Barth simply of deduc-
ing the two natures of Jesus from the doctrine of the
incarnation. Klappert is correct that the affirmation
of the deity and humanity of Jesus ultimately derive
from the unity between God and humanity in the reconciling work of Jesus in the cross.[8] Moreover, the unity of
the reconciling God and reconciled humanity in Jesus
Christ in the event of reconciliation, and thus the
unity of the person and work of Jesus Christ, imply the
humiliation of the Son of God in Jesus Christ and humanity's exaltation in him. Summing up: "The interconnectedness of christology and the doctrine of reconciliation implies and interprets the doctrine of the two
natures and two states."[9]

That Barth intended a dynamic reinterpretation of
the classical doctrine of the incarnation and the christology based on it throughout his entire exposition of
the doctrine of reconciliation is evident in his summary
statement in the second major chapter of the doctrine of
reconciliation.

> From the very first we have understood and
> interpreted the doctrine of the incarnation,
> which we have considered from all angles, in
> historical terms, as an actuality, as an
> operatio between God and man, fulfilled in
> Jesus Christ as a union of God with man. We
> have represented the existence of Jesus Christ
> as His being in His act. ...we have been
> thinking and speaking with this concept of the
> communicatio operationum.[10]

The rigorous way in which Barth holds throughout to
the unity of the person and work of Jesus Christ in the
doctrine of reconciliation along the lines of the

functional christologies of the New Testament is the framework apart form which no single element of his understanding of reconciliation is comprehensible. Typical of many programmatic statements in this vein is the following:

> We hasten to explain that the being of Jesus Christ, the unity of the being of the living God and this living man, takes place in the _event_ of the concrete existence [of God and the concrete existence] of this man. It is a being, but a being in a _history_. The gracious _God_ is in this history, so is reconciled _man_, so are both in their _unity_.[11]

It remains to identify several further consequences of Barth's concentration on the unity of the person and work of Jesus Christ and thus of the interrelationship of the doctrines of christology and reconciliation. In addition to this revision of the orthodox Catholic and Protestant tendency to separate the person and work of Christ, Barth rejects the modern concentration on the saving work of Jesus Christ, or soteriology, in isolation from his person. Such an isolation of soteriology from christology eventually leads to concentration on the latter as that which is of "practical importance" and "'existentially relevant.'"[12] In this context Barth does not single out the Abelardian tradition and its moral influence view of the atonement, or the subjectivism characteristic of Schleiermacher's tradition, or even Bultmann's soteriological concentration. But all of them are representative of a tendency Barth regards as Arian and Pelagian. "Jesus Christ is not what He is--very God, very man, very God-man--in order as such to mean and to do and accomplish something else which is atonement. But [rather] His being as God and man and

God-man consists in the complete act of the reconciliation of man with God."[13]   Finally, Barth sees certain
contours within the unity of the person and work of
Jesus Christ evident in the cross.   It is because Barth
finds the New Testament emphasizing Jesus Christ as the
subject effecting reconciliation that he places the
issue of the identity of the subject effecting reconciliation in the cross at the outset of his doctrine of
reconciliation.   This leads Klappert to conclude that
methodologically Barth does not focus attention on the
distinction between incarnation and cross, but rather on
the distinction between the aspect of the person (par
59:1) and the work (par. 59:2) of reconciliation on the
cross.[14]

II.   THE IDENTITY OF THE PERSON EFFECTING RECONCILIATION ON THE CROSS

Barth begins his interpretation of the doctrine of
reconciliation by accenting that Jesus Christ is the
subject who effects reconciliation.   The focus of paragraph 59:1 is on "The Way of the Son of God into the Far
Country."   The following theses serve to summarize how
Barth views the identity of Jesus Christ as the subject
through whom humanity is reconciled to God.

First, the New Testament traditions concur in
affirming that the man Jesus is qualitatively different
from all other human beings.   This attestation of the
special relationship of Jesus to God, his Father, is
fundamental to the primitive Christian witness to the
uniqueness of Jesus.   This concurs with Jesus' own
testimony concerning his relationship to God.   Apart
from concurrence with the New Testament witness to the
deity of Jesus, no adequate comprehension of him is

possible. Thus Barth rules out all low christologies of the ebionite, adoptionistic or later Arian type. Barth puts it graphically: ". . .to this day there is hardly a point of Christian knowledge of confession which is not positively or negatively, directly or indirectly, related to this one point [i.e., the confession of the deity of Jesus Christ], to this primitive Christian insight."[15] This echoes Barth's earlier refrain: "One cannot subsequently speak christologically, if Christology has not already been presupposed at the outset... ."[16]

Second, primitive Christian confessions of Jesus Christ as "truly God" understood the Gospels as passion stories with lengthy introductions. This led them and Barth to follow the contours of the gospel narrative which views the cross as the completion of the condescension and self-giving of the Son. Klappert is correct to maintain that for Barth the cross indirectly discloses the mystery of the deity of the Son. It simultaneously reveals the deity of God.[17] In short, according to the New Testament witness, Jesus' obedience to God, his Father, which issues in his suffering, crucifixion and death reveals the "humanity of God" as well as the mystery of the presence of God in Jesus, that is, the mystery of his deity.[18]

Third, the condescension of the Son is evident in his unity with the Israelite, Jesus of Nazareth. As representative of God and humanity, he stands in solidarity with sinful Israel and therefore is subject to God's judgment. The limitation involved in the Son's condescension corresponds to God's electing love in the old covenant which involved his continuing condescension and suffering in behalf of Israel. Hence the obedience of the Son in his suffering and death marks the fulfillment of God's suffering love in behalf of his people and

the revelation of his deity. Seen in this way, the Old
Testament is the circle's interpretative circumference
for interpreting the Son's condescension and the cross
is the center to which everything on the circumference
of the circle ultimately refers.

Fourth, the Son's condescension on the way into the
far country fulfilled in the cross does not mean that
God thereby enters into contradiction to himself. It is
rather the case that the Son's submission to the judgment consequent on humanity's sin corresponds to the
being and will of God. Barth's methodological axiom is
that what God does for us in his revelation of himself
corresponds to what he is in himself. God's concealment
in the servant form of his Son corresponds to the deity
of God. God's glory is concealed in the form of his Son
as servant; yet this "concealment, and therefore His
condescension as such, is the image and reflection in
which we see Him as He is."[19] Over against all reduc-
tionist christologies which bypass the cross in the
interpretation of Jesus and of God, his Father, Barth
takes the New Testament witness as teaching that neither
Jesus nor God, the Father, are comprehensible apart from
the event of the cross. Thus it is only on the basis of
the Son's condescension in the cross that it is possible
to speak of obedience and suffering as integral to God's
nature. It is along these lines that Barth has recov-
ered the Pauline and Reformation theologia crucis (theology of the cross). In do doing, he gives powerful
expression to the manner in which the suffering and
cross of Jesus as the fulfillment of his reconciling
work is constitutive both for christology and for the
understanding of God and his triune nature.[20]

III. DIMENSIONS OF THE RECONCILING WORK OF JESUS CHRIST ON THE CROSS

First, throughout Barth insists that the condescension of the Son of God which comes to completion on the cross entails the preservation of his deity.

Second, in his condescension in the cross, Jesus Christ is the Judge who stands in the place of sinful humanity by taking their lost cause upon himself. His work of reconciliation on the cross is pro nobis: that is, for us and for the purpose of human salvation.

Third, Barth speaks of four dimensions of Christ's reconciliation of the world with God. First, Jesus Christ, the Judge, initiates a new order by being the Judge who takes the place of all human beings who in their sin and pride arrogate to themselves the role of being their own judges. Second, Jesus Christ as the Judge "was and is for us in that He took the place of us sinners."[21] Third, Jesus Christ is for us" in that [in our place] he suffered and was crucified and died."[22] Fourth, as the righteous Judge, Jesus Christ in our place does what was right and just in the eyes of God, his Father, in allowing himself to be judged in behalf of sinful humanity. In doing what was right and righteous, he ushers in the new aeon of the world reconciled with God.[23]

Fourth, by interpreting the saving work of God in Jesus Christ in juridical terminology, Barth both utilizes and modifies four traditional terms associated with this theory. First, he modifies the concept of the "judge" by seeing him as the one who ushers in a new order. Second, instead of following tradition and correlating the concept of substitution/representation solely with sin or that which hinders salvation, Barth develops a "christological-personal mode of interpreting "Christ's representative work.[24] Third, Barth, modifies the concept of "satisfaction" by interpreting it as the sinners negation in the cross. It is that act which satisfies (satis-facere) God. Fourth, Barth, reformulates the traditional concept of "righteousness." He does so by viewing Jesus Christ as the one who submits to God's righteousness thereby actualizing the divine righteousness in his own person.

Fifth, Klappert summarizes critical components of Christ's reconciling work. The act of reconciliation takes place through Jesus Christ, the "Judge who is qualitatively other;" his saving activity entails a radical reversal in which Jesus Christ, the subject, "becomes an object in the cross;" in his reconciling work his being is negated and exalted on the cross; and in this dynamic teleological sequence the "justified man" is ushered in. "Put more exactly, in Barth's view Jesus Christ as he exists in this history is the substantive content of the New Testament theologia crucis (theology of the cross)."[25]

Sixth, Jesus Christ represents the actualization of God's self-determination as the one who loves in freedom. In effecting the reconciliation of the world with himself in Jesus Christ, God preserves and fulfills the covenant which is its presupposition. Thus his work of reconciliation in Jesus Christ is the realization of his electing will from the beginning. Hence the work of reconciliation is not solely his response to humanity's sin. Rather, it is the realization of the fellowship God intended with humanity from before the foundation of the world. Viewed in this light, God's reconciling work in Jesus Christ must be seen in terms of God's own self-determination in his electing will and in relationship to his acts of creation, preservation and covenant making. This rules out seeking an understanding of reconciliation which bypasses the actual way in which God realized his own purpose to reconcile humanity to himself. In so doing, he was first of all faithful to himself and to his own purpose. It is on this basis that reconciliation is neither accidental, reversible or in need of supplementation. "Reconciliation through the cross entails the judgment of the judge contra nos (against us), the unity of the righteousness and mercy of God, the wrath of God as the refining fire of his love--understood, of course, in terms of an irreversible subordination of the "No" to the "Yes," of the opus alienum (strange work of God) to his opus proprium (proper work). It is in this way that Barth views the cross in terms of a dynamic teleology."[26]

Seventh, Klappert delineates in incisive fashion the manner in which for Barth reconciliation through Christ not only is that which happens contra nos (against us), but also simultaneously is:

> (a) an objective history which occurred extra nos (apart from us) and for us. As such it has a normative and structural significance which determines all of its anthropological significance; (b) a recountable story which occurred extra nos (apart from us) in Jesus Christ. Through the presence of Christ himself, proclamation which attests him is acknowledged as it recounts this story; (c) the extra nos of the cross which by virtue of its subject is characterized by a content which has to do with a reversal and a dynamic teleology; and (d) the extra nos of reconciliation which implies inclusivity in itself, but does not allow some imposed significance which is simply about it.[27]

Finally, the interpretation of the cross in terms
of this dynamic teleology characterized by an objective,
relatable salvific history, and identified with the
foregoing content and inclusive implications, Barth
opposes to:

> (a) the misuse of the pro me (for me) as a
> methodological principle for interpreting
> reconciliation; (b) a concept of the kerygma
> which presupposes the coincidence of the
> occurrence of the event of salvation with the
> event of its present proclamation; (c) a
> reduction of the pro nobis to a contentless
> and bare "that" of the cross; and (d) the
> interpretation of the exclusivity of the pro
> nobis as a predicate and moment of its
> inclusivity. Barth intends to understand the
> fourfold dimension of the reconciliation which
> God effected on the cross for us in terms of
> this content, these contours and structures,
> and along these lines.[28]

IV. THE RAISING OF JESUS AS THE REVELATION OF HIS
IDENTITY AS THE SUBJECT EFFECTING RECONCILIATION ON
THE CROSS

Barth's primary thesis regarding God's raising of
his crucified Son who became a servant is that it represents the definitive disclosure of the one who effected
reconciliation between God and humanity on the cross.
This entails the development of the following major
affirmations:

First, God's raising of the crucified Jesus from
the dead is a singular act of God. It is revelation in
its exemplary form disclosing the identity of Jesus
Christ as the reconciler who died on the cross.

Second, the raising of Jesus is the revelation of
the one humiliated on the cross as the Son of the

Father: that God raised his crucified Son is the
Father's confirmation and revelation of the one humiliated as the Son of the Father.   It is to the crucified
that the Father grants the name of kurios (Phil. 2:9).

Third, the raising of Jesus unveils the Son's
obedience in relationship to his Father.   His awakening
of the Son is an act of God's pure grace in behalf of
his Son testifying both to the Father's faithfulness
toward his Son and to the Son's obedience towards his
Father.

It is along these lines that Barth interprets the
raising of Jesus from the dead as an exclusively divine
act which reveals the identity of the Son who effected
reconciliation on the cross.[29]

V.   THE RAISING OF JESUS AS THE VALIDATION OF THE ACT
      OF RECONCILIATION ON THE CROSS

It is Barth's contention that God's raising of
Jesus may be viewed as "judicial sentence" indicative of
the divine approbation of the work of reconciliation effected by the Son on the cross.   Klappert's analysis
argues that this entails the following theses.

First, the raising of the crucified Jesus from the
dead is a new act with its own content even though it is
related to the cross.   As such, it is neither to be
identified with the recognition of the significance of
the cross through the disciple's faith (Bultmann) nor as
the completion of the reconciliation effected on the
cross.

Second, the awakening of Jesus is the Father's
acknowledgment of Jesus Christ, the crucified.   It is
the Father's judicial judgment regarding the death of
Jesus on the cross.   As such, it is the Father's

judicial determination of the validity of the work of reconciliation effected by the Son on the cross.

Third, the raising of Jesus from the dead as the validation of the revealing work in the cross is the efficacious proclamation of the teleological subordination of the "No" of God to the "Yes" concealed within his judgment effected on the cross. Hence his "strange work" of judgment (opus alienum) is subordinate to his "proper work" (opus proprium) entailing the establishment of his righteousness for the benefit of humanity. That God raised Jesus from the dead involves first of all the justification of God and his electing will. It is also the justification of Jesus Christ. Finally, it entails the justification of sinful humanity in him. That God's saving work in and through his Son was finally not negated in the cross by the powers of chaos, sin and death is declared in God's verdict pronounced in raising his Son.[30]

VI. THE RESURRECTION AS THE REVELATION OF THE ROYAL MAN
     EXALTED ON THE CROSS

In this section, Barth is concerned to interpret the Easter appearances of the risen Christ as the revelation of the one who is identical with the Son of Man or the "royal man" exalted on the cross. Barth introduces his treatment of "The Exaltation of the Son of Man" as the second major moment of God's reconciling work, namely, "Jesus Christ, the Servant as Lord."[31] Here the focus is on Jesus Christ as the Son of Man, the royal man, in whose exaltation as the Lord the exaltation of humanity is included. Klappert's summary provides a critical analysis of the way in which the lordship of Jesus Christ as the royal man--in his kingly

office exalted on the cross--is revealed through his
resurrection from the dead.

> The resurrection refers to the appearance of
> Jesus Christ raised from the dead to his
> disciples. Whereas Jesus' awakening from the
> dead is the noetic moment revealing the sub-
> ject who reconciles while also attesting the
> divine judgment validating the act of recon-
> ciliation in the cross, his resurrection is
> based upon his being raised and is the revela-
> tion of the royal man exalted on the cross.
> Jesus' resurrection is thus the unveiling of
> the one regnans in cruce (reigning on the
> cross). However, there he was hidden beneath
> the contradiction of the cross. As the reve-
> lation of the lordship of the crucified recon-
> ciler, the resurrection is simultaneously the
> beginning of the lordship of the crucified
> victor preserving the completed reconcilia-
> tion. Thus the resurrection marks the initia-
> tion of the lordship of Jesus Christ as the
> lord of all time. This is the case insofar as
> the lordship of the exalted royal man esta-
> blished in the cross potentates itself in his
> resurrection into an unfinished teleological
> warfare characterized by the revelatory lord-
> ship of the one crucified. Since Jesus Christ
> was conformed to God completely for the first
> time on the cross, it follows that in the
> completion of his earthly activity on the
> cross he was already the exalted and reigning
> royal man. For this reason it is the cross
> and not the incarnation, or the activity of
> the earthly Jesus in word and deed, which is
> the primary referent of the resurrection as
> the revelation of the royal man perfected
> precisely in the cross. The relationship of
> cross and resurrection is the interpretive
> center for comprehending that Jesus is vere
> homo (true man).[32]

VII. THE RESURRECTION OF THE CRUCIFIED AS AN ACTUAL EVENT IN HISTORY

Barth examines the raising of Jesus and his appearances as occurrences in our space-time continuum--and in this sense--"the historical character of the content of the Easter stories."[33] Following Klappert, Barth's methodology and argumentation may be summarized as follows.[34]

The awakening of the crucified Jesus from the dead was an exclusively divine act followed by the resurrection appearances and self-witness of the one crucified and risen. In spite of the fact that the awakening and resurrection appearances originate solely in the divine activity and therewith transcend the ordinary course of human causality and instrumentality, and notwithstanding the eschatological novelty of these occurrences as the coming of Jesus Christ in the glory of God, we are confronted with events occurring in space and time in the same way as the event of the cross of Jesus Christ. As concrete events following the event of the cross, these occurrences take place within the space-time continuum and are not to be interpreted in terms of the rise of Easter faith within the disciples: rather, they are the foundation and presupposition of their faith.

Just as the raising of Jesus as an event in space and time is an implicate of its character as a divine judgment related to the cross, so too, the character of the resurrection as an event occurring in space-time is an implicate of the self-declaration of the risen Lord in his identity with the royal man exalted on the cross. According to Barth, the relationship of the implicates involved here is irreversible: the sovereign acknowledgment by God of the crucified one (the aspect of judgment) and the self-declaration of the risen one in his identity with the one crucified (the revelatory aspect) imply the concrete objectivity of the resurrection as an event in space and time. Hence the spatio-temporal character of Jesus' awakening and resurrection is an implicate of the identity of the one resurrected with the one crucified.

As an exclusive act of God transcending human and historical pragmatics and causality (analogy and correlation), the resurrection is a pre-historical happening; that is, an event whose content is not historically ascertainable. However, the resurrection has a real historical dimension in that it occurred at a particular time (on the third day, during the reign of Pontius Pilate), at a particular place (outside the gates of Jerusalem), in the circle of particular people (the disciples), and in connection with certain "signs" (such as the seeing of the disciples and the Empty Tomb). This historical dimension can certainly be ascertained through historical means. The pre-historical happening of the awakening/resurrection in space and time implies the "historical dimension" of the resurrection, but the historical dimension of the latter does not imply the former. For Barth the "historical dimension" refers neither to a trans-historical realm (Übergeschichte) nor to the sphere of historicity (Geschichtlichkeit) within the bounds of, or dialectically related to, history. Rather, he is speaking of salvation-history (Heilsgeschichte) which encompasses historical facticity while not being identical with it. Therefore, historical phenomena stand fundamentally in a predicative relationship to the raising of Jesus which has the character of a divine judgment and to the resurrection which has the character of a divine revelation. This is

Barth's consistent point that history is a predicate of revelation and not vice versa.

VIII.   SUMMARY THESES ON THE RESURRECTION OF JESUS

Barth's central affirmations regarding Jesus' resurrection may be summarized as follows.[35]

The raising of Jesus from the dead is an exclusive act of God. As such, it is the exemplary form of his revelation and the free divine act of grace effected by the Father on behalf of the Son; and herewith, it is the revelation of the subject who actualizes reconciliation on the cross (thesis 1). In raising Jesus Christ, God is revealed in the one humiliated on the cross. In that the raising of the crucified Jesus reveals the subject of reconciliation hidden in the contradiction of the cross, the connection of the cross and the raising of Jesus are the central context for the interpretation of Jesus as truly God.

If Barth's concern in the first thesis is with the raising of Jesus as the noetic moment of the revelation of the subject effecting reconciliation on the cross, his concern in the second thesis is with the raising of Jesus as the juridical moment attesting the validation of the act of reconciliation on the cross (thesis 2). Hence the raising of Jesus from the dead, in addition to being the revelation of the one hidden in the humiliation of the cross (par. 59:1), is the judicial proclamation of the one whose being for us (pro nobis) is the hidden telos of his being against us (contra nos) (par. 59:2). That is, the raising of Jesus from the dead as God's great positive verdict is the goal of the divine negation in the cross. This new act of God, which is related to the cross but not yet contained in the cross,

encompasses in its content not only the noetic moment,
as in the context of the question concerning the subject
active in reconciliation, and it is not only the expression of the significance of the cross, and finally, not
only the completion of the act of reconciliation in the
cross. It is also far more: as the valid proclamation
of the hidden subordination of the "No" to the "Yes" hid
beneath the appearance of its opposite in the cross, the
raising of Jesus is the justification of God himself
(Rom. 3:36), the justification of Jesus Christ (1 Tim.
3:16), and encompassed therein, the justification of
sinful humanity (Rom. 4:25). In that the raising of
Jesus is the divine proclamation of the "Yes" hidden in
the form of the "No" of the cross, the togetherness of
the cross and the raising of Jesus is the interpretive
center for comprehending that the reconciliation of the
world with God is for us (pro nobis).

The resurrection as the appearance to his disciples
of Jesus Christ raised from the dead by God--in addition
to providing both the knowledge of Jesus as the one
awakened and thus revealing the identity of the subject
of reconciliation and the juridical validation of the
act of reconciliation on the cross and grounded
therein--is the revelation of the royal man exalted on
the cross (thesis 3). Hence the resurrection is the
revelation of the one ruling from the cross while hidden
beneath its opposite. The resurrection as the revelation of the lordship of the crucified reconciler is
simultaneously also the beginning of the lordship of the
crucified one's maintenance of the completed reconciliation, and thus the entry by Jesus Christ into his lordship as the lord of all times (aspect of lordship). The
lordship of the royal man elevated on the cross poten-
tiates itself in the resurrection in the direction of an

unfinished teleological battle of the revealed lordship of the crucified one. Inasmuch as Jesus Christ corresponds to God for the first time on the cross while already ruling in his earthly activity from the cross as the exalted royal man, it follows that it is the cross--and not the incarnation or the activity of the earthly Jesus in word and deed--which is the primary corollary of the resurrection as the revelation of the royal man perfected precisely in the cross. The relationship of cross and resurrection is thus the interpretive center from which Jesus as truly man is ascertained.

Even as the character of the raising of Jesus as an event in space and time is an implicate of its character as a divine judgment, so also the character of the resurrection as an event in space and time is an implicate of the self-proclamation of the risen one in his identity with the royal man exalted on the cross. God's efficacious acknowledgment of the crucified (the juridical aspect) and the self-proclamation of the risen one in his identity with the crucified (revelatory aspect) imply the concrete objectivity of the event of the resurrection in space and time corresponding to the event of the cross. The spatiotemporal "event-character" of the awakening and resurrection is an implicate of the identity of the risen one with the crucified. Inasmuch as the raising of Jesus is an exclusive act of God, it transcends the realm of human and historical pragmatics and causality; hence in terms of its inner content and significance as an act of God, it is a pre-historical event and is not historically verifiable. Nonetheless, it has at the same time as a real, datable and locatable event an historical dimension which is verifiable through historical means.

According to Barth, as a pre-historical event, the raising of Jesus and the resurrection in space and time imply the "historical element of the resurrection" whereas the latter does not imply the former. Inasmuch as the character of the raising of Jesus as an event in space-time is an implicate of its being referred to the cross as an act of divine judgment, and since the character of the resurrection as a space-time event is an implicate of the one who is revealed as elevated on the cross, therefore the event of the resurrection is neither to be subsumed beneath the concept of history (Historie) nor of supra-history (Übergeschichte) nor of historicity. Rather, the interconnectedness of the cross and the awakening/resurrection of Jesus provides the interpretive center for determining the objectivity in space and time of the one raised from the dead.

IX. THE CRUCIFIED AND RISEN JESUS CHRIST AS THE AXIOM OF CHRISTOLOGY

    A. The Differentiated Connection of Cross and Resurrection

Barth speaks of the death and resurrection of Jesus Christ as two different events interconnected in a teleological sequence. The following theses capture Barth's understanding of their relationships.[36]

The differentiated connection of the cross and raising of Jesus is to be understood with reference to the divine subject known in the sequence of these two acts of God. As such, it represents God's creative establishment of identity between the one crucified and the one raised from the dead. As such, this identification is not to be subsumed beneath any other event such

as the incarnation or proclamation of Jesus. Nor is it
to be deduced from something higher such as a concept of
reality or a concept of history. Nor can it be proved
necessary on the basis of some external norm whether
existential or ontological. Nor is it to be derived
from some other context such as the claim and corresponding vindication of Jesus. The differentiated
connection of the cross and the raising of Jesus as
God's creative act of identifying the one resurrected
with the one crucified is, by virtue of the one active
in it (the Father), and the subject known in it (the
Son), the center and axiom of all theology.

The cross and the raising of Jesus stand in a
reciprocal and particular differentiated connection
because the raising of Jesus has a backward reference to
the cross and the cross has a forward reference to the
raising of Jesus. Insofar as the raising of Jesus
reveals the Son who was obedient on the cross, the
subject involved there is disclosed. Insofar as the
raising of Jesus proclaims the "Yes" hidden beneath the
"No" of the cross, the nature of the judgment carried
out there is disclosed. Thus the resurrection is seen
as a positive event with a negative presupposition while
the cross is seen as a negative event in correlation
with the positive event of the resurrection. The differentiated connection of the cross and the raising of
Jesus represents a unity involving a genuine sequence of
two different factors with different contents and functions.

This differentiated connection of cross and awakening is simultaneously the unbreakable unity of an
irreversible teleological sequence insofar as the "No"
is in the service of the "Yes," the judgment of grace is
in the service of the grace of judgment, and insofar as

the negative event of the cross has a positive intention. The differentiated connection between these two events when viewed as an unbreakable unity precludes maintaining a balance, equipoise or static equilibrium between them: rather, we are confronted with an irreversible teleology. These events cannot be construed in terms of a yes and a no. Rather, they constitute a teleologically ordered unity to the extent that in both foundational events the one "yes" of God for the reconciliation of the world is sounded. Thus the connection of the cross and resurrection--on account of their sequence as two foundational events and their backward and forward reciprocal relationships--is a differentiated connection with a irreversible teleology.

B.   Cross and Resurrection and Humiliation and Exaltation

Here the issue is the manner in which Barth develops the relationship of the humiliation and exaltation of Jesus Christ in relationship to the cross and resurrection. Klappert observes that Berkouwer faults Barth for departing from the New Testament's emphasis upon Christ's humiliation being followed by his exaltation in a temporal sequence by making the states coincide. Thus Barth speaks of Christ's exaltation as the unveiling of his glory already occurring within the state of humiliation. Klappert is correct that the issue is more complex than Berkouwer's critique allows. In order to deal with Barth's position, one must ask: in what context does Barth speak of humiliation and exaltation in terms of a temporal coincidence and when does he stress their temporal difference? And how are temporal coincidence and temporal difference related to teach other?[37] It was

stated above and Klappert admits that Barth speaks in
two ways in this regard. On the one hand, he speaks of
the coincidence of Jesus' humiliation and exaltation on
the cross. On the other, he speaks of the cross and
resurrection as parallel to humiliation and exaltation.
It is quite apparent that this framework dominates the
structure of the doctrine of reconciliation developed in
CD 4:1 and CD 4:2. Though we cannot pursue Klappert's
incisive analysis of the varied ways in which the New
Testament speaks in this regard nor Barth's manner of
appropriating the development of the doctrine of
Christ's two states in Protestant orthodoxy, Klappert's
thesis regarding Barth's procedure is helpful.

> Barth's answer to this complex of questions as
> his expositions indicate is determined by the
> relationships between cross and resurrection
> and humiliation and exaltation set forth in
> the New Testament as it is informed by the
> concept of the covenant. Thus Barth under-
> stands exaltation to mean human correspondence
> [to God] within the covenant. In addition,
> Barth's viewpoint is determined both by a
> critical and positive appropriation of the
> Protestant orthodox doctrine of Christ's two
> states.[38]

From this vantage point our earlier development of
this theme and Klappert's summary theses provide a response to Berkouwer's critique.

First, in Barth's view, the awakening of the crucified ("Cross and Awakening") as the revelation of the
majesty of the Son of God on the cross and as the revelation of the glory of the one humiliated on the cross
("Cross as Exaltation") is simultaneously the exaltation
of the Son of God to lordship; that is, God's granting
him dominion as kurios ("Resurrection as Exaltation").

The dimensions of lordship and sovereignty characteristic of Jesus' awakening are implicates of its constitutive revelatory and juridical aspects.

For Barth, the resurrection of the crucified as the revelation of the man exalted on the cross, as the revelation of the one ruling from the cross ("Exaltation as human correspondence, conformity to the covenant") is simultaneously the glorification of the man, Jesus, and his exaltation and translation to the right hand of God ("Resurrection and exaltation"). Thus the dimension of lordship and sovereignty attaching to Jesus' awakening from death is an implicate of its constitutive revelatory aspect related to the one reigning from the cross.

Secondly, for Barth, the differentiated relationship of cross and resurrection--the relationship of the cross as a negative occurrence with a positive intent and of the resurrection as a positive occurrence with a negative presupposition--establishes both: (a) the coincidence of the humiliation and majesty of the Son of God on the cross ("the Cross as Exaltation"); (b) and the coincidence of the humiliation of the Son of God and the exaltation of the man Jesus on the cross ("the Cross as Correspondence"); and also (c) the difference between the humiliation and exaltation of the Son of God on the cross and his being raised ("Awakening as Exaltation"). Viewed in this manner, the coincidence of the condescension of the Son of God and the exaltation of the man Jesus on the cross as the fulfillment of the covenant preserved in the double movement of the reconciling God and reconciled humanity is the substantive center and the material criterion of all other statements about exaltation: hence they are not eliminated on the basis of this center, but rather implied in it and interpreted in its light.

Thirdly, the humiliation of the Son of God and the exaltation of the man Jesus are not to be understood as two states having reference to the incarnation or solely to the human nature of Christ. Rather, the states have their substantive and temporal coincidence in the cross and its central significance. As such, they are implicates of the event of reconciliation in its coinciding double movement of the reconciling God and reconciled man in the cross. The awakening of the crucified ("Cross and Awakening") is the revelation of the majesty of the Son of God on the cross ("Cross as Exaltation"). The dimension of lordship and sovereignty characteristic of the raising of Jesus is thus an implicate of its constitutive revelatory and juridical aspects. The resurrection of the one crucified as the revelation of the one exalted on the cross ("Exaltation as human correspondence") is simultaneously the glorification of the man Jesus and his enthronement to full participation in the lordship of God ("Resurrection and Exaltation"). Hence the aspect of glory and power attending the resurrection is an implicate of its revelatory aspect which is integrally related to the one exalted on the cross.[39]

X.   BARTH'S CHRISTOLOGICAL THINKING: THE EXISTENTIAL UNITY OF THE SON OF GOD AND JESUS OF NAZARETH

In Part III of this analysis, the attempt was made to develop some of the main lines of Barth's doctrine of reconciliation grounded in his understanding of its foundation in Jesus Christ. Attention was focused upon Jesus Christ crucified and risen through whom God's great "Yes" was spoken once and for all. This entailed the suffering and death of the Son who bore the judgment beneath which humanity had fallen thereby making peace

between God's wayward creatures and himself. We only
glanced at the continuing work of the risen lord and
Mediator present through his Spirit which Barth develops
in subsequent volumes of the doctrine of reconciliation.[40] Perhaps enough has been said concerning the
"history of Jesus Christ with which the history of
reconciliation is identical" to comprehend something of
Barth's vision of the movement from "above downwards"
and from "below upwards" both of which are "grounded in
His person in the union of its true deity and true
humanity."[41] For Barth this means that

> it is a matter of the salvation and right of
> man established in the humiliation of the Son
> of God to be the Brother, Representative and
> Head of all men. And it is a matter of the
> right and glory of God asserted in the exalta-
> tion of this Brother, Representative and Head
> of all men, of the true son of Man. As the
> one Jesus Christ is both true Son of God and
> true Son of Man, so there takes place in His
> one history both the humiliation of God and
> the exaltation of man, the conflict and vic-
> tory of God for man, and therewith and thereby
> the achievement of covenant faithfulness on
> both sides, the establishment of peace in this
> twofold form.[42]

It is crucial for understanding Barth's doctrine of
reconciliation that first and last it concerns the
history of Jesus Christ. First and last, therefore, the
church narrates a story of salvation whose divergent
strands lead toward their center in Jesus' history.

> ...the history of reconciliation is His his-
> tory. It is the history of His sending and
> coming, of His life and speech and action, of
> His death and passion and resurrection, of His
> ministry and lordship. In Him God is the One
> who graciously elects man and man is the one
> who is graciously elected by God. He is the

actualisation of the covenant between God and
man, both on the side of God and also on that
of man.[43]

Throughout Barth's depiction of the history of
Jesus Christ, the Son of Man and the Son of God, of
Jesus crucified and risen and yet to come, there is no
doubt that "Jesus is Victor!" This watchword of the
elder J. C. Blumhardt was central to his radical understanding of the kingdom of God and exercised a decisive
influence upon Barth's theological reorientation beginning about 1916. Throughout his Dogmatics, Barth's
indebtedness to the two Blumhardts is evident. Here
Barth adopts this triumphant affirmation as an appropriate summary of the prophetic work of the risen Mediator.
In fact, it points to the meaning of the entire history
of Jesus Christ.

> It tells of the issue but also of the begin-
> ning of the action, and in so doing of the
> dynamic and teleological character which marks
> it from its commencement to its goal, "Jesus
> is Victor" is the first and last and decisive
> word to be said in this respect."[44]

Though Barth frequently stressed that God's victory
in Jesus Christ over the powers of chaos, sin and
death--over all principalities and powers--was assured,
he did not deny that the battle still rages. However,
metaphysical dualism is precluded for the Christian
believer. Typical of his many statements is the following:

> A history is here taking place: a drama is
> being enacted; a war waged to a successful
> conclusion. If from the very first there can
> be no doubt as to the issue of the action,
> there can also be no doubt that there is an

action, and that it is taking place, and can thus be described only in the form of narration.[45]

A.   Christomonism or _Christus_ _Victor_?

Barth's increasing concentration in the Church Dogmatics on Jesus Christ as the final referent of all Christian faith and reflection has repeatedly given rise to the charge of christomonism. Bonhoeffer's charge of a "positivism of revelation" is similar.   Thus numerous critics charge Barth with excessive systematization by theologizing as though the person of Jesus Christ were a principle. Many critics have adopted Balthasar's quip that it appears that Barth has looked into "God's cards."[46]   Hence Barth seems to know at the end, or even the beginning, of theological reflection what seems knowable only when faith gives way to sight!   If this critique is true, Barth's theology would treat Jesus Christ as though he were a principle (_Prinzip_) rather than a person.   Were this the case, Barth would not be "following after his object."   Instead, he would be guilty of treating him as a manipulable principle.

In the final major section of the doctrine of reconciliation, Barth responds to Berkouwer as typical of those making this charge.   He takes Berkouwer's critique against him to mean that he operates with the concept of grace in an "_a_ _priori_ and ontological sense" which "predetermines the contest between God and evil, and this contest, with all that takes place in the creaturely world and therefore in time, can only develop irresistibly, like a piece of clockwork. ..."[47]   Barth notes that Berkouwer "has clearly perceived and continually emphasised that I find, or try to find, a

christological basis for what I say concerning the will
and Word and work of God on the one side, the evil which
strives against these on the other, and finally their
relationship to one another."[48]   Assuming that he and
Berkouwer may differ on what constitutes "'christological' thinking," Barth offers his own perspective.

> I can only speak for myself, and I maintain
> that for me thinking is christological only
> when it consists in the perception, comprehen-
> sion, understanding and estimation of the
> reality of the living person of Jesus Christ
> as attested by Holy Scripture, in attentive-
> ness to the range and significance of His
> existence, in openness to His self-disclosure,
> in consistency in following Him as is de-
> manded. In this formal definition I am confi-
> dent that Berkower and I are in agreement, and
> I also think we can agree that christological
> thinking in this sense is a very different
> process from deduction from a given principle.
> I underline, however, that we are not dealing
> with a Christ-principle, but with Jesus Christ
> Himself as attested by Holy Scripture.[49]

Barth also assumes that he and his critic would concur
that

> christological thinking must always be a
> matter of the perception, apprehension, under-
> standing and estimation of the person who
> according to the witness of Holy Scripture,
> discloses Himself as the crucified and risen
> Son of God and Son of Man, as the one almighty
> Mediator between God and man, indeed, between
> God and all creation, and therefore as the One
> to whom as such all power is given in heaven
> and on earth (Mt. 28:18). We do not really
> speak of Jesus Christ, of His self-disclosure,
> of the witness of Holy Scripture, if we do not
> assume from the very first that we have to do
> with this person.[50]

Moreover, Barth presupposes that he and Berkouwer
would

> also agree that within theological thinking
> generally unconditional _priority_ must be given
> to thinking which is attentive to the exis-
> tence of the living person of Jesus Christ
> (just because it is _this_ existence), so that
> _per_ _definitionem_ christological thinking forms
> the _unconditional_ _basis_ _of_ _all_ other theologi-
> cal thinking, even that which deals with the
> relationship between God and evil.[51]

This necessitates rejection all theological reflection which presumes to speak of concepts such a "God,
man, sin, grace" without reference to Jesus Christ--even
if one were to seek subsequent christological justification of them. Barth surmises that Berkouwer's deep
allegiance to Reformed Orthodoxy qualifies "this uncon-
ditional precedence of christological thinking within
theology generally."[52] Evidence for this charge is to
be found in the orthodox Reformed doctrine of election.
Following Calvin, it was held that "already in the
doctrine of election we have a principle which has
priority over the person and work of Jesus Christ, so
that Jesus Christ is to be understood only as the mighty
executive organ of the divine will of grace, and only a
secondary place can be given to christological
thinking."[53]

Barth rejects the legitimacy of any kind of deduc-
tive theological thinking which presumes that the grace
of God in Jesus Christ is a principle from which every-
thing--including God's triumph over the powers which
oppose him--could be deduced and thereby assured. Barth
is unequivocal regarding his own intention:

422

> I am not trying unilaterally to think through
> the principle of grace to the point at which
> I reach the "triumph of grace" in this rela-
> tionship. I should regard such a procedure as
> quite illegitimate. My desire is that from
> the very first, at every point, and therefore
> in answering this question too [i.e., the
> issue of evil], we should take with uncondi-
> tional seriousness the fact that 'Jesus is
> Victor.' Surely Berkouwer cannot really have
> anything against this. [54]

It is not the case, therefore, that Barth or any
theologian should speak of God's triumph over evil
abstracted from Jesus Christ.

> On the contrary, the living person of Jesus
> Christ in His character as the almighty Media-
> tor between God and man is the one person, and
> that which contradicts and withstands this
> person is the other. But the fact that this
> person is envisaged as such means that the
> reference to the absolute superiority of this
> person cannot mean that we can grasp and
> master either Him or the whole situation. We
> can trust a person, and in the case of this
> person we must do so unconditionally and with
> final certainty, as Blumhardt did when he
> accepted the battle. But we cannot grasp a
> person, and especially not this person, in the
> sense of conceptual apprehension and control.
> Hence we cannot grasp the whole situation in
> this sense, and there is no cause for anxiety
> in this respect. [55]

The theologian's word concerning God's triumph in
Jesus Christ can be only a penultimate word: the final
word is that spoken by God in Jesus Christ himself.
Over against all monisms and thinking about God and the
power of evil in terms of abstract principles, Barth
intends to point to the true conflict between them attested in the Bible. Let these words be representative

of many with respect to Barth's vision of God's triumph in the person of his Son.

> To say "Jesus" is necessarily to say "history," His history, the history in which He is what He is and does what He does. In His history we know God, and we also know evil and their relationship the one to the other--but only from this source and in this way. But at this point a way is trodden. A question is raised and answered. A sentence is pronounced and judgment is executed and suffered. A faith and obedience are demanded and displayed. Prayer is offered. A cross is borne, and on this cross suffering is endured. From the deepest depths a cry is raised to heaven. Nothing is self-evident, obvious or matter-of-course. The day must be carried against the fiercest opposition. A war is waged against sin, death and the devil. It is this war that Jesus is Victor. ...The One who treads this way [who submits to this final conflict, who takes this conflict upon Himself and endures], who acts in it and in this way, in His free act, overcomes the enemy and is thus the Victor, [this One is] the living Jesus Christ. ...The crucified and slain Jesus is the one who triumphs. ... He does this, and we must keep to the fact that He does [this]. But how can we ever imagine that this is an easy "triumph of grace?" How can we overlook or deny that we have to do here with encounter and struggle, and therefore with history.[56]

B.   A Second Naiveté

Whoever confronts Barth's theology constantly is taken aback at the realistic way in which he reads the biblical narratives and seeks to speak about what he hears therein. Some take Barth's reading to be uncritical and indicative of his rejection of historical-criticism. We saw earlier that this lay at the heart of Harnack's opposition to Barth and why he regarded the latter's theology to be unscientific. Many critics of the "later" Barth, including Bultmann as shown above, were critical of Barth for similar reasons. Others, including this writer, view Barth's theology as expressive of a new realism seeking to be faithful to theology's subject matter. On the occasion of the one hundredth anniversary of Barth's birth in 1986, Dalferth put this point well: "In an exemplary way, Barth's theology is realistic theology. It is this in the context of its time, but not as a function of its time. Rather, it is such on the basis of its particular theological realism."[57]

This stance entailed Barth's consistent rejection of making Christianity's truth claims answerable to the claims of reason and modern epistemologies. However, he also insisted contrary to the approach of many contemporaries that all theology was human, fallible construction always in need of correction in light of its subject matter. More importantly, Barth refused to surrender the Christian claim to eschatological truth by moving reductionistically in identifying it with subjective/ existential truth, general ethical or religious convictions or with the values of modern cultural Christianity. Dalferth describes the way in which Barth went "against the stream" of prevailing viewpoints in espousing his consistently held theological realism.

> Barth saw theology as a theology of the <u>Word of God</u> bound to its subject matter: that is, the crucified, risen and therefore living and present Jesus Christ. In keeping with this theme, theology was obligated to a specific objectivity which consisted in gaining a hearing for this eschatological resurrection reality by means of the exegesis of biblical texts attesting it.[58]

Both the "early" and "later" Barth was concerned
with this single reality in all its dimensions. In one
of his last lectures, he spoke of Jesus Christ as ultimate reality. He is the reality with which theology
always has to do. "Jesus is Victor" and "the reality of
the risen, living, active, creative, speaking Jesus
Himself as an actual factor of a unique kind must be the
concern of theology yesterday and today."[59] Dalferth is
correct to remind us that from the outset of Barth's
confrontation with the "strange new world within the
Bible" (1916), he was clear that the reality of the
risen Lord and his coming kingdom did not fit into our
ordinary ways of experiencing reality. He spoke of this
reality in the first edition of his Romans commentary as
that which transcends everything visible and conceivable. Yet this saving eschatological activity of
God in Jesus Christ and his coming kingdom--though not
objectifiable and graspable as objective entities--are
the "true reality" determinative of what constitutes
reality.[60]

Two incidents from Barth's life are typical of his
life-long realistic thinking which took the form of
"faith seeking understanding." The first is found in a
letter written in July, 1934, some six weeks after
Barth's involvement in the drafting of the Barmen Declaration. He had receive a letter from Gerhardt Kuhlmann, a Schlesian theologian and philosopher, along with
his manuscript which dealt critically with Barth's
theology. Kuhlmann asked Barth: "In whom can one still
believe when all the gods of this world are exposed as
idols--including that of your theology?" In the course
of a lengthy response, Barth wrote:

But apart from the plurality of gods, and apart from the God of my Dogmatics or that of any other, one may indeed believe in God himself. What do I intend with my Dogmatics? Surely not to point to my "God," but rather to point to God himself as the God in whom one should and can believe even when all of the gods of this world are exposed before one's eyes as idols. Precisely at that point--and then for the first time! Is it the case that one can believe? Yes, because one believes in Jesus Christ, but I must emphasize again-- because one can believe in Jesus Christ him-self. Can one thus believe? Yes, because apart from all theological constructions and apart from the friendly destruction of faith at the hands of philosophy, one nevertheless today may still read for e.g., Ps. 23, or Ps. 90, or Ps. 139, or Jer. 31, or Is. 53, or Lk. 15, or Rom. 8, or Rev. 21 and allow oneself to be told like a child: it is thus as it stands written there. This likewise untheological and unphilosophical--'it is thus'-- is what I intend when I speak of 'God himself' or of 'Jesus Christ himself'--or much rather would like to speak of and am not able to do so, because only God himself can speak of himself.[61]

The second incident occured over two decades later in 1955--after World War II and in the midst of the Cold War--when Barth published the second of his multivolumed treatment of The Doctrine of Reconciliation. It was this doctrine of his "unfinished" Church Dogmatics which claimed his intense and ultimate devotion and labor. The final Fragment (CD 4:4) appeared in 1968, the year of his death. Midway in his exposition of the doctrine of reconciliation as Barth approached the seventh decade of life, he remarks in a revealing and reflective digression in the section, "The Exaltation of the Son of Man," as follows:

What is the meaning of our keeping Christmas, Good Friday and Easter? What is the meaning of our proclaiming and hearing Jesus Christ as the Word of God spoken to the world and ourselves? What is the meaning of our believing in Him, and loving Him, and hoping in Him? What is the meaning of the Lord's Supper? Do these things really make sense if they are only acts of remembrance and representation, analogous to the many memorials. ...that may be found in the secular sphere? Or is it not the tacit presupposition of all these actions that preceding our remembrance, the One Whom we remember is Himself in action, now, to-day and here?... He is the living Jesus Christ ...in [whom] we now, to-day and here are invited to participate with supreme realism, being personally summoned as individual Christians and gathered as the community. Why with such realism? Because and as He overcomes the barrier of His own time and therefore historical distance. [Because and as He in His action which occurred then in the past is present and future to us. Because and as He in His action which occurred then in the past is among us to-day and will be among us to-morrow]. Did any living Christian or living community ever live except on this presupposition? Would He or they exist at all if this presupposition were not a reality?[62]

At this juncture, Barth pays tribute to a little known Basel pastor-theologian, Abel Burckhardt, who in the mid nineteenth century "composed and edited a collection of songs for children in the local dialect." Barth continues:

This was the text-book in which, at the beginning of the last decade of the last century, I received my first theological instruction in a form appropriate to my then immaturity. And what made an indelible impression on me was the homely naturalness with which these very modest compositions spoke of the events of Christmas, Palm Sunday, Good Friday, Easter, the Ascension and Pentecost as things which might take place any day in Basel or its

environs like any other important happenings.
History? Doctrine? Dogma? Myth? No--but
things actually taking place, so that we could
see and hear and lay [them] up in our hearts.
For as these songs were sung in the everyday
language we were then beginning to hear and
speak, and as we joined in singing, we took
our mother's hand, as it were, and went to the
stall at Bethlehem, and to the streets of
Jerusalem where, greeted by children of a
similar age, the Saviour made His entry, and
to the dark hill of Golgotha, and as the sun
rose to the garden of Joseph. Was this representation, like the unbloody repetition of the
sacrifice of Christ in the Roman doctrine of
the Mass? Was it the kind of faith which in
that rather convulsive doctrine is supposed to
consist in a re-enactment of the crucifixion
of Christ in our own existence? Again, no.
It was all _present_ without needing to be made
present. The "yawning chasm" of Lessing did
not exist. The contemporaneity of Kierkegaard
was not a problem. The Saviour Himself was
obviously _the_ _same_ yesterday and to-day. All
very naive, and not worth mentioning at all in
academic circles? Yes, it was very naive, but
perhaps in the very naivety there lay the
deepest wisdom and greatest power, so that
once grasped it was calculated to carry one
relatively unscathed--although not, of course
untempted or unassailed--through all the
serried ranks of historicism and anti-
historicism, mysticism and rationalism, orthodoxy, liberalism and existentialism, and to
bring one back some day to the matter [die
Sache] itself."[63]

What was the subject (_die_ _Sache_) or subject matter
which repeatedly consumed Barth's attention and confronted him as "Reality" _sui_ _generis_? What caused him
to begin each volume of his Dogmatics, as it were, from
the beginning? In his tribute to Karl Barth on the day
following his death on December 10, 1968, Eberhard
Jüngel, astute interpreter of his theological mentor,
said:

The subject which Barth contemplated for an entire lifetime is a simple one. His entire life revolved about a simple word: the Yes that God says to himself--the Yes that (because he says it to himself) he says also to the human race. To this divine Yes, Barth responded with a thoughtful Yes. And, for the sake of this Yes, he said a No. Karl Barth brought the Word of God to the light as the word Yes. That was his accomplishment.[64]

NOTES

Chapter I

[1]Karl Barth-Rudolf Bultmann, Letters, 1922-1966, ed. by Bernd Jaspert and G. W. Bromiley. Tr. by Bromiley (Grand Rapids: Eerdmans, 1981), p. 1. The letter is dated April 9, 1922. Cited hereafter as Barth-Bultmann Letters.

[2]Rudolf Bultmann, "Karl Barths 'Römerbrief' in Zweiter Auflage," Anfänge der dialektischen Theologie, ed. by Jürgen Moltmann (München: Kaiser, 1962), Part I, p. 140. Cited hereafter: Bultmann, Anfänge, I. Barth's two editions of The Epistle to the Romans are identified as Romans, I and Romans, II. All translations from German originals are mine unless otherwise noted.

[3]Bultmann, Anfänge, I, p. 141.

[4]Bultmann, Anfänge, I, pp. 140-141, for these points. For an analysis of Bultmann's review, see: James Smart, The Divided Mind of Modern Theology (Philadelphia: Westminster, 1967), pp. 117-122. Cited hereafter as DMMT. Other reviews of Barth's Romans I and II may be found in Anfänge. The modified English edition of Anfänge entitled, The Beginnings of Dialectical Theology, vol. I, edited by James M. Robinson, has an excellent introduction to the early developments of dialectical theology and the responses of its critics. Particular attention is given to Barth and Bultmann and their exchanges.

[5]DMMT, p. 117. Smart's critical analysis of the development of the theologies of Barth and Bultmann and their deepening divisions from 1908-1933 is the best English study available.

[6]Bultmann, Anfänge, I, p. 119.

[7]DMMT, p. 118. Bultmann does recognize, however, that Barth does not utilize the term "religion" in the positive way Bultmann does. Cf. Anfänge, I, p. 120.

[8]Bultmann, Anfänge, I, p. 119: cf. Smart, DMMT, p. 118.

[9]Cited in Revolutionary Theology In The Making: Barth-Thurneysen Correspondence, 1914-1925, tr. by James D. Smart (Richmond: Knox, 1964), p. 94. Cited hereafter as RTM. This is among the best resources on the genesis of Barth's theology. The best English secondary source is Thomas F. Torrance, Karl Barth: An Introduction to his Early Theology 1910-1931 (London: SCM,

1962). Excellent insights into Barth's early development are found in Eberhard Jüngel, Barth-Studien
(Gütersloh: Mohn, 1982), pp. 61-209. In English translation, Karl Barth, a Theological Legacy (Philadelphia:
Westminister, 1986), pp. 53-104.

[10]RTM, p. 94.

[11]Bultmann, Anfänge, I, p. 136.

[12]RTM, p. 94. For some of Barth's further comments
on Bultmann's review of the 1922 edition of Barth's
Romans, see his preface to the third edition written in
1923. The Epistle to the Romans, tr. from the sixth
edition by Edwyn C. Hoskyns (London: Oxford University
Press, 1937), pp. 15-20. Cited hereafter as Romans, II.

[13]Romans, II, p. 16.

[14]Romans, II, p. 16.

[15]Romans, II, pp. 16-17.

[16]Romans, II, p. 1.

[17]Romans, II, p. 1.

[18]Romans, II, p. 6.

[19]Jülicher's review of 1920 is found in Anfänge, I,
pp. 87-98. For Barth's comments, see Romans, II, p. 9.

[20]Bultmann, Anfänge, I, p. 141.

[21]Romans, II, p. 7.

[22]Jüngel, Barth-Studien, p. 84.

[23]Romans, II, p. 6.

[24]Romans, II, p. 8. I have transliterated the
Greek.

[25]I have translated the German original to reveal
Barth's emphasis: Der Römerbrief (Zollikon: Evangelischer Verlag, 1954), 2nd ed., p. xiii. Cf. Romans, II,
p. 8.

[26]Romans, II, p. 8.

[27]Romans, II, p. 1.

[28]Romans, II, p. 7.

[29]Romans, II, p. 1.

[30]Romans, II, p. 8.

[31]Romans, II, p. 13. Cf. Jüngel, Barth-Studien, pp.
84ff.

[32]Romans, II, p. 1.

[33]Romans, II, p. 10.

[34]Romans, II, p. 10.

[35]Romans, II, p. 10.

[36]Romans, II, p. 11.

[37]Romans, II, p. 11.

[38]Romans, II, p. 12. The student of the Church Dogmatics will recall Barth's characteristic use of the Latin, nota bene, note well, as a way of calling the reader's attention to something deserving of careful and critical attention and reflection.

[39]Romans, II, p. 12.

[40]Romans, II, p. 24.

[41]Paul S. Minear, "Barth's Commentary on the Romans, 1922-1972; or Karl Barth vs. the Exegetes," in Footnotes to a Theology: The Karl Barth Colloquium of 1972, ed. with an Introduction by Martin Rumscheidt (Canada: Studies in Religion Supplements, 1974), p. 20. Minear provides helpful insights from the vantage point of a Neutestamentler both regarding Barth's exegetical contributions and reactions to him past and present. For a more comprehensive treatment of Barth's mode of Scriptural interpretation in relationship to that of the historical-critical school--especially in the early Barth up to the time of CD I/2--see: Walter Lindemann, Karl Barth Und Die Kritische Schriftauslegung (Hamburg: Reich-Evangelischer Verlag, 1973).

[42]Eberhard Busch, Karl Barth (Philadelphia: Fortress, 1976), p. 126. Cited hereafter as Busch, KB.

[43]Busch, KB, p. 127.

[44]Busch, KB, pp. 127-28.

[45]Busch, KB, p. 128.

[46]Busch, KB, p. 128.

[47]Busch, KB, p. 128.

[48]Busch, KB, p. 129.

[49]Busch, KB, p. 129.

[50]Busch, KB, p. 130.

[51]Busch, KB, p. 130.

[52]Busch, KB, p. 132.

[53]Busch, KB, p. 133.

[54]Busch, KB, p. 133.

[55]Busch, _KB_, p. 133.

[56]Busch, _KB_, pp. 133-34.

[57]Busch, _KB_, p. 134. My brackets.

[58]Busch, _KB_, pp. 136-37.

[59]Busch, _KB_, p. 137.

[60]Busch, _KB_, p. 135.

[61]Busch, _KB_, pp. 134-35.

[62]Busch, _KB_, pp. 135-36.

[63]Busch, _KB_, p. 136.

[64]Busch, _KB_, pp. 137-38.

[65]For this exchange, see _Anfänge_, I, pp. 175-89. Gogarten's answer to Tillich is also included in this collection. Also in _The Beginnings of Dialectical Theology_, vol.I, pp. 133-162.

[66]Busch, _KB_, p. 138.

[67]Karl Barth, _The Word of God and the Word of Man_ (n.p., Pilgrim Press, 1928), p. 100. Cited hereafter _WGWM_. I have corrected the misspelling of Herrmann. Identical reprint as a Harper Torchback in 1957.

[68]Barth, _WGWM_, pp. 122-23. Author's italics.

[69]Barth, _WGWM_, p. 101.

[70]Barth, _WGWM_, p. 98.

[71]Barth, _WGWM_, p. 134. Brackets inserted.

[72]Busch, _KB_, p. 140.

[73]Barth, _WGWM_, p. 186. Author's italics.

[74]Barth, _WGWM_, p. 199. Author's italics.

[75]Barth, _WGWM_, p. 216. Author's italics.

[76]Busch, _KB_, p. 140.

[77]Barth, _WGWM_, pp. 195-96. Author's italics.

[78]Busch, _KB_, p. 142.

[79]Busch, _KB_, p. 142.

[80]Busch, _KB_, p. 143.

[81]Busch, _KB_, p. 143. Bracketed material is mine.

[82]Busch, _KB_, p. 143. Cf. p. 144.

[83]Cited in Busch, _KB_, p. 144. Bracketed material is mine.

[84]Cited in Busch, KB, p. 116; for the influence of Kierkegaard on Romans, II, see pp. 4, 10, and its index. Bracketed material supplied.

[85]Busch, KB, p. 145.

[86]Busch, KB, p. 229. Bracketed material is mine.

[87]Karl Barth. "Abschied von 'Zwischen den Zeiten,'" in Anfänge der dialektischen Theologie, ed. by Jürgen Moltmann (München: Chr. Kaiser Verlag, 1963), Part II, p. 313. Cited hereafter as Anfänge, II. Bracketed material is mine.

[88]Anfänge, II, pp. 316-17. Bracketed material is mine.

[89]Anfänge, II, p. 314.

[90]Anfänge, II, p. 318.

[91]CD 2:1, pp. 27-29; 127ff.; 172ff.

[92]Karl Barth, Die christliche Dogmatik im Entwurf (München: Chr. Kaiser Verlag, 1928), pp. 126ff. Cited hereafter as Christliche Dogmatik.

[93]Christliche Dogmatik, p. 111.

[94]Karl Barth, How I Changed My Mind, Introduction and Epilogue by John D. Godsey (Richmond: John Knox Press, 1966), pp. 42-43. Barth's contributions to the series appeared in The Christian Century in 1938, 1948 and 1958.

[95]CD 1:1, pp. ix-x (G. T. Thomson edition). Bracketed material supplied.

[96]Busch, KB, p. 245.

[97]Cited by Barth, CD 2:1, p. 172. See pp. 172-78 for Barth's significant excursus on Barmen.

[98]CD 2:1, p. 176.

[99]CD 2:1, p. 177.

NOTES

Chapter II

[1](New York: Harper, 1957). For a critical analysis of Harnack's historical and theological positions, see Wayne Glick, The Reality of Christianity (New York: Harper, 1967).

[2]Busch, KB, p. 39.

[3]Busch, KB, p. 34. Bracketed material supplied.

[4]Barth, WGWM, p. 60.

[5]Barth, WGWM, pp. 60-61. Barth's italics.

[6]Barth, WGWM, pp. 68-69.

[7]Busch, KB, pp. 114-15.

[8]Barth, WGWM, p. 88. Barth's italics.

[9]Busch, KB, p. 115.

[10]Busch, KB, p. 115.

[11]Adolf von Harnack and Karl Barth, "The Debate on the Critical Historical Method: Correspondence Between Adolf von Harnack and Karl Barth," in The Beginnings of Dialectic Theology, ed. by James M. Robinson (Richmond: John Knox, 1968), vol. I, p. 167. Cited hereafter Harnack--Barth. Italics and material in brackets will correspond to the German original. Cf., Barth, Theologische Fragen und Antworten (Zollikon: Evangelischer Verlag, 1957), vol. 3, pp. 7-31. The definitive treatment of the Harnack-Barth correspondence and its context is H. Martin Rumscheidt, Revelation and Theology (Cambridge: University Press, 1972). Hereafter referred to as RT. Rumscheidt's translation is more nuanced at points and I have cited it. Occasionally, both translations are cited in the footnotes.

[12]Harnack--Barth, p. 165.

[13]Harnack--Barth, p. 167. Brackets supplied.

[14]Harnack--Barth, p. 171; brackets indicate modified translation.

[15]Harnack--Barth, p. 177.

[16]Harnack--Barth, p. 176.

[17]Harnack--Barth, p. 165.

[18]Harnack--Barth, p. 165. Brackets supplied.

[19]Harnack--Barth, p. 167.

[20]Harnack--Barth, p. 167.

[21]Rumscheidt, RT, p. 46; cf. Harnack--Barth, p. 181.

[22]Rumscheidt, RT, p. 47; cf. Harnack--Barth, p. 181.

[23]Harnack--Barth, p. 168.

[24]Harnack--Barth, p. 168. Brackets supplied.

[25]Harnack--Barth, p. 171.

[26]Harnack--Barth, p. 171.

[27]Harnack--Barth, p. 186.

[28]Harnack--Barth, p. 172. Brackets supplied.

[29]Harnack--Barth, pp. 165-66.

[30]Harnack--Barth, p. 166. These are Harnack's initial questions, 5-11.

[31]Harnack--Barth, p. 168.

[32]Harnack--Barth, p. 172.

[33]Harnack--Barth, p. 168.

[34]Harnack--Barth, p. 168.

[35]Harnack--Barth, p. 172.

[36]Cited from Barth's papers in Busch, KB, p. 81. For the entire manifesto, Rumscheidt, RT, pp. 202-03.

[37]Cited in Rumscheidt, RT, p. 203.

[38]Harnack--Barth, p. 168.

[39]Harnack--Barth, p. 168.

[40]Harnack--Barth, p. 173.

[41]Harnack--Barth, pp. 168-69. Bracketed material from the original.

[42]Harnack--Barth, p. 169.

[43]Harnack--Barth, p. 169. These are Barth's replies to Harnack's intial questions, 5-11.

[44]Harnack--Barth, p. 173.

[45]Adolf von Harnack, Marcion (Leipzig: Hinrichs, 1924), pp. 228f. Cited by Rumscheidt, RT, p. 94.

[46]Rumscheidt, RT, pp. 95-97; cf. esp. pp. 86-100.

[47]Combining the translations of Rumscheidt, RT, p. 47 and Harnack--Barth, p. 181. The origins of labelling Barth a Marcionite are traceable as far back as Jülicher's review of Romans, I, in 1920. In the preface to Romans, II, of 1922, Barth observes: "Harnack's book on

Marcion appeared whilst I was immersed in the writing of my commentary. Those who are familiar with both books will understand why I am bound to refer to it. I was puzzled, on reading the earlier reviews of Harnack's book, by the remarkable parallels between what Marcion had said and what I was actually writing. I wish to plead for a careful examination of these agreements before I be praised or blamed hastily as though I were a Marcionite. At the crucial points these agreements break down. Even before the appearance of Harnack's book, Jülicher had already bracketed my name with Marcion's. Harnack joined me to--Thomas Münzer; Walter Koepler, I think, to Kaspar Schwenckfeld. Before these learned theologians made up their minds to throw me to some ancient and venerable heresiarch they would have done better if they had agreed on their choice. As it is, I remain unscathed, and can only wonder at the varied selection the three theologians have made." (Romans, II, p. 13)

[48]Rumscheidt, RT, p. 48; cf. Harnack--Barth, pp. 181-82.

[49]Rumscheidt, RT, p. 48; cf. Harnack--Barth, p. 182.

[50]Rumscheidt, RT, p. 48; cf. Harnack--Barth, p. 182.

[51]Rumscheidt, RT, p. 49; cf. Harnack--Barth, p. 183.

[52]Rumscheidt, RT, p. 49; cf. Harnack--Barth, p. 183. Barth expresses here his developing polemic against the tradition of natural theology which he opposed in its Roman Catholic and later neo-Protestant or liberal form. The natural theology tradition makes it permissible to speak about a knowledge of God possible on the basis of the universal revelation of God, or the revelation of God in creation. It operates on the principle of the analogy of being (analogia entis) according to which there is continuity between the being of the creature and the being of God. This allows the possibility of the knowledge of God as Creator without any reference to his revelation within the history of the old and new covenants and their center in Jesus Christ. In his Nein! to Emil Brunner in 1934, Barth wrote: "Ever since about 1916, when I began to recover noticeably from the effects of my theological studies and the influence of the liberal-political pre-war theology, my opinion concerning the task of our theological generation has been this: we must learn again to understand revelation as grace, and grace as revelation, and therefore turn away from all "true" or false" theologia naturalis." Karl Barth and Emil Brunner, Natural Theology (London: Centenary Press, 1946), p. 71. For a fuller description

of this controversy on natural theology in the light of Barth's developing doctrine of revelation, see David L. Mueller, <u>Karl</u> <u>Barth</u> (Waco: Word, 1972), pp. 85-93).

[53]Rumscheidt, <u>RT</u>, p. 50; cf. <u>Harnack--Barth</u>, p. 183.

[54]Rumscheidt, <u>RT</u>, pp. 50-51; cf. <u>Harnack--Barth</u>, pp. 183-84. Rumscheidt's translation corrects and clarifies this passage. Brackets added.

[55]<u>Harnack--Barth</u>, p. 166.

[56]<u>Harnack--Barth</u>, p. 169.

[57]<u>Harnack--Barth</u>, p. 169.

[58]<u>Harnack--Barth</u>, p. 173.

[59]<u>Harnack--Barth</u>, p. 166.

[60]<u>Harnack--Barth</u>, p. 169.

[61]<u>Harnack--Barth</u>, p. 170; English translation modified using Rumscheidt, <u>RT</u>, p. 35.

[62]Kähler's book was entitled <u>The</u> <u>So-Called</u> <u>Jesus</u> <u>of</u> <u>History</u> [<u>der</u> <u>historische</u> <u>Jesus</u>], <u>and</u> <u>the</u> <u>Historical</u> [<u>geschichtliche</u>], <u>Biblical</u> <u>Christ</u>. Schweitzer's famous work was <u>The</u> <u>Quest</u> <u>of</u> <u>the</u> <u>Historical</u> <u>Jesus</u>. See Barth's strong subsequent commendation of Kähler's view that the "historical Christ is no other than the biblical Christ attested by the New Testament passages, i.e., the incarnate Word, the risen and exalted One, God manifest in His redeeming action as He is the object of the disciples faith." CD I/2, pp. 64-65.

[63]Rumscheidt translation, <u>RT</u>, p. 35; cf. <u>Harnack--Barth</u>, p. 170.

[64]Rumscheidt translation, <u>RT</u>, p. 39; cf. <u>Harnack--Barth</u>, p. 174.

[65]Rumscheidt translation, <u>RT</u>, p. 39; cf. <u>Harnack--Barth</u>, p. 174.

[66]<u>Romans</u>, II, p. 3.

[67]Barth and Thurneysen dealt with the challenge of Overbeck in <u>Zur</u> <u>inneren</u> <u>Lage</u> <u>des</u> <u>Christentums</u> (1920). Barth's essay in this collection on Overbeck was "Unerledigte Anfragen an die heutige Theologie" ("Unresolved Questions for Modern Theology") available in Barth: <u>Theology</u> <u>and</u> <u>Church:</u> <u>Shorter</u> <u>Writings,</u> <u>1920-1928</u> (New York: Harper, 1962).

[68]Rumscheidt, <u>RT</u>, p. 67. Barth's appropriation of Overbeck's critique of the prevailing liberal theology of the last half of the nineteenth century marked a decisive juncture in Barth's own developing critique

thereof. Jüngel assesses the significance of Overbeck for Barth in "Theologie als 'unmögliche Möglichkeit.' Zwischen Overbeck und die beiden Blumhardts," <u>Barth-Studien</u>, pp. 62-83. For Harnack's post card to Barth, see Barth--Thurneysen, <u>RTM</u>, pp. 127-28.

[69]Rumscheidt, <u>RT</u>, pp. 44-45; cf. <u>Harnack--Barth</u>, pp. 178-79.

[70]Rumscheidt, <u>RT</u>, p. 45.

[71]Rumscheidt, <u>RT</u>, pp. 45-46; cf. <u>Harnack--Barth</u>, p. 180. Bracketed material from the original.

[72]Rumscheidt, <u>RT</u>, p. 35; <u>Harnack--Barth</u>, p. 171.

[73]Rumscheidt, <u>RT</u>, p. 39; cf. <u>Harnack--Barth</u>, p. 174. Brackets supplied.

[74]Rumscheidt, <u>RT</u>, p. 40; cf. <u>Harnack--Barth</u>, p. 175.

[75]Rumscheidt, <u>RT</u>, p. 41; cf. <u>Harnack--Barth</u>, p. 175.

[76]Rumscheidt, <u>RT</u>, pp. 21ff. Rumscheidt's "Introduction" is invaluable for knowledge of the historical and theological context in which the correspondence arose.

[77]Rumscheidt, <u>RT</u>, p. 51; cf. <u>Harnack--Barth</u>, p. 184.

[78]Rumscheidt, <u>RT</u>, p. 51; cf. <u>Harnack--Barth</u>, pp. 184-85.

[79]Rumscheidt, <u>RT</u>, p. 51; cf. <u>Harnack--Barth</u>, p. 185.

[80]Rumscheidt, <u>RT</u>, p. 52; cf. <u>Harnack--Barth</u>, p. 185.

[81]Rumscheidt, <u>RT</u>, p. 52; cf. <u>Harnack--Barth</u>, p. 185.

[82]Rumscheidt, <u>RT</u>, p. 53; cf. <u>Harnack--Barth</u>, p. 187.

[83]Rumscheidt, <u>RT</u>, p. 52; cf. <u>Harnack--Barth</u>, p. 186.

[84]Rumscheidt, <u>RT</u>, p. 53; cf. <u>Harnack--Barth</u>, p. 186.

[85]Rumscheidt, <u>RT</u>, p. 53; cf. <u>Harnack--Barth</u>, p. 185.

NOTES

Chapter III

[1]_Die Auferstehung der Toten_ (Zollikon: Evangelischer Verlag, 1953), 4th. ed., p. iii. Cited hereafter as _AdT_.

[2]_Das Wort Gottes und die Theologie_ (1924); ET, _The Word of God and the Word of Man_ (1928; 1957); _Komm, Schöpfer Geist!_; ET, _Come, Holy Spirit_ (1935). For this period in Barth's life, see Busch, _KB_, pp. 126ff.

[3]Karl Barth, _The Resurrection of the Dead_ (New York: Revell, 1933), p. 6. Cited hereafter as _ROD_. All italicized or underlined text accords with this English translation unless otherwise indicated. Brackets mine.

[4]_ROD_, p. 6.

[5]_ROD_, p. 5; cf. pp. 95-100.

[6]_ROD_, p. 117.

[7]_ROD_, p. 122.

[8]_ROD_, p. 119.

[9]Adriaan Geense, _Auferstehung und Offenbarung_ (Göttingen: Vandenhoeck und Ruprecht, 1971), pp. 16-17. Cited hereafter as _AUO_. Some of the headings in this section stem from Geense.

[10]_ROD_, p. 20.

[11]_ROD_, p. 81.

[12]_ROD_, pp. 87-88.

[13]_Romans_, II, p. 314.

[14]_ROD_, p. 101.

[15]_ROD_, p. 103; cf. pp. 100-03.

[16]_ROD_, pp. 103-04. Geense makes the keen comment here that Barth appreciates the positive role which the biblical imagery is made to serve in this regard; it is not a matter of criticizing it in terms of whether it is meaningful to modern man. See _AUO_, p. 18.

[17]Geense, _AUO_, p. 18. Cf. Barth, _ROD_, pp. 189-90.

[18]_ROD_, p. 104.

[19]_ROD_, p. 105.

[20]_ROD_, p. 106.

[21]_ROD_, p. 106.

[22]ROD, p. 107.

[23]ROD, p. 165. Bracketed material is my translation.

[24]ROD, p. 108.

[25]ROD, p. 109.

[26]ROD, p. 109.

[27]ROD, p. 192. My brackets.

[28]ROD, p. 192.

[29]ROD, p. 193; for the suggestion of this interpretation of Barth, cf. Geense, AUO, p. 19.

[30]ROD, p. 33. My translation.

[31]ROD, p. 194. Italics mine. Translation modified.

[32]ROD, pp. 116-17. Bracketed material substituted for clarity.

[33]ROD, p. 119.

[34]ROD, p. 118; the reader is referred to a series of passages from Romans cited by Barth which are in radical tension with the position of the Corinthian doubters.

[35]ROD, p. 119; for the above stress, cf. Geense, AUO, pp. 19-20.

[36]ROD, p. 202.

[37]Geense, AUO, p. 110.

[38]ROD, pp. 202-03; slight changes in translation based on the original.

[39]ROD, p. 125.

[40]ROD, p. 127.

[41]ROD, p. 130.

[42]ROD, p. 131.

[43]ROD, p. 110.

[44]ROD, p. 131.

[45]ROD, p. 132.

[46]ROD, p. 133.

[47]ROD, p. 134.

[48]ROD, p. 136.

[49]ROD, pp. 138-39.

[50]ROD, pp. 137-38.

[51]ROD, p. 138.

[52]ROD, p. 139.

[53]ROD, pp. 139-40.

[54]ROD, p. 140.

[55]ROD, pp. 140-41.

[56]ROD, p. 142.

[57]ROD, p. 142.

[58]ROD, p. 148.

[59]ROD, p. 149.

[60]ROD, p. 150. Brackets supplied.

[61]ROD, pp. 151-52.

[62]ROD, p. 154.

[63]ROD, p. 154.

[64]ROD, p. 156.

[65]ROD, p. 155.

[66]ROD, p. 154.

[67]ROD, p. 157.

[68]ROD, p. 157; cf. pp. 154; 161.

[69]ROD, p. 168. In this section the KJV version used in ROD, pp. 162-63, is followed.

[70]ROD, p. 169. Brackets supplied.

[71]ROD, p. 167.

[72]ROD, pp. 164-65; cf. the summary statement, pp. 171-72.

[73]ROD, p. 170.

[74]ROD, p. 172.

[75]ROD, p. 172.

[76]ROD, p. 175.

[77]ROD, pp. 174-75.

[78]ROD, p. 181; cf. p. 180.

[79]ROD, p. 183.

[80]ROD, p. 185.

[81]ROD, p. 184. Bracketed material translated from the original.

[82]ROD, p. 184.

[83]ROD, p. 184.

[84]ROD, pp. 183-84.

[85]ROD, p. 185.

[86]ROD, p. 189.

[87]ROD, pp. 185-90.

[88]ROD, p. 190.

[89]ROD, p. 191.

[90]ROD, pp. 191-92.

[91]ROD, p. 192.

[92]ROD, pp. 193-94. German supplied from original.

[93]ROD, p. 194.

[94]ROD, p. 195.

[95]ROD, pp. 196-97.

[96]ROD, p. 199. Brackets supplied.

[97]ROD, p. 200.

[98]ROD, p. 201.

[99]ROD, p. 204.

[100]ROD, p. 207.

[101]ROD, pp. 207-08.

[102]ROD, p. 209.

[103]ROD, p. 212.

[104]ROD, p. 211.

[105]Cited by Barth, ROD, pp. 211-12.

[106]ROD, p. 212.

[107]ROD, p. 213.

[108]ROD, p. 211. Barth notes that Paul's conclusion here parallels Rom. 7:25.

[109]Smart, DMMT, p. 141.

[110]For Bultmann's review, see Faith and Understanding (New York: Harper, 1969), vol. I, pp. 66-67; 80-81. Cited hereafter as FAU, I. See Smart, DMMT, pp. 142-43.

[111]FAU, I, p. 79.

[112]FAU, I, p. 80.

[113]FAU, I, p. 79; cf. pp. 79-80.

[114]FAU, I, p. 81.

444

[115]Cited in Bultmann, _FAU_, I, p. 81.

[116]_FAU_, I, p. 82.

[117]_FAU_, I, p. 82.

[118]_FAU_, I, p. 83.

[119]_FAU_, I, p. 84.

[120]_FAU_, I, p. 90.

[121]_FAU_, I, p. 90.

[122]_FAU_, I, p. 92.

[123]_FAU_, I, p. 86. See Bultmann's reservations regarding Barth's interpretation of "body," pp. 86-92.

[124]_FAU_, I, p. 86.

[125]_FAU_, I, p. 92.

[126]_FAU_, I, p. 92.

[127]_FAU_, I, p. 94.

[128]_FAU_, I, p. 94.

NOTES

Chapter IV

[1]Rudolf Bultmann et. al., Kerygma and Myth, ed. by Hans-Werner Bartsch. Tr. by Reginald H. Fuller (New York: Harper, 1961), vii. Cited hereafter as KM, I.

[2]Cited in Bertold Klappert, editor, Diskussion um Kreuz und Auferstehung (Wuppertal: Aussaat Verlag, 1967). p. 53. Cited hereafter as Diskussion.

[3]Walter Schmithals, An Introduction to the Theology of Rudolf Bultmann (Minneapolis: Augsburg, 1968), p. 250. See his helpful chapter, "The Problem of Hermeneutics: Demythologizing," pp. 249-72.

[4]KM, I, p. 2. Cf. pp. 1-2.

[5]KM, I, pp. 3-8.

[6]KM, I, p. 10.

[7]KM, I, p. 10.

[8]KM, I, p. 11.

[9]KM, I, pp. 11-12.

[10]KM, I, pp. 17-19.

[11]KM, I, p. 19.

[12]KM, I, p. 22.

[13]KM, I, p. 33.

[14]KM, I, p. 35.

[15]KM, I, p. 35.

[16]KM, I, p. 35.

[17]KM, I, p. 36. Brackets inserted.

[18]KM, I, p. 36.

[19]KM, I, p. 36.

[20]KM, I, p. 37.

[21]KM, I, p. 38.

[22]KM, I, p. 39.

[23]KM, I, p. 41.

[24]KM, I, p. 42.

[25]KM, I, p. 42.

[26]KM, I, p. 41. Bultmann expanded the theme of his 1941 essay in his American lectures of 1951 published as

Jesus *Christ* *and* *Mythology* (New York: Charles Scribner's Sons, 1958).

[27]CD 3:2, p. 441.

[28]CD 3:2, p. 443.

[29]CD 3:2, p. 445.

[30]CD 3:2, p. 445.

[31]CD 3:2, p. 446.

[32]CD 3:2, p. 446. Brackets supplied.

[33]CD 3:2, p. 447.

[34]CD 3:2, p. 447.

[35]CD 3:2, p. 446. Brackets supplied.

[36]CD 3:2, p. 447. Bracketed material from the KD.

[37]CD 3:2, p. 446.

[38]CD 3:2, p. 443.

[39]CD 3:2, p. 445. Cf. p. 444.

[40]Klappert, *Diskussion*, p. 106.

[41]CD 3:2, p. 444.

[42]CD 3:2, p. 445.

[43]CD 3:2, p. 445.

[44]CD 3:2, p. 441.

[45]Cf. for e.g., CD 3:2, p. 440. For Barth's exposition of the doctrine of the Person of Christ along Chalcedonian lines, see: CD 1:2, pp. 1-202. For Bultmann's reconstruction of the life of the historical Jesus, see *Jesus* *and* *the* *Word* (New York: Charles Scribner's Sons, 1958).

[46]CD 3:2, p. 441. Brackets supplied.

[47]CD 3:2, p. 443.

[48]CD 3:2, p. 443.

[49]Rudolf Bultmann, *Theology* *of* *the* *New* *Testament*, tr. by Kendrick Grobel (New York: Charles Scribner's Sons, 1951), vol. I, p. 3.

[50]CD 3:2, p. 443.

[51]CD 3:2, p. 443.

[52]CD 3:2, p. 445.

[53]CD 3:2, p. 445.

[54]CD 3:2, p. 446. Brackets supplied.

[55]CD 3:2, p. 446.

[56]CD 3:2, p. 446.

[57]CD 3:2, p. 446. Translation in brackets supplied.

[58]CD 3:2, p. 446.

[59]CD 3:2, pp. 446-47.

[60]CD 3:2, p. 447.

[61]CD 3:2, p. 447.

[62]CD 3:2, p. 447.

[63]Cited by Barth in CD 3:2, p. 447.

[64]CD 3:2, p. 447.

[65]CD 3:2, p. 447. My addition.

[66]CD 3:2, p. 447. Bracketed material from original.

[67]CD 3:2, p. 447.

[68]CD 3:2, p. 447; italics and bracketed words in original.

[69]CD 3:2, p. 441.

[70]CD 3:2, p. 443.

[71]CD 3:2, p. 449; italics mine.

[72]CD 3:2, p. 452.

[73]CD 3:2, p. 452.

[74]CD 3:2, p. 452.

[75]CD 3:2, pp. 452-54.

[76]CD 3:1, p. 80.

[77]CD 3:1, p. 80.

[78]CD 3:1, p. 80.

[79]CD 3:1, pp. 81-82. Brackets supplied.

[80]CD 3:1, p. 81.

[81]CD 3:1, p. 83.

[82]CD 3:1, p. 81.

[83]CD 3:1, p. 82.

[84]CD 3:1, p. 82.

[85]CD 3:1, p. 82.

[86]CD 3:1, p. 82.

[87]CD 3:1, p. 82.

448

[88]CD 3:1, p. 83.

[89]CD 3:1, p. 93; cf. p. 82. For Barth's view of Scripture as the Word of God, see CD 1:1, paragraph 4. For the work of the Holy Spirit in the appropriation of revelation, see CD 2:1, paragraph 16. A more recent helpful summary statement by Barth is in Evangelical Theology: An Introduction, tr. by Grover Foley (Grand Rapids: Eerdmans, 1963), Part I. Cited hereafter as ET.

[90]CD 1:2, p. 817; cf. ET, ch. 3.

[91]CD 3:2, p. 437.

[92]CD 3:2, p. 440.

[93]CD 3:2, p. 439.

[94]CD 3:2, pp. 439-40.

[95]CD 3:2, p. 440.

[96]CD 3:2, p. 441.

[97]CD 3:2, p. 441.

[98]CD 3:2, p. 442.

[99]CD 3:2, p. 448; italics in original.

[100]My translation of KD 3:2, p. 538; cf. CD 3:2, p. 448.

[101]CD 3:2, p. 448; italics in original.

[102]CD 3:2, p. 449; italics in original.

[103]CD 3:2, p. 449; I have inserted the RSV text for the Greek biblical citations in Barth's text and included italics from the original. The last two sentences precede the first part of the citation in Barth's text. Bracketed material from the original.

[104]CD 3:2, p. 450. I have ommitted the Greek in Barth's text.

[105]CD 3:2, p. 450.

[106]CD 3:2, p. 450; cf. pp. 454f.

[107]CD 3:2, p. 455; italics in original.

[108]CD 3:2, p. 452.

[109]CD 3:2, p. 452.

[110]CD 3:2, p. 453.

[111]CD 3:2, p. 453.

[112]CD 3:2, p. 453.

[113]CD 3:2, p. 453.

[114]CD 3:2, p. 454.

[115]CD 3:2, p. 454. For Barth's fuller exposition of the manner in which the resurrection of Jesus is the key to understanding his lordship over time or as the "Lord of Time," see esp. 463-511.

[116]CD 3:3, p. ix.

[117]CD 3:3, p. xi.

[118]Barth-Bultmann Letters, p. 141.

[119]Ibid.

[120]Ibid., p. 142.

[121]Ibid., p. 143.

[122]Ibid., p. 142.

[123]Ibid., p. 142.

[124]Ibid., p. 143.

[125]Ibid., pp. 144-45.

[126]Ibid., pp. 143-44.

[127]Ibid., pp. 144.

[128]Ibid., p. 144.

[129]Ibid.

[130]Ibid., p. 144.

[131]Ibid., p. 144.

[132]Ibid., p. 145.

[133]Ibid.

[134]Ibid., p. 146.

[135]Ibid., p. 145.

[136]Ibid., p. 146.

[137]Ibid., p. 147.

[138]Busch, KB, p. 361.

[139]Busch, KB, p. 351.

[140]Busch, KB, pp. 352-53.

[141]Busch, KB, p. 353. Brackets supplied.

[142]Busch, KB, p. 351.

[143]Busch, KB, p. 352; cf. p. 351 for the preceding quotations.

[144]Karl Barth, "The World's Disorder and God's Design," The Congregational Quarterly, Vol. XXVII, No.

1 (Jan., 1949), pp. 10-11. Cited hereafter as "World's Disorder."

[145]"World's Disorder," p. 11.

[146]"World's Disorder," pp. 11-12.

[147]"World's Disorder," p. 12.

[148]Reinhold Niebuhr, "An Answer to Karl Barth," The Christian Century, vol. LXVI, (Feb. 23, 1949), p. 177. Cited hereafter as "Answer."

[149]Karl Barth, "Continental vs. Anglo-Saxon Theology," The Christian Century, Vol. LXVI (Feb. 16, 1949), p. 408. Cited hereafter as "Continental vs. Anglo-Saxon."

[150]"Continental vs. Anglo-Saxon," p. 408.

[151]Reinhold Niebuhr, "We Are Men and Not God," The Christian Century, Vol. LXV, (October 27, 1948), p. 171.

[152]Ibid., p. 175.

[153]"Continental vs. Anglo-Saxon," p. 404.

[154]"Continental vs. Anglo-Saxon," p. 405.

NOTES

Chapter V

[1]Hans-Werner Bartsch, editor, Kerygma and Myth (London: S.P.C.K., 1962), Vol. II, p. 7. Hereafter this will be cited as KM, II. The symbol KM always refers to the English translation. Among the numerous additional volumes in the German series, one dealt with philosophical responses (III, 1954); (IV, 1955) dealt with the ecumenical discussion; reactions to Bultmann from leading Roman Catholic biblical and systematic theologians is available in (V, 1955). An international symposium dealt with "Demythologizing and Existential Interpretation" in (VI-1) in 1963. The series continued through the 1960's under the editorial leadership of Hans Werner Bartsch. The series is Kerygma Und Mythos (Hamburg: Evangelischer Verlag). The total literature generated by Bultmann and the larger controversy is enormous and still growing. A comprehensive critical analysis of all dimensions of Bultmann's demythologizing program is Gerhard Gloege, Mythologie und Luthertum (1st. ed., 1952). The 3rd. ed. (1963) contains a valuable appendix ("Entmythologisierung") which includes a summary analysis of Gloege's own position and responses to other commentators on the issue of demythologizing; cf., pp. 170-209. Basic bibliography can be found in KM I and II and in Gloege, op. cit. Critical analyses of various aspects of Bultmann's theology by a distinguished group of scholars, including a good representation of Americans, and Bultmann's reply to his critics, are found in: The Theology of Rudolf Bultmann, ed. by Charles W. Kegley (New York: Harper, 1966). The two books by John Macquarrie on Bultmann's theology are among the best available. See: An Existentialist Theology: A Comparison of Heidegger and Bultmann (New York: Harper, 1965), and specifically on demythologizing, The Scope of Demythologizing: Bultmann and His Critics (New York: Harper, 1966).

[2]KM, II, p. 6.

[3]KM, II, p. 6.

[4]KM, II, pp. 1-2.

[5]CD 3:2, p. x.

[6]Busch, KB, p. 388.

[7]Busch, KB, p. 388.

[8]Busch, KB, p. 388.

[9]Busch, _KB_, p. 388.

[10]Busch, _KB_, p. 388.

[11]Rudolph Bultmann, "The Problem of Hermeneutics," in _Essays Philosophical and Theological_ (London: SCM Press, n.d.), p. 252; see esp. the argument, pp. 247ff.

[12]_Ibid._, p. 253.

[13]_Ibid._, p. 254.

[14]_Ibid._, p. 254.

[15]_Ibid._, p. 256.

[16]_Ibid._, pp. 256-57.

[17]_Ibid._, p. 257.

[18]_Ibid._.

[19]_Ibid._. Brackets indicate correction of the English text.

[20]_Ibid._, p. 257. Augustine's phrase may be rendered: "Thou hast made us for Thyself, and our hearts are restless until they rest in Thee."

[21]_Ibid._, p. 258; cf. p. 257.

[22]_Ibid._.

[23]_Ibid._, p. 259.

[24]_Ibid._.

[25]_Ibid._.

[26]_Ibid_, p. 260.

[27]_Ibid._; the citation is from Barth.

[28]_Ibid._.

[29]_Ibid._.

[30]_Ibid._, p. 261.

[31]_Ibid._, p. 261. For essays in this volume indicative of some of Bultmann's hermeneutical concerns and points of tension with Barth, cf. the essay "The Questions of Natural Revelation" (1941), and "Points of Contact and Conflict" (1946), which deals with the issue of the relationship of Christianity to the non-Christian religions. Also, "The Christological Confession of the World Council of Churches" (1950-51). Robert C. Roberts provides a careful analysis of Bultmann's hermeneutics in: _Rudolph Bultmann's Theology: A Critical Interpretation_ (Grand Rapids: Eerdmans, 1976), pp. 125-239.

[32]Busch, <u>KB</u>, p. 389.

[33]Busch, <u>KB</u>, p. 389. My brackets.

[34]<u>KM</u>, II, pp. 83-84.

[35]<u>KM</u>, II, p. 117.

[36]<u>KM</u>, II, p. 118.

[37]<u>KM</u>, II, p. 118.

[38]<u>KM</u>, II, p. 118.

[39]<u>KM</u>, II, p. 118.

[40]<u>KM</u>, II, p. 119.

[41]<u>KM</u>, II, p. 120.

[42]<u>KM</u>, II, p. 120.

[43]<u>KM</u>, II, p. 121.

[44]<u>KM</u>, II, p. 121.

[45]<u>KM</u>, II, p. 121.

[46]<u>KM</u>, II, p. 121. For an extensive analysis of Bultmann's use of Heidegger, see John Macquarrie, <u>An Existentialist Theology: A Comparison of Heidegger and Bultmann</u> (New York: Harper, 1965).

[47]<u>KM</u>, II, p. 121. See Gloege, <u>op. cit.</u>, for a critical comparison of the viewpoints of Bultmann and Luther.

[48]<u>KM</u>, II, p. 122.

[49]<u>KM</u>, II, p. 123.

[50]<u>KM</u>, II, p. 123.

[51]<u>KM</u>, II, p. 89. The so-called "Tübingen Memorandum" is found in <u>Für und wider die Theologie Bultmann's</u> (Tübingen: Mohr, 1952).

[52]<u>KM</u>, II, p. 89.

[53]<u>KM</u>, II, p. 89.

[54]<u>KM</u>, II, p. 90. My brackets.

[55]<u>KM</u>, II, p. 90.

[56]Cited by Barth in <u>KM</u>, II, p. 90.

[57]<u>KM</u>, II, p. 91.

[58]<u>KM</u>, II, p. 84.

[59]<u>KM</u>, II, p. 85.

[60]<u>KM</u>, II, p. 86.

[61]<u>KM</u>, II, p. 86.

[62]<u>KM</u>, II, p. 87.

[63]<u>KM</u>, II, p. 87.

[64]<u>KM</u>, II, p. 91.

[65]<u>KM</u>, II, p. 91.

[66]<u>KM</u>, II, pp. 91-92.

[67]<u>KM</u>, II, p. 93.

[68]<u>KM</u>, II, p. 94.

[69]<u>KM</u>, II, p. 96.

[70]<u>KM</u>, II, p. 96.

[71]<u>KM</u>, II, p. 96.

[72]<u>KM</u>, II, p. 97. Brackets supplied.

[73]<u>KM</u>, II, p. 97.

[74]<u>KM</u>, II, p. 98.

[75]<u>KM</u>, II, p. 98.

[76]<u>KM</u>, II, p. 98.

[77]<u>KM</u>, II, p. 98.

[78]<u>KM</u>, II, p. 98.

[79]<u>KM</u>, II, p. 99.

[80]<u>KM</u>, II, p. 99.

[81]<u>KM</u>, II, p. 99.

[82]<u>KM</u>, II, p. 99.

[83]<u>KM</u>, II, p. 100.

[84]Cited by Barth, <u>KM</u>, II, p. 100; cf. KM, I, p. 41.

[85]<u>KM</u>, II, p. 100. Brackets supplied.

[86]<u>KM</u>, II, p. 100.

[87]<u>KM</u>, II, p. 100.

[88]<u>KM</u>, II, p. 101.

[89]<u>KM</u>, II, p. 101.

[90]See above, Ch. 4.

[91]<u>KM</u>, II, p. 104. Brackets supplied.

[92]<u>KM</u>, II, p. 103.

[93]<u>KM</u>, II, p. 105.

[94]<u>KM</u>, II, p. 105.

[95]KM, II, p. 105.

[96]KM, II, pp. 105-06.

[97]KM, II, p. 106.

[98]KM, II, p. 106.

[99]KM, II, p. 106.

[100]KM, II, p. 108.

[101]KM, II, p. 108.

[102]KM, II, p. 108.

[103]KM, II, pp. 108-09.

[104]KM, II, pp. 109-11.

[105]KM, II, p. 111.

[106]KM, II, pp. 112-13.

[107]KM, II, p. 114.

[108]KM, II, p. 115.

[109]KM, II, p. 114.

[110]KM, II, p. 115.

[111]KM, II, p. 116.

[112]KM, II, p. 116.

[113]KM, II, p. 116.

[114]KM, II, p. 116.

[115]KM, II, p. 117.

[116]KM, II, p. 123.

[117]KM, II, p. 123.

[118]KM, II, p. 124.

[119]KM, II, pp. 124-25.

[120]KM, II, p. 125; my translation.

[121]KM, II, p. 125.

[122]KM, II, p. 126.

[123]KM, II, p. 127.

[124]KM, II, p. 127.

[125]KM, II, p. 127.

[126]KM, II, p. 127.

[127]KM, II, p. 128.

[128]KM, II, p. 128.

[129]Cited in <u>KM</u>, II, p. 130.

[130]<u>KM</u>, II, p. 130.

[131]Busch, <u>KB</u>, p. 389.

[132]That is, <u>KM</u>, II, of 1952.

[133]<u>KM</u>, II, p. 131.

[134]<u>KM</u>, II, p. 132.

[135]<u>KM</u>, II, pp. 131-32.

[136]Barth-Bultmann <u>Letters</u>, p. 86.

[137]Barth-Bultmann <u>Letters</u>, n. 1, p. 102.

[138]Barth-Bultmann <u>Letters</u>, p. 87.

[139]Barth-Bultmann <u>Letters</u>, pp. 87-88. The reference is to the German edition.

[140]Barth-Bultmann <u>Letters</u>, p. 88.

[141]Barth-Bultmann <u>Letters</u>, p. 88.

[142]Barth-Bultmann <u>Letters</u>, p. 89.

[143]Rudolph Bultmann, <u>KM</u>, I, p. 203. Cf. Bultmann's longer German version in H. W. Bartsch, ed., <u>Kerygma und Mythos</u>, vol. II (Hamburg: Reich, 1952), p. 201.

[144]Bultmann, <u>KM</u>, I, p. 204.

[145]Barth-Bultmann <u>Letters</u>, p. 90.

[146]Barth-Bultmann <u>Letters</u>, p. 89. Cf. p. 90.

[147]Barth-Bultmann <u>Letters</u>, pp. 90-91.

[148]Barth-Bultmann <u>Letters</u>, p. 91.

[149]Barth-Bultmann <u>Letters</u>, p. 91.

[150]Barth-Bultmann <u>Letters</u>, p. 92.

[151]Barth-Bultmann <u>Letters</u>, pp. 92-93.

[152]Barth-Bultmann <u>Letters</u>, p. 93.

[153]Barth-Bultmann <u>Letters</u>, p. 93.

[154]Barth-Bultmann <u>Letters</u>, p. 93.

[155]Barth-Bultmann <u>Letters</u>, p. 93.

[156]Barth-Bultmann <u>Letters</u>, p. 94.

[157]<u>KM</u>, I, p. 41.

[158]Barth-Bultmann <u>Letters</u>, p. 94.

[159]Barth-Bultmann <u>Letters</u>, p. 94.

[160]Barth-Bultmann <u>Letters</u>, p. 97.

[161] Barth-Bultmann _Letters_, p. 94.

[162] Barth-Bultmann _Letters_, p. 95.

[163] Barth-Bultmann _Letters_, p. 95.

[164] Barth-Bultmann _Letters_, p. 95.

[165] Barth-Bultmann _Letters_, p. 95. Brackets supplied.

[166] Barth-Bultmann _Letters_, p. 96.

[167] Barth-Bultmann _Letters_, p. 96.

[168] _KM_, II, p. 109.

[169] Barth-Bultmann _Letters_, p. 96.

[170] Barth-Bultmann _Letters_, p. 96.

[171] Barth-Bultmann _Letters_, p. 96.

[172] Barth-Bultmann _Letters_, p. 97.

[173] _KM_, I, pp. 206-07. Bultmann refers Barth to the section, "The 'Act of God,'" in _KM_, I, esp. pp. 206ff., and _Kerygma und Mythos_, II, pp. 185ff.

[174] Barth-Bultmann _Letters_, p. 97. Brackets supplied.

[175] Barth-Bultmann _Letters_, p. 97.

[176] Barth-Bultmann _Letters_, p. 97.

[177] Barth-Bultmann _Letters_, p. 98.

[178] Barth-Bultmann _Letters_, pp. 98-99.

[179] _KM_, I, p. 210; cf. Barth-Bultmann _Letters_, p. 99.

[180] Barth-Bultmann _Letters_, p. 99.

[181] Barth-Bultmann _Letters_, p. 99. Brackets supplied.

[182] Barth-Bultmann _Letters_, p. 99.

[183] Barth-Bultmann _Letters_, p. 100.

[184] Barth-Bultmann _Letters_, p. 100.

[185] Barth-Bultmann _Letters_, p. 100.

[186] Barth-Bultmann _Letters_, p. 101.

[187] Barth-Bultmann _Letters_, p. 101. The reference is to KM, II, pp. 179-208.

[188] Barth-Bultmann _Letters_, p. 101.

[189] Barth-Bultmann _Letters_, p. 102. Cf. the discussion of this 1950 essay, "The Problem of Hermeneutics," above--Ch. 5, II.

458

[190]Barth-Bultmann _Letters_, p. 102. For the critique of Hartlich and Sachs, see _Kerygma Und Mythos_, II, pp. 113-25.

[191]Barth-Bultmann _Letters_, p. 102.

[192]Barth-Bultmann _Letters_, p. 102.

[193]Barth-Bultmann _Letters_, p. 105.

[194]Barth-Bultmann _Letters_, p. 105.

[195]Barth-Bultmann _Letters_, p. 105.

[196]Barth-Bultmann _Letters_, p. 105.

[197]Barth-Bultmann _Letters_, p. 106.

[198]Barth-Bultmann _Letters_, p. 106.

[199]Barth-Bultmann _Letters_, pp. 106-07.

[200]Barth-Bultmann _Letters_, p. 107. Brackets supplied.

[201]Barth-Bultmann _Letters_, p. 108. Brackets supplied.

[202]Barth-Bultmann _Letters_, p. 108.

NOTES

Chapter VI

[1]Among the important sections on the relationship of revelation to history, see CD 1:2, par. 14, "The Time of Revelation," and CD 3:2, par. 47, "Man in His Time," esp. the section, "Jesus, Lord of Time," pp. 437-511. The bearing of Barth's christological perspective on his interpretation of human existence in time is developed in CD 3:2, pp. 511-640. On the relationship of covenant and creation, see the overview in CD 3:1, pp. 42-94. On the relationship of covenant history to world history, cf. CD 3:3, esp. par. 49, pp. 58ff; CD 4:3/1, pp. 38-164, on "The Light of Life;" and CD 4:3/2, pp. 681-762, "The People of God in World-Occurrence." Barth's analysis of the relationship of revelation to the phenomenon of religion has marked parallels to his view of that obtaining between revelation and human history. Cf. CD 1:2, pp. 280-361.

[2]CD 1:2, p. 58. The explication of the prolegomena to Barth's CD in terms of "The Doctrine of the Word of God" in CD 1:1 and CD 1:2 represents an extensive, powerful treatment of his view of revelation. Also to be included here is CD 2:1, par. 25-27, treating "The Knowledge of God."

[3]This receives decisive expression in Barth's sharp distinction between the self-revelation of the triune God and the phenomenon of "human religion." See CD 1:2, pp. 280-361.

[4]Karl Barth, God in Action: Theological Addresses (New York: Round Table Press, 1936), pp. 11-12.

[5]CD 1:2, p. 5.

[6]CD 1:2 p. 3.

[7]CD 1:2, p. 5; cf. p. 819.

[8]CD 1:2, p. 5.

[9]CD 1:2, p. 56.

[10]CD 1:2, p. 57.

[11]Cf. CD 1:2, pp. 10ff., 45.

[12]CD 1:2, p. 57.

[13]CD 1:2, p. 58.

[14]CD 1:2, p. 12.

[15]CD 3:1, p. 59.

[16]CD 3:1, p. 59.

[17]CD 3:1, pp. 59-60.

[18]KD 1:2, p. 13. My translation clarifies Barth's meaning. Cf. CD 1:2, p. 12. Italics added.

[19]CD 1:2, pp. 12, 58.

[20]CD 1:2, p. 30.

[21]CD 1:2, p. 45; original in italics.

[22]CD 1:2, p. 50.

[23]CD 1:2, p. 50, Barth's self-criticism applies to his statement in Romans, II: "There is no special divine history (Gottesgeschichte) viewable as a fragment or quantity of history as a whole. The entire history of religion and of the Church takes place totally in this world. The so-called "salvation-history" (Heilsgeschichte) is nothing less than the crisis of all history--not a history in or alongside of history." (Romans, II, p. 57.) I have modified the translation from the original. Italics in original. Cf. the above statement with the latter which indicates Barth's more realistic and concrete view of revelation in history in the CD by virtue of the stress on the incarnation. "Precisely as the time of grace that breaks upon us, it is the crisis that breaks into general time. This is where the offence of revelation arises." (CD 1:2, p. 67.)

[24]CD 2:1, pp. 634-35.

[25]CD 1:2, p. 12.

[26]CD 3:1, p. 59.

[27]In Christ and Time, Cullmann commends Barth for stressing "the temporal quality of eternity" in the CD in contrast to his earlier writings. But he holds that the "philosophical influence which controls the conception of time" in those writings is still operative since Barth takes as his starting point a fundamental distinction between time and eternity, and refuses to regard eternity as "time stretching endlessly forward and backward." Cullmann's view is that eternity "is understood in the Biblical sense only when the symbol of the straight line is applied to both time and to eternity. ..." The lurking danger in Barth's distinction between eternity and time is that "eternity may again be conceived as qualitatively different from time, and so as a result there may again intrude that Platonic conception of timeless eternity which Karl Barth in the Dogmatik is nevertheless plainly striving to discard." (Philadelphia: Westminster, 1950), pp. 62-63. Italics

added. While not mentioning Cullmann, Barth seems to have him in mind in saying: "In the last resort when we think of eternity we do not have to think in terms of either the point or the line, the surface or space. We have simply to think of God Himself, recognising and adoring and loving the Father, the Son and the Holy Spirit. It is only in this way that we know eternity. For eternity is His essence." (CD 2:1, p. 639.) It is certainly clear that Barth does not surrender the qualitative difference between eternity and time while also asserting that "the Word became time." (CD 1:2, p. 50.)

[28]For an analysis of Barth's disagreements with Cullmann and Bultmann, see H.-J. Kraus, "Das Problem der Heilsgeschichte in der Kirchlichen Dogmatik," in Antwort, ed. by E. Wolf et. al., (Zürich: Evangelischer Verlag, 1956), pp. 70-75. Cited hereafter as Antwort.

[29]CD 1:2, p. 12. For Barth's amplification of the relationship of Jesus Christ to both testaments, see CD 1:2, pp. 45-121.

[30]CD 1:2, pp. 70-72.

[31]CD 1:2, pp. 72, 74-78.

[32]CD 1:2, p. 102.

[33]CD 1:2, p. 103.

[34]CD 1:2, p. 109.

[35]CD 1:2, pp. 110-12.

[36]CD 1:2, p. 114.

[37]CD 1:2, p. 114.

[38]CD 1:2, p. 116.

[39]CD 1:2, p. 116.

[40]CD 1:2, p. 119.

[41]CD 1:2, p. 117. Brackets supplied.

[42]CD 1:2, p. 47.

[43]CD 1:2, p. 47.

[44]CD 1:2, p. 47.

[45]CD 1:2, p. 50.

[46]CD 1:2, p. 50.

[47]CD 1:2, p. 58.

[48]CD 1:2, p. 59.

[49]CD 1:2, p. 59.

[50]CD 1:2, p. 59.

[51]CD 1:2, p. 61.

[52]CD 1:2, p. 63.

[53]CD 1:2, p. 63.

[54]CD 1:2, p. 63.

[55]Barth, ET (1963), p. 66.

[56]ET, pp. 67-68.

[57]CD 1:2, p. 64.

[58]ET, p. 71. "That revelation can be understood only in the form of miracle is the result of its being, according to the witness of the New Testament, revelation in the resurrection of Jesus Christ from the dead." (CD 1:2, p. 64.) The confession that God reveals himself "does not imply blind credence in all the miracle stories related in the Bible. ...A man might even credit all miracles and for that reason not confess the miracle." (CD 1:2, p. 65.)

[59]For the following, see CD 1:2, pp. 53-54.

[60]Barth's translation. See CD 1:2, p. 53.

[61]CD 1:2, p. 53. I have transliterated the Greek.

[62]Cf. CD 1:2, p. 53.

[63]CD 1:2, p. 53.

[64]See CD 2:1, p. 54 for Barth's exegesis.

[65]CD 1:2, p. 55.

[66]CD 1:2, p. 52.

[67]CD 1:2, p. 52.

[68]CD 1:2, p. 55.

[69]CD 3:1, p. 60.

[70]Kraus, Antwort, pp. 76-77. Italics mine. Kraus' entire citation is italicized.

[71]CD 1:2, p. 58.

[72]CD 3:1, p. 42; Barth's text is italicized.

[73]CD 3:1, pp. 94-325.

[74]CD 3:3, p. 36. Bracketed material and italics in original; KD 3:3, p. 42.

[75]CD 3:3, p. 195; cf. pp. 192-95.

[76]CD 2:2, pp. 7-8. Cf. 3:3, pp. 192ff. This thesis is at the heart of Barth's distinctive christocentric

doctrine of election. For the extensive development of this thesis, see CD 2:2, pp. 94-194.

[77]CD 3:3, pp. 195-96; brackets supplied.

[78]For a critical treatment of this issue and an indication of some problematic features of Barth's approach, cf. Wilhelm Dantine, "Der Welt-Bezug des Glaubens: Überlegungen zum Verhältnis von Geschichte und Gesetz im Denken Karl Barths," in K. Luthi, ed., Theologie Zwischen Gestern und Morgen (München: Kaiser, 1968), see esp. pp. 267-78.

[79]CD 3:4, p. xii.

[80]Busch, KB, p. 374.

[81]Busch, KB, p. 374.

[82]Busch, KB, p. 377.

[83]Busch, KB, p. 377.

[84]CD 4:1, p. 3; brackets supplied.

[85]CD 4:1; 4:2; 4:3/1; 4:3/2; 4:4 (Fragment).

[86]CD 4:1, p. ix.

[87]CD 4:1, p. x.

[88]CD 4:1, p. 3. The editors note (CD 4:1, vii) that they have translated Barth's use of the term, Versöhnung, with the words "reconciliation" and "atonement" depending on the context. The reader should note that the more comprehensive term, "reconciliation," usually is more representative of Barth's emphasis.

[89]CD 4:1, p. 3.

[90]CD 4:1, p. 81.

[91]CD 4:1, p. 81.

[92]CD 4:1, p. 81.

[93]Busch, KB, p. 387.

[94]CD 4:1, pp. ix-x.

[95]CD 1:1, p. xiv (Thompson edition).

[96]CD 3:1, par. 41.

[97]An instructive introduction to Barth's Church Dogmatics is provided by John Godsey, Karl Barth's Table Talk (Edinburgh: Oliver and Boyd, 1963), esp. pp. 1-12, along with Barth's replies to Godsey's questions.

[98]CD 4:1, p. 79; Barth's text is italicized.

NOTES

Chapter VII

[1]These are Barth's headings; cf. CD 4:1, p. 157.

[2]CD 4:2, p. 23; cf. pp. 21-25.

[3]CD 4:2, p. 25.

[4]CD 4:1, p. 128; cf. pp. 128-130.

[5]CD 4:1, p. 128.

[6]CD 4:1, p. 198; italics in original. Cf. KD 4:1, p. 216.

[7]Bultmann, KM, I, p. 36.

[8]CD 4:1, p. 157; it should be noted that Barth uses the German word, _Geschichte_, and not _Historie_ in the above statement and generally when speaking of reconciliation as "history."

[9]CD 4:1, p. 157. For Barth's view of salvation-history, cf. H. J. Kraus, "Das Problem der Heilsgeschichte in der 'Kirchlichen Dogmatik,'" in _Antwort_, ed. by E. Wolf et. al., (Zürich: Evangelischer Verlag, 1956), pp. 69-83. Cited hereafter as _Antwort_.

[10]CD 4:1, p. 157; italics in original. Cf. KD 4:1, p. 171.

[11]CD 4:1, p. 157.

[12]CD 4:1, pp. 157-58. In CD 3:1, p. 60, Barth made this point forcefully: "The history of salvation is _the_ history, the true history, which encloses all other history. ... The history of salvation is _the_ history."

[13]CD 2:2, p. 3. Italics in original.

[14]CD 2:2, p. 94. Italics in original. For an extensive treatment of Barth's doctrine of election, see Walter Kreck, _Grundentscheidungen in Karl Barth's Dogmatik_ (Neukirchen: Neukirchener Verlag, 1978), esp. pp. 188-283. Hereafter cited _GKBD_.

[15]CD 4:1, p. 158.

[16]CD 4:1, p. 158. Brackets supplied.

[17]CD 4:1, p. 158.

[18]CD 4:1, p. 157. Italics in original. Or: "The reconciliation of man with God takes place as God Himself actively intervenes...that He Himself becomes man. God

became man. That is what is, i.e., what has taken place in Jesus Christ." CD 4:1, p. 128.

[19]CD 4:1, p. 157.

[20]CD 4:1, p. 157.

[21]CD 4:1, pp. 158-59. Bracketed material supplied for clarity.

[22]CD 4:1, p. 159.

[23]CD 4:1, p. 211.

[24]CD 4:1, pp. 159-60. Barth refers to Jesus as "qualitativ Anderer." Cf. KD 4:1, p. 174. Barth is playing on his initial designation of God as "Wholly Other" in his commentary on Romans.

[25]CD 4:1, p. 160.

[26]CD 4:1, p. 160. Klappert observes that the latter trilogy of titles both reflects the dominance of juridical titles which will control Barth's exposition of the work of Christ which follows beneath the caption, "The Judge Judged in our Place" (par. 59:2), and recalls the Old Testament covenant as the "presupposition of reconciliation" (par. 57:2). Earlier Barth described the relationship between God and his covenant partner thus: "When God becomes his Partner, as the Lord of the covenant who determines its meaning, content and fulfilment, He necessarily becomes the Judge of man, the Law of his existence." CD 2:2, p. 511. Thus Klappert contends that for Barth the trilogy "Lord, Lawgiver and Judge" derived from the Old Testament "represents the true substantive content of the christological titles of the New Testament." Bertold Klappert, Die Auferweckung des Gekreuzigten (Neukirchen: Neukirchener Verlag, 1974), p. 140. Cf. pp. 139-40. Cited hereafter as AdG.

[27]CD 4:1, p. 160. Italics and bracketed terms in original. Cf. KD 4:1, p. 174. Noteworthy here is that Barth does not include the titles Priest (4:1), King (4:2), and Prophet (4:3) which dominate his own exposition of the doctrine of reconciliation. Klappert observes Barth's preference for the titles, Christ, Lord, Son of God and Word of God which dominate other sections of the CD. Thus in CD 2:2, Barth speaks of Jesus Christ as Israel's crucified Messiah and of Christ as the risen Lord of the church. The title, Christ, points Barth to the fulfillment of the OT covenant and to the divine election. In addition to its OT antecedents, the kyrios title for Barth points especially to the resurrection of Jesus: see CD 3:2, pp. 437ff., CD 1:1, par. 9, 11-12. For Christ as Second Adam, see Barth's Christ and Adam

(New York: Macmillan, 1968). For the title, Son of God, CD 4:1, pp. 52, 71, 129f. For the title, Word of God, see esp. the exegesis of Jn. 1:1-2 in CD 1:2, par. 15 and parallels. The title, Word of God, is treated in CD 1:1, pp. 124-35, 4:2, pp. 205ff., 4:3/1, pp. 80ff., 96ff. For further discussion of the titles in recent German literature, see Klappert, _AdG_, pp. 140ff.

[28]CD 4:1, p. 160. Material in the second set of brackets translated from the original. Italics in original. Cf. KD 4:1, p. 174. As textual support Barth cites: Col. 2:9; Jn. 14:9; Jn. 5:23; 1 Cor. 1:2; Rom. 10:12; Acts 9:14, 21; 22:16; Jn. 20:28; Acts 7:59; 2 Cor. 12:8; Jn. 14:13f.

[29]Eicholz, _Antwort_, p. 64, note 28.

[30]CD 4:1, p. 162.

[31]CD 2:1, pp. 126ff.

[32]CD 4:1, p. 161.

[33]CD 4:1, p. 161.

[34]For these citations, see CD 4:1, pp. 161-63.

[35]CD 4:1, p. 163. Bracketed material in the original. Cf. KD 4:1, p. 178.

[36]CD 4:1, pp. 162-63. It is therefore not surprising that in Barth's subsequent treatment (CD 4:3) of the appropriation of reconciliation in terms of the prophetic office of Jesus Christ, he views Jesus Christ as the Prophet attesting his own way and work. "...Jesus Christ Himself guarantees that He is the one Word of God...He shows Himself to be this by acting towards us as such. ...If Jesus Christ is the one Word of God, He alone, standing out from the ranks of all other supposed and pretended divine words, can make Himself known as this one Word." CD 4:3/1, pp. 103-04. Cf. the entire section, par. 69:2, esp. pp. 72ff.

[37]Klappert, _AdG_, p. 150.

[38]Hans Grass, _Theologie und Kritik_ (Göttingen: Vandenhoeck und Ruprecht, 1969), p. 138. My translation. Cited hereafter as _TK_.

[39]CD 4:1, p. 177; cf. p. 163.

[40]CD 4:1, p. 163.

[41]CD 4:1, p. 164. Brackets inserted.

[42]CD 4:1, p. 164.

[43]CD 4:1, p. 164.

[44]CD 4:1, p. 164.

[45]CD 4:1, p. 164.

[46]CD 4:1, p. 165.

[47]CD 4:1, p. 164.

[48]Passages cited included: Phil. 2; 2 Cor. 8:9; Heb. 2:14; 5:8; Lk. 2:7; Mtt. 2:13ff.; Jn. 17:5; Heb. 4:15; 1 Jn. 4:2f.; 2 Jn. 7; Rom. 8:3; Gal. 3:13; Mtt. 3:15; Jn. 3:14; 8:28; 12:32; 1 Pet. 1:19f.; Rom. 8:32; Mk. 9:12; Gal. 2:20; Eph. 5:2 et.al..

[49]CD 4:1, p. 166; italics mine. Bracketed material supplied to clarify the translation. Cf. KD 4:1, p. 181.

[50]CD 4:1, p. 245.

[51]CD 4:2, p. 252; cf. pp. 249ff.

[52]Klappert, AdG, p. 154. Italics in original. Klappert's well-documented thesis is that Pannenberg and others err in interpreting Barth's christology primarily in terms of the classical christology of the incarnation. See the extensive argument in AdG, pp. 85-101.

[53]See the previous note for references. Klappert credits Eberhard Jüngel, an incisive Barth interpreter, for first developing the thesis Klappert later expanded and modified. Cf. AdG, pp. 160-64.

[54]CD 4:1, p. 186.

[55]CD 4:1, p. 186.

[56]CD 4:1, p. 186; modified translation and italics from KD 4:1, p. 203.

[57]CD 4:1, pp. 186-87.

[58]CD 4:1, p. 176.

[59]CD 4:1, p. 130.

[60]See esp. CD 4:1, par. 57:2.

[61]CD 4:1, p. 166.

[62]CD 4:1, p. 168.

[63]CD 4:1, p. 168.

[64]CD 4:1, p. 170.

[65]CD 4:1, p. 169.

[66]CD 4:1, p. 170. My brackets.

[67]CD 4:1, p. 172.

[68]CD 4:1, pp. 174-75.

[69]CD 4:1, p. 175.

[70]Klappert, _AdG_, p. 168.

[71]CD 4:1, p. 184.

[72]CD 4:1, p. 187; italics in original. Cf. KD 4:1, p. 204.

[73]CD 4:1, p. 193.

[74]CD 4:1, p. 193.

[75]CD 4:1, p. 193.

[76]CD 4:1, pp. 179-80.

[77]CD 4:1, p. 180.

[78]CD 4:1, p. 180.

[79]CD 4:1, p. 183.

[80]CD 4:1, p. 181. Bracketed translation is mine.

[81]CD 4:1, p. 182.

[82]CD 4:1, p. 182.

[83]CD 4:1, p. 182. Bracketed translation is mine.

[84]CD 4:1, p. 183. The definitive significance of 2 Cor. 5:18-19 for the structure of Barth's doctrine of reconciliation is clear in par. 59. In 59:1, Barth stresses that _God_ was in Christ (the stress is on the Person of Christ); in 59:2, the stress is on the saving work of reconciliation.

[85]CD 4:1, p. 183.

[86]CD 4:1, p. 184.

[87]Klappert, _AdG_, p. 175. Bracketed term is Klappert's.

[88]CD 4:1, p. 184.

[89]CD 4:1, p. 184.

[90]Cited in Klappert, _AdG_, p. 176; citing Heinrich Vogel, _Christologie_, I, p. 189. Brackets supplied.

[91]Cited in Klappert, _AdG_, p. 176, from Vogel, _ibid_, p. 192.

[92]CD 4:1, p. 185.

[93]CD 4:1, p. 185.

[94]CD 4:1, p. 185. The bracketed letter was inadvertently capitalized in the translation. Cf. Klappert, _AdG_, pp. 176-77. See 2 Cor. 5:21; Gal. 3:13.

[95]CD 4:1, p. 185; italics in original. Cf. KD 4:1,

p. 202.

[96]CD 4:1, p. 185.

[97]CD 4:1, p. 186.

[98]CD 4:1, p. 186.

[99]CD 4:1, p. 187.

[100]CD 4:1, p. 188.

[101]Klappert, AdG, p. 180.

[102]For Barth's attempt to ground this thesis exegetically, see his references (CD 4:1, pp. 188-192) to Phil. 2; 1 Cor. 1:23; 2:2. The self-abasement enjoined upon Christians is a corollary of Christ's self-abasement and is a "fellowship with the Crucified" (p. 190).

[103]CD 4:1, p. 192; italics in original. My brackets. Cf. KD 4:1, p. 210.

[104]CD 4:1, p. 193; cf. Klappert, AdG, p. 184. Italics in original, KD 4:1, p. 211.

[105]CD 4:1, p. 195.

[106]CD 4:1, p. 193; italics in original. Cf. KD 4:1, p. 211. For the exegetical support for speaking of the obedience of Jesus here, see pp. 193-94.

[107]CD 4:1, p. 195; I am translating "offenbares Geheimnis" as "revealed mystery" rather than the translator's "open secret." Cf. KD 4:1, p. 213.

[108]CD 4:1, p. 199; italics in original. My brackets. Cf. KD 4:1, p. 218.

[109]CD 4:1, p. 199. The comma and italics are in the original. Cf. KD 4:1, p. 218.

[110]CD 4:1, p. 195.

[111]CD 4:1, p. 195. Bracketed material supplied.

[112]CD 4:1, p. 194.

[113]CD 4:1, p. 195.

[114]CD 4:1, p. 185.

[115]CD 4:1, p. 196.

[116]CD 4:1, p. 196.

[117]CD 4:1, p. 198; italics in original. Cf. KD 4:1, p. 216.

[118]CD 4:1, p. 197; italics in original. Bracketed punctuation supplied. Cf. KD 4:1, p. 215.

[119]CD 4:1, p. 199.

[120]CD 4:1, pp. 199-200; for the review of Barth's positive presuppositions, see pp. 197-200.

[121]CD 4:1, p. 201; italics from original. Cf. KD 4:1, p. 219.

[122]CD 4:1, p. 201.

[123]CD 4:1, p. 202.

[124]CD 4:1, p. 202.

[125]CD 4:1, p. 204. The reference is to CD I:1, par. 8-12.

[126]Cited by Klappert, AdG, p. 187.

[127]Klappert, AdG, p. 187.

[128]CD 4:1, pp. 203-04. Brackets indicate modified translation. Cf KD 4:1, pp. 222-23. For a parallel treatment dealing with the analogies appropriate to interpreting the incarnation, see CD 4:2, pp. 58-60. For an illuminating and nuanced treatment of analogies Barth utilizes to describe the relationship between man and God, God and man in Jesus Christ, and between humans which are grounded in, and correspond to, the dimensions of the immanent Trinity, see Jüngel, Barth-Studien, pp. 210-32. Cf. the summary statement on p. 216. For a comprehensive analysis and critical discussion of Barth's use of analogy in the CD, see: Wilfred Harle, Sein und Gnade (Berlin: De Gruyter, 1975), pp. 172-226.

[129]CD 4:1, p. 203.

[130]CD 4:2, p. 45; substituting "inner" for "inter."

[131]CD 4:2, p. 59; cf. the discussion pp. 58-60. Christophe Freyd treats Barth's view of the triune God in relationship to his reconciling work in full, esp. pp. 118-132. Throughout he juxtaposes Barth and Hegel. See: Gott als die Universale Wahrheit von Mensch und Welt (Stuttgart: np., 1982). Jüngel comments on Barth's clarification of the way in which the immanent Trinity can be posited only in the light of revelation: "One of the weaknesses of the marvelous trinitarian architecture which defines Karl Barth's Church Dogmatics in both its dogmatic structure and its individual systematic arguments is that the foundation of the doctrine of the Trinity in the Prolegomena can lead to the misunderstanding that the knowledge of the Trinity of God was deduced from the axiomatically presupposed proposition "God reveals himself as the Lord" with help of the formal differentiation of subject, object, and predicate in the revelatory event. Such a

misunderstanding is avoided when the humanity of Jesus is not only interpreted dogmatically within the context of faith in the triune God (see chiefly CD IV/2), but faith in the triune God is first presented as dogmatically founded in the context of the humanity of Jesus." God as the Mystery of the World (Grand Rapids: Eerdmans, 1983), pp. 351-52. Cited hereafter as GMW. That Barth's intention is to make the humanity of Jesus constitutive for interpreting God's triunity is clear in CD 4:1.

[132]CD 4:1, p. 211. Bracketed material and italics from the German: KD 4:1, p. 231.

NOTES

Chapter VIII

[1]CD 4:1, p. 211.

[2]CD 4:1, p. 212. Bracketed translation inserted.

[3]Klappert, AdG, p. 195.

[4]CD 4:1, p. 212.

[5]CD 4:1, p. 222. The phrase is from The Creed of Nicaea (325 and the Nicene Creed 381 A.D.). My brackets.

[6]CD 4:1, p. 157.

[7]CD 4:1, p. 224. Bracketed text from original, KD 4:1, p. 246.

[8]CD 4:1, p. 224.

[9]CD 4:1, p. 218; my brackets.

[10]CD 4:1, p. 225; my brackets.

[11]CD 4:1, p. 226.

[12]CD 4:1, p. 226.

[13]CD 4:1, p. 227.

[14]CD 4:1, p, 227.

[15]CD 4:1, p. 227. Italics in original, KD 4:1, p. 249. Brackets indicate my modifications of the translation.

[16]The conclusion of W. Popkes, Christus Traditus, is that the major weakness of modern christology is that the true deity of Jesus Christ has become problematical. As a result, the soteriological relevance of the work of Christ is called in question. Klappert shows that Barth attacks this position directly in his insistence that God does not surrender his deity in his reconciling activity in Jesus Christ. The reconciliation is efficacious for the world, for us, and for me because it is securely grounded in the fact that Jesus Christ was truly God. This point was made throughout the above exposition of "The Way of the Son of God into the Far Country" (59:1). See Klappert, AdG, p. 196, citing Popkes, pp. 292ff.

[17]CD 4:1, pp. 222-23.

[18]CD 4:1, p. 223; italics and bracketed material in original, KD 4:1, p. 245.

[19]CD 4:1, p. 228.

[20]CD 4:1, p. 227; italics in original, KD 4:1, p. 249.

[21]CD 4:1, p. 228; my brackets.

[22]CD 4:1, p. 224; italics in original, KD 4:1, p. 245. Punctuation modified.

[23]CD 4:1, p. 245.

[24]CD 4:1, p. 285; transliteration of the Greek and brackets supplied.

[25]CD 4:1, p. 285. Cf. CD 4:3/1, p. 183.

[26]CD 4:1, p. 273. Italics in original, KD 4:1, p. 300. I supplied the numeration. Cf. CD 4:1, pp. 231-283 for this section.

[27]CD 4:1, p. 273; my brackets. The editors note (vii) that Barth's use of the German word, Stellvertretung, encompasses both the meanings of representation and substitution. The ensuing exposition should make Barth's meaning clear.

[28]CD 4:1, p. 273. Klappert refers to the oral communication of W. Kreck: "The fourfold answer [of Barth] describes not only the four essentials of the New Testament doctrine of the atonement, but at the same time encompasses the four termini [main points] of traditional christology: (a) Judge; (b) Substitution; (c) Satisfaction; (d) Righteousness." Klappert adds that it is instructive to see how Barth utilizes and transforms both NT and historical materials. AdG, p. 198.

[29]CD 4:1, p. 231; italics in original, KD 4:1, p. 254.

[30]CD 4:1, p. 225; italics in original, KD 4:1, p. 247.

[31]Cf. the survey in this chapter, "Jesus' History as a Passion Narrative," I, B.

[32]CD 4:1, p. 389. Barth therefore develops the doctrine of sin within the doctrine of reconciliation; cf. CD 4:1, par. 60; 4:2, par. 65; 4:3/1, par. 70.

[33]CD 4:1, p. 231; my brackets. Cf. 4:1, par. 60.

[34]CD 4:1; cf. Gen. 3:5ff..

[35]CD 4:1, p. 220.

[36]CD 4:1, p. 232.

[37]CD 4:1, p. 232.

[38]CD 4:1, p. 232; my brackets.

[39]CD 4:1, p. 235.

[40]CD 4:1, p. 233.

[41]Klappert, AdG, p. 200.

[42]CD 4:1, p. 217.

[43]CD 2:1, p. 393: see the correlation of "The Mercy and Righteousness of God," pp. 368-406, and also "The Grace and Holiness of God," pp. 351-368.

[44]CD 4:1, p. 217.

[45]CD 4:1, p. 216.

[46]CD 4:1, p. 233; italics in original, KD 4:1, p. 256.

[47]CD 4:1, p. 234.

[48]CD 4:1, p. 235; italics in original, KD 4:1, p. 259.

[49]CD 4:1, p. 235.

[50]CD 4:1, p. 235.

[51]CD 4:1, p. 238.

[52]CD 4:1, p. 238; italics in original, KD 4:1, p. 262. Cf. the section above: "Jesus' History as a Passion Narrative," Ch. 8, I, B.

[53]CD 4:1, p. 235; my brackets. Italics in original, KD 4:1, p. 258.

[54]CD 4:1, pp. 239-40; my brackets with alternative translation.

[55]CD 4:1, p. 236.

[56]CD 4:1, p. 236.

[57]CD 4:1, p. 236.

[58]CD 4:1, p. 237. The decisive doctrine of election, CD 2:2, (1942) anticipates all essentials of Barth's strongly substitutionary view of the atoning work of Christ in his doctrine of reconciliation published eleven years later in 1953. See esp., "Jesus Christ, Electing and Elected," CD 2:2, pp. 94-145, and also pp. 145-194.

[59]CD 4:1, p. 237; cf. p. 238.

[60]CD 4:1, p. 240. Italics in original. In adopting the christological grounding of the knowledge of sin, Barth sides with Luther and against Erasmus. See Luther's The Bondage of the Will. Cf. Barth's reference

to Luther's commentary on Gal. 3:13 in CD 4:1, pp. 238-40.

[61]CD 4:1, p. 492.

[62]CD 4:1, p. 492; brackets supplied.

[63]CD 4:1, pp. 499-500.

[64]CD 4:1, p. 500; italics in original, KD 4:1, p. 557. Barth rejects the interpretation of original sin as the biological transmission of depravity, and prefers to interpret it strictly as the first sin of every person. He clearly rejects that by virtue of the fall humans cease to be in the image of God. The creature remains such, but is nonetheless a sinner in its total being. Cf. pp. 492ff. and CD 4:1, par. 60:3, "The Fall of Man."

[65]CD 4:1, p. 403.

[66]CD 4:1, p. 492; cf. p. 405.

[67]CD 4:1, p. 406; brackets inserted.

[68]CD 4:1, pp. 240-43. Klappert identifies three points where Barth's more adequate and deeper view necessitates his critique of some traditional ideas associated with the understanding of atonement. (1) Since Jesus Christ died as a total being in order to effect the reconciliation of each person as sinner in his/her whole being, it is no longer possible to distinguish sin from the sinner. In this way Barth moves away from the understanding of sin conceived impersonally as an obstacle requiring removal to a "christological-personal" view of substitution. Thus it is not 'sin' as an obstacle which is removed by Christ, but the sinner. Here we are in the sphere of personal relationships. (2) This also involves the correction of the traditional idea of substitution oriented to "guilt and punishment, meritum and imputatio," and its replacement by a "christological-personal" one according to which Jesus Christ himself personally bears and carries sin away thereby effecting atonement. (3) In contrast to Socinianism which views the saving work of Jesus Christ as an example to be followed, Barth sees the saving work of Christ as engaging, judging and transforming man himself. See AdG, pp. 205-08.

[69]CD 4:1, p. 244; italics in original, KD 4:1, p. 269. Brackets indicate words missing in the English.

[70]CD 4:1, p. 244. Barth notes that while the witness of the Gospels to Christ moves on a line toward

this event, the Epistles proceed from that event: Barth contends that his exposition has adopted this sequence.

[71]CD 4:1, p. 238.

[72]CD 4:1, pp. 244-45.

[73]CD 4:1, p. 245. For an extensive discussion of recent views opposed to Barth's in Pannenberg and others, cf. Klappert, AdG, pp. 210ff.

[74]Klappert, AdG, p. 210.

[75]CD 4:1, p. 244.

[76]CD 4:1, p. 245; cf. p. 248. Italics in original, KD 4:1, p. 269.

[77]CD 4:1, p. 245; brackets from original, KD 4:1, p. 270.

[78]KD 4:1, p. 260. Cf. CD 4:1, p. 237; my translation accords with the original.

[79]CD 4:1, p. 245.

[80]CD 4:1, p. 245.

[81]CD 4:1, p. 246; italics in original, KD 4:1, p. 271.

[82]CD 4:1, p. 246. I have modified the last part of the final sentence in brackets to make it accord more closely to the German. Cf. KD 4:1, p. 271.

[83]CD 4:1, p. 246. Italics in original. I have modified the translation of the last sentence; KD 4:1, p. 271.

[84]CD 4:1, p. 251. Bracketed words supplied from original. Cf. KD 4:1, p. 276.

[85]CD 4:1, pp. 246-47. Italics in original, KD 4:1, p. 271. Cf. the section, "Beyond the God of Theism," above in chapter 7, section C, 4.

[86]CD 4:1, p. 247.

[87]CD 4:1, p. 247.

[88]KD 4:1, p. 272. My translation. Cf. CD 4:1, p. 247.

[89]CD 2:1, p. 257.

[90]CD 2:1, p. 257; italicized in English text.

[91]CD 2:1, p. 351; italicized in English test.

[92]CD 2:2, p. x.

[93]CD 2:2, p. 94; Barth's text is italicized. Compare this overview with the introduction above on both the "Significance" and the "Structure" of the doctrine of reconciliation in ch. 6, IV.

[94]Jürgen Moltmann, The Crucified God (New York: Harper, 1973), p. 268. Hereafter cited as TCG. See Moltmann's discussion of the divine apathy in TCG, pp. 267ff. See above, the sections, "Beyond the God of Theism" and "The Definition of the Deity of Christ: His Suffering and Cross," in ch. 7.

[95]CD 2:2, p. 123.

[96]CD 4:1, p. 246.

[97]CD 4:1, p. 247. Italics added.

[98]GMW, pp. 101-02. Jüngel also refers the reader to this point made in his earlier treatment of Barth, The Doctrine of the Trinity: God's Being is in Becoming (Grand Rapids: Eerdmans, 1976). For an example of Jüngel's creative re-thinking of the passion of God and God's triune nature in the light of the crucified Christ, see his section, "The Crucified Jesus Christ as 'Vestige of the Trinity,'" in GMW, pp. 343-68.

[99]CD 4:2, p. 357. Final brackets in original; cf. KD 4:2, p. 399.

[100]Moltmann, TCG, p. 203. Moltmann feels that his own theology of the cross deepens that of Barth in making the cross of Jesus more crucial for conceiving of God as triune. Cf. pp. 203ff.

[101]CD 2:1, pp. 402-03. In CD 2:1, pp. 368-407, Barth develops how God's righteousness and mercy are related on account of their confluence in Jesus Christ. This is expanded in terms of the cross of Jesus Christ in 4:1.

[102]The German is Gottes Sein ist im Werden (God's Being is in Becoming). The English version is less aptly entitled: The Doctrine of the Trinity.

[103]CD 2:1, pp. 398ff.; CD 4:1, par. 59:2 and par. 60:1.)

[104]CD 4:1, pp. 253-54.

[105]CD 4:1, p. 253; italics in original, KD 4:1, p. 278.

[106]CD 4:1, p. 253.

[107]CD 4:1, p. 248.

[108]CD 4:1, p. 248. Bracketed translation supplied.

[109]CD 4:1, p. 249. Italics in original. I have modified the first and last sentences in my translation. Cf. KD 4:1, p. 274. For a further analysis of differences between Barth and Bultmann, see Klappert, AdG, pp. 264ff. Barth contends that primitive NT communities knew the death of Jesus Christ to be redemptive apart from much explanation. Thus such statements as "the word of the cross" as the preaching of Christ crucified (1 Cor. 1:18-23), God gave his Son "for us all" (Rom. 8:32), or "for me" (Gal. 2:20), or he "suffered for you" (1 Pet. 2:21), or he "died for us" (1 Thess. 5:9), or he "tasted of death for every man" (Heb. 2:9), or he gave his life "for his friends" (Jn. 15:13), and Jesus Christ as the Good Shepherd who gave his life for the sheep (Jn. 10:11)--all pointed to this truth. Cf. CD 4:1, p. 250.

[110]CD 4:1, p. 251. Material in brackets in original, KD 4:1, p. 276.

[111]CD 2:1, p. 399.

[112]CD 4:1, p. 253. Italics in original, KD 4:1, p. 278.

[113]CD 4:1, p. 253.

[114]CD 4:1, pp. 253-54. Italics from the original. Bracketed material either insertions of missing material or changes based on the original. Cf. KD 4:1, pp. 279-280.

[115]CD 4:1, p. 254; italics in original, KD 4:1, p. 280.

[116]CD 4:1, p. 254.

[117]CD 4:1, pp. 254-55; italics in KD 4:1, p 280.

[118]For Barth's exegetical bases in this section, see: CD 4:1, pp. 249-50; 252-53; 255-56. For Gustav Aulen's depiction of the "classical" view of the atonement, see: Christus Victor (1931).

[119]KD 4:1, p. 282; cf. CD 4:1, p. 256. Italics in original.

[120]CD 4:1, p. 256.

[121]CD 4:1, p. 257.

[122]CD 4:1, p. 256; italics and bracketed material in original, KD 4:1, p. 282.

[123]CD 4:1, p. 257; italics in original, KD 4:1, p. 283.

[124]CD 4:1, p. 256.

[125]CD 4:1, p. 257; italics in KD 4:1, p. 283.

[126]CD 4:1, p. 257; earlier (p. 219) Barth spoke of the righteous action of Jesus as "His bowing before the judgment of this Judge." Italics in KD 4:1, p. 283.

[127]CD 4:1, p. 258. Italics in original, KD 4:1, p. 284.

[128]CD 4:1, p. 258; italics in KD 4:1, p. 284.

[129]CD 4:1, p. 259; italics in KD 4:1, p. 285.

[130]CD 4:1, p. 259. Klappert notes Barth's close agreement with Luther as follows: "The *iustitia* *hominis* corresponding to the *iustitia* *dei* as the omnipotence which creates order means thus: *deum* *justificare* (Luther), to put God in the right against oneself. ...Jesus Christ is the "righteous man" who affirms God's judgment, who puts God in the right against himself and thus corresponds to the righteousness of God." Cf. *AdG*, pp. 223-24.

[131]CD 4:1, p. 273; italics in original. The last sentence modified to accord with the original, KD 4:1, p. 300.

[132]CD 4:1, p. 273. Brackets indicate change from the original. Cf. KD 4:1, p. 300.

NOTES

Chapter IX

[1]In this chapter I have utilized some headings from Klappert, AdG, pp. 293-345.

[2]CD 4:1, p. 300; italics in original, KD 4:1, p. 330.

[3]CD 4:1, p. 300.

[4]CD 4:1, p. 300; bracketed material inserted.

[5]CD 4:1, p. 300.

[6]CD 4:1, p. 300; italics in original, KD 4:1, p. 331.

[7]CD 4:1, p. 301; I have transliterated the Greek.

[8]CD 4:1, p. 302.

[9]CD 4:1, p. 302.

[10]CD 4:1, p. 301.

[11]CD 4:1, p. 301; bracketed material is my modification of the translation of KD 4:1, p. 333.

[12]CD 4:1, p. 301; Cf. Barth's earlier comment on 2 Cor. 5:19 in CD 3:2, p. 449.

[13]Klappert, AdG, p. 301. For Klappert's defense of his interpretation of Barth versus his detractors, see pp. 85-101.

[14]CD 4:1, p. 303.

[15]CD 4:1, p. 303.

[16]CD 4:1, p. 303; the Greek is transliterated. My bracketed translation here and throughout follows Barth's distinction. I have translated Auferwecken and its cognates either as "awakening" or as "raising from the dead."

[17]CD 4:1, p. 304.

[18]CD 4:1, p. 304.

[19]CD 4:1, p. 304.

[20]For Barth's exegesis on these first two theses, cf. CD 4:1, pp. 299-304. For literature dealing with exegetical and theological issues Barth addresses, cf. Klappert, AdG, pp. 287-307.

[21]CD 4:1, p. 304; italics and bracketed word in original, KD 4:1, p. 335.

²²CD 4:1, p. 304.

²³CD 4:1, p. 307.

²⁴CD 4:1, p. 309; italics in original, KD 4:1, p. 340.

²⁵CD 4:1, p. 305.

²⁶CD 4:1, pp. 305-06.

²⁷CD 4:1, p. 305.

²⁸CD 4:1, p. 305.

²⁹CD 4:1, p. 305; bracketed word supplied.

³⁰CD 4:1, p. 306.

³¹This is my resumé of Klappert, AdG, pp. 314-15; cf. CD 4:1, p. 309.

³²CD 4:2, p. 155. See the major section, CD 4:2, par. 64, pp. 3-377, for Barth's exposition of this second dimension of Christ's reconciling work. Eberhard Jüngel delineates some of Barth's major emphases regarding Jesus Christ as "The Royal Man' in Karl Barth, a Theological Legacy (Philadelphia: Westminster, 1986), pp. 127-138. Cited hereafter: Karl Barth.

³³CD 4:2, p. 3; Barth's text is in italics.

³⁴CD 4:2, p. 132.

³⁵CD 3:2, p. 444.

³⁶CD 4:2, p. 140.

³⁷KD 4:2, p. 170; cf. CD 4:2, p. 152.

³⁸CD 4:2, p. 152.

³⁹CD 4:2, p. 152; bracketed material from KD 4:2, p. 170.

⁴⁰CD 4:2, p. 133.

⁴¹For the above, Klappert, AdG, pp. 316-17.

⁴²CD 4:2, p. 135; bracketed punctuation is mine.

⁴³CD 4:2, p. 140ff.

⁴⁴CD 4:2, p. 140; italics in original, KD 4:2, p. 157.

⁴⁵CD 4:2, p. 141.

⁴⁶CD 4:2, p. 141.

⁴⁷CD 4:2, p. 141; italics in original, KD 4:2, pp. 157-58.

[48]CD 4:2, p. 141; bracketed and italicized material in KD 4:2, p. 158.

[49]CD 4:2, p. 141.

[50]CD 4:2, p. 141.

[51]CD 4:2, pp. 292-94.

[52]CD 4:2, p. 292.

[53]CD 4:2, p. 293.

[54]CD 4:2, p. 293.

[55]CD 4:2, p. 290.

[56]CD 4:2, p. 292.

[57]CD 4:2, p. 292.

[58]CD 4:2, p. 285.

[59]CD 4:2, pp. 298-99.

[60]CD 4:2, pp. 298-99.

[61]CD 4:1, p. 316.

[62]CD 4:1, p. 313.

[63]KD 4:2, p. 168. The English translation cited in CD 4:2, p. 151, does not note Barth's more literal rendering of the Greek.

[64]CD 3:2, par. 47, p. 437.

[65]CD 4:2, p. 265.

[66]CD 4:2, p. 153.

[67]CD 4:2, p. 153.

[68]CD 4:2, p. 154; my brackets.

[69]CD 3:2, par. 47, to which Moltmann refers in his critique.

[70]CD 3:2, p. 489.

[71]CD 3:2, p. 490.

[72]CD 3:2, p. 490.

[73]CD 3:2, p. 490.

[74]CD 3:2, p. 490.

[75]For these summary statements, see Klappert, AdG, pp. 324-25. The translation is mine.

[76]CD 4:1, p. 351.

[77]CD 4:1, p. 333.

[78]CD 4:1, p. 333.

[79]CD 4:1, pp. 333-34.

[80]CD 4:1, p. 334.

[81]CD 4:1, pp. 351-52.

[82]CD 4:1, p. 351.

[83]CD 4:1, p. 351; bracketed material supplied.

[84]Klappert, AdG, p. 332.

[85]CD 4:2, p. 142.

[86]CD 4:2, p. 143.

[87]CD 4:2, pp. 143-44; italics in original, KD 4:2, pp. 160-61.

[88]CD 3:2, p. 449.

[89]CD 3:2, p. 448; brackets supplied. Cf. the positive statement re the identity and continuity between the crucified and risen Jesus, ibid.

[90]CD 4:2, p. 145.

[91]CD 4:2, p. 143; bracketed material and italics in original, KD 4:2, p. 160.

[92]CD 4:2, pp. 143-148; cf. Klappert, AdG, p. 333.

[93]CD 4:2, p. 149.

[94]CD 4:1, p. 334; bracketed material in original, KD 4:1, p. 369.

[95]CD 4:1, p. 334.

[96]CD 4:1, p. 334-35.

[97]CD 4:1, p. 335.

[98]Klappert, AdG, p. 334.

[99]CD 4:1, p. 335.

[100]CD 4:1, p. 336; bracketed material and italics in original, KD 4:1, p. 370.

[101]CD 4:1, p. 335; italics in original, KD 4:1, p. 370.

[102]CD 4:1, p. 336; my bracketed material.

[103]CD 4:1, p. 336; italics in original, KD 4:1, p. 371.

[104]CD 4:2, p. 143; brackets supplied.

[105]CD 4:1, p. 298.

[106]CD 4:1, pp. 337-38.

[107]CD 3:2, p. 446.

[108]CD 3:2, p. 496.

[109]CD 4:1, p. 336; cf. KD 4:3/1, p. 358.

[110]CD 4:1, p. 336; italics in original, KD 4:1, p. 371.

[111]Cf. CD 4:2, pp. 146ff.

[112]CD 4:2, p. 149; italics in original, KD 4:2, p. 167.

[113]CD 4:2, p. 148.

[114]KD 4:2, p. 166. Modifications of the translation in CD 4:2, p. 149 are mine. Italics in original.

[115]CD 3:2, p. 451.

[116]For this translation, cf. the summary in Klappert, AdG, pp. 342-47.

NOTES

Chapter X

[1]CD 4:1, p. 309; italics in original, KD 4:1, p. 341. I am indebted to Klappert AdG, pp. 348-377, for the headings and the lines of some of the argument in this section.

[2]CD 4:1, p. 310; italics in original, KD 4:1, p. 342.

[3]CD 4:1, p. 298.

[4]CD 4:1, p. 298.

[5]CD 4:1, p. 298; italics in original, KD 4:1, p. 329.

[6]CD 4:1, p. 305; material in brackets in original, KD 4:1, p. 336.

[7]CD 4:1, p. 316.

[8]CD 4:1, p. 346.

[9]CD 4:1, p. 346; italics in original, KD 4:1, p. 382. Barth puts the citation from the First Article of the Declaration of Barmen in quotes, but does not identify the source in the original. The English of the CD does not include the quotation marks I supplied.

[10]CD 4:1, p. 346.

[11]Klappert, AdG, pp. 350-51.

[12]CD 4:3/1, p. 288.

[13]CD 4:3/1, p. 44; italics and exclamation point in original, KD 4:3/1, p. 47.

[14]CD 4:1, pp. 309-10; italics and material in brackets from original, KD 4:1, pp. 341-42.

[15]CD 4:1, p. 310; italics in original, KD 4:1, p. 342.

[16]CD 4:1, p. 310; italics in original, KD 4:1, p. 342.

[17]CD 4:1, p. 310; italics in original, KD 4:1, p. 341. In order to describe the death of Jesus as a negative event with a positive intention and the resurrection as a positive event with a negative presupposition, Barth utilizes several contrasts: judgment--beyond judgment; negative--positive aspects of the event of reconciliation; the judgment of grace--the grace of judgment; freedom from--freedom for; delivered up for

our sins--raised for our justification (Rom. 5:25);
question--answer; puzzle--solution.

[18]CD 4:1, pp. 310-11; italics in original, KD 4:1,
pp. 342-43.

[19]CD 4:1, p. 311; see pp. 311-12 for further exegesis, especially of Rev. 21:4ff.

[20]CD 4:1, pp. 311-12; italics in original, KD 4:1,
pp. 343-44.

[21]KM, I, p. 38.

[22]CD 4:1, p. 311; italics in original. I have
modified the translation in brackets to accord with the
original. Cf. KD 4:1, p. 343. Cf. Klappert, AdG, p.
353.

[23]CD 4:1, p. 304.

[24]CD 4:1, p. 343; italics in original, KD 4:1, p.
379. Bracketed material indicates my modification of
the translation; the last sentence is also slightly
modified.

[25]CD 4:1, p. 312; italics in original, KD 4:1, p.
344.

[26]CD 4:1, p. 313; italics in original, KD 4:1, p.
345. Cf. CD 4:1, pp. 312-18, for this section.

[27]Cited in CD 4:1, p. 313.

[28]CD 4:1, p. 313; italics in original, KD 4:1, p.
345.

[29]CD 4:1, p. 314. I have altered the sequence of
Barth's text.

[30]CD 4:1, p. 314.

[31]CD 4:1, p. 293; cf. pp. 287ff.

[32]CD 4:1, p. 315; italics in original, KD 4:1, p.
347. Barth cites Heb. 10:19-29 as an impressive statement of this view common to the New Testament.

[33]CD 4:1, p. 315; italics in original, KD 4:1, p.
347.

[34]CD 4:1, p. 316; italics and bracketed material
supplied from the original, KD 4:1, p. 348.

[35]Klappert, AdG, p. 356; the brackets indicate
Klappert's examples. The final citation is from W.
Kreck's class lectures on Barth's theology. For more
extensive discussion of the literature, see Klappert, pp.
355-58.

[36]CD 4:1, p. 289.

[37]CD 4:1, pp. 285-86; italics in original, KD 4:1, pp. 313-14.

[38]CD 4:1, p. 316; italics in original, KD 4:1, p. 348. Since Barth does not give primary attention in this context to the manner in which the Holy Spirit is the bridge between God and us today and therewith to the link between what God has accomplished in the Son and how he makes this effective today, we have not developed it either. Clearly, this is the underlying presupposition of everything Barth says here about the work of the risen Christ present through the Spirit. It is true to say that the most dynamic treatment of Barth's pneumatology is to be found in the volumes on the doctrine of reconciliation (4:1; 4:2; 4:3; 4:4), particularly in the treatment of the appropriation of salvation through the work of the Spirit in the Church, the individual Christian, as well as in the world. Barth's theology cannot therefore be reduced to christology even though the christological focus is dominant: he develops his pneumatology in relationship to his christology along trinitarian lines. In one of the most insightful treatments of Barth's pneumatology to date, Rosato provides an analysis and critique of Barth as a "pneumatocentric theologian." Writing as a sympathetic Catholic interpreter, Rosato shows that Barth's "entire life's work simply cannot be categorized as christocentric; it is pneumatocentric as well" (p. 181). Much like Moltmann, Rosato criticizes Barth (Part III) for his failure to develop an adequate view of God as *Spiritus Creator* alongside of his stress on the Spirit as *Spiritus Redemptor*. Furthermore, had Barth moved more in the direction of an "eschatological" doctrine of the Trinity rather than stressing "an originative doctrine of the Trinity" (p. 184), his pneumatology would have been more dynamic and open-ended. Despite his failings, Rosato regards Barth's pneumatology to be among the most comprehensive in 20th-century theology along with those of Karl Rahner and Tillich (p. 182). Philip J. Rosato, *The Spirit as Lord* (Edinburgh: T. & T. Clark, 1981).

[39]CD 4:1, p. 318; italics in original, KD 4:1, p. 350.

[40]KD 4:1, p. 350; cf. CD 4:1, p. 318.

[41]CD 4:1, p. 318; brackets inserted. I am translating *Gegenwart* in this context as "presence" rather than as "present" as in the original, KD 4:1, p. 351. Italics in the original.

[42]CD 4:1, p. 318.

[43]KD 4:1, p. 351. I have shifted the sequence of phrases in this citation. Italics in original. Cf. 4:1, p. 318.

[44]KD 4:1, p. 352. Bracketed material and italics in original. Cf. CD 4:1, p. 319.

[45]CD 4:3/1, p. 293; cf. p. 292.

[46]CD 4:1, p. 310.

[47]CD 4:1, pp. 342-43. Italics and bracketed material in the original, KD 4:1, p. 378.

[48]CD 4:1, p. 350.

[49]CD 4:1, p. 343; italics and bracketed words in the original, KD 4:1, p. 378.

[50]CD 4:1, p. 342; italics and bracketed material in original, KD 4:1, p. 378.

[51]CD 4:1, p. 342.

[52]KD 4:1, p. 378. My translation modifies that found in CD 4:1, p. 342.

[53]KD 4:1, p. 341; cf. CD 4:1, p. 309.

[54]CD 4:1, p. 342; italics from original, KD 4:1, p. 378.

[55]CD 4:1, p. 343; material in brackets and italics in original, KD 4:1, p. 379.

[56]KD 4:1, p. 379; cf. CD 4:1, p. 343.

[57]CD 4:1, p. 343; italics in original, KD 4:1, p. 379.

[58]CD 4:1, p. 343-44; bracketed material and italics in original, KD 4:1, p. 379.

[59]CD 4:1, p. 344. Barth students will recall that a copy of Grünewald's _Crucifixion_ hung on the wall above Barth's desk from the Safenwil days unto the end of his life. That this is not incongruous with the above indictment is no doubt due to the fact that Barth interpreted the hand of John the Baptist pointing to the crucified as symbolic of the manner in which all Scripture pointed to Christ. Cf. Busch, _KB_, p. 116, and his Frontispiece for a reproduction of Grünewald's painting.

[60]CD 4:1, p. 344; italics in original, KD 4:1, p. 380.

[61]CD 4:1, p. 344; italics in original, KD 4:1, pp. 379-80.

[62]CD 4:1, p. 344.

[63]CD 4:1, p. 344.   Italics and bracketed material in the original, KD 4:1, p. 380.

[64]CD 4:1, p. 345; italics in original, KD 4:1, p. 381.

[65]CD 4:1, p. 346.

[66]CD 4:1, p. 346; italics in original, KD 4:1, p. 382.

[67]For this translation and summary analysis, see Klappert, AdG, pp. 362-63.

NOTES

Chapter XI

[1] I have utilized many of Klappert's (AdG) headings in this conclusion. All translations and paraphrases are mine.

[2] Klappert, AdG, p. 87.

[3] Klappert, AdG, p. 89-90.

[4] CD 4:1, p. 5.

[5] CD 4:1, p. 122. Italics and bracketed material in original, KD 4:1, p. 134.

[6] CD 4:1, p. 123: italics in original, KD 4:1, p. 134.

[7] CD 4:1, p. 123; my brackets. For Barth's explicit statements about his modifications of classical christology, see CD 4:1, pp. 123-25, 126-28, 132-38; CD 4:2, pp. 104-10.

[8] Klappert, AdG, pp. 100-01.

[9] Klappert, AdG, p. 94; italicized in AdG.

[10] CD 4:2, p. 105; cf p. 106.

[11] CD 4:1, p. 126: italics and bracketed material in original, KD 4:1, p. 138.

[12] CD 4:1, p. 124.

[13] CD 4:1, pp. 126-27; bracketed word in original, KD 4:1, p. 138.

[14] Klappert, AdG, p. 387.

[15] CD 4:1, p. 161, italics from original, KD 4:1, p. 175.

[16] CD 1:2, p. 123.

[17] Klappert, AdG, p. 388; cf. p. 193.

[18] CD 4:1, pp. 164-66.

[19] CD 4:1, p. 188.

[20] Cf. Klappert, AdG, pp. 131-93. Cf. the summary theses, pp. 192-93.

[21] CD 4:2, p. 235; italics in original, KD 4:1, p. 259.

[22] CD 4:1, p. 244; bracketed material and italics in original, KD 4:1, p. 269.

[23]See above, ch. 8.

[24]Klappert, AdG, p. 225.

[25]Klappert, AdG, p. 225.

[26]Klappert, AdG, pp. 285-86.

[27]Klappert, AdG, p. 286; cf. p. 390.

[28]Klappert, AdG, p. 286.

[29]See esp. CD 4:1, pp. 299-304; cf. Klappert, AdG, pp. 293-308. See above, Part III, ch. 4 pp.   .

[30]Klappert, AdG, pp. 314-15; cf. CD 4:1, pp. 304-09. See ch. 9 above.

[31]CD 4:2, ch. XV, par. 64; pp. 3-377.

[32]Klappert, AdG, pp. 391-92; cf. pp. 315-25. Cf. CD 4:1, pp. 309-33; 4:2, pp. 131-54.

[33]CD 4:1, p. 351.

[34]Klappert, AdG, pp. 342-45.

[35]For the summary and analysis, see Klappert, AdG, pp. 345-47.

[36]Klappert, AdG, pp. 362-63; cf. pp. 348-62. See above this chapter.

[37]Klappert, AdG, pp. 363-64.

[38]Klappert, AdG, p. 364. Cf. the careful analysis of both traditions, pp. 364-68.

[39]Klappert, AdG, pp. 375-77. For Barth's view of orthodoxy and other predecessors, see ibid., p. 375.

[40]CD 4:2, 4:3/1, 4:3/2, 4:4.

[41]CD 4:3/1, p. 4.

[42]CD 4:3/1, p. 4.

[43]CD 4:3/1, p. 4.

[44]CD 4:3/1, p. 168. For Barth's recounting of the victory of Jesus in the healing of Blumhardt's counselee, Gottliebin Dittus, of purported demon posession, see ibid., pp. 168-171. Barth dedicates an appreciative chapter to the elder Blumhardt in Protestant Theology in the Nineteenth Century (Valley Forge: Judson, 1973).

[45]CD 4:3/1, p. 168.

[46]See Hans Urs von Balthasar, The Theology of Karl Barth (New York: Holt, Rinehart and Winston, 1971), pp. 151-203.

[47]CD 4:3/1, p. 174.

[48]CD 4:3/1, p. 174; italics in KD 4:3/1, p. 199.

[49]CD 4:3/1, p. 174; italics in original, KD 4:3/1, p. 199.

[50]CD 4:3/1, p. 174-75: italics in original, KD 4:3/1, pp. 199-200.

[51]CD 4:3/1, p. 175; italics in original, KD 4:3/1, p. 200.

[52]CD 4:3/1, p. 175.

[53]CD 4:3/1, p. 175. Barth develops this point at length in his doctrine of election; cf. especially CD 2:2, pp. 94-145. See my analysis in Karl Barth (Waco: Word, 1972), pp. 96-110.

[54]CD 4:3/1, p. 175.

[55]CD 4:3:1, p. 176, italics in original, KD 4:3/1, p. 201.

[56]CD 4:3/1, pp. 179-80. Italics and bracketed material from original, KD 4:3/1 p. 205. The assurance of the final triumph of God grounded in the crucified, risen and reigning lord is developed throughout this section of the doctrine of reconciliation entitled, "Jesus is Victor," CD 4:3/1, pp. 165-274.

[57]Ingolf U. Dalferth, "Theologischer Realismus und realistische Theologie," Evangelische Theologie, (Hft.4/5, 1980), p. 402.

[58]Ibid., p. 403.

[59]Cited by Dalferth from K. Barth, Das christliche Leben. Die Kirchliche Dogmatik, 4:4, Fragment aus dem Nachlass, (1959-1961), (Zürich: EVZ-Verlag, 1979), p. 443 in ibid., p. 407. My translation.

[60]K. Barth, Der Römerbrief (Zürich: EVZ-Verlag, 1963), pp. 59-60. This is a reprint of the first edition of 1919.

[61]Cited from the Barth Archives, Basel, in Heinrich Stoevesandt, "Gott und die Götter," Evangelische Theologie, (Hft.4/5, 1980), p. 475.

[62]CD 4:2, p. 112. Bracketed material is my translation of the original; italics in original, KD 4:2, pp. 124-25.

[63]CD 4:2, pp. 122-23. Italics and bracketed material in KD 4:2, pp. 124-25.

[64]Jüngel, Karl Barth, p. 18.

Index of Names

*Names cited in the NOTES are not included in this index.

Index of Subjects

496

500

SELECTED BIBLIOGRAPHY

Writings of Karl Barth

Barth, Karl. Die Auferstehung der Toten. Zollikon: Evangelischer Verlag, 1953 (4th ed.).

_____. Die christliche Dogmatik im Entwurf. München: Chr. Kaiser Verlag, 1928.

_____. Church Dogmatics. Trans. Geoffrey Bromiley. Edinburgh: T. & T. Clark, 1936-1969. 13 volumes.

_____. The Epistle to the Romans. Trans. from the sixth edition by Edwyn C. Hoskyns. London: Oxford University Press, 1957.

_____. Evangelical Theology: An Introduction. Trans. by Grover Foley. Grand Rapids: Eerdmans, 1963.

_____. How I Changed My Mind. Introduction and Epilogue by John Godsey. Richmond: Knox, 1966.

_____. Karl Barth--Rudolf Bultmann Letters, 1922-1966. Edited by Bernd Jaspert and G. W. Bromiley. Trans. by G. W. Bromiley. Grand Rapids: Eerdmans, 1981.

_____. Kirchliche Dogmatik. Zollikon--Zürich: Evangelischer Verlag, 1932-1967. 13 volumes.

_____. Protestant Theology in the Nineteenth Century. Valley Forge: Judson, 1973.

_____. The Resurrection of the Dead. Trans. by H. J. Stenning. New York: Revell, 1933.

_____ and Eduard Thurneysen. Revolutionary Theology in the Making: Barth-Thurneysen Correspondence, 1914-1925. Trans. by James D. Smart. Richmond: Knox, 1964.

_____. Der Römerbrief. Bern: Baschlin, 1919.

502

_____. "Rudolf Bultmann--an Attempt to Understand Him." _Kerygma_ and _Myth_. Ed. Hans-Werner Bartsch. Trans. R. H. Fuller. London: S.P.C.K., 1962. Vol. II.

_____. The _Word_ of _God_ and _the_ _Word_ of _Man_. Trans. by Douglas Horton. N. P.: Pilgrim Press, 1928.

Other Selected Writings

Balthasar, Hans Urs Von. The _Theology_ of _Karl_ _Barth_. Trans. by John Drury. New York: Holt, Rinehart and Winston, 1971.

Bartsch, Hans-Werner, editor. _Kerygma_ and _Myth_. Trans. by Reginald Fuller. New York: Harper, 1961. Vol. I.

_____. _Kerygma_ and _Myth_. Trans. by Reginald Fuller. London: S.P.C.K., 1962. Vol. II.

Brunner, Emil and Karl Barth. _Natural_ _Theology_. Trans. by Peter Frankel. London: Centenary, 1946; reprinted by University Microfilms International, Ann Arbor, Michigan and London, 1979.

Bultmann, Rudolf. _Essays_ _Philosophical_ and _Theological_. London: SCM Press, (n.d.).

_____. _Faith_ and _Understanding_. New York: Harper, 1969.

_____. _Jesus_ _Christ_ and _Mythology_. New York: Scribner's, 1958.

_____. "New Testament and Mythology." _Kerygma_ and _Myth_, edited by Hans-Werner Bartsch. New York: Harper Torchback, 1961.

Busch, Eberhard. _Karl_ _Barth_. Trans. by John Bowden. Philadelphia: Fortress, 1976.

Geense, Adriaan. _Auferstehung_ und _Offenbarung_. Göttingen: Vandenhoeck and Ruprecht, 1971.

Grass, Hans. _Theologie_ und _Kritik_. Göttingen: Vandenhoeck and Ruprecht, 1969.

Harnack, Adolf Von and Karl Barth. "The Debate on the Critical Historical Method. Correspondence Between Adolf von Harnack and Karl Barth." The Beginnings of Dialectic Theology, edited by James M. Robinson. Trans. by Keith R. Crim et. al. Richmond: John Knox, 1968.

Harnack, Adolf Von. Liberal Theology at its Height, edited by Martin Rumscheidt. London: Collins, 1989.

Jüngel, Eberhard. God as the Mystery of the World. Grand Rapids: Eerdmans, 1983.

_____. Karl Barth, a Theological Legacy. Trans. by Garrett E. Paul. Philadelphia: Westminster, 1986.

_____. The Doctrine of the Trinity: God's Being is in Becoming. Grand Rapids: Eerdmans, 1976.

Klappert, Bertold. Die Auferweckung des Gekreuzigten. Revised edition; Neukirchen-Vluyn: Neukirchener Verlag, 1974.

_____, editor. Diskussion um Kreuz und Auferstehung. Wuppertal: Aussaat Verlag, 1967.

Kreck, Walter. Grundentscheidungen in Karl Barths Dogmatik. Neukirchen-Vluyn: Neukirchener Verlag, 1978.

Küng, Hans. Justification: The Doctrine of Karl Barth and a Catholic Reflection. Trans. by E. E. Tolk and D. Granskou. New York: Nelson, 1964.

Jenson, Robert W. Alpha and Omega: A Study in the Theology of Karl Barth. New York: Nelson, 1963.

_____. God After God: The God of the Past and the God of the Future, Seen in the Work of Karl Barth. Indianapolis and New York: Bobbs-Merrill, 1969.

Lindemann, Walter. Karl Barth Und Die Kritische Schriftauslegung. Hamburg: Reich-Evangelischer Verlag, 1973.

Macquarrie, John. An Existentialist Theology: A Comparison of Heidegger and Bultmann. New York: Harper, 1965.

504

_____. The Scope of Demythologizing: Bultmann and
His Critics. New York: Harper, 1966.

Moltmann, Jürgen, editor.   Anfänge der dialektischen
Theologie. München: Kaiser, 1962.

_____. The Crucified God. Trans. by R. A. Wilson and
John Bowden. New York: Harper, 1973.

Robinson, James M., editor.   The Beginnings of
Dialectical Theology. Trans. by Keith R. Crim and
Louis De Grazia. Richmond: Knox, 1968. Vol. I.

Rosato, Philip J. The Spirit as Lord. Edinburgh: T.
& T. Clark, 1981.

Rumscheidt, H. Martin, editor. Footnotes to a Theology:
the Karl Barth Colloquium of 1972. Canada: Studies
in Religion Supplements, 1974.

_____. Revelation and Theology: An Analysis of the
Barth--Harnack correspondence of 1923. Cambridge:
Cambridge University Press, 1972.

Smart, James D. The Divided Mind of Modern Theology:
Karl Barth and Rudolf Bultmann, 1908-1933.
Philadelphia: Westminster, 1967.

Torrance, Thomas F. Karl Barth: An Introduction to His
Early Theology, 1910-1931. London: SCM Press,
1962.

Wolf, Ernst, Ch. Von Kirschbaum and Rudolf Frey, editors.
Antwort. Zollikon-Zürich: Evangelischer Verlag,
1956.

TORONTO STUDIES IN THEOLOGY

22. Manfred Hoffmann (ed.), **Martin Luther and the Modern Mind: Freedom, Conscience, Toleration , Rights**

23. Eric Voegelin, **Political Religions,** T. J. DiNapoli and E. S. Easterly III (trans.)

24. Rolf Ahlers, **The Barmen Theological Declaration of 1934: The Archeology of a Confessional Text**

25. Kenneth Cauthen, **Systematic Theology: A Modern Protestant Approach**

26. Hubert G. Locke (ed.), **The Barmen Confession: Papers from the Seattle Assembly**

27. Barry Cooper, **The Political Theory of Eric Voegelin**

28. M. Darrol Bryant and Hans R. Huessy (eds.), **Eugen Rosenstock-Huessy: Studies in His Life and Thought**

29. John Courtney Murray, **Matthias Scheeben on Faith: The Doctoral Dissertation of John Courtney Murray,** D. Thomas Hughson (ed.)

30. William J. Peck (ed.), **New Studies in Bonhoeffer's** *Ethics*

31. Robert B. Sheard, **Interreligious Dialogue in the Catholic Church Since Vatican II: An Historical and Theological Study**

32. Paul Merkley, **The Greek and Hebrew Origins of Our Idea of History**

33. F. Burton Nelson (ed.), **The Holocaust and the German Church Struggle: A Search for New Directions**

34. Joyce A. Little, **Toward a Thomist Methodology**

35. Dan Cohn-Sherbok, **Jewish Petitionary Prayer: A Theological Exploration**

36. C. Don Keyes, **Foundations For an Ethic of Dignity: A Study in the Degradation of the Good**

37. Paul Tillich, **The Encounter of Religions and Quasi-Religions: A Dialogue and Lectures,** Terrence Thomas (ed.)

38. Arnold van Ruler, **Calvinist Trinitarianism and Theocentric Politics: Essays Toward a Public Theology,** John Bolt (trans.)

39. Julian Casserley, **Evil and Evolutionary Eschatology: Two Essays,** C. Don Keyes (ed.)

40. John Quinn and J.M.B. Crawford, **The Christian Foundation of Criminal Responsibility: Historical and Philosophical Analyses of the Common Law**

41. William C. Marceau, **Optimism in the Works of St. Francis De Sales**

42. A. James Reimer, **The Emanuel Hirsch and Paul Tillich Debate: A Study in the Political Ramifications of Theology**

43. George Grant, *et al.*, *Two Theological Languages* **by George Grant and Other Essays in Honour of His Work,** Wayne Whillier (ed.)

44. William C. Marceau, **Stoicism and St. Francis De Sales**

45. Lise van der Molen, **A Complete Bibliography of the Writings of Eugen Rosenstock-Huessy**